The
Diary
of
Anaïs Nin

Works by Anaïs Nin

The
Diary
of
Anaïs Nin

1931–1934

Edited and with an Introduction by Gunther Stuhlmann

The Swallow Press
and
Harcourt, Brace & World, Inc.
New York

A Harvest Book

ISBN   0-15-626025-5

Library of Congress Catalog Card Number: 66-12917

Printed in the
United States of America

KLMNOPQRST

Introduction

For more than three decades, Anaïs Nin's monumental diary, or journal, has been the object of much rumor, gossip, and conjecture. Since the early 1930s, when she showed sections of the journal for the first time to some of her close friends and associates in Paris, the word has spread that here was one of the unique literary documents of our century. In an often-quoted article in the English magazine *Criterion,* in 1937, Henry Miller ventured the opinion that the diary would "take its place beside the revelations of St. Augustine, Petronius, Abélard, Rousseau, Proust." Others, who over the years watched the diary grow to its present state of some 150 volumes—adding up to more than 15,000 pages in typewritten transcript—contributed their share to the growing legend surrounding this remarkable, lifelong undertaking.

Anaïs Nin herself has often stated that the body of her published, artistic work—the five novels which make up the *roman fleuve, Cities of the Interior,* and her other books and stories—were merely outcroppings of the diary, and that her real life, as a writer and a woman, was contained in the pages of the journal. "I have a natural flow in the diary," she wrote more than thirty years ago, "what I produce outside is a distillation, the myth, the poem." And after an argument about one of her early works of fiction, she noted in the diary: "Sometimes when people talk to me, I feel that I have done all they ask of me here, in the journal, when they ask me to be authentic, passionate, explosive, etc."

Much of the speculation about this legendary work, no doubt, derived from the fact that Miss Nin, in her intense and multileveled life, moved freely, and sometimes mysteriously, in the cosmopolitan world of international art and society. "Friendships, relationships, and travel," she has said, "are my greatest pleasure. The world I live in, in every city, is that of writers, painters, musicians, dancers, and actors." As a child, born in Neuilly, a suburb of Paris, she had accompanied her famous father, the Spanish composer-pianist Joaquin Nin, on his glamorous concert tours through Europe. As a youngster, she had escaped from the poor gentility of her Danish-born mother's rooming house in New York into the enchanted gardens of her fantasies, and eventually had become an artists' model and, later, a Spanish dancer. As a fledgling writer, she had, in the 1930s, re-entered the intellectual and social climate of Paris, captivated, and influenced, by Proust, Lawrence, and Giraudoux. In 1929, she had settled in Louveciennes, and there —as, after the outbreak of World War II, in her studio on the edges of New York's Greenwich Village—had provided a gathering place for many "unknown," and often subsequently "famous," creative people. Indeed, the roster of those who appear, at one time or another, in Miss Nin's diary represents an impressive cross-section of the literary and artistic life of the past forty years.

But those who may have set their sights merely upon the usual "exposures" of famous lives, the "tell-all" confessions of an insider, will undoubtedly be disappointed by this long-awaited first publication of a section of Miss Nin's diary. To be sure, Anaïs Nin writes at length, and often with startling candor, about her relationships, her friends and acquaintances, the "famous" and the "ordinary" people who have crossed her path. She is, indeed, "authentic, passionate, explosive." But her concern is not that of the literary gossip. She does not simply treat us to another "keyhole" view of the literary life.

The true significance, the uniqueness, the "revelation" of her diary is of another kind. Certainly, Miss Nin provides much important and valuable biographical, and autobiographical, detail to our knowledge of an artistic era, she portrays and records with flashing insight people, conversations, events. Yet in the end it does not seem to matter that the struggling writer she befriends is Henry Miller, that the tortured poet who confides in her is Antonin Artaud, the propounder of the "theatre of cruelty," or that Dr. Otto Rank is her psychiatrist. The "revelation" of Miss Nin's diary, essentially, lies in the fact that here, for the first time, we have a passionate, detailed, articulate record of a modern woman's journey of self-discovery.

"What I have to say," Miss Nin writes, "is really distinct from the artist and art. *It is the woman who has to speak*. And it is not only the woman Anaïs who has to speak, but I who have to speak for many women. As I discover myself, I feel I am merely one of many, a symbol. I begin to understand women of yesterday and today. The mute ones of the past, the inarticulate, who took refuge behind wordless intuitions, and the women of today, all action, and copies of men. And I, in between . . ."

Indeed, Miss Nin's diary is more than the whetstone of an emerging writer, though she is always aware of the artistic problem of "what to include, what to tell, how to tell it." It is more than a notebook of ideas, dreams, and experiences, though, as she has stated, much of her conscious literary work is drawn from the pages of the diary. And it is more than a mere record of her days, her conversations, her encounters, though she captures them with vivid immediacy. The diary is the log of her journey through the labyrinth of the self, of her effort to find, and to define, the woman Anaïs, the real and the symbolic one who balances "between" action and contemplation, involvement and self-preservation, emotion and intellect, dreams and reality, and who sometimes despairs of ever reconciling these disparate elements.

There is an entry in the diary, in the mid-1930s, which may explain not only Miss Nin's attitude to the "outside" world—to the gathering political and economic storms which, much to the dismay of her critics, found no direct reflection in her artistic work—but also the basic, underlying function of the journal itself. "What makes people despair," she wrote, "is that they try to find a universal meaning to the whole of life, and then end up by saying it is absurd, illogical, empty of meaning. There is not one big, cosmic meaning for all, there is only the meaning we each give to our life, an individual meaning, an individual plot, like an individual novel, a book for each person. To seek a total unity is wrong. To give as much meaning to one's life as possible seems right to me. For example, I am not committed to any of the political movements which I find full of fanaticism and injustice, but in the face of each human being, I act democratically and humanly. I give each human being his due. I disregard class and possessions. It is the value of their spirit, of their human qualities I pay my respect to, and to their needs as far as I am able to fulfill them. If all of us acted in unison as I act individually, there would be no wars and no poverty. I have made myself personally responsible for the fate of every human being who has come my way."

The diary is Anaïs Nin's book. It is her created life, the filter through which she strains her experience into a meaningful pattern. It is also her shield and her confessional.

The diary had its inception on the boat that brought Anaïs Nin, her mother and two brothers, from Spain to America. At the age of eleven Miss Nin already was possessed by what she later called "an immediate awareness," both "terrible and painful." Her father, the idol of her early years, had deserted the family, had turned his attention to another, a very young woman. At first, she tried to win back her father: "The diary began as the diary of a journey, to record everything for my father. It was really a letter, so he could follow us into a strange land, know about us." But the "letter" was never sent (her mother told her it would get lost), and the diary became also "an island, in which I could find refuge in an alien land, write French, think my thoughts, hold on to my soul, to myself."

Isolated from her father, from her European childhood, from the supportive strictures of her early Spanish Catholicism, forced to adapt to a new country, a new language, Anaïs Nin rapidly acquired a sense of her own separateness. "My dear diary," she wrote at the time, "it is Anaïs who is speaking to you, and not somebody who thinks as everybody should think. Dear diary, pity me, but listen to me."

As the fanciful youngster blossomed into a vivacious young woman, "possessed by a fever for knowledge, experience and creation," Anaïs Nin also began to build for herself an "image," a "persona" which enabled her to face the world. The sense of drama, the imagination she had displayed as a child, now asserted itself, instinctively as well as consciously, in her adult life. Like the characters in her fiction, like Sabina in *A Spy in the House of Love*, she gave herself wholeheartedly to the "roles" she felt she was expected to play—daughter, wife, artist, enchantress, bohemian, friend, caretaker, etc.—to the expectations and demands that others made upon her.

"There were always, in me," she noted soberly at the age of twenty-nine, "two women at least, one woman desperate and bewildered, who felt she was drowning, and another who would leap into a scene, as upon a stage, conceal her true emotions because they were weaknesses, helplessness, despair, and present to the world only a smile, an eagerness, curiosity, enthusiasm, interest."

While the world watched with fascination the gay, charming, intelligent, mysterious Anaïs, the other women in her—the shy, the strong, the practical, the unsure, the observing, the detached, the childish—clamored for recognition in the pages of the diary. It is the gathering place of her fragmented self, her retreat from the demands of living.

"This diary is my kief, hashish, and opium pipe. This is my drug and my vice. Instead of writing a novel, I lie back with this book and a pen, and dream, and indulge in refractions and defractions . . . I must relive my life in the dream. The dream is my only life. I see in the echoes and reverberations, the transfigurations which alone keep wonder pure. Otherwise all magic is lost. Otherwise life shows its deformities and the homeliness becomes rust . . . All matter must be fused this way through the lens of my vice or the rust of living would slow down my rhythm to a sob."

Her escape into the diary, she realizes at times, is fraught with danger ("You have hampered me as an artist") and she fears that in "talking to this friend I have, perhaps, wasted my life." But even when her sense of isolation and despair of ever meshing the various aspects of her self into a meaningful whole prompt her to undergo psychoanalysis, she balks at being without her crutch, without her diary.

"I only regret that everybody wants to deprive me of the journal," she wrote in June, 1933, "which is the only steadfast friend I have, the only one which makes my life bearable, because my happiness with human beings is so precarious, my confiding moods rare, and the least sign of non-interest is enough to silence me. In the journal I am at ease."

Tenaciously, she hangs on to her diary. Like a talisman, she carries it with her. She writes on trains, at café tables, while waiting for an appointment, and as soon as she returns from an excursion into "life," she turns to the journal. The "lens of her vice" not only allows her to filter her experiences ("When I write afterwards, I see much more, understand better, I develop and enrich"), it also gives her writing its rare sense of immediacy.

"I live more on time. What is remembered later does not seem as true to me. I have such a need of truth. It must be that need of immediate recording which incites me to write almost while I am living, before it is altered, changed by distance or time."

This vivid freshness, coupled with her enriching reflection, seems to have determined not only the marvelously natural flow Miss Nin has achieved in her diary ("Writing for a hostile world discouraged me. Writing for the diary gave me the illusion of a warm ambiance I needed to flower in"), but, to some extent, also the nature of her material. In an essay "On Writing," published in 1947, she wrote: "The diary taught me that it is in the moments of emotional crisis that human beings reveal themselves most accurately. I learned to choose the heightened moments because they are the moments of revelation."

Anaïs Nin's passionate pursuit of truth, her peeling away of the many layers of a character in search of the illusive human core, often strikes her as painful and dangerous. "It hurts me to be giving myself away." The woman in her wearies of the ultimate exposure. "What kills life," she had written, "is the absence of mystery." Even when she decides to show her father, whom she had seen again in 1933, some of the childhood diaries originally written for him, she has her doubts. "These days," she wrote in a letter to him, "I feel like abdicating as a writer. It suddenly seems monstrous to me to expose the feelings one has, even those in the past, even the dead ones."

Though many of her friends and admirers had urged her for years to begin with the publication of what they considered her true life work as a writer—see, for instance, the recurring references in Henry Miller's *Letters to Anaïs Nin* (Putnam, 1965)—Miss Nin, for various reasons, hesitated. There were problems of personal privacy, legal hurdles, and there was the enormous bulk of the manuscript, which made a chronological, complete publication of the work an economic impossibility. So the original manuscript remained in Miss Nin's iron strong-boxes, first in France (where, in the turmoil of the early days of World War II, the whole diary was lost, for some time, at a rural railroad station), and subsequently in the United States. Maxwell Perkins, the editor who had struggled with the manuscript coffers of Thomas Wolfe, once suggested to Miss Nin a one-volume condensation of the diary, but quickly changed his mind and protested that nothing should be cut. Alas, a complete publication of the work, even today, remains impossible. We can only hope that some day the entire diary will be made available. For the moment, we must be content with, and grateful for, the possible.

The present volume—the first in a projected series drawn from the body of the work—begins in 1931, at a time when Miss Nin herself is about to publish her first book, an appreciation of D. H. Lawrence, which gained her first public recognition as a writer. It seemed a logical starting point. It ends, in the winter of 1934, when Miss Nin leaves Paris for what turned out to be a brief stay in New York. The present text represents approximately half of the material contained in the ten original manuscript volumes (No. 30 to No. 40) covering this period. In preparing this volume for publication, Miss Nin, and the editor, still faced certain personal and legal considerations inherent in the nature of the diary. Several persons, when faced with the question of whether they wanted to remain in the diary "as is"—since Miss Nin did not want to change the essential nature of her presentation—chose to be deleted altogether from the manuscript (including her husband and some members of her family). The names of some incidental figures have been omitted or changed, since, as any reader will soon see, the factual identity of a person is basically unimportant within the context of the diary. Miss Nin's truth, as we have seen, is psychological. The dates in brackets, given by the editor, also are merely intended to indicate the flow of time (or date a specific event), and do not always correspond to the numerous dates in the original manuscripts, where retrospective entries sometimes confuse the actual chronology. Some excerpts from the earlier childhood diaries have been translated from the original French and included by Miss Nin to provide background information and facilitate the understanding of certain situations, notably Miss Nin's relationship to her father. A short bibliography of Miss Nin's books is given elsewhere in this volume.

"I believe literature, as we have known it, will die, is dying," Anaïs Nin noted in her diary many years ago. Yet in creating this diary she has, perhaps, already given us a new kind of literature: her own articulate record of an individual past which, in its timeless, universal validity, provides us with a blueprint for our own future. "We are going to the moon," Anaïs Nin has written. "That is not very far. Man has so much farther to go within himself."

GUNTHER STUHLMANN

New York
October 1965

The
Diary
of
Anaïs Nin

[Winter, 1931–1932]

Louveciennes resembles the village where Madame Bovary lived and died. It is old, untouched and unchanged by modern life. It is built on a hill overlooking the Seine. On clear nights one can see Paris. It has an old church dominating a group of small houses, cobblestone streets, and several large properties, manor houses, a castle on the outskirts of the village. One of the properties belonged to Madame du Barry. During the revolution her lover was guillotined and his head thrown over the ivy-covered wall into her garden. This is now the property of Coty.

There is a forest all around in which the Kings of France once hunted. There is a very fat and very old miser who owns most of the property of Louveciennes. He is one of Balzac's misers. He questions every expense, every repair, and always ends by letting his houses deteriorate with rust, rain, weeds, leaks, cold.

Behind the windows of the village houses old women sit watching people passing by. The street runs down unevenly towards the Seine. By the Seine there is a tavern and a restaurant. On Sundays people come from Paris and have lunch and take the rowboats down the Seine as Maupassant loved to do.

The dogs bark at night. The garden smells of honeysuckle in the summer, of wet leaves in the winter. One hears the whistle of the small train from and to Paris. It is a train which looks ancient, as if it were still carrying the personages of Proust's novels to dine in the country.

My house is two hundred years old. It has walls a yard thick, a big garden, a very large green iron gate for cars, flanked by a small green gate for people. The big garden is in the back of the house. In the front there is a gravel driveway, and a pool which is now filled with dirt and planted with ivy. The fountain emerges like the headstone of a tomb. The bell people pull sounds like a giant cowbell. It shakes and echoes a long time after it has been pulled. When it rings, the Spanish maid, Emilia, swings open the large gate and the cars drive up the gravel path, making a crackling sound.

There are eleven windows showing between the wooden trellis covered with ivy. One shutter in the middle was put there for symmetry only, but I often dream about this mysterious room which does not exist behind the closed shutter.

Behind the house lies a vast wild tangled garden. I never liked formal gardens. At the very back is a wooded section with a small brook, a small bridge, overrun with ivy and moss and ferns.

The day begins always with the sound of gravel crushed by the car.

The shutters are pushed open by Emilia, and the day admitted.

With the first crushing of the gravel under wheels comes the barking of the police dog, Banquo, and the carillon of the church bells.

When I look at the large green iron gate from my window it takes on the air of a prison gate. An unjust feeling, since I know I can leave the place whenever I want to, and since I know that human beings place upon an object, or a person, this responsibility of being the obstacle when the obstacle lies always within one's self.

In spite of this knowledge I often stand at the window staring at the large closed iron gate, as if hoping to obtain from this contemplation a reflection of my inner obstacles to a full, open life.

No amount of oil can subdue its rheumatic creaks, for it takes a historical pride in its two-hundred-year-old rust.

But the little gate, with its overhanging ivy like disordered hair over a running child's forehead, has a sleepy and sly air, an air of being always half open.

I chose the house for many reasons.

Because it seemed to have sprouted out of the earth like a tree, so deeply grooved it was within the old garden. It had no cellar and the rooms rested right on the ground. Below the rug, I felt, was the earth. I could take root here, feel at one with the house and garden, take nourishment from them like the plants.

The first thing I did was to have the basin and fountain unearthed and restored. Then it seemed to me that the house came alive. The fountain was gay and sprightly.

I had a sense of preparation for a love to come. Like the extension of canopies, the unrolling of ceremonial carpets, as if I must first create a marvelous world in which to house it, in which to receive adequately this guest of honor.

It is in this mood of preparation that I pass through the house, painting a wall through which stains of humidity show, hanging a lamp where it will throw Balinese shadow plays, draping a bed, placing logs in the fireplace.

Every room is painted a different color. As if there were one room for every separate mood: lacquer red for vehemence, pale turquoise for reveries, peach color for gentleness, green for repose, grey for work at the typewriter.

Ordinary life does not interest me. I seek only the high moments. I am in accord with the surrealists, searching for the marvelous.

I want to be a writer who reminds others that these moments exist; I want to prove that there is infinite space, infinite meaning, infinite dimension.

But I am not always in what I call a state of grace. I have days of illuminations and fevers. I have days when the music in my head stops. Then I mend socks, prune trees, can fruits, polish furniture. But while I am doing this I feel I am not living.

Unlike Madame Bovary, I am not going to take poison. I am not sure that being a writer will help me escape from Louveciennes. I have finished my book *D. H. Lawrence: An Unprofessional Study.* I wrote it in sixteen days. I had to go to Paris to present it to Edward Titus for publication. It will not be published and out by tomorrow, which is what a writer would like when the book is hot out of the oven, when it is alive within one's self. He gave it to his assistant to revise.

As soon as I go to Paris too often, my mother looks disapprovingly out of her window, and does not wave good-bye. She looks, at times, like the old women who raise their curtains to stare at me when I take Banquo for a walk. My brother Joaquin plays the piano continuously, as if he would melt the walls of the house.

I take walks along the railroad tracks on bad days. But as I have never been able to read a timetable, I never walk here at the right time and I get tired before the train comes to deliver me from the difficulties of living, and I walk back home. Does this fascination for a possible accident come from the traumatic time when I missed such a death as a child? We had a servant in Neuilly (when I was two years old, and my brother Thorvald just born). My father must have seduced her and then forgotten her. Anyway, she sought revenge. She took my brother and me on an outing and left the carriage, and me beside it, in the middle of the railroad track. But the signal gateman saw us, and as he had seven children of his own, he took a chance on his own life and rushed out in time to kick the carriage out of the way and carry me off in his arms. The event remained in our memory. I still remember the beds covered with toys for the seven children of the man who saved our lives.

Richard Osborn is a lawyer. He had to be consulted on the copyrights of my D. H. Lawrence book. He is trying to be both a Bohemian and a lawyer for a big firm. He likes to leave his office with money in his pocket and go to Montparnasse. He pays for everyone's dinner and drinks. When he is drunk he talks about the novel he is going to write. He gets very little sleep and often arrives at his office the next morning with stains and wrinkles on his suit. As if to detract attention from such details, he talks more volubly and brilliantly than ever, giving his listeners no time to interrupt or respond, so that everyone is saying, "Richard is losing his clients. He cannot stop talking." He acts like a man on a trapeze who must not look down at the public. If he looks below he will fall. He will fall somewhere between his lawyer's office and Montparnasse. No one will know where to look for him for he hides his two faces from all. There are times when he is still asleep in some unknown hotel with an unknown woman when he should be at his office, and other times when he is working late at his office, while his friends are waiting for him at the Café du Dôme.

He has two recurrent monologues. One is patterned after a trial for plagiarism. It seems that a great many people have copied his novels, his plays, and his ideas. He is preparing a long brief to sue them. "They" always steal his briefcase. One of the novels stolen from him is now published, and one of his plays is being acted on Broadway. That is why he does not show his present novel to me or to anyone.

His other monologue concerns his friend Henry Miller. Henry Miller is writing a book one thousand pages long which has everything in it that is left out of other novels. He has now taken refuge in Richard's hotel room. "Every morning when I leave he is still asleep. I leave ten francs on the table, and when I return there is another batch of writing done."

A few days ago he brought me an article by Henry Miller on Buñuel's film *L'Âge d'Or*. It was as potent as a bomb. It reminded me of D. H. Lawrence's "I am a human bomb."

There is in this piece of writing a primitive, savage quality. By contrast with the writers I have been reading, it seems like a jungle. Only a short article, but the words are slung like hatchets, explode with hatred, and it was like hearing wild drums in the midst of the Tuileries gardens.

You live like this, sheltered, in a delicate world, and you believe you are living. Then you read a book (*Lady Chatterley*, for instance), or you take a trip, or you talk with Richard, and you discover that you are not living, that you are hibernating. The symptoms of hibernating are easily detectable: first, restlessness. The second symptom (when hibernating becomes dangerous and might degenerate into death): absence of pleasure. That is all. It appears like an innocuous illness. Monotony, boredom, death. Millions live like this (or die like this) without knowing it. They work in offices. They drive a car. They picnic with their families. They raise children. And then some shock treatment takes place, a person, a book, a song, and it awakens them and saves them from death.

Some never awaken. They are like the people who go to sleep in the snow and never awaken. But I am not in danger because my home, my garden, my beautiful life do not lull me. I am aware of being in a beautiful prison, from which I can only escape by writing. So I have written a book about D. H. Lawrence out of gratitude, because it was he who awakened me. I took it to Richard and he prepared the contracts, and then he talked about his friend Henry Miller. He had shown my manuscript to Henry Miller and Miller had said, "I have never read such strong truths told with such delicacy."

"I would like to bring him to dinner," said Richard. And I said yes.

So delicacy and violence are about to meet and challenge each other.

The image this brings to my mind is an alchemist workshop. Beautiful crystal bottles communicating with each other by a system of fragile crystal canals. These transparent bottles show nothing but jeweled, colored liquids or clouded water or smoke, giving to the external eye an abstract aesthetic pleasure. The consciousness of danger, fatal mixtures, is known only to the chemist.

I feel like a well-appointed laboratory of the soul—myself, my home, my life—in which none of the vitally fecund or destructive, explosive experiments has yet begun. I like the shape of the bottles, the colors of the chemicals. I collect bottles, and the more they look like alchemist bottles the more I like them for their eloquent forms.

When I saw Henry Miller walking towards the door where I stood waiting, I closed my eyes for an instant to see him by some other inner eye. He was warm, joyous, relaxed, natural.

He would have passed anonymously through a crowd. He was slender, lean, not tall. He looked like a Buddhist monk, a rosy-skinned monk, with his partly bald head aureoled by lively silver hair, his full sensuous mouth. His blue eyes are cool and observant, but his mouth is emotional and vulnerable. His laughter is contagious and his voice caressing and warm like a Negro voice.

He was so different from his brutal, violent, vital writing, his caricatures, his Rabelaisian farces, his exaggerations. The smile at the corner of his eyes is almost clownish; the mellow tones of his voice are almost like a purring content. He is a man whom life intoxicates, who has no need of wine, who is floating in a self-created euphoria.

In the middle of a serious discussion between Richard and Joaquin, he began to laugh. Seeing the perplexity on Richard's face, he said, "I'm not laughing at you, Richard, but I just can't help myself. I don't care a bit who's right. I'm too happy. I'm just so happy right at this moment, with all the colors around me, the fire in the fireplace, the good dinner, the wine, the whole moment is so wonderful, so wonderful . . ." He talked slowly, as if enjoying his own words. He installed himself completely in the present. He appeared gentle and candid. He admitted he had only come because of Richard's promise of a good dinner. But now he wanted to know the whole house, everyone living in it, what each one did, and asked question after question with casual unrelentingness. Henry Miller talked with Joaquin about music, about his compositions and his concerts. He went to shake my mother's hand, he visited the garden, looked over the books. He was full of curiosity. Then, sitting by the fire, he began to talk about himself:

"Last night I spent the night in a *cinéma de quartier*. I had nowhere else to go. Richard was entertaining his girl. I watched the film three times because the actress reminded me of my wife, June. Then I slipped down into the seat and went to sleep. They never clean up the place until morning and even then the *femme de ménage* only grunts when she sees me and lets me off. Did you ever stay in a movie house when it's empty? Films are like a dose of opium, then as you come out in the street it's a shock, and you are brutally awakened from your dream. But when you stay, you never wake up. The dream goes on working. I would fall asleep for a while and then see images on the screen, and I could not tell the difference between the film and a dream. I saw my wife, June, as she looked when she announced to me one morning in New York: 'You always wanted to go to Paris and become a writer, well, I have the money. But I can't go with you. I'll follow you later.' The story on the screen was about a woman who lied, she lied, and damn it, she made the lie come true. She wanted to become an actress so she invented that she had a love affair with the best known of all the actors, and publicized it so well, in such heightened colors, that the actor himself came to confront her. Then she explained to him why she had done it, describing at the same time the 'scenes' which had taken place between them, with such charm that he stayed on and fulfilled all she had invented as if it had been a prophecy. My wife, June, can confuse me in this way. She stayed in New York to earn money for my trip. Don't ask me how she earns money. Every time I tried to find out, I ran into such complicated stories, intrigues, miraculous barters, that I gave up trying to understand. Everything she did had that air of prestidigitation. 'You want to go to Paris, Henry? I'll find a way. The rent is due. Let me see the landlord.' She reminded me of the gypsies I saw in the south of France. When they come home, they lift up their skirt and, presto, there's a chicken or two they have stolen. I felt that June's stories were lies, but I could not disprove them. I felt that her bargaining power came not from objects or ingenuity but from giving herself. She would tell me to keep on writing and forget about all this, but I could not write. I spent all my time trying to figure out how she solved these problems without going to work like everybody else. She never answered direct questions. She reminded me of the Arabs who believe that true intelligence consists of concealment of your thoughts. But damn it, you conceal your thoughts from an enemy, not a husband, lover, friend. She always said she concealed her thoughts from me because whatever she did tell me, I would turn around and caricature. But I only do this when I'm angry. If she read a book, sooner or later I would discover it had been given to her by somebody else and that her opinion of the book belonged to the giver. Other times she even told people that it was she who had first made me read Dostoevsky and Proust. I don't know why I am talking in the past tense. She's coming in a few weeks."

The two sides of himself showed simultaneously: acceptance and passivity in life, rebellion and anger at whatever happened to him. He endured, and then must avenge himself, probably in his writing. The writer's delayed reaction.

June is an irritant. He turns away into the uncomplicated worlds he enjoys. "I like the prostitutes. There is no pretense there. They wash themselves in front of you."

Henry is like a mythical animal. His writing is flamboyant, torrential, chaotic, treacherous, and dangerous. "Our age has need of violence."

I enjoy the power of his writing, the ugly, destructive, fearless cathartic strength. This strange mixture of worship of life, enthusiasm, passionate interest in everything, energy, exuberance, laughter, and sudden destructive storms baffles me. Everything is blasted away: hypocrisy, fear, pettiness, falsity. It is an assertion of instinct. He uses the first person, real names; he repudiates order and form and fiction itself. He writes in the uncoordinated way we feel, on various levels at once.

I have always believed in André Breton's freedom, to write as one thinks, in the order and disorder in which one feels and thinks, to follow sensations and absurd correlations of events and images, to trust to the new realms they lead one into. "The cult of the marvelous." Also the cult of the unconscious leadership, the cult of mystery, the evasion of false logic. The cult of the unconscious as proclaimed by Rimbaud. It is not madness. It is an effort to transcend the rigidities and the patterns made by the rational mind.

Henry has a strange mixture of all these things. He can be swept off his feet easily by a book, a person, an idea. He is a musician and a painter.

He notices everything, the fat-bellied bottles for the wine, the hissing of the damp logs in the fireplace. He selects from everything only what can be enjoyed. He even enjoys Emilia's slightly crossed eyes. She reminds him of figures in Goya paintings. He enjoys the colors on the wall, the oranges and the blues.

He finds joy in everything, in food, in talk, in drink, in the sound of the bell at the gate, the liveliness of Banquo, who comes in slapping the furniture with his tail.

He thinks I must know a great deal about life because I once posed for painters when I was sixteen. The extent of my innocence would be incredible to him. I tried to look up in the dictionary some of the words he uses, but they were not there.

After he left I destroyed my enjoyment, thinking he would not be interested in me, that he had lived too much, too roughly, too completely, like a Dostoevskian character, the lower depths, and he would find me inexperienced. What does it matter what Henry thinks of me. He will know soon enough exactly what I am. He has a caricatural mind. I will see myself in caricature. Why cannot I express the fundamental me? I play roles too. Why should I care? But I do care. I care about everything. Emotionalism and sensibility are my quicksands. I am fascinated with the "toughness" of Henry and June. It is new to me.

It takes great hatred to make caricature and satire.

I have no hatreds. I have compassion. Everything with me is either worship, passion, or else compassion, understanding. I hate rarely. But I respond to Henry's fiery rebellions. His angers. I can't fathom the paradox of his enjoyment and his angers. My rebellions were concealed, inhibited, indirect. His are open revolutions. He laughs at my concern for Emilia's feelings. I did not want her to hear him laughing at her head being out of proportion to her body. I never hate enough to mock, caricature, or even describe what I hate at length. I am more preoccupied with loving. I can't rave as Henry does against conventional novelists. I picked out D. H. Lawrence and devoted myself to him. I don't rave against politics. I ignore it. I elect something I can love and absorb myself in it. I am absorbed by Henry, who is unsure of himself, self-critical, sincere, and carries within him some great force. I am very busy loving. What does he need? Everything. He is almost a hobo. Sleeps anywhere, at a friend's house, a railroad-station waiting room on a bench, in a movie house, in a park. He has hardly any clothes. They are not his own.

He is rewriting his first book [*Crazy Cock*]. He lives from day to day, borrowing, begging, sponging. He wants a set of Proust. I add railroad tickets to them so that he can come and see me when he wants to. He has no typewriter. So I give him mine. He likes big meals, so I cook sumptuous ones. I would like to give him a home, an income, security so that he could work.

Henry came again today. He talked about his second wife, June. June was full of stories. She told him several versions about her childhood, birthplace, parents, racial origins. Her first version was that her mother was a Roumanian gypsy, that she sang in cafés and told fortunes. Her father, she said, played the guitar. When they came to America, they opened a night club, mostly for Roumanians. It was a continuation of their life in Roumania. But when Henry asked her what did she do in that environment, did she sing, did she tell fortunes, did she learn to dance, did she wear long braids and white blouses, she did not answer. Henry wanted to know where she had learned the beautiful English she spoke, like English spoken on the stage by English actors. He took her to a Roumanian restaurant and waited for her response to the music, the dances, the songs, to the swarthy men whose glances were like dagger thrusts. But June had forgotten this story by then and looked on the scene with detachment. When Henry pressed her for the truth, she began another story. She told him that she was born on the road, that her parents were show people, that they traveled all the time, that her father was a magician in a circus, her mother a trapezist.

(Had she learned there her skill in balancing in space, in time, avoiding all definitions and crystallizations? Had she learned from her father to deal in camouflage, in quick sleight of hand? This story, Henry said, came before the one in which she asserted her father had been anonymous. Not knowing who she was, he might turn out to be the man she most admired at the time.)

Henry said that another time she had told him her father was a Don Juan, that it was his faithlessness which had affected her childhood, giving her a feeling of impermanency, distrust of man. He reminded her of this when she talked about her "magician" father. This did not trouble her. "That was true, too," said June. "One can be a faithless magician."

From the very first day I could see that Henry, who had always lived joyously and obviously *outside*, in daylight, had been drawn into this labyrinth unwittingly by his own curiosity and love of facts. He only believed in what he saw, like a candid photographer, and he now found himself inside a row of mirrors with endless reflections and counter-reflections.

June must be like those veiled figures glimpsed turning the corner of a Moroccan street, wrapped from head to foot in white cotton, throwing to a stranger a single spark from fathomless eyes. Was she the very woman he had been seeking? He felt a compulsion to follow her, from story to story. From a mobile, evanescent childhood to a kaleidoscopic adolescence, to a tumultuous and smoky womanhood, a figure whom even a passport official would have difficulty in identifying.

Henry has the primitive urge of the conqueror. From the first day, he was trapped by what he believed to be a duel between reality and illusion. It was difficult to conquer and invade a labyrinth. The brain of man is filled with passageways like the contours and multiple crossroads of the labyrinth. In its curved folds lie the imprints of thousands of images, recordings of a million words.

Certain cities of the Orient were designed to baffle the enemy by a tangle of intricate streets. For those concealed within the labyrinth, its detours were a measure of safety; for the invader, it presented an image of fearful mystery.

June must have chosen the labyrinth for safety.

In seeking to understand Henry's talk about June, and his obsessional curiosity, I gave him the feeling that I understood her. Yet he said, "You are not at all the same."

"Perhaps she felt," I said, "that once her stories were finished, you would lose interest."

"But it was just the opposite, I felt that the day she would tell me the truth I would really love her, possess her. It was the lies I fought."

What was she seeking to conceal? Why had he assumed the role of detective?

Henry seems so candid. He talks without premeditation. He seems the incarnation of spontaneity. He seems direct, open, naked. He never withholds what he thinks or feels. He passes no judgment on others, and expects none to be passed on him. But he is a caricaturist. June may have feared his sense of caricature.

Even I could see the danger of his angers. He paints savagely those who do not give him what he asks of them, whether it is the truth, or help. He is suspicious of poetry and beauty. Beauty, he seems to say, is artifice. Truth only lies in people and things stripped of aesthetics.

Was he the lover of June's body but curious about its essence? And frustrated in the knowledge of this essence?

While he talked, I remembered reading that the Arabs did not respect the man who unveiled his thoughts. The intelligence of an Arab was measured by his capacity to elude direct questions. This was true of Indians, of Mexicans. The questioner was always suspect. June must have been of such races. Did she truly originate thousands of years ago from the people who veiled their faces and their thoughts? Where does she come from, that she understands well this racial dedication to mystery?

Henry has a habit of asking naïve questions, of prying. When his curiosity is satisfied he seems to be saying, "You see, there was nothing behind that." He is one who would walk behind the magician's props; he would expose Houdini.

He hates poetry and he hates illusion. His own savage self-confessions demand the same of others. This passion for unveiling, exposing, must be the one which compels him to enter June's smoke-screened world.

When he first talked, it seemed like the natural preoccupation of a lover: does she love me? does she love me alone? does she love others as she loves me? does she love anyone?

But there is more. He marks in Proust the passages referring to Albertine's habit of never saying: I love, I want; but others wanted, others loved her, etc.; thus she eluded all responsibility, all commitments.

He treats the whole world as men are said to treat prostitutes, desiring, embracing, and then discarding, knowing only hunger and then indifference.

He is a gentle savage, who lives directed entirely by his whims, moods, his rhythms, and does not notice others' moods or needs.

We sit at the Viking Café. It is all of wood, low-ceilinged, and the walls are covered with murals of the Vikings' history. They serve strong drinks which Henry likes. The lighting is dim. One has a feeling of being on an old galleon, sailing Nordic seas.

Henry talks about June and I listen and seek to understand.

Was he a very hurt man? Hurt men were dangerous, like wounded animals in the jungle.

June may fear to see a distorted image of herself in him. He has already written about her in a way which I would find intolerable. Without *charity*, without feeling. I see distorted images of others in his talk. They are all like Hieronymus Bosch. Only the ugliness appears. I can understand, when I listen to him, the Oriental fear of letting others paint you or photograph you.

Poor June is not like me, able to make her own portrait. Henry, I can see, is already suspicious of my quickness of mind, my pirouettes, even though I answer his questions directly.

While Henry is so concerned to know whether June has other lovers, whether she loves women, or takes drugs, it seems to me that he overlooks the true mystery: why are such secrets necessary to her?

In spite of the seriousness of these talks, pondering the mysteries of June, each meeting we have is like a holiday. Henry arrives in a workman's suit one day, another time in Richard's discarded suit, which is too big for him.

He shows me the black sooty angel who guards the house called The Well. It is a round house with a small medieval courtyard, dark as a well and as dank. The angel is all black with time. The rain can only clean his eyelids, and so he stares at the darkness with white eyes. Henry is in love with Mona Paiva, a reigning courtesan of a hundred years ago whose photograph he found on the quays. His pockets are full of notes on the meals he would like to eat one day:

> *Merlans à la Bercy*
> *Coquilles de Cervelles au Gratin*
> *Flamri de Semoule*
> *Galantine de Volaille à la Gelée*
> *Anguilles Pompadour*
> *Selle de Mouton Bouquetière.*

I don't think he knows what the dishes really are. He is fascinated with the *sound* of words. He notes fragments of conversation on menus, toilet paper, envelopes. He takes me to the Mariner's flophouse to eat an omelet with pickpockets. He plays chess at the café where old actors meet for a game to the tune of tired classical musicians playing quartets. At dawn he likes to sit and watch the tired prostitutes walking home.

He has an eagerness to catch everything without make-up, without embellishment, women before they comb their hair, waiters before they don artificial smiles with their artificial bow ties. His quest for naturalism must have come to a stop before June's heavily painted eyes, and I can well see her as he talks, a woman whom daylight cannot touch.

"She hates daylight."

In Henry's glaring, crude daylight upon externals, and in her preference for the night, I can see the core of their conflict.

From his novel I see, too, that until he met June, women confounded themselves in his mind; they were interchangeable; his desire never became a desire to know them intimately; they were faceless, without identity except as sexual objects.

He was never concerned about the identity or individuality of his women, but because June would not acknowledge any, he began to search for one.

Why did she fix his attention? Did she have a more voluptuous body, a more penetrating voice, a more dazzling smile than other women? He paints her in his novel in opulent colors.

I wonder if it is not so much that June hides a great deal from him, but that he fails to see what is there, as I begin to see a June who does not baffle me. Perhaps when she talks so much about the others who love her, it is not to conceal whether she loves them or not, but because this is what interests her. Her desire to BE loved. Among the chaotic confessions, the rambling talks, the flow of fiction, I detect a June who escapes direct questions but who offers other clues.

His first letter to her was delirious. She showed it to her mother. June wanted to know if Henry was a drug addict. This question startled Henry, because his intoxications come from images, words, colors. It occurred to him that June must have taken drugs if the idea of wild flights of imagination was linked in her mind inevitably with the use of drugs.

He asked her how the idea had come to her. As an artist he held the proud notion that every image came out of his own spontaneous chemistry, not from any synthetic formula.

June eluded the question. "She often talks about drugs but never acknowledges any intimate experience with them." This became one of Henry's obsessional mysteries to unravel.

I can see that, up to the moment of his encounter with June, he was at ease in his physical, evident world, and how she made him doubt all of it.

They must have been drawn together by his need to expose illusion, her need to create it. A satanic pact. One of them must triumph: the realist or the mythmaker. The novelist in Henry turned detective, to find what lies behind appearance, and June creating mysteries as a natural flowering of her femininity.

How else to hold his interest for a thousand nights? And I feel he is already drawing me into this investigation.

I can see her symbolic resistance to the revelations of her thoughts and feelings creating in Henry a suspense similar to that of the strip-tease women who expose on the stage certain areas of their bodies and vanish when they are about to be seen completely nude.

He enters the labyrinth with a notebook! In her place I might close up too. If he annotates enough facts, he will finally possess the truth. His notes: black stockings, overfull bags, missing buttons, hair always falling down or about to topple down, a strand always falling over the eye, hasty dressing, mobility, no repose. Will not tell what school she went to, where she was raised as a child. Has two distinct manners, one refined, gracious, the other (when she loses her temper) crude like a street urchin. They correspond to her attitude about clothes. At times she has holes in her stockings, wears unwashed jeans, uses safety pins to hold everything together. At other times she rushes to buy gloves, perfume. But all the time her eyes are carefully made-up, like the eyes on Egyptian frescoes.

"She demands illusion as other women demand jewels."

For Henry, illusions and lies are synonymous. Art and illusion are lies. Embellishment. In this I feel remote from him, totally in disagreement with him. But I am silent. He is suffering. He is a man with a *banderilla* stuck in his body, a poisoned arrow, something he cannot rid himself of. He sometimes cries out, "Perhaps there is nothing at all, perhaps the mystery is that there is no mystery at all. Perhaps she is empty, and there is no June at all."

"But, Henry, how can an empty woman have such a vivid presence, how can an empty woman cause insomnia, awaken so many curiosities? How could an empty woman cause other women to take flight, as you tell me, abdicating immediately before her?"

He notices that I smile at the obviousness of his questions. For a moment his hostility turns against me.

I said, "I do feel that perhaps you did not ask the correct questions of the Sphinx."

"What would you ask?"

"I would not be concerned with the secrets, the lies, the mysteries, the facts. I would be concerned *with what makes them necessary. What fear.*"

This, I feel, Henry does not understand. He is the great collector of facts, and the essence sometimes escapes him.

From his notes for a future novel:

June brings to the studio a treasure house of curios, paintings, statues, with vague stories as to how they had been acquired. Just recently I found that she had obtained a statue from Zadkine saying she would sell it and, of course, never did. She makes use of the soft part of the bread for a napkin. She falls asleep at times with her shoes on, on unmade beds. When a little money comes in, June buys delicacies, strawberries in the winter, caviar and bath salts.

[December 30, 1931]

Henry came to Louveciennes with June.

As June walked towards me from the darkness of the garden into the light of the door, I saw for the first time the most beautiful woman on earth. A startlingly white face, burning dark eyes, a face so alive I felt it would consume itself before my eyes. Years ago I tried to imagine a true beauty; I created in my mind an image of just such a woman. I had never seen her until last night. Yet I knew long ago the phosphorescent color of her skin, her huntress profile, the evenness of her teeth. She is bizarre, fantastic, nervous, like someone in a high fever. Her beauty drowned me. As I sat before her, I felt I would do anything she asked of me. Henry suddenly faded. She was color and brilliance and strangeness. By the end of the evening I had extricated myself from her power. She killed my admiration by her talk. Her talk. The enormous ego, false, weak, posturing. She lacks the courage of her personality, which is sensual, heavy with experience. Her role alone preoccupies her. She invents dramas in which she always stars. I am sure she creates genuine dramas, genuine chaos and whirlpools of feelings, but I feel that her share in it is a pose. That night, in spite of my response to her, she sought to be whatever she felt I wanted her to be. She is an actress every moment. I cannot grasp the core of June. Everything Henry had said about her is true.

By the end of the evening I felt as Henry did, fascinated with her face and body which promises so much, but hating her invented self which hides the true one. This false self is composed to stir the admiration of others, inspires others to words and acts about and around her. I feel she does not know what to do when confronted with these legends which are born around her face and body; she feels unequal to them.

That night she never admitted, "I did not read that book." She was obviously repeating what she had heard Henry say. They were not her words. Or she tried to speak the suave language of an English actress.

She tried to subdue her feverishness to harmonize with the serenity of the house, but she could not control her endless smoking and her restlessness. She worried about the loss of her gloves as if it were a serious flaw in her costume, as if wearing gloves were enormously important.

It was strange. I who am not always sincere was astonished and repelled by her insincerity. I recalled Henry's words: "She seems perverse to me." The extent of her falsity was terrifying, like an abyss. Fluidity. Elusiveness. Where was June? Who was June? There is a woman who stirs others' imagination, that is all. She was the essence of the theatre itself, stirring the imagination, promising such an intensity and heightening of experience, such richness, and then failing to appear in person, giving instead a smoke screen of compulsive talk about trivialities. Others are roused, others are moved to write about her, others love her as Henry does, in spite of himself. And June? What does she feel?

June. At night I dreamed of her, not magnificent and overwhelming as she is, but very small and frail, and I loved her. I loved a smallness, a vulnerability which I felt was disguised by her inordinate pride, by her volubility. It is a hurt pride. She lacks confidence, she craves admiration insatiably. She lives on the reflections of herself in the eyes of others. She does not dare to be herself. There is no June to grasp and know. She knows it. The more she is loved, the more she knows it. She knows there is a very beautiful woman who took her cue last night from my inexperience and concealed the depth of her knowledge.

Her face startlingly white as she retreated into the darkness of the garden, she posed for me as she left. I wanted to run out and kiss her fantastic beauty and say: "June, you have killed my sincerity too. I will never know again who I am, what I am, what I love, what I want. Your beauty has drowned me, the core of me. You carry away with you a part of me reflected in you. When your beauty struck me, it dissolved me. Deep down, I am not different from you. I dreamed you, I wished for your existence. You are the woman I want to be. I see in you that part of me which is you. I feel compassion for your childish pride, for your trembling unsureness, your dramatization of events, your enhancing of the loves given to you. I surrender my sincerity because if I love you it means we share the same fantasies, the same madnesses."

Henry hurts her but he keeps her body and soul together. Her love for him is her only wholeness.

June and I have paid with our souls for taking fantasies seriously, for living life as a theatre, for loving costumes and changes of selves, for wearing masks and disguises. But I know always what is real. Does June?

I wanted to see June again. When she came out of the dark again, she seemed even more beautiful to me than the first time. Also she seemed more at ease. As she went up the stairs to my bedroom to leave her coat, she stood halfway up the stairs where the light set her off against the turquoise wall. Her blonde hair piled high and carelessly on her head, pallid face, peaked eyebrows, a sly smile, with a disarming dimple. Perfidious, I felt, infinitely desirable, drawing me to her as towards death. Downstairs, Henry's laughter and lustiness were earthy, simple, and there were no secrets, no dangers in Henry. Later she sat in the high-backed chair, against the books, and her silver earrings shimmered. She talked without tenderness or softness to Henry, mocked him, was relentless. They were telling about a quarrel they had before coming, about other quarrels. And I could see then, by the anger, violence, bitterness, that they were at war.

Joaquin, who is reticent, uneasy before intensity, who eludes ugliness and violence, prevented their violence from exploding. If he had not been there, I felt there would have been a fierce and inhuman battle.

At dinner Henry and June were famished and ate quickly and talked little. Then we went together to the Grand Guignol, which June had never seen. But these extremes of comedy and horror did not move her. It was probably tame, compared with her life. She talked to me in a low voice.

"Henry does not know what he wants, likes or dislikes. I do. I can select and discard. He has no judgment. It takes him years to reach a conclusion about people." Secretly we were mocking Henry's slowness, and she was asserting the perfidious alliance of our lucidities, our quickness, our subtleties.

"When Henry described you to me," said June, "he left out all that was important. He did not see you at all!"

So we had understood each other, every detail and every nuance.

In the theatre she sat with a pale, masklike face, but impatient. "I am always impatient in theatres, at movies. I read very little. It always seems pale and watered down, compared with . . ."

"With your life?"

She had not intended to finish the phrase.

"I want firsthand knowledge of everything, not fiction, intimate experience only. Whatever takes place, even a crime I read about, I can't take an interest in, because I already knew the criminal. I may have talked with him all night at a bar. He had confessed what he intended to do. When Henry wants me to go and see an actress in a play, she was a friend of mine at school. I lived at the home of the painter who suddenly became a celebrity. I am always inside where it first happens. I loved a revolutionist, I nursed his discarded mistress who later committed suicide. I don't care for films, newspapers, 'reportages,' the radio. I only want to be involved while it is being lived. Do you understand that, Anaïs?"

"Yes, I do."

"Henry is *literary*."

I divined her life at that moment. She only believed in intimacy and proximity, in confessions born in the darkness of a bedroom, in quarrels born of alcohol, in communions born of exhausting walks through the city. She only believed in those words which came like the confessions of criminals after long exposure to hunger, to intense lights, to cross-questioning, to violent tearing away of masks.

She would not read books on travel but she sat alert in the café to catch the appearance of an Abyssinian, a Greek, an Iranian, a Hindu, who would bear direct news from home, who would be carrying photographs from his family, and who would deliver to her personally all the flavors of his country.

"Henry is always making characters. He made one out of me."

Intermission. June and I want to smoke. Henry and Joaquin do not. We create a stir as we walk out together and stand in the little cobblestone street breathing the summer air.

We face each other.

I say to her, "You're the only woman who ever answered the fantasies I had about what a woman should be."

She answered, "It's a good thing that I'm going away. You would soon be disillusioned. You would unmask me. I am powerless before a woman. I don't know how to deal with a woman."

Is she telling the truth? I feel she is not. In the car she had been telling me about her friend Jean, the sculptress and poetess.

"Jean has the most beautiful face," and she added hastily, "I am not speaking of an ordinary woman. Jean's face, her beauty, were more like that of a man." She paused. "Jean's hands were so very lovely, so very supple because she handled clay a lot. The fingers tapered, a little like yours."

What feelings stir in me at June's praise of Jean's hands? Jealousy? And her insistence that her life is full of men, that she does not know how to act before a woman? I feel like saying, as Henry does so bluntly, "You lie."

She says, staring intently, "I thought your eyes were blue at first. They are strange and beautiful, grey and gold, with those long black lashes. You are the most graceful woman I have ever seen. You glide when you walk."

We talked about the colors we love. She always wears black and purple. I love warm colors, red and gold.

We returned to our seats. She continues to whisper to me, indifferent to the show. "I know Henry thinks I'm mad because I want only fever. I don't want objectivity, I don't want distance. I don't want to become detached."

When she says this, I feel very close to her and I hate Henry's writing, and my own, which makes us stay aware, to register. And I want to become immersed with her.

Coming out of the theatre I take her arm. Then she slips her hand over mine, and we lock hands. The chestnut trees are shedding their pollen in wispy parachutes, and the street lamps in the fog wear thin gold halos around them like the heads of saints.

Does she find with me a rest from the tensions? Does she have this need of clarity when the labyrinth becomes too dark and too narrow?

I was infinitely moved by the touch of her hand. She said, "The other night at Montparnasse I was hurt to hear your name mentioned by men like Titus. I don't want to see cheap men crawl into your life. I feel rather . . . protective."

In the café her pallor turns ashen. I see ashes under the skin of her face. Henry had said she was very ill. Disintegration. Will she die? What anxiety I feel. I want to put my arms around her. I feel her receding into death and I am willing to enter death to follow her, to embrace her. I must embrace her, I thought, she is dying before my eyes. Her tantalizing, somber beauty is dying. Her strange, manlike strength.

I am fascinated by her eyes, her mouth, her discolored mouth, badly rouged. Does she know that I feel lost in her, that I no longer understand what she is saying, feeling only the warmth of her words, their vividness?

She shivers with cold under her light velvet cape.

"Will you have lunch with me before you leave?"

"I am glad to be leaving. Henry loves me imperfectly, brutally. He hurts my pride. He desires ugly common women, passive women. He can't stand my strength."

"I resent men who are afraid of women's strength."

Jean loves June's strength. Is it strength, or is it destructiveness?

"Your strength, Anaïs, is soft, indirect, delicate, tender, womanly. But it is strength just the same."

I look at June's neck which is strong, I listen to her voice which is dark, heavy, husky. I look at her hands which are larger than most women's, and almost those of a peasant woman.

June does not reach the same sexual center of my being as man reaches. She does not touch that. What, then, does she move in me?

I resent Henry injuring her enormous and shallow pride. Henry looks with interest at my homely maid, Emilia. June's superiority arouses his hatred, even a feeling of revenge. He looks lingeringly at stupid, gentle Emilia. His offense makes me love June.

I love June for what she has dared to be, for her hardness and cruelty, her relentlessness, her egoism, her pride, her destructiveness.

I am suffocated by my compassions. She is a personality expanded to the limit. I worship that courage to hurt which she has, and I am willing to be sacrificed to it. She will add me to her other admirers, she will boast about my subjection to her. She will be June plus all that I am, all that I give her. I love this magnified woman, bigger than other women.

When she talks, she has the same expression of intensity she must have while making love, that forward thrust of her whole head which gives her the appearance of a woman at the prow of a ship. The coal brown of her eyes turns to cloudy violet.

Is she drugged?

It was not only that June had the body of the women who climbed every night upon the stage of music halls and gradually undressed, but that it was impossible to situate her in any other atmosphere. The luxuriance of the flesh, its vivid tones, the fevered eyes and the weight of the voice, its huskiness, became instantly conjugated with sensual love. Other women lost this erotic phosphorescence as soon as they abandoned their role of dance-hall hostesses. But June's night life was internal, it glowed from within her and it came, in part, from her treating every encounter as either intimate, or to be forgotten. It was as if, before every man, she lighted within herself the lamp lighted by waiting mistresses or wives at the end of the day, only they were her eyes, and it was her face which became like a poem's bedchamber, tapestried with twilight and velvet. As it glowed from within her, it could appear in totally unexpected places, early in the morning, in a neglected café, on a park bench, on a rainy morning in front of a hospital or a morgue, anywhere. It was always the soft light kept through the centuries for the moment of pleasure.

We agreed to meet, June and I. I knew she would be late and I did not mind. I was there before the hour, almost ill with tension and joy. I could not imagine her advancing out of the crowd in full daylight and I thought, could it be possible? I was afraid that such a mirage could not be. I was afraid that I would stand there exactly as I had stood in other places, watching a crowd and knowing no June would ever appear, because June was a product of my imagination.

As people came into the place, I shivered at their ugliness, at their drabness, their likeness to each other in my eyes. Waiting for June was the most painful expectancy, like awaiting a miracle. I could hardly believe she would arrive by those streets, cross such a boulevard, emerge out of a handful of dark, faceless people, walk into that place. What a profound joy to watch the crowd scurrying and then to see her striding, resplendent, incredible, towards me. I could not believe it. I held her warm hand. She was going to call for mail. Didn't the man see the wonder of her? Nobody like her ever called for mail at the American Express. Did any woman ever wear shabby shoes, a shabby black dress, a shabby blue cape, and an old violet hat as she wore them? I could not eat before her. But I was calm outwardly, with that Hindu placidity of bearing that is so deceptive. She drank and smoked. I was so calm before her, yet I could not eat. My nervousness gnawed me deeply, it devoured me. She is quite mad, in a sense, I thought; subject to fears and manias. Her talk was mostly unconscious. The contents of her flowering imagination are a reality to her. But what is she building so carefully? A heightened sense of her own personality, a glorifying of it? In the obvious and enveloping warmth of my admiration she expanded. She seemed at once destructive and helpless. I wanted to protect her! I, protect her whose power is infinite! At moments her power was so strong that I actually believed it when she told me her destructiveness was unintentional. I believed her. Did she try to destroy me? No, she walked into my house and I was willing to endure any pain at her hands. If there is any calculation in her whose destiny is beyond her control, it comes only afterwards, when she becomes aware of her power and wonders how she can use it. I do not think her power is directed. Even she is baffled by it.

I see her as someone to be pitied and protected. She is involved in tragedies and perversities she cannot understand or control. I know her weakness. She is weak before reality. Her life is full of fantasies. I do not believe her relationship to Jean is sexual. I believe it is a fantasy in which she escapes from Henry's relentless inquisitions.

June's elusiveness, her retreat into fantasy, suddenly enrage me, because they are mine. A new anger and a new strength are aroused by her unwillingness to face her acts and feelings. I want to force her into reality (as Henry does). I, who am sunk in dreams, in half-lived acts, I want to do violence to her. What do I want? I want to grasp June's hands, find out whether this love of woman is real or not. Why do I want that? Am I driving obscure, mysterious emotions out into the open (as Henry wants to do and does constantly)? Do I get angry with her self-deceptions, which are like mine? Her subtlety makes me desire frankness; the quicksands of her evasions make me, for the first time, demand clarity. At times I feel as she does, like taking flight from selves I do not know, and at other times I feel like Henry, like pursuing and exposing these selves to crude daylight.

Yet, in the taxi, I could hardly think clearly when she pressed my hand to her breast, and I kept her hand and I was not ashamed of my adoration, my humility, for she is older, she knows more, she should be leading me, initiating me, taking me out of smoky fantasies into experience.

She said she wanted to keep the rose dress I wore the first night she saw me. I told her I wanted to give her a going-away present and she said she wanted some of the perfume she smelled in my house, to evoke memories. And she needs shoes, stockings, gloves, a warm coat. Sentimentality? Romanticism? If she means this . . . Why do I doubt her? Perhaps she is very sensitive, and hypersensitive people become false when others doubt them. They vacillate. And one thinks them insincere. Yet I want to believe her. At the same time, it does not seem so very important that she should love me. It is not her role. I am so filled with my love of her. At the same time I feel that I am dying. She says of me, "You are at once so decadent and so alive." She is so decadent and so alive. Our love would be death.

Henry was jealous and intolerant. June is the stronger, harder me. He takes all he wants, but he reviles her for doing the same. He makes love to a woman almost in front of her at a party. June takes drugs. She loves Jean. She talks underworld language when she tells stories. And yet she has kept that incredible, out-of-date, uncallous sentimentalism. "Give me the perfume I smelled in your house. Walking up the hill to your house the other night, in the dark, I was in ecstasy. I have never liked a woman Henry has liked. Yet, in this case, I felt, he had not said enough."

When I talk now, I feel June's voice in me. I feel my voice growing heavier, and my face less smiling. I feel altered facially. I feel a strange presence making me walk differently.

In my dream last night I was at the top of a skyscraper and expected to walk down the façade of it on a very narrow fire ladder. I was terrified. I could not do it.

June's character seems to have no definable form, no boundaries, no core. This frightens Henry. He does not know all she is.

Do I feel my own self definite, encompassable? I know its boundary lines. There are experiences I shy away from. But my curiosity, creativeness, urge me beyond these boundaries, to transcend my character. My imagination pushes me into unknown, unexplored, dangerous realms. Yet there is always my fundamental nature, and I am never deceived by my "intellectual" adventures, or my literary exploits. I enlarge and expand my self; I do not like to be just one Anaïs, whole, familiar, contained. As soon as someone defines me, I do as June does; I seek escape from the confinements of definition. Am I good? Kind? Then I seek to see how far I can go into unkindness (not very far), into hardness. But I do feel I can always come back to my true nature. Can June come back to her true nature?

And what is my true nature? What is June's? Is mine idealism, spirituality, poetry, imagination, sense of beauty, a need of beauty, a fundamental Rimbaud innocence, a certain purity? I need to create, I hate cruelty. But when I have wanted to go deep into evil, this evil changes as I approach it. Henry and June change as I come near to them. I destroy the worlds I want to enter. I arouse creativeness in Henry, romanticism in June.

June, by her voluptuous body, her sensual face, her erotic voice, arouses perversity and sensuality. What is it that makes this a destructive experience? She has the power to destroy. I have the power to create. We are two contrasting forces. What will be our effect on each other? I thought June would destroy me.

The day we had lunch together, I was ready to follow her into any perversity, any destruction. I had not counted on my effect on her. I was so filled with my love for her I did not notice my effect on her.

June came to my house on Monday. I wanted an end to the mysteries, a climax to the suspense. I asked her cruelly and brutally, as

Henry might have asked, "Do you love women? Have you faced your impulses towards women?"

She answered me so quietly. "Jean was too masculine. I have faced my feelings. I am fully aware of them. But I have never found anyone I wanted to live them out with, so far. I am not sure what it is I want to live out."

And then she turned away from my questions and said, gazing at me, "What a lovely way you have of dressing. This dress—its rose color, its old-fashioned fullness at the bottom, the little black velvet jacket, the lace collar, the lacing over the breasts. How perfect, how absolutely perfect. I like the way you cover yourself, too. There is very little nudity, only your neck, really. I love your turquoise ring, and the coral earrings." Her hands were shaking, she was trembling. I was ashamed of my directness. I was intensely nervous. She told me that at the restaurant she had wanted to look at my bare feet in sandals but that she could not bring herself to stare. I told her I had been afraid to stare at her body, and how much I had wanted to. We talked brokenly, chaotically. She now looked at my feet in sandals and said, "They are flawless. I have never seen such flawless feet. And I love the way you walk, like an Indian woman."

Our nervousness was unbearable.

I said, "Do you like these sandals?"

"I have always loved sandals and worn them, but lately I could not afford them and I am wearing shoes someone gave me."

I said, "Come up to my room and try another pair I have, just like these."

She tried them on, sitting on my bed. They were too small for her. I saw she was wearing cotton stockings and it hurt me to see June in cotton stockings. I showed her my black cape, which she found beautiful. I made her try it on. Then I saw the beauty of her body I had not dared to look at, I saw its fullness, its heaviness; and the richness of it overwhelmed me.

I could not understand why she was so ill and so timid, so frightened. I told her that I would make her a cape like mine. Once I touched her arm. She moved it away. Had I frightened her? Could there be someone more sensitive and more afraid than I? I could not believe this. I was not afraid at that moment.

When she sat on the couch downstairs, the opening of her black, clinging dress showed the beginning of her full breasts. I was trembling. I was aware of the vagueness of our feelings and desires. She talked ramblingly, but now I knew she was talking to cover a deeper talk, talking against the things we could not express.

I came back from walking with her to the station dazed, exhausted, elated, happy, unhappy. I wanted to ask her forgiveness for my questions. They had been so unsubtle, so unlike me.

We met the next day at the American Express. She came in her tailored suit because I had said that I liked it.

She had said that she wanted nothing from me but the perfume I wore and my wine-colored handkerchief. But I reminded her she had promised she would let me buy her sandals.

First of all, I took her to the ladies' room. I opened my bag and took out a pair of sheer black stockings. "Put them on," I said, pleading and apologizing at the same time. She obeyed. Meanwhile I opened a bottle of perfume. "Put some on."

June had a hole in her sleeve.

I was happy, and June was exultant. We talked simultaneously. "I wanted to call you last night." "I wanted to send you a telegram last night." June said, "I wanted to tell you how unhappy I was on the train, regretting my awkwardness, my nervousness, my pointless talk. There was so much, so much I wanted to say."

We had the same fears of displeasing each other, of disappointing each other. She had gone to the café in the evening to meet Henry. "I felt as if drugged. I was full of thoughts of you. People's voices reached me from afar. I was elated. I could not sleep all night. What have you done to me?"

She added, "I was always poised, I could always talk well. People never overwhelmed me."

When I realized what she was revealing to me, I was overjoyed. *I* overwhelm *her?* She loved me then? June! She sat beside me in the restaurant, small, timid, unworldly, panic-stricken, and I was moved, I was almost unbearably moved. June different, upset, changed, yielding, when she had made me so different, she had made me impulsive, strong.

She would say something and then beg forgiveness for its stupidity. I could not bear her humility. I told her, "We have both lost ourselves, but that is when one reveals most of one's true self. You've revealed your incredible sensitiveness. I am so moved. You are like me, wishing for such perfect moments, and frightened for fear of spoiling them. Neither one of us was prepared for this, and we had imagined it too long. Let's be overwhelmed, it is so lovely. I love you, June."

And not knowing what else to say, I spread between us on the seat the wine-colored handkerchief she wanted, my coral earrings, my turquoise ring. It was blood I wanted to lay at June's feet, before June's incredible humility.

Then she began to talk beautifully, not hysterically, but deeply.

We walked to the sandal shop. In the shop the ugly woman who waited on us hated us and our obvious happiness. I held June's hand firmly. I commanded: "Bring this. Bring that." I was firm, willful with the woman. When she mentioned the width of June's feet I scolded her. June could not understand the Frenchwoman, but she sensed that she was disagreeable.

We chose sandals like mine. She refused everything else, anything that was not symbolic or representative of me. Everything I wore she would wear, although she said she had never wanted to imitate anyone else ever before.

When we walked the streets, bodies close together, arm in arm, hands locked, I was in such ecstasy I could not talk. The city disappeared, and so did the people. The acute joy of our walking together through the grey streets of Paris I shall never forget, and I shall never be able to describe it. We were walking above the world, above reality, into pure, pure ecstasy.

I discovered June's purity. It was June's purity I was given to possess, what she had given to no one else. To me she gave the secret of her being, the woman whose face and body have aroused instincts around her which left her untouched, which terrified her. As I had sensed, her destructiveness is unconscious. She is imprisoned in it, and detached, and bewildered. When she met me, she revealed her innocent self. She lives in fantasies, not in the world Henry lives in.

Henry had written of a dangerous and venomous woman. To me she confided her detachment from the realities of Henry's world, her complete absorption in fantasies, her madnesses.

So many people had sought the way into June's true nature and had not guessed the strength and fullness of her imaginative world, her isolation, the June who lives in symbols, who shrinks from crudeness. I brought June into my world. June did not take me into her violent and harsh world because it is not hers. She came to me because she likes to dream.

All at once I knew, too, that the sensual and perverse world in which she reigns is closed to me again. Do I regret it? She came to me when I was hungry for reality. I wanted real experiences which would free me of my fantasies, my daydreaming. She turned me away from Henry, who ruled that world of earthy, lusty harsh facts. She has thrown me back into visions, dreams. But if I were made for reality, for ordinary experience, I would not have loved her. I have a greater need of illusion and dreams, then, than I have of Henry's animal world.

She said yesterday, "There are so many things I would love to do with you. With you I would take drugs."

June does not accept a gift which has no symbolic significance. June washes laundry to be able to buy herself a bit of perfume. June is not afraid of poverty and drabness, is untouched by it, is untouched by the drunkenness of her friends (her drunkenness is so different, it's more like an exaltation). June selects and discards people with evaluations unknown to Henry.

When June tells her endless anecdotes now, I understand they are ways of escape, disguises for a self which lives secretly behind that smoke-screen talk.

I think so much about her, all day, all night. As soon as I left her yesterday, there was a painful void, and I shivered with cold. I love her extravagances, her humility, her fears of disillusion.

The struggle for expression was not as acute for me before I met June. Her talk is like my secret writing. At times incoherent, at times abstract, at times blind. Let incoherence be, then. Our meeting each other has been emotionally too disturbing. Both of us had one inviolate self we never gave. It was our dreaming self. Now we have invaded this world in each other. She is too rich to be fully known in a few days. She says I am too rich for her. We want to separate and regain our lucidity.

But I have fewer fears than she has. I would not separate from her of my own free will. I want to give myself away, to lose myself.

Before her I repudiate all I have done, all that I am. I aspire to more. I am ashamed of my writing. I want to throw everything away and begin anew. I have a terror of disappointing her. Her idealism is so demanding. It awes me. With her I feel timelessness. Our talk is only half-talk. When she talks on the surface, it is because she is afraid of the rich silences between us. In the silence, the quietness of my gestures calms her agitation. If she had wanted to, yesterday, I would have sat on the floor at her feet and placed my head against her knees. But she would not let me. Yet at the station while we waited for the train, she begged for my hand. I turned away and ran, as if in panic. The station master stopped me to sell me some charity tickets. I bought them and gave them to him, wishing him luck with the lottery. He got the benefit of my wanting to give to June, to whom one cannot give anything.

Yet I have given her life. She died in Paris. She died the night she read Henry's book [manuscript version of *Tropic of Cancer*], because of his brutality. She wept and repeated over and over again, "It is not me, it is not me he is writing about. It's a distortion. He says I live in delusions, but it is he, it is he who does not see me, or anyone, as I am, as they are. He makes everything ugly."

What a secret language we talk. Undertones, overtones, nuances, abstractions, symbols. Then we return to Henry with an incandescence which frightens him. Henry is uneasy. What is this powerful magic we create together and indulge in? How can Henry be excluded from it when he has genius? What do June and I seek together that Henry does not believe in? Wonder wonder wonder.

At first I protested and rebelled against poetry. I was about to deny my poetic worlds. I was doing violence to my illusions with analysis, science, and learning Henry's language, entering Henry's world. I wanted to destroy by violence and animalism my tenuous fantasies

34

and illusions and my hypersensitivity. A kind of suicide. The ignominy awakened me. Then June came and answered the cravings of my imagination and saved me. Or perhaps she killed me, for now I am started on a course of madness.

June eats and drinks symbols. Henry has no use for symbols. He eats bread, not wafers. June never liked Madeira wine before, but because I serve it at home she drinks it, and asks for it at the café. The taste of me. The tastes and smells of my house. She found a café where there was an open fire, and the burning logs smelled like my house.

When I look up at her, she says I look like a child. When I look down, I look very sad.

The intensity is shattering us both. She is glad to be leaving. She is always in flight. She is in flight from Henry. But I cannot bear the separation because it is physical, and I need her presence. It is Henry she is in flight from.

When we met for half an hour today to discuss Henry's future, she asked me to take care of him, and then gave me her silver bracelet, a part of her. It has a cat's-eye stone, so symbolical of her. I refused the bracelet at first, because she has so few possessions, but then the joy of wearing her bracelet filled me. I carry it like a symbol. It is precious to me.

June was afraid that Henry should turn me against her. "How?" I said. "By revelations." What does she fear? I said, "I have my own knowledge of you. Henry's knowledge of you is not mine."

Then I met Henry accidentally, and I felt him hostile, and I was startled. June said that he was uneasy and restless, that she only told him what would not give him anxiety because he is more jealous of women than of men. Henry, who thought me a rare person, now doubts me. June, sower of madness.

June may destroy me and my faith in her. Today I shivered when she said that when she talked to Henry about me, she tried to be very natural and direct so as not to imply anything unusual. So she said to Henry, "Anaïs was just bored with her life, so she took us up." That seemed false to me. It was the only ugly thing I have ever heard her say. I have seen a beautiful June. Henry's portrait is of an ugly June.

I do not think that, in spite of the passion so often described by Henry, June and Henry have really ever fused, yielded to each other, possessed each other. Their individualities are too strong. They are at war with each other, love is a conflict, they lie to each other, they mistrust each other.

June wants to go back to New York to accomplish something, be lovely for me, become an actress, have clothes. But I don't care about all this. I say, "I love you as you are."

Hell is a different place for each man, or each man has his own particular hell. My descent into the inferno is a descent into the irrational level of existence, where the instincts and blind emotions are loose, where one lives by pure impulse, pure fantasy, and therefore pure madness. No, that is not the inferno. While I am there, I am as unconscious of misery as a man who is drunk; or, rather, my misery is a great joy. It is when I become conscious again that I feel unutterable pain.

I began to awaken from my dream yesterday.

June and I had lunch together in a softly lighted, mauve, diffused place which surrounded us with velvety closeness. We took off our hats. We drank champagne. We ate oysters. We talked in half-tones, quarter-tones, clear to us alone. She made me aware of how she eludes all Henry's efforts to grasp her logically, to reach a knowledge of her. She revealed a fluidity, a will to elude, as persistent and as shrewd as other people's frankness and self-revelations. She admires Eleonora Duse because she was great. "D'Annunzio," June said, "was only Duse's mediocre penman. Even some of his plays were born of Duse and would never have been written if she had not existed." What did she mean? That Henry was D'Annunzio and she Duse?

"But," I agreed bitterly, "Duse is dead, and D'Annunzio has done the writing, and he is famous and not Duse."

Did she want me, the writer, to make her famous? To write about her? To make her portrait so people would not believe Henry's portrait?

I am the poet who sees her. I am the poet who will write things which would never have been written if June had not existed. Yet I exist too, independently of my writing.

June sat filled with champagne. I have no need of it. She talked about the effects of hashish. I said, "I have known such states without hashish. I do not need drugs. I carry all that in myself." At this she was irritated. She does not realize that, being an artist, I want to be in those states of ecstasy or vision while keeping my awareness intact. I am the poet and I must feel and see. I do not want to be anaesthetized. I am drunk on June's beauty, but I am also aware of it.

But I am also aware that there are quite a few obvious discrepancies in her stories. Her carelessness leaves many loopholes, and when I put the stories together, they do not fit. I formed a judgment, a judgment which she fears always, which she is in flight from. She lives without pattern, without continuity. As soon as one seeks to coordinate June, she is lost. She must have seen it happen many times. She is like a man who gets drunk and gives himself away. Was that why she wanted to drug me, intoxicate me, blind me, confuse me?

At lunch we were talking about perfumes, their substance, their mixtures, their meaning. She said casually, "Saturday when I left you, I bought some perfume for Jean." (Jean, the masculine girl she had told me about.) She told me that she had been as affected by my eyes as I was by her face. I told her I felt her bracelet clutched my wrist like her very own fingers, holding me in slavery. She wanted my cape around her body. Then we went out and walked.

She had to buy her ticket for New York.

We walked into several steamship agencies. June did not have enough money for even a third-class passage to New York and she was trying to get a reduction. Then I watched her as in a dream. I was smoking constantly because June does. I saw her lean over the counter, her face in her hands, appealing, so very close to the man's face that his eyes devoured her boldly. And she so soft, persuasive, alluring, smiling up in a secret way at him, for him. I saw her.

An intolerable pain. I watched her begging. I realized my jealousy but not her humiliation.

We walked out again. We crossed the street. We asked the policeman for the Rue de Rome.

I told her I would give her the money she needed, all of my month's allowance.

We walked into the steamship agency, with June barely finishing some story or other. I saw the man stunned by her face and her soft, yielding way of asking him, of paying and signing and receiving instructions. I stood by and watched her. My dream had been like down around me, my dream of June's inviolateness, aloofness, nobility. I stood by and watched the Frenchman ask her, "Will you have a cocktail with me tomorrow?" June was shaking hands with him. "Three o'clock?" "No, at six," she answered. She smiled at him cajolingly, intimately, seductively. Then as we walked out, she explained hurriedly, "He was very useful to me, very helpful. He is going to do a lot for me. He may slip me into first class at the last minute. I couldn't say no. I don't intend to go, but I couldn't say no."

"You must go, now that you said yes," I said absurdly, and the absurdity of my anger nauseated me. I almost wept. I took June's arm and said, "I can't bear it, I can't bear it." I did not know what it was I could not bear. I was blind and angry. At what? Not at June. It was her beauty. She could not prevent its effect on others. But I was angry at an undefinable thing. Was it at her begging? I thought of the prostitute, honest because in exchange for money she gives her body. June gave only promises, false promises. She teased.

June! There was such a tear in the down. She knew it. So she took my hand against her warm breast. She did this to soothe and console me.

And she talked, she talked about things which did not relate to what I felt. "Would you rather I had said no, brutally, to the man? I am sometimes brutal, you know, but I couldn't be, in front of you. I didn't want to hurt his feelings."

And, as I did not know what angered me, I was silent. It was not a question of accepting or refusing a cocktail. One had to go back to the origin of why she should need the help of that man. One of her phrases came back to my mind: "No matter how badly things are going for me, I can always find someone who will pay for my champagne."

Of course! She was a woman accumulating debts which she never intended to pay as honest prostitutes do, for afterwards she boasted of her sexual inviolability. She was a gold-digger. Great pride in the possession of her own body, but not too proud to humiliate herself with prostitute eyes over the counter of a steamship company.

She was telling me that she and Henry had quarreled over buying butter. They had no money and . . .

"No money? But Saturday I gave you enough for a month. And today is Monday."

"We had things to pay up that we owed," said June. I thought she meant the hotel room. Then suddenly I remembered the perfume. Why didn't she say to me, "I bought perfume and gloves and stockings Saturday." She did not look at me when she intimated they had debts to pay. Then I remembered other phrases: "People say that if I had a fortune I would spend it in a day and no one would ever know how. I could never account for the way I spend money."

This was the other face of June's fantasies.

We walked the streets and all the softness of her breast could not lull the pain.

I walked into the American Express. The fat man at the door greeted me. "Your friend was here this morning and she said goodbye to me as if she were not coming back."

"But we had agreed to meet here!"

A terrible anxiety overcame me. If I were never to see June walking towards me! It was like dying. What did it matter, after all, what I had thought the day before. But it may have offended her. She was unethical and irresponsible, but my pride about money was absurd and anachronistic. I should not have tampered with her nature. I should not have expected her to be like me, scrupulous and proud. She alone is without fetters. I am a fettered, an ethical being. I could not have let Henry go hungry. I should have accepted her entirely. If only she would come and meet me for half an hour, for a moment. I had dressed ritually for her. If she came I would never again question her behavior.

Then June came, all in black velvet, black cape and her hat with

39

a feather shading her eyes, her face paler and more transparent than ever. The wonder of her face and smile, her smileless eyes.

I took her to a Russian tearoom where, before, I had felt the lack of beauty of most people, their lack of vividness, aliveness. The Russians sang as we felt. June wondered whether they were as emotionally fervent as their voices. The richness and violence of their singing stirred us. June used the word scorch.

"At first I was afraid of being tubercular, but now I am glad because it makes me more aware of life, it has taught me to live more intensely. That is all I want now, a fiery life."

Russian voices and June's incandescent face. Violet rugs and stained-glass windows, dusty lights and the plaintive chant of strings. June is the essence of all these, of candles, incense, flambées, fine liqueurs, exotic foods.

The people around us seem ugly and dead compared with her.

June rushing towards death, smiling. Henry could not keep pace with her recklessness because he held on to the earth. He wants laughter, and food, and plain joys. So he holds her back. But June and I seek exaltations and the madness of Rimbaud.

I always endowed madness with a sacred, poetic value, a mystical value. It seemed to me to be a denial of ordinary life, an effort to transcend it, to expand, to go far beyond the limitations of *La Condition Humaine*. The madness of June at this moment seemed beautiful. I did not even say to her as one should say to a human being in danger, "You must take care of your health." If she wanted to dissolve like this, in a heightened and burning form of life, I would follow her wherever she wanted to go.

It was time to part. I put her in a taxi. She sat there about to leave me and I stood by in torment. "I want to kiss you, I want to kiss you," said June. And she offered her mouth which I kissed for a long time.

To keep June beside me, I think about her as if she were walking with me. I imagine saying to her: You are a magnificent character, a portentous character. (She was always saying she was like the characters in Dostoevsky.) You have power, freedom. You have kissed away all my scruples, guilts, conscience. Your love of Henry is masochistic. You are responsible for the greatness of his book.

When June left, I wanted to sleep and dream for many days, but I still had something to face, my friendship with Henry. I asked him to come to Louveciennes because I knew he was in pain. I wanted to offer him peace and a lulling house, but of course I knew we would talk about June.

We walked through the forest, walked off our restlessness, and we talked. There is in both of us an obsession to understand June. He has no jealousy of me, because he said, "You brought out wonderful things in June. It was the first time June ever attached herself to a woman of value." He seemed to expect I would have an influence over June's life. When he saw that I understood her and that I was willing to be truthful with him, we talked freely.

Just once I paused, hesitant, wondering if my confidences to Henry were a betrayal of June. Henry caught the hesitation and agreed with me that in the case of June, "truth" had to be totally disregarded because she lived in fantasies and illusions. But that truth could be the only basis of our friendship.

And, as we sat by the fire later, there was an understanding between us: we both craved truth. It was a necessity to us. We should collaborate, with our two minds, in understanding June. What was June? What was June's value? Henry loves her with passion, he wants to know June, the perpetually disguised woman. June, the powerful, fictionalized character. In his love for her he has endured so many torments that the lover took refuge in the writer. The writer is like a detective. But it is the husband, the jealous and betrayed husband, who has written so ferociously about her and Jean, about his efforts to prove her Lesbianism, his fruitless attempts.

I said, "If there is an explanation of the mystery, it is this: the love between women is a refuge and an escape into harmony and narcissism in place of conflict. In the love between man and woman there is resistance and conflict. Two women do not judge each other. They form an alliance. It is, in a way, self-love. I love June because she is the woman I would like to be. I don't know why June loves me."

I gave him the one thing June cannot give him: honesty. There is a strange detachment from the ego in me. I am so ready to admit what an egotistical woman would not admit: that June is a superb and inspiring character who makes every other woman insipid. That I would like to live her life, but for my compassion and my conscience. She may destroy Henry the human being, but she fascinates Henry the writer, and he is more enriched by the ordeals she imposes on him than by happiness.

But like June I have infinite possibilities for all experience, like June I have the power to burn like a flame, to enter all experience fearlessly, decadence, amorality, or death. The Idiot and Nastasia are more important to me than the self-denial of Abélard and Héloïse. The love of only one man or one woman is a limitation. To be fully alive is to live unconsciously and instinctively in all directions, as Henry and June do. Idealism is the death of the body and of the imagination. All but freedom, utter freedom, is death.

Yet Henry gets very angry and says June has no value. Her power is great but it is destructive. She has fallen into the weakest, easiest form of life, into fantasy-making. But I love her power of non-resistance, of yielding. Evil is life as well as good. I want to live without idealism and without ethics. But I am not free. I am incapable of destruction.

Henry expected me to impose my strength on June. I do not need drugs and artificial stimulation. That is my natural role. Yet my desire to do these very things with June, to penetrate the evil which attracts me, is the same which lured Henry when he first met her in the dance hall, when they made love in the park at night and she asked him for fifty dollars.

I go out into the world to seek life, and the experience I want is denied me because I carry in me a force which neutralizes it. I meet June, the near prostitute, and she becomes pure. A purity which mystifies Henry, a purity of face and being which is awesome, just as I saw her one afternoon on the corner of the divan, pale, transparent, innocent. June's real demon is a voraciousness for life, a possession by life, the tasting of its bitterest flavors. June, who lives by the impulses of her nature, would not be capable of the efforts Henry and I are making to understand her. Henry tries to impose on her an awareness which, if she accepted it, would close up this flow of fantasies, obscure impulses. He only succeeds in making her aware of a wholeness she cannot live by.

I told Henry: "June destroys reality; her lies are not lies, they are roles she wants to live out. She has made greater efforts than any of us to live out her illusions. When she told you that her mother had died, that she never knew her father, that she was illegitimate, she wanted to begin nowhere, to begin without roots, to plunge into invention. Anyone could be her father. She loved the suspense, the possible surprise. She did not want to be classified, she did not want to be associated with any race, nationality, or background either. Her pallor, her upward curving eyebrows, her cape, her jewelry, her erratic eating, her destruction of the boundary lines between night and day, her hatred of sunlight, are all escapes from rigid patterns."

Henry said: "Nobody can ever say to June: '*Listen,* listen deeply and attentively.' I did it occasionally by violence. How did you make her listen? How did you stop the nervous flow of her talk? Talking about you, she was humble."

What had I done? Nothing. Looked at her, felt in sympathy with her quest for the marvelous, her chaos which I did not seek to organize with a man's mind, but which I accepted as I accepted her courage to descend into all experience. She has that courage. She has obeyed every impulse to drink, take drugs, to be a vagabond, to be free at the cost of poverty and humiliation.

"I understand her. She cannot be considered as a whole. She is composed of fragments. Only passion gives her a moment of wholeness. Perhaps, being as she is, she may lose your human love, but she has gained your admiration of June the character."

"Compared with June, all other women seem insipid. She had tears in her eyes when she spoke of your generosity, and kept repeating: 'She is more than a woman, much more than a woman.'"

"She humiliates you, starves you, deserts you, torments you, and yet you thrive. You write books about her. I do not have her courage to hurt even for good reasons, to hurt and to be aware of hurting, and to know its ultimate necessity."

"And the Lesbianism?"

"I can't answer that. I don't know. It was not that, with us."

Henry believes me.

"Her sensuality is far more complicated than yours. So much more intricate."

June was always telling stories; June with drugged eyes and a breathless voice:

"One day in summer I left my hotel room with a phonograph I was going to lend to a friend. I was wearing a very light summer dress, and no stockings because I had no money for stockings. I saw a taxi waiting before a bar and got into it to wait for the driver. Instead of the driver, a policeman came. He poked his head inside the window and said: 'What's the matter with you? Are you sick?' 'I'm not sick,' I answered. 'I'm waiting for the taxi driver. I'm carrying a phonograph to a friend. It's heavy and I didn't want to walk with it. I took the first taxi I saw.' But the policeman was worried and stared at my pale face. 'Where do you live?' I got angry and offered to show him where I lived, if he wished, and he insisted on it and carried the phonograph for me. I took him to the basement room where we lived and where Henry was still lying in bed, wearing a red Roumanian embroidered shirt which made him look like a Russian. The table was piled high with manuscripts, books, bottles, ash trays; and he could see we were intellectual Bohemians. On the table there was a long knife which Jean had brought back from Africa. The policeman looked it over, and then smiled and went away."

I sat silent and June began another story.

"A man came to my door one day and asked if I wanted M or O. I said I didn't know what he meant. He said, laughing: 'Of course you do, morphine or opium. I'll bring you ten dollars' worth tomorrow if you want it.' I said I didn't want it, but he said he would bring it anyway. The next day a man forced his way into my place and said: 'You've ordered ten dollars' worth of M and O. I'll get you into trouble for this.' 'No, you won't,' I said. And I called up a man who has influence in the government. When the man heard the name of my friend, he became frightened and begged me not to say a word, said that he would not bother me again, and went away."

I sat silent. I wondered whether her stories, like Albertine's stories to Proust, contained each one of them a secret key to some happening in June's life which it is impossible to clarify. She takes drugs, I know, and she may have had trouble with the police. Some of these stories are in Henry's book. She does not hesitate to repeat herself. She is drugged with her fictions and romances. She hates explanations. I don't know why I feel they are not true. I stand humbly before this spinner of tales and wonder whether I could not invent better stories for her.

At moments she seems non-human, because she is so unconscious of her acts, amoral, unfettered by human considerations or hesitations. She does not hesitate to send Henry to Paris and then leave him without the money she had promised to send him. She imposed on him a sharing of their life with Jean. She lives as if in a dream, in uncalculated impulses and whims, plunging into relationships, destroying unintentionally in her fiery course. One man committed suicide for her. She is so busy just BEING, talking, walking, making love, drinking, that she can achieve nothing else. She had once thought of becoming an actress but could not take the discipline, rehearsals, deadlines, appointments, care of her hair and dressing, etc. She speaks of protecting Henry but does it erratically, spasmodically. She is baffled because she cannot satisfy him, because he rebels against her obsessions, eccentric course, irrational behaviors. In her "possessed" life she is unable to pause, to reflect. She refuses to contemplate the meaning or direction of her life. She lives within chaos.

I may be stopped on my course by all kinds of thoughts, pity, consideration for others, fears for those I love, protectiveness, devotion, sense of duty, of responsibility. But as Gide says, thought arrests action and being. So June is BEING. Nothing can control her. She is our fantasy let loose upon the world. She does what others only do in their dreams. Mindless, the life of our unconscious without control. There is a fantastic courage in this, to live without laws, without fetters, without thought of consequences.

What demonic accounts does June keep so that Henry and I, human beings, look with awe on her impulsiveness and recklessness, which enrich us more than the tender devotions of others, the measured loves, the considerate cautiousness of others.

The other side of June, I see the grandiose side of June the character. I will not tear her to pieces as Henry has. I will love her and enrich her.

The wonder and mystery of June's madness. I feel closer to her than to Henry's earthy simplicities because of my duality. Someday I may follow her to the very end of her voyage.

Gide says: "The characters of Dostoevsky are moved fundamentally either by pride or lack of pride."

Henry's bordellos must seem laughable to June. So easy, so direct, so natural. I am sure her acts are less easily defined, more intricate, more sensuous. It is an erotic light which shines around her. Henry counts on me to understand. I must know, he thinks. It must be clear to me. To his great surprise, I say things which resemble what June said: "It is not the same thing." There is a world which is closed to him, a world of shadings, gradations, nuances, and subtleties. He is a genius and yet he is too explicit. June slips between his fingers. You cannot possess without loving.

I carry about rich, heavy letters from Henry. Avalanches. I have tacked up on the walls of my writing room two big sheets covered with words which he gave me, and a panorama of his life, with lists of friends, mistresses, unwritten novels, written novels, places he has been to, and those he wants to visit. It is covered with notes for future novels.

I stand between June and Henry, between his primitive strength in which he feels secure (this is reality), and June's illusions and delusions. I am grateful for Henry's fullness and richness. I want to answer him with equal abundance and flow. But I find myself keeping certain secrets, as June did. Fear of ridicule? I delay revelations. I know he thinks June seduced me, that through me he will finally know. As in Proust, when he took more pleasure in being with Albertine's girl friend, who might tell him something about Albertine that he did not know, than in being with Albertine, who by this time concealed all her life from him. I did promise to take him into our world, my world. It is quite possible that I may be even more secretive than June. More fearful than June to reveal myself.

I have always been tormented by the image of multiplicity of selves. Some days I call it richness, and other days I see it as a disease, a proliferation as dangerous as cancer. My first concept about people around me was that all of them were coordinated into a WHOLE, whereas I was made up of a multitude of selves, of fragments. I know that I was upset as a child to discover that we had only one life. It seems to me that I wanted to compensate for this by multiplying experience. Or perhaps it always seems like this when you follow all your impulses and they take you in different directions. In any case, when I was happy, always at the beginning of a love, euphoric, I felt I was gifted for living many lives fully. (June?) It was only when I was in trouble, lost in a maze, stifled by complications and paradoxes that I was haunted or that I spoke of my "madness," but I meant the madness of the poets.

It is too simple for Henry to say June is a faithless woman. We may both be faithful to the living moment, to life, and not to one love. Henry is always painting a portrait of a June scattered in fragments, beyond all reassemblage.

"Passion gives me moments of wholeness."

Perhaps we have built a false concept of wholeness and, under the pressure of an artificial unity, people like June explode and fly in all directions.

Some day we may be reassembled into a more truthful whole.

I never said to June, "You lie," but "You imagined, you invented," as I wish my parents had said to me when I fabricated tales of meeting jungle animals in the street, etc.

Multiple personalities, multiple lives born of an extravagant hunger. Poor June has increased the dose of love as the poor addict increases his dose of drugs.

Henry's background, he told me, is German. To me, he seems like a Slav, or is it that Dostoevsky has been interwoven with their lives. He has the German sentimentality. He goes from sentimentality to callousness. His imagination is German, his writing resembles George Grosz. He has a love of ugliness. He likes vulgarity, slang, apache quarters, squalor, toughness, the *bas fonds* of everything. He likes the smell of cabbage, of stew, of poverty and of prostitutes.

Henry's letters give me a feeling of plenitude I get rarely. They are extraordinary. I take great joy in answering them, but the bulk of them overwhelms me. I have barely answered one when he writes another. Comments on Proust, lists of books, descriptions, moods, his own life, his indefatigable sexuality, the way he immediately gets mixed up, tangled in action. Too much action, to my mind. Undigested. No wonder he marvels at Proust. No wonder I watch his life knowing I can never live like that, for my life is slowed up by thought and the need to understand what I am living.

Letter to Henry:

You ask impossible and contradictory things. You want to know what dreams, what impulses, what desires June has. But how could she tell you when she lives like a submarine, sunk always at the deepest level of instinct and intuition. Perhaps I may be able to tell you all that, for I always come up for air, I am not always just living, loving, pursuing my fantasies. I may sit down one day and try to tell you just that I would much rather go on living blindly. And you beat your head against the walls of June's world, and you want me to tear all the veils. You want to force delicate, profound, vague, obscure, mysterious, voluptuous sensations into something you can seize and violate. But will you caricature it? Why do you want such clarity from me? You were the first to say one day: "Chaos is rich. Chaos is fecund." The mysteries of June inspired you. You never gave any other woman so much attention. Then why do you want to dispel this mystery? Will you be content if you find that June is a Lesbian, that she takes drugs, that she may be psychotic, that she has a hundred lovers. I never understood Proust's need to know, to be present almost, when Albertine was loving someone else.

June simply IS. She has no ideas, no fantasies of her own. They are given to her by others, who are inspired by her face and body. She acquired them. Henry says angrily, "She is an empty box." And he adds, "You are the full box." To think of her in the middle of the day lifts me out of ordinary living. Who wants the ideas, the fantasies, the contents, if the box is beautiful and inspiring. I am inspired by June the empty box. The world has never been as empty as since I have known her. Precisely because a world full of ideas, talent, fantasies, is not a full world. June supplies the beautiful incandescent flesh, the fulgurant voice, the abysmal eyes, the drugged gestures, the presence of the body, the incarnation of our dreams and creations. What are we? Only the creators. She IS. What a dull world without June. No beauty. No voice. No presence. All the poetry written, all the erotic imaginings, all the obsessions, illusions, nightmares, manias, what are they if there is no June, the warm being walking and touching us? Sterile, all our cries, all our staggering words, all the heat and fervor of storytelling, sterile our creations, if there were no June passing through, like the supreme materialization of them all, with a demonic indifference to human order, human limitations and restrictions.

I get letters from Henry every day. I answer him immediately. I gave him my typewriter and I write by hand. I think of June day and night. I am full of energy. I write endless letters.

Last night after reading Henry's novel I could not sleep. It was midnight. I wanted to get up and go to my writing room and write to Henry about his first book. There are two doors to open and they creak. I lay still and forced myself to sleep, with phrases rushing through my head like minor cyclones. I could understand and see, as if I had been there, the devastating charade lovers enter upon. Henry's and June's was on the theme of truth and non-truth, illusion and reality. The meshing only took place in the interlockings of desire. Sudden, violent desires. No time to turn down coverlets, to close windows, to turn out the lights. Against the wall, on the carpet, on a chair, on a couch, in taxis, in elevators, in parks, on rivers, on boats, in the woods, on balconies, in doorways at night, they grappled body to body, breath to breath, tongue against tongue, as if to enclose, enmesh, imprison once and forever, essences, odors, flavors which eluded them at other times.

They were locked at least for an instant in a common pulsation. No mysteries concealed in these rites of the body. Palpable rites, hands full of evidence.

I could see them, lying back to back. He still immersed in her. Her breath quieting down. He wants to remain within her, to lie blind in the furls of her flesh. On what wings does she take flight from Henry? As if the sensual act had been but a mouth applied to an opium pipe.

Henry complains, "She was never tender or warm after love-making. She would rise after it, cool and collected." Was it at this moment that Henry attacked her? Attacked a June who separated from him, who denied him a state of friendship? Either passion or war? And who had declared war first?

I have learned from Henry to make notes, to expand, not to brood secretly, to move, to write every day, to do, to say instead of meditating, not to conceal the breaking up of myself under emotion. He arouses tremendous strength in me. I write against and with him. I live against and with him. I am conscious of his life. I feel rich with it. His letters and the notes on the back of them, his wealth of activity, give me a feeling of warmth and fervor which I love, a feeling of expansion, of ampleness, plenitude. I could not live any longer in an empty world. I must have much to love, much to hate, much to grapple with. I am deeply happy. I no longer have the feeling of emptiness around me.

I am so far away from my soft and gentle home. Yet for June too, I was an archangel. They all want to sanctify me, to turn me into an effigy, a myth. They want to idealize me and pray to me, use me for consolation, comfort. Curse my image, the image of me which faces me every day with the same over-fineness, over-delicacy, the pride, the vulnerability which makes people want to preserve me, treat me with care. Curse my eyes which are sad, and deep, and my hands which are delicate, and my walk which is a glide, my voice which is a whisper, all that can be used for a poem, and too fragile to be raped, violated, used. I am near death from solitude, near dissolution. My being was sundered in two by Henry and June, in absolute discord, in profound contradiction. It is impossible for me to follow one direction, to grow in only one direction.

June said to me, "How can I be faithful to Henry when he does not love all of me, when so much of me he passes judgment on, hates, even."

"Yes," I agreed, "the truly faithless one is the one who makes love to only a fraction of you. And denies the rest."

To me Henry confesses that he has a haunting fear that June is a creation of his own brain. "She is loaded with riches given to her by others. The only difference between her and other women is that instead of furs and jewels she prefers paintings, poems, novels, compositions, statues, praise, admiration."

"Then she does exist in her selections," I said to Henry. "Doesn't she exist in her selection of you? Of me? What kind of certitude do you seek? She is suspicious of words. She lives by her senses, by her intuition. We don't have a language for the senses. Feelings are images, sensations are like musical sounds. How are you going to tell about them?"

"For example," said Henry, not hearing, "once she told me that she was tubercular. But she will not say if she is cured, and how long she was ill, and all she concedes is that it taught her to live more intensely."

"Perhaps, Henry, she may think you will love her better if there is the danger of losing her."

"Whenever she comes back from the café with new friends, her introduction always is: '*They* talked to me, *they* sought me out.'"

As if she were a passive wax receiving others' imprints. To Henry this always seemed a way to conceal her own interest.

"Perhaps she is telling the truth then. Like an actress, she may need to be nourished by a public, by praise, by admiration. They may be a necessity to her as a proof of her visibility. I know that the idea of June doubting her existence may seem impossible to you. But I feel that many of her efforts are not directed towards experiencing her own existence within herself but in obtaining outward proofs of it, outward proofs of her beauty, power, gifts, etc."

This need (which I have, and would not tell Henry) increases like the addict's need of drugs. June had to increase the dose of friendships, admirers, devotees, lovers.

"What are you seeking, Henry? Are you chafing under your bondage? What will you gain if you discover that June can love more than one person? What are you seeking? To disentangle yourself? They say that people who have more than one self are mad, but you yourself, how many Henrys are there in you? And you think of yourself as the sanest of men!"

"I want the key, the key to the lies."

"Passion and violence never opened a human being."

"What opens human beings?"

"Compassion."

Henry laughed. "Compassion and June are absolutely incompatible. Absolutely absurd. As well have compassion for Venus, for the moon, for a statue, for a queen, a tigress."

"Strange irony, in Spanish, compassion means with passion. Your passion is without compassion. Compassion is the only key I ever found which fits everyone."

"And what would you say aroused your compassion for June?"

"The need to be loved . . ."

"You mean faithlessness . . ."

"Oh, no. Don Juan was seeking in passion, in the act of possession, in the welding of bodies, something that had nothing to do with passion and was never born of it."

"A Narcissus pool."

"No, he was seeking to be created, to be born, to be warmed into existence, to be imagined, to be known, to be identified; he was seeking a procreative miracle. The first birth is often a failure. He was seeking the love which would succeed. Passion cannot achieve this because it is not concerned with the true identity of the lover. Only love seeks to know and to create or rescue the loved one."

"And why seek that from me?" said Henry. "I don't even care to feed a stray cat. Anybody who goes about dispensing compassion as you do will be followed by a thousand cripples, nothing more. I say, let them die."

"You asked for a key to June, Henry."

"You also think of June as a human being in trouble?"

This is the kind of image Henry will not pursue. It must be returned quickly to the bottle of wine, like an escaped genie that can only cause trouble. Henry wants pleasure. Drink the wine, empty the bottle, return to it these images of tenderness, recork it, throw it out to sea. Worse luck, it would surely be me who would spot it as a distress signal, pick it up lovingly, and read into it a request for compassion.

Even though Henry laughed at my words, drowned them in a Pernod, he found that when he returned to his writing about June he had lost some of that mythological larger-than-nature proportion which he liked to give to her. What had happened? June seemed less powerful, more vulnerable.

Once June had a fever. The fever, too, he never believed in; he considered it part of her dramatizations, a mere exaggeration of her natural state. That night I saw her, the fever rouged her cheeks and dampened her hair. I believed in it.

The figures in his books are always outsized, whether tyrant or victims, man or woman. Could people change size according to our vision of them?

Henry always saw his mother immense in the scale of the universe. He had been shocked on one of his visits to find her smaller than he remembered her. He believed it was her aging which was shrinking her. If a person continues to see only giants, it means he is still looking at the world through the eyes of a child. I have a feeling that man's fear of woman comes from having first seen her as the mother creator of men. Certainly it is difficult to feel compassion for the one who gives birth to man.

Difficult to keep the friendship of Henry, and the friendship of June.

Yesterday at the café he tore bits of our story from me. Henry cannot make me love her less, but he can make her appear unreal. He can persist in proving that June does not exist, that she is only an illusion, an image invented by us, a beautiful jewel casket filled with others' gifts. He talked about how easily June was influenced, how Jean, the mannish woman in New York, affected her talk, her vocabulary, her habits.

And then Henry said, "You mystify me."

What am I? Is he going to hate me? When we first met, he was so enthusiastic about me.

I am trapped between the beauty of June and the talent of Henry. In a different way, I am devoted to both, a part of me goes out to each one, the writer in me is interested in Henry. Henry gives me a world of writing, June gives me danger. I must choose and I cannot. For me to confide in Henry all the feelings I have about June would be like betraying her, and a secret part of myself. And what does he want? Just knowledge, a ferocious curiosity? No, I cannot believe that. I feel a certain tenderness in him. I do not know when he will turn around and ridicule. Do I fear his ridicule?

Letter to Henry:

Perhaps you didn't realize it but, for the first time today, you shocked and startled me out of a dream. All your notes, your stories about June, never hurt me. Nothing hurt me until you touched upon the non-existence of June. June under the influence of others, yielding. June as she was when you first met her; then June reading Dostoevsky and changing her personality, and June under the influence of Jean. You lived with her, Henry; surely you do not believe that there is no June, just someone who reflects whatever you wish her to be, takes the imprint or her cue from others. Is it your terror too, that she may be a creation of your own brain? But what of her selection of you, and of me? She chose you from other men; she distinguished me. You were delighted when she admired me. You were delighted because she was revealing a side of herself. There is a June who is difficult to identify in the maze of her many relationships, her many roles, but there is a June who is not just a beautiful image. How can she seem unreal to you who had lived with her, and to me whom she kissed? Oh, I do sense another June. But why did you talk to her so much that first night you met her at the dance hall? What was she like then? She must have been far more vivid than all the other women around her?

More letters from Henry, parts of his book as he writes it, quotations, notes while listening to Debussy and Ravel, on the back of menus of small restaurants in shabby quarters. A torrent of realism. Too much of it, too much action. He will not sacrifice a moment of life, eating, walking, movies, people, to his work. He is always rushing and writing about future works, writing more letters than novels, doing more preparation and investigating than actual writing. Yet the form of his last book, discursive, free, associative, casual, reminiscent, like talking, is marvelous.

I get tired of his obscenities, of his world of "shit, cunt, prick, bastard, crotch, bitch," but I suppose it is the way most people talk and live. A symphonic concert today, and reading the poetry and music of Proust, confirmed my mood of detachment. Again and again I have entered realism, and found it arid, limited. Again and again I return to poetry. I write to June. I try to imagine her life now. But poetry took me away from life, and so I will have to live in Henry's world. When I come home, Emilia says, "There is a letter for Madame." I run upstairs hoping it is a letter from Henry.

I want to be a strong poet, as strong as Henry and June are in their realism. What baffles me about Henry is the flashes of imagination, the flashes of insight, the flashes of dreams. Fugitive. And the depths. Rub off the German realist, the man who "stands for shit," as people say of him, and you get a lusty imagist. At moments he can say the most delicate and profound things. But this gentleness is treacherous because when he sits down to write, he denies this; he does not write with love but with anger, he writes to attack, to ridicule, to destroy. He is always against something. Anger incites him; fuels him. Anger poisons me.

Henry feels that he has not got June in his novel. There is one world closed to him. It is the oblique, indirect world of subtle emotions and ecstasies, those which do not take a physical form, a plain physical act. He said he would never stop banging his head against it. I said, "There are some things one cannot seize by realism, but by poetry. It is a matter of language."

Each time Henry describes June in his language, he fails to make her portrait. Elusive, voluptuous, mysterious June. Sometimes while reading his manuscript, I feel there is too much naturalism. It obscures moods, feelings, psychic states.

Café Viking. Henry. He still remembers passages in my novel, wants to have the manuscript, to be able to read it over.* Says it is the most beautiful writing he has read lately. Talks about the fantastic potentialities of it. Talks about his first impression of me standing at the doorsteps.

"So lovely, and then sitting in the big black armchair like a princess. I want to destroy the illusion. At the same time, I am aware of your great honesty. I cannot talk well. I want to write to you."

I read him what I wrote on the effect of reading his notes. He was interested, said I could only write like that, with that imaginative intensity, because I had not lived out what I was writing about. "The living out in excess kills the imagination and the intensity," said Henry. But at the contact of my fervor, he felt like going home and writing with that imaginative power.

Henry misunderstands so much. My smile when he talks about June "at first fighting all my ideas, fighting them off violently, and later absorbing them and expressing them as if they were her own." When I smiled, he looked at me aggressively, as if my smile had been critical and said, "It happens to all of us!" My smile meant: I have done that too. But I believe he loves to quarrel. My mellowness is strange to him. He finds that, like a chameleon, I change color in the café. I lose the colors I had in my own home. I do not fit into the café life. I do not fit into his life.

His life. The lower depths, the underworlds. Violence, ruthlessness, gold-digging, debauch. What a torrent of bestial life. His language, descriptions of a world I never knew. The streets of Brooklyn. Broadway. The Village. Poverty. Associations with illiterates, with all kinds of people.

Mine was, from childhood, growth in an atmosphere of music and books and artists, always constructing, creating, writing, drawing, inventing plays, acting in them, writing a diary, living in created

* This first novel by Anaïs Nin, untitled, remained unpublished.

dreams as inside a cocoon, dreams born of reading, always reading, growing, disciplining myself to learn, to study, skirting abysses and dangers with incredible innocence, the body always sensitive but in flight from ugliness. The eroticism of Paris awakened me but I remained a romantic. I studied dancing, painting, sculpture, costuming, decoration. I created beautiful homes.

When I talk about June, Henry says, "What a lovely way you have of putting things."

"Perhaps it is another way of evading facts."

"No, perhaps you see more."

"You and June wanted to protect me, why?"

"Because you seemed so utterly fragile."

Henry's older mind watching me.

Henry talks about Saint Francis, meditates on the idea of saintliness. Why, I ask him.

"Because I consider myself the last man on earth."

And I am thinking of the sincere admissions I get from him, of his capacity to be awed, which means he is not corrupt, not cynical. When I have been most natural, serving food, cooking, lighting a fire, he still says: "I do not feel natural with you yet." He says this humbly, delicately, and I see such a different Henry from the one in the notes.

He lives rather quietly. He is sometimes not in the present. The writer registers. His feelings are not always in the moment. Afterwards, when he is writing, he seems to realize, to warm up; he begins to react and dramatize.

Our talks: he in his language of the streets, I in mine. I never use his words. His watchfulness and my candid impulsiveness. I think that my "registering" is more unconscious, more intuitive, more instinctive. It does not appear on the surface as his does.

The slipperiness and agility of my mind against his relentless dissection. My belief in wonder against his crude, realistic details. The joy when he seizes upon my essence.

"Your eyes seem to be expecting miracles."

Will he perform them?

Second afternoon at the café.

"I take pleasure in telling you the truth, Henry. I have told you all I know about June."

"Yes, I know that," said Henry. "I am sure of that."

We talked about writing. Henry said, "I like to have my desk in order before I begin; only my notes around me, a great many notes."

"I work the same way. My diary is my notebook. Everything goes into it that I may use for novels." Delight in talk of techniques. Our craft.

Does he suffer from his own inexorable frankness? Does he have no moments of feeling he is violating sacred intimacies? He seems full of delicacies with me.

"We have a common objective passion for truth," I said. "I have been trying to be honest, day by day, in the diary. You are right when you speak of my honesty. I make an effort, at least. It is feminine to be oblique. It is not trickery. It is a fear of being judged. What we analyze, will it die? Will June die? Will our feelings die suddenly, if you should make a caricature of them? There is a danger in too much knowledge. You have a passion for absolute knowledge. You will be hated because of this. There are truths human beings can't bear. And sometimes I do feel your relentless analysis of June leaves something out. You go about it like a surgeon with a scalpel. And as you cut, you kill what you cut into. What will you do after you have exposed all there is to expose about June? Truth. What ferocity in your quest of it. At times I'm sure you want to resuscitate your blind worship, your blindness. In some strange way, I am not with you, I am against you. We are destined to hold two truths. When you caricature, tear apart, I hate you. I want to fight your realism with all the magic forces of poetry."

He carries one vision of the world as monstrous, and I carry mine. They oppose each other, and also complement each other. If at moments I see the world as he does, will he sometimes see the world as I do?

Henry said, "Would you like me to take you to 32 Rue Blondel?"

"What will we see there?"

"Whores."

Henry's whores. I feel curious and friendly towards Henry's whores.

The taxi drops us in a narrow little street. A red light painted with number 32 shines over the doorway. We push a swinging door. It is like a café full of men and women, but the women are naked. There is heavy smoke, much noise, and women are trying to get our attention even before the *patronne* leads us to a table. Henry smiles. A very vivid, very fat Spanish-looking woman sits with us and she calls a woman we had not noticed, small, feminine, almost timid.

"We must choose," says Henry. "I like these well enough."

Drinks are served. The small woman is sweet and pliant. We discuss nail polish. They both study the pearly nail polish I use and ask the name of it. The women dance together. Some are handsome, but others look withered and tired and listless. So many bodies all at once, big hips, buttocks, and breasts. "The two girls will amuse you," says the *patronne*.

I had expected a man for the demonstration of sixty-six ways of making love. Henry barters over the price. The women smile. The big one has bold features, raven black hair in curls which almost hide her face. The smaller one has a pale face with blonde hair. They are like mother and daughter. They wear high-heeled shoes, black stockings with garters at the thighs, and a loose open kimono. They lead us upstairs. They walk ahead, swinging their hips.

Henry jokes with them. They open the door on a room which looks like a velvet-lined jewel casket. The walls are covered with red velvet. The bed is low, and has a canopy which conceals a mirror on the ceiling of the bed. The lights are rosy and dim. The women are at ease and cheerful. They are washing themselves in the bidet which is in the room. It is all done so casually and with so much indifference that I wonder how one can become interested. The women are joking, between themselves. The big woman ties a rubber penis around her waist. It is of an impossible pink. They lie on the bed after slipping their shoes off, but not the black stockings.

And they begin to take poses.

"L'amour dans un taxi."

"L'amour à l'Espagnole."

"*L'amour* when you do not have the price of a hotel room." (For this, they stand up against the wall.)

"*L'amour* when one of them is sleepy."

The small woman pretended to be asleep. The big woman took the smaller woman from behind, gently and softly.

As they demonstrate they make humorous remarks.

It is all bantering and mockery of love until . . . The small woman had been lying on her back with her legs open. The big woman removed the penis and kissed the small woman's clitoris. She flicked her tongue over it, caressed it, kissed. The small woman's eyes closed and we could see she was enjoying it. She began to moan and tremble with pleasure. She offered to our eyes her quivering body and raised herself a little to meet the voracious mouth of the bigger woman. And then came the climax for her and she let out a cry of joy. Then she lay absolutely still. Breathing fast. A moment later they both stood up, joking, and the mood passed.

I feel that when Henry talks to me he seeks another language. I feel him evading the words which come easier to his lips and searching for more subtle tones. I feel I have taken him into a new world. He walks cautiously into it, gently.

I said to him: "Don't think that when I talk so much about beauty and poetry in relation to June that I am merely trying to romanticize, to make it all appear innocent or ideal. I am only trying to describe feelings which are not so simple to describe. For you the sexual act is everything. But sometimes the senses can make a great deal of the mere touch of a hand."

Henry observes that it is impossible for me to hurt or destroy. He had tears in his eyes when he said this.

It gives me far more pleasure to see him working, and I cannot understand wanting to use one's power for destruction when it is so much more pleasurable to watch Henry writing a hundred pages after our talks together.

With me he explores the symphonies of Proust, the intelligence of Gide, Cocteau's fantasies, Valéry's silences, the illuminations of Rimbaud.

He said, "I have never made friends with an intelligent

woman before. All the other women were inferior to me. I consider you my equal.

"With June," he said, "the battles began immediately."

Literature has fallen away. We are entirely sincere with one another.

Joaquin questions my giving to Henry. Why curtains for Henry? Why shoes for Henry? Why writing paper and books for Henry? And me? And me? Joaquin does not understand how spoiled I am. Henry gives me the world. June gave me madness. They gave me two beings I can admire. How grateful I am to find two people who interest me unreservedly. They are generous to me in a way I cannot explain to Joaquin. Can I explain to Joaquin that Henry gives me his water colors, and June her only bracelet?

Henry reproaches June for falling down in her acting because once she gave herself away in a café. Men who knew me made flippant remarks about wanting to sleep with me. June stopped them in an angry way which revealed her love of me. As if I were sacred.

[April, 1932]

I met Fred Perlès today. He is timid, sad-eyed, a sad clown. He echoes Henry, mimics him.

We were sitting in the kitchen of their new home. Fred works for the *Tribune* and he took this small workman's apartment in a workman's quarter, Clichy, next door to Montmartre and the Place Blanche. It is a plain, bare house. One walks up the uncarpeted stairs, and the thin walls let all the noises through. Fred and Henry have two rooms and a kitchen. It is barely furnished, with only essentials, beds, tables, chairs. In the kitchen there is a round table. Once we are sitting down there is no room to walk around.

This is a sort of housewarming. Henry is opening a bottle of wine. Fred is tossing a salad. Fred seems pale beside Henry, pale and sickly.

Henry said, "Here is the first woman with whom I can be absolutely sincere."

"Laugh, Anaïs," said Fred. "Henry says he loves to hear you laugh, that you are the only woman who has a sense of gaiety, a wise tolerance."

A few pans, unmatched dishes from the flea market, old shirts for kitchen towels. Tacked on the walls, a list of books to get, a list of menus to eat in the future, clippings, reproductions, and water colors of Henry's. Henry keeps house like a Dutch housekeeper. He is very neat and clean. No dirty dishes about. It is all monastic, really, with no trimmings, no decorations. Plainness. The white and light grey walls.

Yesterday Henry came to Louveciennes. A new Henry, or, rather, the Henry I sensed behind the one generally known, the Henry behind the one he has written down. This Henry can understand: he is sentient.

He looked so serious. His violence has burnt itself out. The coarseness, in the alchemy, became strength. He had received a letter from June, in pencil, irregular, mad, like a child's moving, simple cries, of her love for him. "Such a letter blots out everything." I felt the moment had come to expose the June I knew, to give him June, "because it will make you love her more. It's a beautiful June. Other days I felt you might laugh at my portrait, jeer at its naïveté. Today I know you won't."

I let him read all I had written about June.

What is happening? He is deeply moved, torn apart. He believes.

"It is in this way that I should have written about June," he says. "The other is incomplete, superficial. You have got her."

"You leave softness, tenderness out of your work, you write down only the hatred, the rebellions, the violence. I have only inserted what you leave out. What you leave out is not because you don't feel it, or know it, or understand, as you think. It is left out only because it is more difficult to express, and so far, your writing has come out of violence and anger."

I confide in him completely, in the profound Henry. He is won over. He says, "Such love is wonderful. I do not hate or despise that. I see what you give each other. I see it so well. Let me read on. This is a revelation to me." I tremble while he is reading. He understands too well. Suddenly he says, "Anaïs, I have just realized that what I give is something coarse and plain, compared to that. I realize that when June returns . . ."

I stop him. "You don't know what you have given me! It is not coarse and plain." And then I add, "You see a beautiful June now."

"No, I hate her."

"You hate her?"

"Yes, I hate her," Henry says, "because I see by your notes that we are her dupes, that you are duped, that there is a pernicious, destructive direction to her lies. Insidiously, they are meant to deform me in your eyes, and you in my eyes. If June returns, she will poison us against each other. I fear that."

"There is a friendship between us, Henry, which is not possible for June to understand."

"For that she will hate us, and she will combat us with her own tools."

"What can she use against our understanding of each other?"

"Lies," said Henry.

We were both so aware of her power over both of us, of the friend-

ship which bound Henry and me, of the friendship which bound
me to June. When Henry realized that I had trusted him because I
understood him, he said, "What penetration you have, Anaïs, how
wise you are."

It was I who defended June against one of Fred's remarks
to Henry.

"June is evil," Fred said. "June is bad for you."

"She is not bad for you, Henry," I said. "Her lies, her un-
necessary complications as you call them, interest the writer in you.
Novels are born out of conflict. She was so busy living that she never
took time to listen to you, to understand you. June will be good for
your novels, and I will be good for you."

Henry was in a subdued mood.

"If I had the means to help you get June back to Paris, would you
want me to do it?"

Henry winced.

"Don't ask me, Anaïs, don't ask me." He was suffering.

The full body of June would triumph over creation.

"How you get at the core of everything," said Henry.

"What feeling," he exclaimed, while he read the diary.

To sneer, to rebel, to revolt; that has been his only work so far.
And not to care. To destroy is easy.

When we talked once about my writing in the peace of my house,
I said, "Perhaps you could not work with peace, you need excitement, interruptions, noise."

"It would be a different writing," said Henry.

Does he want the peace and delicacies I am seeking to escape from?
Does he hunger for gentleness and subtlety? Will he turn around and
betray all this, destroy it?

I teased him. "Perhaps all I have written is untrue, untrue of
June, untrue of me, all illusion and delusion."

"No," he said. "Whatever you see, or whatever you do is right."

"Am I not the Idiot?"

"No, you see more, you just SEE more," said Henry. "What you
see is there all right. Yes. For the first time I see some beauty in it."

Dostoevsky was a portentous author for Henry and for June.
When I first met them, I felt they were living in his climate, with the

same fervors, extravagances, and impersonations of his characters. Today Henry seemed completely Henry and no one else.

"I cannot express tenderness," mused Henry. "Only extravagance. Only passion and energy."

Henry says, "It is quite clear, of course, that I am a failure."

"But I don't want you to be. I won't let you be one. I want you to write, to live and be recognized."

If what Proust says is true, that happiness is the absence of fever, then I will never know happiness. For I am possessed by a fever for knowledge, experience, and creation.

I think I have an immediate awareness in living which is far more terrible and more painful. There is no time lapse, no distance between me and the present. Instantaneous awareness. But it is also true that when I write afterwards, I see much more, I understand better, I develop and enrich.

I live more on time. What is remembered later does not seem as true to me. I have such a need of truth! It must be that need of immediate recording which incites me to write almost while I am living, before it is altered, changed by distance or time.

We sit in the Clichy kitchen having lunch. Books pile up, records on the floor. Charts and drawings on the walls.

The talk is about Proust and it brings out this confession from Henry: "To be entirely honest with myself, I like to be away from June. It is then I enjoy her best. When she is here, I am morbid, oppressed, desperate. I am satiated with experience and pain."

June has worn him out, worn out his jealousies, and his capacity for suffering. What he has left is a capacity for enjoying peace.

I palliate the sufferings of others. Yes, I see myself always softening blows, dissolving acids, neutralizing poisons, every moment of the day. I try to fulfill the wishes of others, to perform miracles. I exert myself on performing miracles (Henry will write his book, Henry will not starve, June will be cured, etc.).

"Living a lie which is not a lie but a fairy tale," wrote Henry.

Today I met Fred and we walked towards Trinité together to buy things for the apartment. The sun came out from behind a cloud.

I quoted from his writing on a sunny morning in the market, which touched him. He tells me that I am good for Henry.

"You are wonderful," says Fred, "you are beautiful."

Brought Henry a copy of the magazine *transition*. I like adding to his writing, enriching it.

Reading Proust marked by Henry:

On the other hand, it is not by chance that intellectual and sensitive beings always give themselves to insensitive and inferior women. Such men need to suffer. Such intellectual and sensitive beings are generally little inclined to lie. This takes them all the more by surprise, that even though very intelligent, they live in the world of possibilities, react little, live in the pain that a woman has just inflicted upon them, rather than in the clear perception of what she wanted . . . Through this, the mediocre woman that one was surprised to see them love, enriches their universe much more than would have an intelligent woman.

Lies . . . All this creates, in the face of a sensitive intellectual, a universe all in depths which his jealousy would like to plumb and which is not without interest to his intelligence.

All this I sensed and said to Henry.

I see similarities between Henry and myself in softness and yieldingness in human relationships. I see his utter subjection to June balanced by continuous revenges upon her in his writing. Henry talks of beating June, but it is only verbal or in writing. He is weak before her. And he is completely lacking in protectiveness towards woman. He has let himself be protected always. That may be why she can say: "I have loved him like a child." Will Henry continue to assert his manhood only by destruction, anger, and then when June appears, bow his head and endure?

Right now only hatred fires him to write. He reads Mabel Dodge Luhan on Lawrence [*Lorenzo in Taos*] and is immediately aroused. He writes me a long letter which is like a brainstorm. His furies are out of proportion. He wills the whole world to fire and floods because the article Fred writes laboriously for the *Chicago Tribune* for a pittance is destroyed the next day if it is not printed. Dionysian furies and orgies. "Life is foul, life is foul," he cries.

I guess I must have been sleeping a hundred years in the world of the poets, and did not know about hell on earth.

I had been thinking of letting Henry read all I have written about him. And then I hesitated, because I could hear him saying: "Why are you so grateful?" He would mock my thanksgivings. And then Fred writes about him, "Poor Henry, I feel sorry for you. You have no gratitude because you have no love. To be grateful one must first know how to love."

Henry marks this in Proust:

I was happier to have Andrée near me than I would have been had Albertine been miraculously found again. For Andrée could tell me more things about Albertine than Albertine had told me. On the other hand, the idea that a woman had perhaps had relations with Albertine caused me no more than the desire to have them myself with this woman.

And:

Since desire always goes towards that which is our direct opposite, it forces us to love that which will make us suffer.

Henry says, "Fred and I have terrific arguments. He insists so much. Am I the better writer, or is he? It bothers me sometimes."

"You have more power, more strength, more energy. He is more like a French writer, subtle, wry, witty, oblique."

"But meanwhile it is Fred who has written three wonderful pages about you. He raves about you. He worships you. I am jealous of these three pages. I wish I had written them."

"You will," I said confidently.

"For example, your hands. I had never noticed them. Fred gives them so much importance. Let me look at them. Are they really as beautiful as that? Yes, indeed," said Henry, so naïvely that I laughed.

"You appreciate other things, perhaps."

Henry said, "I am so sick of the vulgar, drab poverty of my life. You give me something rare."

"The destroyers do not always destroy. June has not destroyed you, ultimately. The core of you is a writer, and the writer is thriving."

Fred draws strength from Henry's torrential writing and tropical furies. And Henry is puzzled and curious about Fred's agile, foxy, oblique remarks. Henry is a loud speaker compared with Fred's timid ways.

"Henry, tell Fred we can go and look for curtains tomorrow." (It is Fred who attends to feminine details of settling in the apartment.)

"I'll come, too," said Henry, who had first said he would not waste time looking for curtains.

"Tell him to meet me at the same place, at the same time as last time . . ."

"About four o'clock."

Henry's face is sometimes oddly impenetrable, at other times flushed and excited, at others pale and chastened, as if the hot blood had withdrawn from him. He is observant, analytical, watchful, and often suspicious. His blue eyes occasionally turn moist with feeling. Then I remember a story about his childhood. His parents (his father, a tailor) would take him on their Sunday outings, dragging him about all day and late at night. They sat in relatives' and friends' houses to play cards and smoke. The smoke would grow thick and hurt Henry's eyes. They would put him on the bed in the room next to the parlor, with wet towels over his inflamed eyes. And now his eyes get tired of proofreading work at the newspaper, and I would like to free him and I can't.

I have just stood before the open window of my bedroom and I have breathed in deeply all the honeysuckle-perfumed air, the sunshine, the snowdrops of winter, the crocuses of spring, the primroses, the crooning pigeons, the trills of the birds, the entire procession of soft winds and cool smells, of frail colors and petal-textured skies, the knotted snake greys of old vine roots, the vertical shoots of young branches, the dank smell of old leaves, of wet earth, of torn roots, and fresh-cut grass, winter, summer, and fall, sunrises and sunsets, storms and lulls, wheat and chestnuts, wild strawberries and wild roses, violets and damp logs, burnt fields and new poppies.

Henry disturbs the wisdom I seek to maintain, my passion for truth (it is true that June is beautiful and worthy of passion). He

68

mistrusts suavity, prefers explosiveness. The smile I always carry he challenges; he tears it away like a holiday mask.

He shatters the reserve with which I handle my explosiveness so as not to hurt others. He exposes the withdrawn Anaïs who lives several fathoms deep. He likes to churn the ground. His role is to keep everything moving, for out of chaos comes richness, out of upheavals new seeds.

The same thing which makes Henry indestructible is what makes me indestructible. The core of us is an artist, a writer. And it is in our work, by our work, that we reassemble the fragments, re-create wholeness.

I gave myself totally and annihilatingly to my mother. For years I was lost in my love of her. I loved her uncritically, piously, obediently. I gave myself. I was weak, depersonalized. I had no will. She chose the dresses I wore, the books I read; she dictated my letters to my father, or at least read and censored them, revised them. I only began to rebel and assert myself when I went out to work at sixteen. I could not go out with boys as other girls did. I repudiated Catholicism, Christianity. It is my weakness I hate, not her engulfing domination.

It takes character to write a long, lifelong diary, a book, to create several homes, to travel, to protect others, and yet I have no character in human relationships. I cannot scold a maid, tell a hurtful truth, assert my wishes, be angry at injustice or treachery.

I heard Joaquin say: "Anaïs is a dreamer, she has no sense of reality. It is reality she thinks Henry is revealing to her."

I expected to meet Fred, but it is Henry who comes to the rendezvous. He tells me that Fred has work to do. And then he adds, "But that's not altogether true. I didn't let him come. I enjoyed his disappointment. Have you ever noticed, he looks at you with the eyes of a dog you are beating when you are cruel. I enjoyed his misery, to imagine him working and not being able to see you."

For the first time I notice stains on Henry's hat, and the torn greasy pockets. Another day this would have touched me, but his gloating over Fred's misery chills me. He talks marvelously about [Samuel] Putnam and [Eugene] Jolas, and his own work, and the work of Fred. But then the Pernod affects him and he tells me, "Last night I sat in a café with Fred after work and the whores talked to me, and Fred looked at me severely because they were ugly ones, diseased I could say, and he thought I should not be talking to them. Fred is a snob sometimes. But I like whores. You don't have to write them letters. You don't have to tell them how wonderful they are."

"What is Fred like when he is drunk?"

"Merry, yes, but always a bit contemptuous with the whores. They feel it."

"Whereas you are friendly?"

"Yes, I talk to them like a cart driver."

I saw, for the first time, a malevolent Henry. He had come to hurt Fred.

He repeated several times, as if reveling in it: "Fred is working, how it must gripe him." I did not want to choose the curtains without Fred, but Henry insisted. "I found as much pleasure doing evil . . ." said Stavrogin. And this is for me a pain, not a pleasure.

One of Henry's stories was how he used to like borrowing from a certain man and then spending half the sum he gave him to send the man a telegram. When these stories rise out of drunken mists, I see in him a gleam of deviltry, a secret enjoyment of cruelty.

June buying perfume for Jean while Henry was hungry, or taking pleasure in concealing a bottle of Scotch in her trunk while Henry and his friends, penniless, were wishing desperately for something to drink. What startles me is not what they do, which could be merely thoughtless or selfish, it is the pleasure which they find in doing it. June carried it much further, into blatant perversity, when she wrestled with Jean at Henry's parents' home and willfully shocked them. This love of cruelty must bind them indissolubly. Would they take pleasure in destroying me? For jaded people, the only pleasure left is to demolish others.

Am I facing reality? Am I Stavrogin, who would not act but who watched Stepanovitch with fascination, as if letting him act for him?

Am I, at bottom, still that fervent little Spanish Catholic child who chastised herself for loving toys, who forbade herself the enjoyment of sweet foods, who practiced silence, who humiliated her pride, who adored symbols, statues, burning candles, incense, the caress of nuns, organ music, for whom Communion was a great event? I was so exalted by the idea of eating Jesus's flesh and drinking His blood that I couldn't swallow the Host well, and I dreaded harming it. On my knees, lost to my surroundings, eyes closed, I visualized Christ descending into my heart so realistically (I was a realist then!) that I could see Him walking down the stairs and entering the room of my heart like a sacred visitor. The state of this room was a subject of great preoccupation for me. I fancied that if I had not been good, this room would appear ugly in the eyes of Christ; I fancied He could see as soon as He entered whether it was clear, empty, luminous, or cluttered, dark, chaotic. At that age, nine, ten, eleven, I believe I approximated sainthood. And then, at sixteen, resentful of controls, disillusioned with a God who had not granted my prayers (the return of my father), who performed no miracles, who left me fatherless and in a strange country, I rejected all Catholicism with exaggeration. Goodness, virtue, charity, submission, stifled me. I took up the words of Lawrence: "They stress only pain, sacrifice, suffering and death. They do not dwell enough on the resurrection, on joy and life in the present."

Today I feel my past like an unbearable weight, I feel that it interferes with my present life, that it must be the cause for this withdrawal, my closing the doors.

Until now, I had the feeling of beginning anew, with all the hopes and freshness and freedom which erases the past mysteries and restrictions. What has happened?

And what sorrow, and coldness. I feel as if I carried inscribed over me: my past killed me.

I am embalmed because a nun leaned over me, enveloped me in her veils, kissed me. The chill curse of Christianity. I do not confess any more, I have no remorse, yet am I doing penance for my enjoyments? Nobody knows what a magnificent prey I was for Christian legends, because of my compassion and my tenderness for human beings. Today it divides me from enjoyment of life.

I have suddenly turned cold towards Henry because I have witnessed his cruelty to Fred. No, I do not love Fred, but Fred is a symbol of my past because he is romantic, sensitive, vulnerable. The first time I saw him, he was so shy, and then he became devoted to me. So the day when Henry willfully hurts Fred, my friendship comes to a stop. It seems absurd. But the fear of cruelty has been the great conflict of my life. I witnessed the cruelty of my father towards my mother, I experienced his sadistic whippings of my brothers and myself, and I saw his cruelty towards animals (he killed a cat with a cane).

The sympathy I felt for my mother reached hysteria when they quarreled, and the terror of their battles, of their angers, grew so great it became paralyzing later, when I became incapable of anger or cruelty myself. I grew up with such an incapacity for cruelty that it is almost abnormal. When I should show character, I show weakness because of my fear of cruelty. Seeing a small manifestation of it in Henry brought out an awareness of all his other cruelties (he beat his pregnant first wife). It was to avoid this conflict that I almost became a recluse. Regression. I fell back into early memories, early states of being, into childhood recollections, and all this prevents me from living in the present. I give too much importance to cruelty.

All this sounds very reasonable. Certainly I feel cold and withdrawn, and I need to confide in someone. I need guidance.

The next day I rushed to Clichy and Henry, Fred and I laughed all this away.

All I wanted was humor and wisdom.

Joaquin thinks that Henry is a destructive force who has elected its opposite (me) to test his power on. Joaquin and my mother think I have succumbed to tons of literature (it is true that I love literature), that I may be saved (Joaquin is not sure how), in spite of myself.

I smiled sardonically.

All this is utterly incomprehensible to Henry. For me, he is a living force, not a destructive one.

I am amazed how many streets he can walk through in a day, how many letters he can write, how many books he can read, how many people he can talk to, how many cafés he can sit in, how many movies he can see, how many exhibitions. He is like a torrent in continuous movement.

He confessed that he was only cruel when he was jealous. He had been jealous of Fred's admiration of me.

His concept of morality is simply not to be a hypocrite. He admits he has no loyalties. He admits he is capable of anything, at a given time: to steal, betray, etc.

Henry, with his clowning, whips the world into a carnival.

We are sitting in a monastically simple room where, a moment before, Henry's typewriter crackled like a castanet. Henry is urging me to display the worst in myself, and I am angered that I have so little to tell. (As a girl I went to confession and could not find any reprehensible acts, but highly censurable dreams!)

There was a bottle of red wine on the floor. Fred was reading from my diary.

It touches me when Henry is humble before something he has never seen before.

"Your house, Anaïs. I know I am a boor, and that I don't know how to behave in such a house, and so I pretend to despise it, but I love it. I love the beauty and fineness of it. It is so warm that when I come into it I feel taken up in the arms of a Ceres, I am ensorcelled."

Henry is no Proust, lingeringly tasting all things; he lives by gusts, by leaps. He never stops to understand; he disperses his time and energy with prodigality.

I always run away from the simplest phrases because they never contain all of the truth. To me the truth is something which cannot be told in a few words, and those who simplify the universe only reduce the expansion of its meaning.

Writers do not live one life, they live two. There is the living and then there is the writing. There is the second tasting, the delayed reaction.

The intention of June's lies is often pointless. The first time we met, she told me a story about a man who followed her so obstinately that she finally went to his apartment. He had a copy of Spengler which Henry had been forced to sell. He gave June beautiful gifts. He wanted her to select clothes for a woman he loved who had no taste, no originality. June tells me she saw him a few times and *then stopped for the sake of the other woman.* I sensed a distortion in the story, but I could not tell what she meant it to prove. Her Quixotisms? The story, somehow, sounded false. Does she lie because, as Proust says, we lie most to those we love best? Does she lie to embellish her image, or out of fear of consequences, or to romanticize her life? Both she and Henry acted so sensitively with me that I cannot believe in the other aspect of their lives.

Proust:

Of how many pleasures, of what a sweet life she has deprived us, I said to myself, by reason of this savage obstinacy to deny her inclination.

Marguerite S. is a dark-haired girl whose father is a writer and who earns her living by translating from the English. I met her at the home of my neighbor, Madame Pierre Chareau, one afternoon. She is helping me to copy the diary. She has been visiting Dr. René Allendy for psychoanalysis. After her work, we often sit and talk in the garden. She has a great deal to say about him, and is well read, and we have long talks. Once a week she goes to visit him, and I do notice a change in her.

Her father had known him in the army. At that time he wanted to be a doctor, but he became interested in psychoanalysis and believed in its effectiveness.

Dr. Allendy has written *Le Problème de la Destinée (Etude sur la Fatalité Intérieure)*. He believes in destiny being motivated from within and directed by unconscious tropisms. Deep and unknown impulses push the individual towards repetitive experiences. Man tends to project those patterns outside of himself and to place the blame for all that happens to him on external forces.

Man can control his destiny, says Allendy, to the extent that he becomes aware of these tropisms, but it requires a real initiation, similar to Buddhist discipline which enables disciples to escape their karma through knowledge. Psychoanalysis can overcome what we call bad luck, or tragedy, or fatality.

He was born in 1889 in Paris. He studied medicine, later practicing in hospitals. His thesis in 1912 was on *"Les Théories Alchimique dans l'Histoire de la Médecine."* He is interested in homeopathy and astrology and founded the Société Française de Psychanalyse.

I went to the Sorbonne to hear him lecture. He is tall, bearded.

He does not look French at all. He is a Breton, but he looks like a Russian peasant. It is interesting that he studied Russian as a young man, and later traveled through Russia and organized a welcome-committee for Russian students.

Marguerite has tried to persuade me to see him too. She reminds me that in New York I had a breakdown. But I feel that all I needed was to live, and if I were neurotic I would not have written a book, or created a beautiful house, or dared to live full as I am doing.

"I have no brakes on," I said. "Analysis is for those who are paralyzed by life."

Today, for the first time, I rang the bell of Dr. Allendy's house. I was led by a maid through a dark hallway into a dark salon. The dark brown walls, the brown velvet chairs, the dark red rug received me like a quiet tomb, and I shivered. The only light came from a greenhouse on which it opened. It was filled with tropical plants, surrounding a small pool with goldfish in it. A pebble path circled the pool. The sun filtered through the green leaves gave a subdued greenish light, as if I were at the bottom of the ocean. It seemed apt to leave ordinary daylight behind for the exploration of submerged worlds.

Dr. Allendy's office was soundproofed by a heavy black Chinese curtain, embroidered in gold thread with a few papyrus branches. When the time came, he slid a door open and then lifted the curtain and stood there, very tall, his eyes the most alive part of his face, the eyes of a seer. He has very brilliant, even, small teeth, and bold features. He is heavy, and his bearded face gives him a patriarchic air. It was almost a surprise to see him, a moment later, sitting quietly behind the Morris chair on which I sat, rustling note paper and pencils, and talking softly. It would have seemed more appropriate for him to be doing horoscopes, or preparing an alchemist formula, or reading a crystal ball, because he looked more like a magician than a doctor.

We talked first of all about his books, his lectures, and my reaction to them.

I talked about my work, and my life in general. I said I had always been very independent and had never leaned on anyone.

Dr. Allendy said, "In spite of that, you seem to lack confidence."
He had touched a sensitive spot. Confidence!

Dr. Allendy rose from his chair and said, smiling, "Well, I am glad you can stand on your own feet, that you don't need any help."

I started to weep. I wept. He sat down again.

Confidence.

My father did not want a girl. My father was over-critical. He was never satisfied, never pleased. I never remember a compliment or a caress from him. At home, only scenes, quarrels, beatings. And his hard blue eyes on us, looking for the flaws. When I was ill with typhoid fever, almost dying, all he could say was: "Now you are ugly, how ugly you are." He was always on tour, pampered by women. My mother made scenes of jealousy. When I was nine years old and almost died of an appendicitis not diagnosed early enough, and we arrived at Arcachon, where he was vacationing, he made it plain he did not want us. What he meant for my mother I also took for myself. Yet I had a hysterical sorrow when he finally abandoned us. I always feared his hardness and his criticalness. I could not bring myself to see him again.

"And so," said Dr. Allendy, "you withdrew into yourself and became independent. I can see you are proud and self-sufficient. You fear the cruelty of older men, so, at the first sign of cruelty in anyone, you are paralyzed."

"Can a child's confidence, once shaken and destroyed, have such repercussions on a whole life? Why should my father's insufficient love remain indelible; why was it not effaced by all the loves I received since he left me?"

"You seem very well balanced, and I don't believe you need me."

I suddenly felt a great distress at being left alone again, to solve my own difficulties.

I asked if I might come again.

There is a baffling thing about analysis which is a challenge to a writer. It is almost impossible to detect the links by which one arrives at a certain statement. There is a fumbling, a shadowy area. One does not arrive suddenly at the clear-cut phrases I put down. There were hesitancies, innuendos, detours. I reported it as a limpid dialogue, but left out the shadows and obscurities. One cannot give a progressive development.

Is it that Dr. Allendy works with something which escapes consciousness?

Dr. Allendy said, "Women have contributed nothing to psychoanalysis. Women's reactions are still an enigma, and psychoanalysis will remain imperfect as long as we have only men's knowledge on which to base our assumptions. We assume that a woman reacts like a man, but we do not know. Man's vanity is greater than a woman's —because his whole life is based on a manly cult of conquering, from the Dark Ages, when the one who could not hunt and was not strong died. His vanity is immense, and the wounds to it are vital and fatal."

Psychoanalysis does force one to be more truthful. Already I realize certain feelings I was not aware of, like the fear of being hurt.

I despise my own hypersensitiveness, which requires so much reassurance. It is certainly abnormal to crave so much to be loved and understood.

I have written the first two pages of my new book, *House of Incest,* in a surrealistic way. I am influenced by *transition* and Breton and Rimbaud. They give my imagination an opportunity to leap freely.

What do I feel when I see Henry's cold blue eyes on me? My father had icy blue eyes.

Henry talks beautifully to me, in a cool, wise mood.

"Sunday night after you left us, I slept a while and then I went out for a walk. I realized a terrible truth: that I don't want June to come back. At certain moments I even feel that if June should come back and disappoint me, and if I should not care for her any more, I would be almost glad. Sunday night I wanted to send her a cable telling her I did not want her any more. What I have discovered with you is that there can be friendship between men and women. June and I are not friends."

We were walking to the Place Clichy, Fred, Henry and I. Henry makes me aware of the street, of people. He is smelling the street, observing. He shows me the whore with the wooden stump who stands near the Gaumont Palace. He shows me the narrow streets winding up, lined with small hotels, and the whores standing by the doorways, under red lights. We sit in several cafés, Francis Carco cafés, where the pimps are playing cards and watching their women on the sidewalk. We talked about life and death, as D. H. Lawrence talked about it, the people we know who are dead, those who are alive. Henry said, "If Lawrence had lived and known you, he would have loved you."

At Clichy we were sitting in the kitchen with Fred. A small window looks down on the courtyard. We had finished a bottle of wine. We were smoking heavily, and Henry had to get up and wash his eyes with cold water, the irritated eyes of the little German boy.

I could not bear this and I said impetuously, "Henry, let's drink to the end of your newspaper work. You will never do it again. I will take care of you."

This had an extraordinary effect on Fred. His mouth began to tremble. He began to sob. He laid his head on my shoulder and the tears which rolled down his cheeks were enormous and heavy. I had never seen such tears. "Don't be hurt," I said, but I did not know why I said this. Why should he be hurt that Henry might be free of a job which was ruining his eyes?

Henry did not understand either. "What is the matter, Fred? I believe you're angry because you think I washed my eyes before Anaïs to arouse her pity, to take advantage of her susceptibility."

I met Henry and his friends at the café.

Henry told me that Fred had not returned to Clichy the night before.

"Don't take him too seriously," said Henry. "He loves tragedy. His feelings are very keen but all on the surface, all emotional, and they pass quickly."

Later Fred joined us. We ate dinner together at a bistro. But Fred was depressed. Henry was deciding which movie we would see. Fred said he would not come with us, that he had work to do.

Henry went to buy cigarettes.

I said, "Fred, won't you come with us? Why are you so hurt?"

"It is better I should not come. I am too unhappy. You know my feelings." He kissed my hand.

A little later, as the red wine took effect, he threw off his mood to please me, and said, "Let's not go to the movies, let's go to Louveciennes."

The three of us rushed for the train.

It was only nine in the evening but everyone in the house was asleep.

Magic.

I felt the magic of my house lulling them. We sat by the fire. The fire made us talk quietly, intimately.

I opened the iron boxes and showed them my journals. Fred seized upon the first volume and began to cry and laugh over it. Henry read all about himself in the red journal. We sat in the salon and read and talked.

Henry and Fred were both at work when I arrived at Clichy for dinner. Henry was looking over fragments to be inserted in his book. The strength of his writing! The paradox between his gentleness and his violent writing. We all cooked dinner together. Fred had been typewriting pages about me. He made a beautiful portrait of me. He said, "Those are for everyone to read. I am going to write secret ones for you alone.

"Do you like me, Anaïs," he asked pleadingly.

"Of course I do, Fred."

Henry is very gay. He is making plans for future books; he talks about Spengler, *transition*, Breton, and dreams.

He has heavy "take-offs" and I sometimes suggest he begin somewhere else, to cut out laborious beginnings.

It is these tranquil, relaxed hours with Henry and Fred which are the most fecund. Henry falls into a thoughtful quietness, musing, chuckling over his work. He has, at times, something of a gnome, a satyr, and a German scholar. At such moments his body appears fragile, and the energy of his writing and his talk and imagination seem almost too much for it. As he sits there sipping coffee, I see a new aspect of him: I see his richness, the impulses which blow like gusts and carry him everywhere, his letters to people all over the world, his curiosity, his exploration of Paris day and night, his relentless investigation of human beings.

His charts on the walls are enormous, filled with names, incidents, titles of books, allusions, relationships, places, restaurants, etc. A giant task, a universe, if he can ever write it all.

But June may come back and blow all this down like a simoom wind.

There will remain the things Henry said which I cull here. He talks about God, about Dostoevsky, and the finesse of Fred's writing, which he admires.

He can draw a distinction between dramatic, sensational, potent writing like his own, and the delicacy of Fred's writing. Can June perceive such nuances? Henry says, "She likes orgies, orgies of talk, orgies of noise, orgies of sex, orgies of sacrifice, orgies of hatred, orgies of weeping."

Henry said, "Fred has a finesse which I lack, the quality of an Anatole France."

"But he lacks the power you have."

His passion runs through a chill, intellectual world like lava. It is his passion which seems important to the world today. It raises his books to the level of a natural phenomenon, like a cyclone, an earthquake. Today the world is chilled by mind and by analysis. His passion may save it, his appetite for life, his lust.

Henry was telling me about a book I had not read. It was Arthur Machen's *Hill of Dreams*. I was listening, and suddenly he said, "I am talking almost paternally to you."

At that moment I knew Henry had perceived the part of me that is half child, the part of me who likes to be amazed, to be taught, to be guided. I became a child listening to Henry, and he became paternal. The haunting image of an erudite, literary father reasserted itself, and the woman became a child again.

I felt as if he had discovered a shameful secret. I ran away from Clichy.

My childlike attitude towards older men. I can see nothing in it but immaturity, a need brought on by the absence of a father.

Dr. Allendy's office. His big desk, and a big shaded lamp. The wall where the window is, the window which looks on the street, is the one I look at as I sit on the armchair. On the arm of the chair is a small ash tray. Dr. Allendy sits behind this chair, where nothing betrays his presence except the rustle of paper and the sound of his pencil as he makes notes.

His questions come from behind the armchair, disembodied, and so I can give all my attention to his words. I am not able to notice other things, his face, his clothes, his gestures. I have to concentrate on what he says.

Dr. Allendy: "What did you feel after our first talk?"

Anaïs: "I felt that I needed you, that I didn't want to be left alone again to face the problems of my life."

Dr. Allendy: "It is quite clear from all you tell me that you loved your father devotedly, abnormally, and that you hated the sexual reasons which caused him to abandon you. For you felt his reason for having mistresses, for traveling away from you (even with the excuse of concert tours), the reason for your mother's unhappiness and scenes, the reason for his final departure, was sexual. This may have created in you a certain obscure feeling against sex."

Anaïs: "Not against it, but a fear of being hurt through it, by it, because of it."

He probes, asks questions, sometimes gives up an inquest into a particular theory, surrenders a theme of domination in favor of a theme of courting and fearing suffering from love.

Anaïs: "It seemed to me that men only loved big, healthy women with enormous breasts. When I was a girl, my mother worried about my slenderness and quoted the Spanish proverb: 'Bones are for the dogs.' I doubted being able to please, or win a big love for myself, so I accepted what was given to me, gratefully. It was to forget this that I decided to be an artist, a writer, to be interesting, charming, accomplished. I was not sure of being beautiful enough . . ."

At times Dr. Allendy laughs at what I say, at the way I say it.

He says I have a sense of humor. But from my dreams he culls a consistent desire to be punished, or abandoned. I dream of a cruel Henry. I see men as sadists.

Dr. Allendy: "This comes from a sense of guilt for having loved your father too much. I am sure that to make up for this, you loved your mother much more, later."

Anaïs: "It is true. I was blindly devoted to her, loved her tremendously."

Dr. Allendy: "And now you seek punishment. And you enjoy the suffering, which reminds you of the suffering you endured with your father. You were very jealous, as a little girl, of the women he loved."

Dr. Allendy's statements sound unsubtle. I feel oppressed, as if his questions were like thrusts, as if I were a criminal in court. Analysis does not help me. It seems painful. It stirs up my fears and doubts. The pain of living is nothing compared to the pain of this investigation.

Anaïs: "I cannot believe I had a fear of men. I was always very susceptible physically. It was only my romanticism, my desire for a real love, which prevented me from yielding to many temptations."

Dr. Allendy asks me to relax and to tell him what goes on in my mind.

Anaïs: "I am analyzing what you said, and I do not agree with your interpretations."

Dr. Allendy: "You are doing *my* work, you are trying to be the analyst, to identify with me. Have you ever wished to surpass men in their own work, to have more success?"

Anaïs: "Indeed not. I protected and sacrificed much for my brother's musical career, made it possible. I am now helping Henry and giving him all I can, to do his own work. I gave Henry my typewriter. There I think you are very wrong."

Dr. Allendy: "Perhaps you are one of those women who are a friend, not an enemy of man."

Anaïs: "More than that, I wanted to be married to an artist rather than be one, collaborate with him."

There are ideas which Dr. Allendy abandons. But every time he touches upon the theme of confidence, he sees the turmoil and distress I feel. I lie back and I feel an inrush of pain, despair, defeat. Dr. Allendy has hurt me. I cry. I feel weak. It is time to go. I stand up and face him. His marine-blue eyes are very soft. He feels pity for me; he says, "You have suffered a great deal." But I did not want pity; I wanted him to admire me, to think me a unique woman.

When I leave him, I am in a dream. If, behind the black Chinese curtain he looked like a powerful magician, at the front door in the daylight, he looks like a kindly, protective, gentle-mannered doctor. It seems symbolically right to enter his home and wait in a dark salon, to sit in a dark library, and then, having traversed these dark, fantastic, fearful regions, to emerge into daylight, into a neatly groomed garden, a quiet street.

Dr. Allendy: "Why did you cry the last time?"
Anaïs: "I feel that some of the things you said were true."
Analysis is distasteful to me. I would prefer to tell Dr. Allendy simply about the day spent with Henry, and Fred. Fred's weeping when I said I would take care of Henry.

I begin with docility but I feel a growing resistance to probing.
Dr. Allendy: "Did you hate me for making you cry?"
Anaïs: "No, I think I liked that. It made me feel that you were stronger than I."

As the hour progresses I feel he is awakening a consciousness of obstacles and difficulties which I could easily forget if he let me, that all he is doing is re-awakening my fears and doubts. But he reminds me that, at the first sign of cruelty in Henry, I wanted to give up the friendship.

Whenever Dr. Allendy tells me to close my eyes and relax, I begin to do my own analysis.

Now he is probing the splitting of personalities, the imaginative poetic writing on the one hand, and the realistic writing in the diary. He begins to sense the importance of my work. Meanwhile I am saying to myself that he is telling me little that I do not know, little that I have not written already. But this is not true, because he has made clear to me the idea of guilt, of guilt and punishment.

I elude Dr. Allendy's further questions. He fumbles. He can find nothing definite. He suggests many hypotheses. Yet I had come in a mood of surrender; I had come intensely tired from the night before, on purpose (I could have postponed the séance). I thought I would be less mentally on guard, more malleable, less wary. Also, when he probed to know my feelings about him and I told him about my interest in his books, I had a mischievous awareness that he expected me to be interested in him, and I did not like playing the game while knowing it was a game. Yet my interest in his books was sincere. I also told him that I did not care any more to impress him, to gain his admiration. That I admitted my need of him.

Anaïs: "At this moment I have less confidence in myself than ever. It is intolerable."

Henry never analyzes, probes, or seeks to understand. He said, "You've noticed my love of finding fault, of criticizing, or ridiculing, yet I assure you I have less desire to exert them on you than anybody." This is a paradox, because he seems to be the one who does not pass judgment or accept that others should judge him. The man is full of contradictions.

He was washing dishes. Fred and I were drying them. His vest was unbuttoned because the discarded suit given to him is too small for him. The lapels are frayed. He has a surreptitious, half-ashamed expression when he takes the garbage can away. He is ashamed of his orderliness, which forces him to wash the dishes, to tidy the kitchen. He says, "June objected to this in me, she said it was unromantic, that no real artist would bother with all this. She affected a royal disorder."

I have to admit that I myself behave as Henry does, but that June's rebellion against these chores seems wonderful to me.

"I have overdrawn the cruelty of June, the evil in June," says Henry, "because I was interested in evil. I take goodness for granted. But that is just the trouble, there are no really evil persons in the world. June is not really evil. Fred is right, eh, Fred? June tries desperately to be evil. It was one of the first things she told me the night we met. She wanted me to think her a femme fatale. I am inspired by Evil. It preoccupies me as it preoccupied Dostoevsky."

The sacrifices June made for Henry. Were they sacrifices, abnegation, selflessness, or were they romantic gestures which heightened her personality? Henry incited me to probe this. June refused the humble duties of a wife. She made sensational or spectacular acts of devotion. Flamboyant ones. Going to "gold-dig" for Henry, arranging liaisons, etc. She would protect Henry only intermittently. In between, he could starve. She urged Henry not to work. She wanted to support him.

I said to Henry, "But why are you so savage about her defects? Why do you write less about her dramatic qualities, her superb recklessness, her magnificent generosities?"

"That's just what June said. She often repeated: 'And you forget this, and you forget that. You only remember the wrongs.' "

"She did tell me that you were fascinated with evil, and that is why she tried to invent an evil life, to interest you."

I could not bring myself to say that there were times when I was tempted to abdicate from my own goodness or faithfulness in order to create for myself a richer life, to have more to tell, to find a way to match the eventfulness of their life, the enormous amount of relationships, incidents, experiences. I could see already how contagious a full life can be. When I walk about Paris, I see and sense much more now than I did before, my eyes having been opened by Henry's revelations.

But all these fantasies were dispelled when I found Henry in such a serious mood. He asked me to "roll up my sleeves" and go to work with him on the coordination of his book. Fred was working on his book.

Henry tends to overflow, to expand so much that he gets lost. I am able to see what is irrelevant, over-developed, and confused. My own style is terser, more condensed, and it helps him.

June would have interrupted the writing mood, precipitated Henry into more experience, more life, delayed his assimilation and digestion of experience (which he needs), shone with the glitter of motion and drama; and Henry would have cursed her, but said, "June is an interesting character."

Anaïs: "Today, I frankly hate you. I am against you."
Dr. Allendy: "But why?"

Anaïs: "I feel that you have taken away from me the little confidence I did have. I feel humiliated to have confessed to you. I have rarely confessed."

Dr. Allendy: "Why do you never confess? You have told me that you are reserved, that in most relationships it is you who receive confidences. People confess their fears and doubts to you. But you rarely do. Why? Are you afraid to be less loved?"

Anaïs: "Yes. Quite definitely. I keep a kind of shell around me, because I want to be loved. If I exposed the real Anaïs, I might not be loved."

Dr. Allendy: "Have you ever thought of how you feel when people confess to you? Does it make you love them less?"

Anaïs: "No, on the contrary. I feel sympathy, compassion, I understand them better, it makes me feel closer to them."

Dr. Allendy: "Have you ever thought of what a relief it would be if you could be entirely open and natural with everybody?"

Anaïs: "Yes, sometimes I feel human relationships are too great a strain."

Dr. Allendy: "After all, what do you fear so much? Come on, tell me, let's look at them frankly. What is the worst of your fears?"

Anaïs: "My greatest fear is that people will become aware that I am fragile, not a full-blown woman physically, that I am emotionally vulnerable, that I have small breasts like a girl. And so I cover all this up with understanding, wisdom, interest in others, with my mind's agility, with my writing, my reading: I cover the woman up, to reveal only the artist, the confessor, the friend, the mother, the sister. I am even more unhappy since I have seen the woman who is my ideal of a woman, June, who has the dark husky voice, the full strong body, who has vigor and endurance, can stay up all night and drink all night."

Dr. Allendy: "Do you realize how many women envy your silhouette? Your grace? How many men find a woman who looks like a girl infinitely attractive?"

(This kind of direct assurance I have often received, and it does not convince me or I would have been convinced long ago, when I was the most popular model for the painters, so much in demand that I could not keep up with my engagements. I know he must find a more profound way of healing my shattered confidence.)

Dr. Allendy was amazed at the extent of my lack of confidence.

Dr. Allendy: "Of course, to an analyst, it is very clear, even in your appearance."

Anaïs: "In my appearance?"

Dr. Allendy: "Yes, everything you wear, the way you walk, sit, stand is seductive and it is only people who are unsure who act constantly in a seductive manner and dress to charm."

We laughed at this.

I felt softer and more relaxed.

I talked about my father's passion for photography and how he was always photographing me. He liked to take photos of me while I bathed. He always wanted me naked. All his admiration came by way of the camera. His eyes were partly concealed by heavy glasses (he was myopic) and then by the camera lens. Lovely. Lovely. How many times, in how many places, until he left us, did I sit for him for countless pictures. And it was the only time we spent together.

Later, when I gave a concert of Spanish dances in Paris, I imagined I saw his face in the audience. It seemed pale and stern. I stopped in the middle of my dance, frozen, and for an instant I thought I could not continue. The guitarist playing behind me thought I had stage fright and he began to encourage me with shouts and clapping. Later, when I saw my father again, I asked him if he had been at this concert.

He answered me, "No, I was not there, but if I had been I would have disapproved absolutely. I disapprove of a lady being a dancer. Dancing is for prostitutes, professionals. I would not have allowed you on the stage. Besides, you can't read music."

I told him that I had an amazing ear, and could learn anything by ear.

Dr. Allendy suggested that I might have wanted him there, that I had willed him there.

Dr. Allendy: "You may have wanted to dance for him, to charm him, to seduce him, unconsciously. And when you became aware that the dancing was an act of seduction, you felt guilt, and it was guilt which made you give up dancing as a career. Dancing became synonymous with seducing the father. You must have felt guilt for his admiration of you as a child, his admiration may have awakened your feminine desire to please your father, to hold him away from his mistresses."

And so guilt, guilt had cut short a life I wanted, for after the concert I was offered an engagement with the Spanish Ballet of the Opéra. I would have traveled, I would have been pampered, I would have lived an adventurous and physical, colorful life.

Could Dr. Allendy really have rescued me then, freed me of the EYE of the father, of the eye of the camera which I have always feared and disliked as an *exposure*. An exposure of what? Of the desire to charm, of coquettishness, of vanity, of seductiveness?

Dr. Allendy said I wanted my father there, I wanted to dazzle him. And that today, when I do charm, dazzle, or win anyone, I do not want to win, really; I have too much guilt.

Anaïs: "And writing! Writing I was not afraid to do?"

Dr. Allendy: "No, that did not seem as if you put yourself forward to charm men, but your work, a creation, something removed from you. It is something you do alone, not in public. There is distance and objectivity. But I have no doubt that if you should succeed in it, you would also give it up."

Then suddenly I remembered that my father wrote too, although it was not his profession. He wrote two books, one called *Pour L'Art,* and the other *Idées et Commentaires,* both on the aesthetics of art. I had seen him at work on them, and it was my mother who typed for him.

The rest of our talk escapes me.

Henry said, "Anaïs, I have watched you, observed you. You are blossoming so quickly that you will soon exhaust all I have to teach you, and you will pass on to other friendships. There are no limits to what your life might be! I have seen how you can swim in a large life. Listen, if anybody else did the things you have done for your mother and your brother, I would call them foolishly romantic, but somehow you make them seem so terribly right. Your diary-writing, for instance, it is so rich, so terribly rich. You say my life is rich, but it is only full of events, incidents, facts, experiences, people. What is really rich are those pages you write on so little material."

Henry had been questioning me on my devotion to my mother and my brother. When he began to say I should not make sacrifices for them, I should live as I please, I was silent.

He talked of what I meant to his growth. He feels a sense of growing deeper. "I can talk to you, it is so good to be able to talk."

It was the first time he had been the object of a portrait and he loved being written about so fully. "Always what is human in the diary is wonderful."

June would be surprised if she came in, to hear us talking about her. Fred lies on the couch reading. Henry sits by his desk. I sit on the floor. We all talk so quietly, divested of all glamour and dramatics, like craftsmen at work. June would scatter the silences, the pages of Henry's book, the pages of the journal, would make us all hate each other and worship her, and stir up the furnace in which novels are born but not written.

I too am interested in evil, and I want my Dionysian life, drunkenness and passion and chaos; and yet here I am, sitting at a kitchen table and working with Henry on the portrait of June, while Fred is making a stew.

My restlessness, which was vague and lyrical, has become sharp-pointed and intolerably clear. I want to be June.

Never have I seen as clearly as tonight that my diary-writing is a vice. I came home worn out by magnificent talks with Henry at the café; I glided into my bedroom, closed the curtains, threw a log into the fire, lit a cigarette, pulled the diary out of its last hiding place under my dressing table, threw it on the ivory silk quilt, and prepared for bed. I had the feeling that this is the way an opium smoker prepares for his opium pipe. For this is the moment when I relive my life in terms of a dream, a myth, an endless story.

As I can never catch up with the typing of the diary, Marguerite is very helpful, and she needs the work. We type in different rooms, but sit in the garden afterwards, talking. She talks about her life.

Her father was director of a college in the provinces, and very severe with her. He demanded perfection. She is now trying to live alone. He had subdued her mother so completely that he had instilled in her a great fear of love and marriage. Dr. Allendy is helping her. Copying my diary seems to help her too, as when I am frightened I throw myself into action, whereas she withdraws. She is doing research work in libraries which she will not discuss. She is full of secrets.

I confide in Dr. Allendy. I talk profusely about my childhood. Quote from early writings obvious phrases about my father. So intelligible now, my love for him. And also the consequent sense of guilt. I wrote at age eleven: "I feel I do not deserve my Christmas presents." I gave up my faith in God because He did not accomplish a miracle and bring my father back to me on my thirteenth birthday. That was my prayer and it was never answered. I began to write the diary on the ship bringing us to America, at the age of eleven, for him, to tell him the story of my wanderings far from him. I tried to mail the diary volumes to him. My mother did not let me, saying they might get lost. When I took communion at Mass, I imagined it was not Christ who visited me in this heart shaped like a room, but my father. I was aware that I had not only lost him, but a way of life, music, musicians, colorful visitors, prestige, a European life, as compared with life in America, unknown, with drab and colorless friends, and my mother struggling to support us.

We discuss finances and I tell Dr. Allendy the cost of the visits will prevent me from seeing him more than once a week. He not only reduces his fee by half but offers to let me pay him by working for him. He has research to do in the library and has some articles which must be rewritten. I am very flattered. I have full confidence in my ability as writer. Dr. Allendy listens to my talk about June.

Anaïs: "June is my ideal of what a woman should be. I am underweight. A few more pounds would add greatly to my self-confidence. I feel like an adolescent girl. Will you add medicine to your psychic treatment? My breasts are too small."

Dr. Allendy: "Are they absolutely undeveloped?"

Anaïs: "No." As I flounder in my descriptions, I say: "To you, a doctor, the simplest thing is to show them to you." And I do. And then Dr. Allendy began to laugh at my fears.

Dr. Allendy: "Perfectly feminine, small but well shaped, well outlined in proportion to the rest of your figure, such a lovely figure, all you need is a few more pounds of it. You are really lovely, so much grace of movement, charm, so much breeding and finesse of line." And I begin to laugh too. But my hands are cold, my heart is beating and my face is flushed from the ordeal of the test. He is amazed by the disproportion of my self-criticism. How did these doubts begin?

I had brought him a copy of my book on D. H. Lawrence. He gave me two books he had written. *Problème de la Destinée. Capitalisme et Sexualité.*

I told him that he was helping me to live; that I had been able to confide in Henry and Fred and that Henry had written me marvelous letters on my childhood diaries.

Dr. Allendy had observed the unnaturalness of my personality. As if enveloped in a mist, veiled. He said I had two voices, one like that of a child before its first communion, timid, almost aphonic, the other deeper, richer. This one appears when I have a great deal of confidence. In this state I can imitate the singing of Dinah, the Negro singer. Dr. Allendy thinks that I have created a completely artificial personality, like a shield. I conceal myself. I have constructed a style, a manner, affable, gay, charming, and within this I am hidden.

An enormous sorrow brands me at the age of nine (the loss of my father and of a glamorous European life) and makes me deviate from this light airy course forever. Grace and charm become secondary, superficiality vanishes, I begin to seek compensations. If my father left, it must be that he did not love me, and if he did not, it must have been because I was not lovable. I was going to interest him in other ways. I was going to become interesting. And I grew in depth through sadness and self-doubt. As a courtesan, at the age of nine, I had already experienced failure so I must try other ways to interest men.

But why am I not satisfied with my achievements then? Because, originally, what I truly wanted was a life of pleasure, luxury, travel, adulation, adventures.

I asked Dr. Allendy to help me as a doctor of medicine. Was this quite a sincere action? Did I have to show him my breasts? Did I want to test my charm on him? Wasn't I pleased that he reacted so admiringly? That he gave me his books afterwards?

Is Dr. Allendy really curing me?

Many times Henry talks nonsense. He is flushed, eloquent, drunk, nonsensical. He gets drunk on words.

Summer heat. Cafés. Henry has a few pages to show me, the first pages of his next book [*Black Spring*]. He expected me to have written at least ten pages in my diary after the last talks. But something has happened to the woman with a notebook. I feel like letting Henry do the writing. I want to enjoy the summer day. Words are secondary.

Henry is correcting my first novel with care. Henry is a demon driven by curiosity, always pumping people. Henry is always pretending callousness. Is that an American disease? They are ashamed to show feeling.

"Anaïs, what you really look like is a Greek. There is something very Grecian about you. But the Greeks, they say, are treacherous! I have not written to June yet. Your book is really beautiful. There are memorable pages in it, and it is sharp and ironic, at times very strong. Most women's writing is so petty. Yours never is."

And then later, "Listen, Anaïs, I know I am worth more than June. I won't stand for anything when she returns. She must be made to suffer. It will be good for her. You will see. I am another man. I won't let her override me. I don't like what she does to me when she is here. She humiliates me."

Henry lacks confidence. He is uneasy in certain places, certain situations, and when he is uneasy, he becomes insulting. If we meet chic people, or enter a chic place, or if the waiter is snobbish, or we run into a celebrity, he becomes contrary and difficult.

We either go to Clichy and have lunch with Fred, or sit in cafés, or he comes to Louveciennes.

Sometimes I see a gnomelike Henry, and I can imagine him as a child, impetuous, restless, mobile, prankish.

Fred looks like someone who has been beaten. He looks sensitive and frightened. His eyes plead, and yet it is like the pleading of a priest, who conceals his humor and mockery. I think he takes pleasure in Henry's "toughness." He likes Henry's caricatures. He laughs with his head bowed. Henry may be teaching us both how to become tougher, how to laugh, how to feel less.

I am dropping my shell. I love those long nights of talk at the café, watching the dawn arrive, watching the sleepy workmen going to work, or having their white wine at the bistro. Children are going to school, with their black aprons and their bags of books on their backs like mountain climbers. I carry away my red journal, but that is only a habit, for I carry away no secrets, as Henry reads the journal. I carry a few pages of Fred's book [*Sentiments Limitrophes*], delicate as a water color, and a few pages of Henry's book which is like a volcano. I feel like a flower or a fruit. The old pattern of my life is shattered. I live by improvisation, impetus, surrealist whims.

Great things are going to grow out of all this. I feel the fermentation. I look at the workmen carrying their tools and their lunch boxes, and I feel that we are working too, although they may not think so when they see us sitting at a café table with a bottle of wine, talking.

Fred and Henry walk me to the Gare Saint-Lazare. The train which takes me home to Louveciennes is a small, quaky, shaky miniature train, the Proustian train, and it shakes the phrases in my mind for future books. Image of Henry talking to himself. Henry's seven pages about his childhood. Fred's hands held over me like a priest about to give benediction, his sad eyes apologizing for Henry's rough remarks; but what Fred has not divined is my strength.

Image of Henry protruding like a giant. Henry leaning forward. Henry's notes on big sheets of paper, on menus. Diabolical notes, plagiarisms, distortions, caricatures, nonsense, lies, profundities.

The table at Clichy is stained with wine. Henry ends his phrases in a kind of hum, as if he puts his foot on the pedal of his voice and creates an echo. In this way none of his phrases end abruptly.

He immediately creates a climate of ease and slackness. When he laughs, he shakes his head like a bear. He might pass unnoticed in a crowd, with his hat on one side, his step dragging a little, his laughter. He sits like a workman before his drink, he talks to the waiter and everyone is at ease with him. He gives to the word "good" a mellowness which makes the whole room glow. He gives himself to the present moment. He takes what comes.

One afternoon Henry came to Louveciennes after reading pages from my childhood diary. "I still see you as a child of eleven." I felt anxiety. As if this child had been a secret and was now revealed. How could I exorcise it? I saw a sentimental Henry, awed and intimidated. I became ironic and mocking, wise, and teased him.

"Where are the black cotton stockings?" he asked. "And the basket with the diary in it?"

There was no remedy. I had brought this child so vividly before Henry that she had an existence of her own.

Henry said, "It's strange, but with you I feel relaxed. Most women make men feel strained and tense. And I feel at my best because of that."

He had received a cable from June: "I miss you—I must join you soon." And he was angry.

"Why angry?"

"I don't want June to come and torture me."

"What I am afraid of, Henry, is that June will break our friendship."

"Don't give in to her, keep your wonderful mind. Be strong."

"I could say the same to you. Yet I know your wisdom will be of no use to you."

"It will be different this time."

Has Henry really become aware that he is a man of talent, imagination?

I know his deviltries, too, his begging and borrowing and gold-digging; but I know a Henry who is not in his books, who is unknown to June or to Fred. I am not blind. He has shown me a different Henry. When he wears his hat, it hides his thinning hair at the top and he looks thirty and irresponsible. When his hat is off, he looks like a balding professor, with his glasses and his gravity.

Fred comes into the kitchen. The kitchen table is covered with manuscripts, books, notes, and once you sit at the table, there is no room to move again. The three of us were looking at the map of Europe. Fred pointed to the places he and Henry wanted to see.

I asked Henry to write something in the diary.

Henry wrote:

"I imagine that I am now a very celebrated personage and that I am being given one of my own books to autograph. So I write with a stiff hand, a little pompously . . ."

Dr. Allendy's private house, three floors, with a small front garden and a back garden, the kitchen in the basement, his office and parlor on the first floor, bedrooms on the second floor, resembles the house in Brussels where we lived when I was eight and nine years old. It also resembles the house my father lives in now, in Passy, in a quiet well-bred street where gardeners take care of the plants, where cars wait with chauffeurs in them, where no children play in the street, and no beggars are allowed.

When I first arrive, the window is open and I can see the upper half of his bookcase, which reminds me of my father's bookcase in Brussels and how I spent hours in it when he was out of the house, reading on a chair which was resting on another chair so I could reach the books on the top shelf which were forbidden to us. It was then I read Zola, without understanding half of it, spent hours wondering why the lovers who had been caught in a mine explosion had been found clasped together so tightly they could not be separated, or why the woman who had been given a sleeping draught by Monte Cristo was later found to be pregnant. Impossible to fill in these blank spaces. But I read.

When I first came to Paris we had rented the bachelor apartment of Mr. Hansen, an American who was going away for the summer. It was all we could find. He had left his clothing, his books, his personal belongings in the closets.

Trying to tidy up one day, I was cleaning out the shelves

and found the very top shelf, in a very dark corner, stacked with French paperbacks. I took them down, examined them, and then realized from the lurid drawings of naked women that I must read them in secret too, and could not leave them lying around the apartment for Joaquin to see, or my mother.

One by one, I read these books, which were completely new to me. I had never read erotic literature in America. These were the novelettes which were sold on the counters by the Seine, on the bookshelves of the famous quays. They overwhelmed me. I was innocent before I read them, but by the time I had read them all, there was nothing I did not know about sexual exploits. Some were well written, others purely informative, and others sensational and unforgettable. I had my degree in erotic lore.

These books affected my vision of Paris, until now a purely literary one. They opened my eyes and my senses, they sensitized me so that I became aware of *maisons closes,* red-light districts, prostitutes on the boulevards, the meaning of drawn curtains in the middle of the afternoon, hotels by the hour, the role of Parisian hairdressers (the great procurers), and the acceptance of the separation between love and pleasure.

I was far from my other method of education, from the days when I read books from the New York Public Library alphabetically, having no one to guide me.

Mr. Hansen's bachelor books were illustrated, in color: some in eighteenth-century style, some in contemporary style. I became familiar with boots, whips, garters, black stockings, frilled panties, alcoves, mirrors on the ceilings, peepholes in the walls, and the inexhaustible varieties of erotic experiences.

In those days, when a window opened and a couple stood embracing in front of it, I could sense the whole atmosphere, and get vicarious shivers of pleasure. I developed such antennae that when I went to people's houses I could divine which couples were faithful and which ones having love affairs, and often detect the lover or the mistress. It was as if I had developed a sixth sense in matters of vibrations and sexual currents between people. I was often right. I could detect the presence of desire like a *sourcier.*

I became familiar with the aspect of hotel rooms, the deep-set alcoves still prevalent, the deep quilts, the suppers at midnight, the varieties of luxuries or absence of luxuries.

My knowledge of life had been primarily literary, and it was no wonder that later, when I entered life, there were times when "scenes" seemed like the scenes of novels, not me living my own life, and times when I recognized rooms I had already seen in prints, on the covers of Mr. Hansen's books.

Dr. Allendy's books, alas, as I could see from the covers, covered the same ground but the classification was different. What came under the heading of PLEASURE in Mr. Hansen's library, here was categorized as ABERRATIONS, SADISM, MASOCHISM, PERVERSIONS, ABNORMALITIES, etc. And I wondered whether Dr. Allendy, in having to look upon the sexual habits of his patients as symptoms or clinical problems, did not lose his interest in sex.

Even today I cannot enter a hotel room without feeling that first shiver of delight awakened by the books of Mr. Hansen, and it was then, I believe, that I began to like the prostitutes, as Henry likes them. The blanks in the Zola novel were filled by this exploration of dime novels. The man who was found dead in the embrace of the prostitute had to be pried away from her by a doctor, but the dime novel was far more informative.

I came to see Dr. Allendy in a state of elation. I told him first about the article I am doing for him which I found difficult. I did do the research on the Black Plague which he needed, so he could develop his ideas on death. He told me of a simpler way of doing this article.

My reading of his books has raised him very much in my estimation. He is no poet but he is full of wisdom and insight. Particularly on the theme of fatality being interior and therefore alterable, conquerable. A comforting concept.

I told him a dream: I was in a hall, beautifully dressed. It was the King who wanted to dance with me and who loved me. He whispered loving phrases in my ear. I was very happy and I laughed. I danced alone too, for everyone to see my happiness and lightness. Then I was driving home in a carriage, which could hardly hold my wide fluffy dress. It rained heavily. The rain came into the carriage and spoiled my dress. The carriage began to move slowly, to float in water. I wanted to get back to the castle. But I did not mind the water.

Dr. Allendy says that the love of the King was the conquest of my father. The watery drive is sinking into the unconscious (water is the unconscious) and being at one with it, not minding living in it. Fecundation, perhaps?

I feel loved, fecundated, fecund.

Dr. Allendy says I do not seem to need him any more. But he does point out to me that by entering Henry's world (poverty, Bohemianism, living by expediencies), I have moved in the opposite direction from my father's world (luxury, society life, aesthetics, security, aristocratic friendships, etc.).

Henry's world seems more sincere to me. I never liked my father's worldliness, his need of luxury, his salon life, his love of titles, his pride in his own aristocracy, his dandyism, his elaborate social life.

[May 20, 1932]

The concert hall [Salle Chopin] is all white and gold. The chairs of red plush. It is my brother Joaquin who is playing. He has not come out yet. The hall and the entrance were small, and my father insisted on "receiving" people as if he were the sponsor of the concert. He knew what my mother's reaction would be, but he could not resist the temptation to anger her in public, in front of Joaquin, in front of his friends. Joaquin sent him a message: "Kindly take your seat like everybody else or I will have you thrown out." It had its effect, but it ruined Joaquin's concert for him. It made him nervous and when he first came out, he was pale and tense. But then he warmed up and began to play magnificently. He was wildly applauded.

Henry was sitting in the balcony where I could not see him. I had asked Dr. Allendy to come, although it was not orthodox, and he had accepted. When I saw him walking down the aisle with his wife, I realized how tall he was: he towered over everyone. Our eyes met. There was sadness in his, a great seriousness, which I liked and which moved me.

During the entr'acte, Henry came downstairs. He seemed timid in the crowd. I shook his hand. He seemed strange and distant. When I faced my father, we bowed formally, barely smiling. Would Dr. Allendy give me strength? That night I felt the child in me, still frightened, while the woman appeared radiant to all. There was so much sadness in Dr. Allendy which I had not observed in his office. I saw that he was startled by my evening dress, the hair piled high in ringlets, and my poise. I wanted to hide inside my velvet cape. I felt the weight of my full balloon sleeves. The hypnotic glow of the many lights. Fatigue at meeting so many people, receiving compliments for Joaquin, talking. I observed my father's cold, pale, aristocratic stiffness. The scene at the door has reawakened all the anxieties of my childhood at the battles between my father and mother. I felt the same anxiety. [Many years later my father admitted having done all this "on purpose."—A.N.]

I cut out a photograph of Dr. Allendy from the newspaper. In the car, driving home, Joaquin covers me with his Spanish cape.

Dr. Allendy told Marguerite that I was a very interesting subject, that I responded so sensitively and so quickly. That I was almost cured! But at the concert, I had the certitude that I was trying to dazzle Dr. Allendy, that I was concealing some secret part of my real self. I still find something to hold back. I hold back from everyone a full knowledge of myself. Yet I gave Henry the red journal to read. That was an exception. There must always be a secret, as with June.

Henry wrote me a letter after the concert:

Anaïs, I was dazzled by your beauty. You stood there like a Princess. You were the Infanta of Spain, not the one I was pointed out later. So many Anaïses you have shown me and now this one. As if to prove your Protean versatility. Do you know what [Michael] Fraenkel said to me? "I never expected to see a woman as beautiful as that. How can a woman of such femininity, such beauty, write a book on D. H. Lawrence?" I sought out the father. I think I spotted him. His long dark hair was the clue. He looks like Segovia. You belong in another world. I see nothing in myself to recommend your interest. That seems fantastic to me. It is some divine prank, some cruel jest you are playing on me.

I finally wrote the article for Dr. Allendy. It was a restating from French to English, coordinating Dr. Allendy's notes, excerpts from his book and a magazine article, for an American magazine. I had to be thoroughly familiar with the subject to do this, and as the subject was death, the most profound and difficult theme in psychology, it took me several days to assimilate the material. Several times I wanted to give up, acknowledge myself defeated. I was happy when it was done.

When I brought it to Dr. Allendy, I said: "Don't analyze me today. Let's talk about you. I am enthusiastic about your books. Let's talk about death."

Dr. Allendy assented. Then we discussed the concert. He said my father looked like a young man. Henry made him think of a German painter, George Grosz. Soft—perhaps dual? Henry an unconscious homosexual?

My article was very good, said Dr. Allendy, but why didn't I want to be analyzed?

Was it because he had won my confidence, because I have begun to lean on him, because I asked him to be at Joaquin's concert as I feared trouble between my father and mother?

Dr. Allendy: "As soon as you begin to depend, you work to reverse the process and want me to need you, depend on you. You feel more comfortable then. You need to conquer because you have been conquered. What were your thoughts about me at the concert?"

Anaïs: "I wondered whether you could give me strength, because there was sadness in your eyes. I thought when I saw you in public that you too were shy. You looked different out in the world, more human, as if you were unhappy at times . . ."

Dr. Allendy: "You wanted to find my weakness . . ."

Anaïs: "But to be unhappy is not a sign of weakness! What I felt was sympathy, and that is the way I treat all my friends. It is when they are in trouble that my tenderness is aroused."

To help Henry, I have cut down on clothes, entertaining, gardener, and luxury foods.

I describe to Dr. Allendy, Henry's life, and his friends: Fred working for the newspaper, picking up young girls, making love to them before everyone, how they all accept dinners from anyone at all, how they borrow, and sponge, and live by expedients of all kinds. Michael Fraenkel buys leftover books of no value at all, like outdated dictionaries, and makes his living selling them to nuns in far-off convents in Puerto Rico.

Dr. Allendy began to probe a painful contrast between Henry's life and my father's life, the life I was brought up in. We only saw talented people, people of quality, musicians, writers, professors.

But I like these lower depths of Henry's life. It seems real to me. What is Dr. Allendy hinting at? That I had to go to the other end of the world, to opposite poles, to forget my father, to escape from his image, his values? I am denying all the values he emphasized: will, control, manners, achievement, aesthetics, elegance, social or aristocratic values, bourgeois values.

What would my father say of the odds and ends of cups with unmatched saucers, cigarettes on the edge of the tables, linoleum table-clothes, the homeliness of the furniture, also odds and ends, the ugly couch covers, the rug, the glasses from Woolworth?

It is true I am walking with Henry and Fred, or with Henry and his other friends through streets my father has never walked through, sit at bars he has never gone to, talk with people who would never have been admitted to his home.

Fraenkel loved my home, the idea of a house, a home as a pivot, a base, a hub. Henry, the vagabond, was amazed at Fraenkel's asser-tion that this was necessary to creation, that rolling and drifting pre-vented growth, that this was the way to grow, expand.

Henry has always respected the house, but Fraenkel was moved to tears, and talked of how he would make this his base and draw into it all the interesting people of the world, and make "symbols" of them.

"Why symbols?" asked Henry.

"Because that is the only way to hold on to them. As ideas they be-long to you, they become incorporated into your world. As human beings . . . well . . . modern life makes friendships precarious."

"And why hold on?" asked Henry. "I never hold on."

"You live without pattern, without direction, that is your role, just to flow, a weather vane, without compass. You must go on being wild, rudderless. There is a consistency in your disorder. But someone will have to look after you."

"I will," I said.

Fraenkel looked Faustian, with his small beard, his narrow face, his cape, his sensual mouth, a face all pointed, foxy, on a small undernourished body, with frail but willful hands pointing to di-rections, asserting, with his sharp index finger pointing. Romantic actor's gestures are vehement, almost too powerful for the frailness of his body. He has written about Werther, much about death, and he could be Werther. He has no need to commit suicide. He has al-ready died. I have never seen anyone so withered from within, so dead in life.

"To grow!" he says, and his hands, held clasped and pointed as if for a prayer, point sharply into space. Henry has never thought about growth, or about death either. Henry always seeks in men these intellectual concepts which he never adheres to. At first it was [Walter] Lowenfels, now Fraenkel. Fraenkel has a "system" of thought. He is all mind. An abstraction. It is almost terrifying. I can understand his seeking Henry, but I do not understand Henry seeking him. Fred hates Fraenkel; Fraenkel shows up Fred's fuzzy thinking.

I feel that an initial shock has shattered my wholeness, that I am like a shattered mirror. Each piece has gone off and developed a life of its own. They have not died from the shock (as, in some cases I have seen, women who died from betrayals, go into mourning, abdicate all love, never renew contact with man again), but separated into several selves, and each one developed a life of its own.

It is not fear that keeps me from gathering myself together and surrendering to one life. It is that there is an Anaïs who cannot bring all the pieces together, who can be devoted, love, and still feel alone and divided.

Does Dr. Allendy see this, that there is one Anaïs who can be depended on living at Louveciennes a domestic life, filled with duties, devoted to mother, brother, to the past. There is another Anaïs who lives a café life, an artist's life, timeless, not to run away from my father but because I put artistic values above all others. Because writing, for me, is an expanded world, a limitless world, containing all.

Perhaps I am like my mother, and not like my father.

My mother first saw my father in a music shop in Havana, Cuba. He was nineteen years old. He had come from Barcelona to escape from military service. The music shop owner would let him practice on the piano in the back of the room. He was handsome, dark-haired and blue-eyed, with a very fair skin, a small straight nose, fine regular features, beautiful teeth, and beautiful manners.

My mother was a society girl. Her father was the Danish consul in Havana. Her mother had once been one of the most beautiful French girls in New Orleans. They lived in a house on the Malecon, a broad avenue along the sea. My mother was twenty-seven years old and still unmarried. She had mothered all her three brothers and three sisters when her mother ran away. My mother Rose, Rosa she was called, had a beautiful voice and studied singing. She loved music. She wore a dress similar to many I saw in her trunks later, all lace, with long lace sleeves, with a lace collar which came all the way to her chin and was supported by small white bones. The shoulders were puffed, the waist tremendously small. (The girls pulled on the laces of the corsets for each other until they could hardly breathe, and when they went to dances they pulled the corset laces so tight they could not eat beforehand, and that was the real reason for their fainting so easily.) She carried a white lace umbrella. She had a very full figure, a buoyant temperament; she was vital and cheerful. She had never fallen in love: she had refused to marry rich men, titled men, diplomatic service men, military men.

While she was buying music, she heard the piano. The owner of the shop allowed her and her sister to enter the back room. She listened to my father play Beethoven's "Moonlight Sonata." He played Chopin particularly sensitively and romantically. For my mother it was love at first sight. For my father I never knew. He once said, "Rosa's sister was prettier, but Rosa had a strength, a courage, a decisiveness I needed."

He was invited to the house, even though he did not have the proper clothes. My mother said he would tutor her in singing. The family opposed their courtship. My mother's father was desperately unhappy. She faced all opposition courageously, married her penniless musician, and they went off to live in Paris, where I was born. An artist in Cuba, at that time, had no prestige at all. For a bourgeois family, the marriage was a disgrace. Grandfather sent them money, and shipped them a piano as a wedding present.

They never returned to Cuba until my grandfather became ill with cancer. My brother had just been born. My mother took him and myself to the house on the Malecon. My father came later and spent his time trying to seduce my mother's younger sister. I caught typhoid fever and almost died of it. My mother was the only one who had the courage to give the doctor permission to give an injection which relieved my grandfather's unbearable suffering. Her love was brave and virile.

[May 25, 1932]

Letter from Madame Pierre Chareau, my neighbor, whose husband built the first glass-brick house, in 1931:

I have just finished reading your book on Lawrence, and I must rearrange the vision I had of you over the fence as the frail child-woman. You seem to be so capable of objective judgment (rare in any woman at any age) that it is almost impossible to realize that it is a young woman, a fair young woman who has felt and, almost as spontaneously as I am writing this word of thanks, has written the finest cry in the world, perhaps the only one that counts for the artist: *I understand.* Would that Lawrence could have read it. It would have covered, at least for a moment, the cry of the hounds . . .

Late at night. I am in Louveciennes. I am sitting by the fire in my bedroom. The heavy curtains are drawn. The room feels heavy and deeply anchored in the earth. One can smell the odors of the wet trees, the wet grass outside. They are blown in by the wind through the chimney. The walls are a yard thick, thick enough to dig bookcases into them, beside the bed. The bed is wide and low.

Henry called my house a laboratory of the soul.

Enter this laboratory of the soul where every feeling will be X-rayed by Dr. Allendy to expose the blocks, the twists, the deformations, the scars which interfere with the flow of life. Enter this laboratory of the soul where incidents are refracted into a diary, dissected to prove that everyone of us carries a deforming mirror where he sees himself too small or too large, too fat or too thin, even Henry, who believes himself so free, blithe, and unscarred. Enter here where one discovers that destiny can be directed, that one does not need to remain in bondage to the first wax imprint made on childhood sensibilities. One need not be branded by the first pattern. Once the deforming mirror is smashed, there is a possibility of wholeness; there is a possibility of joy.

It is Dr. Allendy who does the dissecting and the explorative operations. I bring them home, and sift them to catch impurities and errors in the diary. And then I tactfully, poetically, artistically, transmit what I have learned to Henry. By the time it reaches him, it does not have a clinical odor, it is not expressed in the homely jargon of analysts. He balks at some of it, but when it is properly adorned, seasoned, dramatized, he is interested. So I tell Dr. Allendy all my life, and Henry tells me all of his.

Man can never know the kind of loneliness a woman knows. Man lies in a woman's womb only to gather strength, he nourishes himself from this fusion, and then he rises and goes into the world, into his work, into battle, into art. He is not lonely. He is busy. The memory of the swim in amniotic fluid gives him energy, completion. The woman may be busy too, but she feels empty. Sensuality for her is not only a wave of pleasure in which she has bathed, and a charge of electric joy at contact with another. When man lies in her womb, she is fulfilled, each act of love is a taking of man within her, an act of birth and rebirth, of child-bearing and man-bearing. Man lies in her womb and is reborn each time anew with a desire to act, to BE. But for woman, the climax is not in the birth, but in the moment when man rests inside of her.

Fred, Henry, other friends, and I at the café. Talking, discussing, arguing, storytelling until the electric lights went out in the street, the night was dispersed, and a dim, shy, sienna-colored dawn entered the window. The dawn! The dawn, I repeated. Henry thought it was the dawn itself which was a new experience. I could not explain what I felt. It was the first time I had not felt the compulsion to escape; it was the first time I had abandoned myself to fraternity, exchange, confessions, without feeling suddenly the need to take flight. All night I had stayed there, without experiencing that abrupt end to fusion, that sudden and painful consciousness of separation, of reaching ultimately and always the need of my own world, the inability to remain outside, estranged, at some moment or other, from everyone. This had not happened, this dawn had come as the first break in the compulsion and tyranny of inadaptation. (The way I once concealed from myself this drama of perpetual divorce was to blame the clock. It was time to go, in place of now I must go, because relationship is so difficult for me, so strained, so laborious, its continuance, its flow.) I never knew what happened. At a party, at a visit, at a play, a film, came a moment of anguish. I cannot sustain the role, the pretense that I am at one with others, synchronized. Where was the exit? Flight. The imperative need of flight. Was it the failure to remove the obstacles, the walls, the barriers, the effort? Dawn had come quietly, and found me sitting at ease with Henry and Fred, and it was the dawn of freedom from a nameless enemy. At midnight I had always been metamorphosed into a solitary, estranged wanderer.

I was like a stranger in a strange country who was welcomed, who felt at home, who shared festivities, births, marriages, deaths, banquets, concerts, birthdays, and then suddenly became aware that I did not speak their language, that it was all a game of courtesy.

What locked me out? Over and over again I was thrust, and thrust myself, into roomfuls of people with a genuine desire to amalgamate with them, but my fears proved greater than my desire and, after a conflict, I fled. Once alone, I reversed the process and suffered to be locked out and abandoned by those who were talking and laughing in a commonly shared enjoyment and pleasures. It was I who made the move out of the enchanted circles, but because I felt as if this circle were electrified against burglars, something I could not cross, could not defy. I longed to be a part of every intense, every joyous moment, every moment of life; longed to be the woman who was weeping or laughing; the woman who was being kissed amorously before everyone; the woman who was given a flower to wear; the woman who was being helped into the bus; the woman who was leaning out of a window; the one who was being married; the one who was giving birth.

The hero of this book may be the soul, but it is an odyssey from the inner to the outer world, and it is Henry who is dispelling the fogs of shyness, of solitude, taking me through the street, and keeping me in a café—until dawn.

Before Henry, I thought art was the paradise, not human life, that in art alone could pain become an abstraction.

It was a man's way of mastering pain, to put art and space and time and history and philosophy between himself and human life.

Art was the prescription for sanity and relief from the terrors and pains of human life.

I was ready to see Dr. Allendy again. He questioned me relentlessly. He feels there is a secret. The theme of flight does not satisfy him. I feel that something in me escapes from his definitions. I dread the scalpel. I am living, installing myself in life. He is probing the moment at the concert when I imagined him sad and troubled. What exactly did I imagine? That he had financial worries, concerns over his work, or sentimental troubles?

Today I find flaws in Dr. Allendy's formulas. I am irritated by his quick categorizing of my dreams and feelings. When he is silent I do my own analysis. If I do, he will say I am trying to find him defective, inadequate, to revenge his forcing me to confess my jealousy of his wife. At that moment he was much stronger than I. He agreed that I was much freer than before.

Henry is dissolving my old gravity with his literary pranks, his satirical manifestoes, his contradictions, paradoxes, his mockery of ideas, his change of moods, his grotesque humor.

I now make fun of my own earnestness, my efforts at understanding others, at not wounding people.

We heard that Richard Osborn had gone mad. Henry danced like a clown and said, "Richard has gone mad? Hurrah. Let's go and see him. Let's have a drink first, and put ourselves in the right mood. This is rare, superb, it doesn't happen every day. I hope he is really insane and not faking."

I was at first disconcerted, and then I found his humor a way to defeat tragedy. I would like to know the secret of his not caring. I care too much. It is the same with Michael Fraenkel. He first appears in Henry's book as the man who was eating his dinner when Henry arrived and who continued to eat his dinner without offering Henry a share of it.

Henry wrote a parody of my first novel.

Henry's first novel, Lowenfels once said, was corny and purple writing, it was trash, it was pulpy. I can hardly believe that. Lowenfels claims to have initiated him to modern writing. Putnam's *European Caravan* seems to contain definitions which apply to Henry's writing. I am referring to improvisation, surrealistic associations of images, wild flights of fancy. His humor is like Tristan Tzara's *"une entreprise de démolition."*

The other night we talked about literature's elimination of the unessential, so that we are given a concentrated "dose" of life. I said, almost indignantly, "That's the danger of it, it prepares you to live, but at the same time, it exposes you to disappointments because it gives a heightened concept of living, it leaves out the dull or stagnant moments. You, in your books, also have a heightened rhythm, and a sequence of events so packed with excitement that I expected all your life to be delirious, intoxicated."

Literature is an exaggeration, a dramatization, and those who are nourished on it (as I was) are in great danger of trying to approximate an impossible rhythm. Trying to live up to Dostoevskian scenes every day. And between writers there is a straining after extravagance. We incite each other to jazz-up our rhythm. It is amusing that, when Henry, Fred, and I talked together, we fell back into a deep naturalness. Perhaps none of us is a sensational character. Or perhaps we have no need of condiments. Henry is, in reality, mild not temperamental; gentle not eager for scenes. We may all write about sadism, masochism, the Grand Guignol, *Bubu de Montparnasse* (in which the highest proof of love is for a pimp to embrace his woman's syphilis as fervently as herself, a noblesse-oblige of the apache world), Cocteau, drugs, insane asylums, *House of the Dead,* because we love strong colors; and yet when we sit in the *Café de la Place Clichy,* we talk about Henry's last pages, and a chapter which was too long, and Richard's madness. "One of his greatest worries," said Henry, "was to have introduced us. He thinks you are wonderful and that you may be in danger from the 'gangster author.' "

Today Dr. Allendy was incisive and powerfully effective. I will never be able to describe that hour. There was so much intuition and obscurity in the sequences.

Dr. Allendy: "Until you can act perfectly naturally according to your own nature, you will never be happy."

Anaïs: "But what is my own nature? Whatever life I was leading before I met Henry and June was stifling me. I felt that I was dying."

Dr. Allendy: "But you are not a femme fatale either. The femme fatale enjoys rousing men's passions, exasperating them, proving her power, tormenting them; and men do not love her profoundly, anyway. You have already discovered that you are loved profoundly. Do not play games which are not natural to you. You could never be June."

Anaïs: "I have always been afraid of becoming one of those women who are hopelessly dominated by one man."

Dr. Allendy: "What woman have you known who was hopelessly dominated by one man?"

Anaïs: "My mother. She only had one love in all her life, my father. She was never able to love anyone else. She was at his mercy. When he deserted her, her love turned to hatred, but he was still the only man in her life. When I asked her once why she had not married again, she said: 'After living with your father, with your father's charm, and his way of making everything wonderful and interesting, his talent for creating illusion, all other men seemed dull and prosaic and shallow. You cannot imagine how charming your father was!' "

Dr. Allendy: "And so she spent the rest of her life hating him, and fearing his influence over you."

Anaïs: "That was why she took us to America. She wanted to bring us up in a totally different culture. She herself had been brought up in Brentwood, a Catholic convent for society girls, in New York."

Dr. Allendy: "The more you act like yourself, the nearer you will come to fulfillment of your real needs."

Anaïs: "But I am not sure what this self is. For the moment I seem to be busy tearing down what I was."

Dr. Allendy: "I do not despair of reconciling you to your own image."

What a beautiful phrase! To reconcile me to my own image. And if he can help me to find this image? The words were not as important as the sensations he created in me, a loosening of innumerable tensions. His voice was gentle and compassionate. Before he had finished I was sobbing.

My gratitude was immense. He was silent while I sobbed, and then he asked me a gentle question: "I did not say anything to hurt you?"

This has been a time of pleasure, broken only by superimpositions from the past. I want to linger over it.

I am dressing more simply. I have felt much less the need of an original way of dressing. I can wear ordinary clothes now. Why? Costume was, for me, very symbolical. It meant many things. It had, first of all, a poetic significance: colors for certain occasions, evocations of other styles, countries (Spanish flavor, Moroccan touches, etc., etc.). It was a sign of individuality (I never wore what everybody wore; I designed my own costumes). I did not follow fashions. I did not wear neutral colors, neutral suits, plain or homely or nondescript things. I wanted striking clothes which distinguished me from other women. Costumes added to my confidence, as I suffered so keenly all through my girlhood to be badly dressed with the cast-off clothes my aunts sent me from Cuba. I had to go to American schools with clothes designed for the tropics, pastel colors, silks, and all of them burnt by the sun so that very often they would split and tear during a party, or at graduation exercises. They were always party dresses, summer dresses, dresses which only the Latins would invent, garish colors. Later my mother selected my clothes, and again they did not resemble or represent me. I invented many original things to wear, had my watch set in a wide, soft, Russian link bracelet, put fur on my winter shoes, made dresses out of Spanish shawls, etc.

The first time I went to see Dr. Allendy, I dressed in my most dazzling clothes. He looked rather amazed. I was reminded of the fantastic dressing of actresses, of the wife of Maeterlinck, who would say to her friends: "Would you care to assume the responsibility of taking my arm in the street?" (She created such a scandal by her dress!)

The pathological basis of creation! I could have been a famous dress designer! The only problem was that my imagination created costumes which did not fit in my simple life, were not intended to be worn in the little train from Louveciennes to Paris, or to Dr. Allendy's office. What I sought in clothes was an evocation of the fairy tale. In New York, in winter, posing for a painter, I once arrived at nine in the morning in a vivid red velvet dress.

Some of this may have been a result of being raised in Latin clothes for the tropics, in contradiction to the New York winter, and the American love of neutral clothes. But here I was, dressed like a Russian princess, the first time I came to Dr. Allendy; and today, here I am, dressed like royalty in exile, seeking anonymity. Dr. Allendy noticed the change. Then he ventured to say (for all the art of analysis consists in saying a truth only when the other person is ready for it, has been prepared for it by an organic process of gradation and evolution) that he thought I had also dressed to accentuate my "strangeness," my separateness from the crowd, but in a way which reminded him of what the primitives wore to frighten their enemies! At this I laughed. I could see the paint, the feathers, the beads, the bone necklaces, the fur headgear and teeth, and clinking bells!

Dr. Allendy: "Strangeness always frightens people. You may have thought this originality impressed, but it may have estranged people."

Anaïs: "I never thought of that. I am attracted by unconventionality. When I become 'normal,' what will become of my art of dressing? I don't really want to become normal, average, standard. I want merely to gain in strength, in the courage to live out my life more fully, enjoy more, experience more. I want to develop even more original and more unconventional traits."

Dr. Allendy: "Then you will feel alone, as you have felt before. Isolated. Do you want that?"

Dr. Allendy said that it was necessary to become equal to life, that the romantic was defeated by life, really died of it, whether by tuberculosis in the old days, or by neurosis today. I had never thought before of the connection between neurosis and romanticism. Wanting the impossible? Dying when unable to reach it? Not wanting to compromise?

Henry's responses to all things, his capacity for seeing so much in everybody, in everything. I had never looked at a street as Henry does: every doorway, every lamp, every window, every courtyard, every shop, every object in the shop, every café, every hidden-away bookshop, hidden-away antique shop, every news vendor, every lottery-ticket vendor, every blind man, every beggar, every clock, every church, every whore house, every wineshop, every shop where they sell erotica and transparent underwear, the circus, the night-club singers, the strip tease, the girlie shows, the penny movies in the arcade, the bal musettes, the artist balls, the apache quarters, the flea market, the gypsy carts, the markets early in the morning.

When we come out of the cafe, it is raining. Rain does not bother him. Hunger or thirst only. Shabby rooms don't bother him. Poverty does not bother him. You drink a fiery Chartreuse at a zinc counter. In life he follows his impulses, always. The only thing which surprises me is that he has no desire to meet other writers, musicians, painters, his equals. When I talk about this, he shows no interest. Would you like to meet Julian Green? Hélène Boussinesq, the translator of Sherwood Anderson; Florent Schmitt, who lives near us in Louveciennes; Manuel de Falla, or others? "No," says Henry. "What would they see in me?"

It all began with my reading of D. H. Lawrence. But Henry is no Lawrence. Lawrence was a romantic, and he sought to fuse body and soul. Henry asserts the primitive instincts. He leaves feeling out of his writing. No symbolism in Henry, no mythology. We do have a feeling at times of not being ordinary people. When we looked at photographs of D. H. Lawrence's house, Henry said he would some-day show me his house in Brooklyn, where he lived out his child-hood, and that he wanted to see 158 West Seventy-fifth, where I wrote the journal he is now reading.

I confessed to Dr. Allendy my desire for experience and my curiosities.

Anaïs: "I am curious about your life. I would like to know whether you get restless, whether you ever stayed up all night, wandered through night clubs, had mistresses, etc."

Dr. Allendy: "I cannot answer such questions; for the sake of analysis, it is best if I remain an impersonal figure. I must remain enigmatic. An intimate knowledge of my life would not be an answer to your questions. Experience is, in itself, good, but what is important is your attitude. Any experience which answers to a deep need of your nature is right, but there are times when I feel you are driven by other motives. I suspect sometimes you have forced yourself into experiences for unnatural reasons."

Anaïs: "I want to grow, mature. I want to match Henry and June's life. I also at times feel I want to make an effort to overcome my fears, and my recoils. I am afraid that if I followed my natural bent, I would withdraw from the world. Henry embraces everything, the ugly, the sick, the vulgar. I admire that. I made a world so beautiful, filled only with people of quality, with beauty and finesse, and it was static."

Dr. Allendy: "Perhaps Henry's lack of discrimination, of evaluations, is bad."

It was the first time Dr. Allendy passed a judgment on Henry.

Anaïs: "Which of my experiences were not genuine, how could I distinguish between them?"

Dr. Allendy: "The genuine ones give pleasure."

Anaïs: "You once called me a *'petite fille littéraire.'* Did you mean I was trying to live out novels and biographies and not my own self?"

Dr. Allendy: "At times, yes."

He would say nothing more. This was something I had to discover for myself. I have felt, at times, the difference between curiosity and real feeling.

But he probed why I had "forgotten" my last appointment with him. I was beginning to lean on him. I was grateful to him. Why did I stop for a week? To stand on my own feet again, to fight alone, to take myself back, to depend on no one. Why? The fear of being hurt. Fear that Dr. Allendy should become a necessity and that, when the "cure" was finished, our relationship would end and I must lose him. He reminds me that it is a part of the cure to make me self-sufficient, so that by the time the visits are over I will not need him. But by not trusting him, now I have revealed that I am still motivated by fears.

I also wanted to know whether he would miss me.

Dr. Allendy: "If you dropped me now, I would suffer as a doctor from not succeeding in my cure of you, and I would suffer personally because you are interesting. So you see, in a way, I need you as much as you need me. You could hurt me by dropping me."

Anaïs: "I have lost everyone I ever cared for. Every house, every country I loved. First I loved our house in Neuilly. I was very sociable then. I was four years old and I would go out in the street and invite everybody for tea. I loved our house in Brussels, always full of music and musicians. I lost that, and my father. I was happy in Spain. I loved my grandmother. The life we led there was so much happier than in New York. My mother was teaching singing at the Granados Academy of Music. We had a small apartment with balconies from which we could see the mountains and the sea. We had a maid, Carmen, who sang all day as she worked. We had prestige and interesting friends. My father's family came from there. My father told me that we were distantly related to the Guells, who were aristocrats. The Guells had a house with a private chapel, and a magnificent library which the Jesuits burned because it was too liberal. There was a statue erected to a Guell. We would hear stories about their past. The family divided into two branches, one wealthy and the other artists. One became a court painter, José Nin y Guell. And who, naturally, became poor."

I understand that I am reliving with Dr. Allendy situations of happiness and fear of loss. In my childhood diary I wrote: "I have decided that it is better not to love anyone, because when you love people, then you have to be separated from them, and that hurts too much."

[June, 1932]

Yesterday at eleven in the morning, Joaquin had been playing the piano. He passed under my window and shouted: "Come out to the garden with me and let's sit in the sun. I don't feel well." I was busy, but I dropped what I was doing. We sat in the garden. At lunch he would not eat.

It was appendicitis. Clinique de Versailles in the ambulance. The longest half hour in my life. Fear of losing him. When the door opened and he was brought out on the stretcher with his face so white, I panicked. Perhaps he is dead. I looked at the faces of the nurses and doctors. The doctor said, "Your brother will be all right."

When he was placed on his bed, I stood looking at him. He was breathing with difficulty, and it terrified me. I watched over him. He is not only my brother; he is my child. I took care of him. I was his nurse and his second mother. In his eyes, dilated with pain, there was a fear of death. I love my brother, and there are times when I know this love of my brother makes me feel man is a brother; it created a pact which has disarmed my power to do man any harm. Man, my brother. Needing care and devotion. My mother and I are sitting there in the hospital room, as if to echo every spasm of pain. To feel life and love and pain in the womb, always, as if in our own body.

A summer evening. Fred, Henry, and I are eating in a small restaurant open on the street. We are part of the street. It is not Henry, Fred, and I eating, but the street full of people eating, talking, drinking. It is the whole world eating, drinking, and talking. We are eating also the noises of the street: the voices, the automobiles, the cries of the vendors, children's cries, the cooing of doves, the flutter of pigeons' wings, the barking of dogs. We are all fused. The wine which runs down my throat runs down all other throats. The warmth of the day is like a man's hand on my breast; the warmth of the day and the smells of the street caress everybody; the restaurant is wide open and the street penetrates into the restaurant. The wine bathes them all like an aphrodisiac ocean: Henry, Fred, the street, the world, and the students preparing for the Quatz Arts Ball. The street is invaded with Egyptians in barbaric jewels and little else. Their skins are dyed in golden suntans. They overflow from buses and taxis. They invade the café. They help themselves to our decanter of wine, to other decanters of wine, steal a lamb chop, fried potatoes, laugh, and continue on their way.

Henry is drunk. He is reminiscing, "One day when Fred had just got his pay, he took me to a cabaret. We began to dance and we took two girls to Clichy. When we were sitting in the kitchen having a snack, they asked us to talk business. They asked a big price. I wanted to let them go but Fred paid them what they wanted and they stayed. One was an acrobatic dancer and she showed us some of her tricks naked, with only slippers on."

Shouts and laughter from the students. They want to pull me away. "We'll dress her up as Cleopatra, she looks like Cleopatra. Look at that nose!" When I held on to my chair, they knocked the wine bottle over. We had to push our way through the crowd.

"This Paulette," said Henry, "she and Fred are cute together. I don't know how it will end. She is younger than she said; in fact, she was a virgin. She let Fred think she was a prostitute. She ran away from home. We were worried that her parents should make trouble for Fred when they found out. He makes me take care of her in the evenings while he is at work. I have taken her to the movies but the truth is, she bores me. She is so young. We have nothing to say to each other. She is jealous of what Fred wrote about you. The goddess . . ."

Henry told me this while Fred went to meet Paulette and bring her to us. Paulette was thin, and homely and frightened.

If Henry can steal razor blades, keep the extra money a taxi driver gave him by mistake, write treacherously about June and his best friends, there is also a Henry who is something entirely different, which he himself may repudiate one day. He shows the world only his toughest side. The side I know is more like his water colors.

He is a mass of contradictions.

"The diary may die," said Henry.

"Why should it? I am afraid to forget. I do not want to forget anything."

Henry said, "This is my Golden Age between wars."

I was talking a little like June, and Henry would think all this complicated and interesting. I could, if I wanted to, stop and simplify the whole thing for him. But I preferred to let myself go in that bit of drunken incoherence which I now find so relaxed and enjoyable. Henry experienced the same split when he wrote me a paragraph once in a letter, and immediately realized it would make an excellent preface to something or other. Henry and I have this double awareness, with only moments of complete abandon. And that may be why we are attracted to the madness of the poets, Rimbaud, Tristan Tzara, Dadaism, Breton. The free improvisations of the surrealists break down the artificial order and symmetry of consciousness. In chaos there is fertility. How difficult it is to be "sincere" when each moment I must choose between five or six souls. Sincere according to which one, reconciled to which one?—as I once asked Dr. Allendy.

I began to see that my costumes had been an armor. I remembered that once when Henry wanted to take me to Montparnasse in a plain dress I wore, I felt I could not face all his friends unless I "dressed up." I had lost my true rhythm. But what was my true rhythm? This was too direct a question for Dr. Allendy to answer. He said he could only answer it obliquely. He felt himself that I was fundamentally simple and charming, feminine and soft. All the rest was literary, intellectual, imaginative. If I were really callous, I would not show such pity, sympathy, and tenderness in every situation. There was nothing wrong with playing roles, except that I must not take them seriously. Too often I become sincere, and go all the way.

He asked me where I had been most happy. Real, quiet happiness. I said in Switzerland, in nature, where I lived without make-up, without fancy clothes, stripped of all roles and play-acting.

"You see," said Dr. Allendy, "you want to please, you want to be loved, and you take poses, even your interest in perversion is a pose.

You lack faith in your fundamental values. You put too much faith in externals."

Here I balk a little. If psychoanalysis is going to divest me of all decoration, costume, adornment, flavor, characteristic, then what will be left?

[July, 1932]

I am waiting in Dr. Allendy's salon, in which the green-tinted glass of the hothouse makes everything look under water. The cats are prowling around. I am amazed that they have not swallowed the goldfish in the small pond. I hear the trickle of a small sculptured fountain. I hear a woman's voice in his office, behind the big black Chinese curtains. I feel jealous. I am annoyed because I hear them laughing. *They* laugh oftener, it seems to me, than we do when we talk together. He is late, too, for the first time. And I am bringing him an affectionate dream—the first time I have allowed myself to think of him tenderly. Perhaps I should not tell him the dream. It puts me in his hands, it is giving him too much, while he . . . My bad feelings vanish when he appears. I tell him the dream.

In the dream we were sitting face to face in his office. He was holding my hands. He had neglected all his other patients to sit and talk to me. He was completely absorbed in me. There was a mood of intimacy.

I confide in him. I do not withdraw from competition. I trust that he does admire me. This, he says, is an improvement. A few months ago I would have withdrawn. Now I am telling him that I dreamed of closeness after he showed such understanding of me the last time.

But how strange that he should be late for the first time today. This brings him to the idea of destiny: "what we fear might happen, does happen." I always fear to be abandoned or at least neglected, and so it happens . . . *I make it happen*. To what extent we thus shape our destiny is a mystery, even to Dr. Allendy. He goes so far as to assert that, if I had not feared to be neglected or liked less than his other women patients, he would not have been delayed. This is very obscure and hypothetical. Certainly a fatality haunts me. This set me dreaming about fatality. Do human beings pick up "waves" from others' thoughts? Did Dr. Allendy pick up waves of my thoughts while I sat waiting: be late, and then I will be able not to trust you, confide in you, love you, and be in another's power?

They are obsessed with mobility. After lying down, they have to arise; after walking, they sit down again, or lie down, and almost immediately must walk again.

The haunted drug addicts are usually haunted by fear of police, fear of raids [June's story about police questioning her in the taxi].

Drug causes illusion of being bitten by insects—an illusion caused by itchiness brought on by the drug itself. (Itchiness of the nose, dry lips.) May lead to tuberculosis, epilepsy or suicide.

June shows many of these symptoms.

Henry was overwhelmed. June talked so constantly about drugs, like a criminal who returns to the scene of the crime. She needed to mention the subject while all the time violently denying that she took drugs (two or three times, perhaps, was all she ever admitted). Henry began to piece the fragments together. When I saw his despair, I was frightened.

"We may be wrong, you know, there are neuroses which present similar symptoms." And then I added, "And if it is true, we should pity her, not be so hard on her."

But Henry passed the only ethical judgment I ever heard him pass on self-destruction, that taking drugs denoted a terrible weakness in one's nature. That this made the relationship hopeless. I felt such pity for him, too, when he told me he had been examining June's love for him and become aware that she had no real love for him.

I said, "She has her own way of loving you, inhuman and fantastic, but strong too."

"She loves herself more," said Henry.

Henry and I talked about the writer's life. How his life is arrested by his work, the periods during which he dies humanly. Henry, when he is deep in his book, takes on the air of a zombie, a man whose soul has been taken away from him. But I thought it was only a temporary death, for the work, in turn, causes one to re-enter the flow of life enriched, as though the arrest were only a suspended activity while one creates a richer life.

To be strong when he is writing, Henry may have paid the ransom of great weakness in the world. I, too, the moment I rise from my desk, I am disarmed.

Henry will stay on at a party until the very dregs show. I tend to leave it before it becomes ugly. He wants to touch bottom. I want to preserve my illusion.

What have I touched off in him; will it change his writing?

His life with June seems now like a wild meteoric deviation, comparable to my flights from my real self.

If we could only write simultaneously all the levels on which we live, all at once. The whole truth! Henry is closer to it. I have a vice for embellishing.

Besides the reading of D. H. Lawrence, there was another element which had prepared me for Henry's gutter language, the Rabelaisian animalism of it. And this was my father's language when he was with intimate men friends, or when he lost his temper. In Spain it is a common thing for men to use obscene language on every occasion but not in the presence of women. Men on every level of social or educational refinement. My mother deplored this, did all in her power to prevent our hearing or learning it, but admitted that it was a very Spanish trait. It was a rather startling contradiction to his ultra-refined manners.

There was a storm last night while we sat in the café. Marble-sized hail. Sea fury of the trees.

I had been reading one of the few passages I did understand in Spengler, on the relation between architecture and the character of the people. How the houses of the Orientals represented their emotional attitude. No windows on the outside, open on the inside, into a patio, a secret intimate life. And then the rooms all linked together by this patio. Luxury concealed. Thoughts concealed.

Henry began to parody an elegant man talking condescendingly to a prostitute, with hauteur, a parody of women in sexual convulsions, and stories began to pour out. A tumultuous childhood in the streets of Brooklyn. Tough games in empty lots, battles, bicycle rides, nothing at first to indicate a future novelist. Action. Slyness. Deviltries. Stealing pennies from blind news vendors. Lies. Deceptions. Sexual hunger. Aside from shabbiness, ugliness, poverty, nothing there to justify his angers. I seek the origin of his bitterness.

All of us, Henry, Fred and I, are sitting in the garden of Louveciennes. Henry says, "This is no ordinary garden. It is mysterious, significant. There is mentioned in a Chinese book a celestial kingdom, or garden, suspended between heaven and earth: this is it."

Night again. Walks. We show Henry the manor house which has two towers. They stand out sharply in the moonlight. I tell how I have never been inside of this house, and yet I know how it is furnished, what the tower room looks like, with walls made of wood panels, and, inside of these walls, secret drawers, closets, bookcases. But recently my aunt brought me the handwritten diary of my great-grandfather, the one who left France during the revolution and went to Haiti, then to New Orleans, and then to Cuba, where he built the first railroads. His description of the manor house they had left in Anjou was the exact replica of this house, and the photograph my aunt took was a duplicate of this house. She described the inside of the tower room, and the furniture. Everything corresponded to the taste of that period. But how did I know this? Was it a racial memory?

The village of Louveciennes is asleep. Dogs bark as we pass. I listen to Henry. There are definitely two Henrys. Towards certain women, he is tough and hard-boiled. Towards others, he shows a naïve romanticism. At first June appeared like an angel to him, even in her dance hall background. I see him now as a man who can be enslaved by a passion. But in all the stories he tells me, it is the woman who has taken the initiative. He even admits that this is what he likes about the prostitutes. It was June who put her head on his shoulder and asked for a kiss the first night they met. His toughness is external only. But like all soft passive people, he can commit the most dastardly acts at certain moments, prompted by his weakness, which makes him a coward. He leaves a woman in the most cruel manner because he cannot face the moment of breaking the connection.

But all his actions seem dictated by the torrential, instinctual flow of his energy. I cannot believe a man could be so ruthless, yet he seems to live by some other laws, a primitive life, other tribal habits than those familiar to me. He respects nothing. To live. He once said that only angels or devils could catch the tempo of June's life, and it is the same with him. This is nature, with its blind storms, earthquakes, tidal waves, appetites. Yet he gives the dog half of his steak, and expands the world, and brings joy.

Then this scattered man, easily swayed, now collects himself to talk about his book. Our talks have a firm, exhilarating interplay, resilience. His riotous living, curiosity, gusto, amorality, sentimentality, rascalities, enough to fill a hundred books. He has never known stagnation. Introspection does not need to be a still life. It can be an active alchemy. Henry generates enthusiasm.

Why does Henry say: "I want to leave a scar on the world!"

I received this morning the first pages of his new book [*Tropic of Capricorn*]. What pages! He is whole, powerful, every word hits the mark. The splendor of it.

One night Henry, Marguerite, and I sat talking in a café. The talk was desultory until Henry began to ask questions about psychology. Everything I had read during the year, all my talks with Dr. Allendy, my own explorations of the subject, my own theories; all this I expressed with amazing vehemence and assurance. It was all on the theme of destiny. What we call our destiny is truly our character, and that character can be altered. The knowledge that we are responsible for our actions and attitudes does not need to be discouraging, because it also means that we are free to change this destiny. One is not in bondage to the past which has shaped our feelings, to race, inheritance, background. All this can be altered if we have the courage to examine how it formed us. We can alter the chemistry provided we have the courage to dissect the elements.

Henry stopped me. "I don't trust either Dr. Allendy's ideas nor your thinking. Why, I saw him only once. He is a brutish, sensual man, lethargic, with a fund of fanaticism in the back of his eyes. And you—why, you put things so clearly and beautifully to me—so crystal clear—it looks simple and true. You are so terribly clever, so nimble. I distrust your cleverness. You make wonderful patterns—everything is in its place—it looks convincingly clear—too clear. And meanwhile, where are you? Not on the clear surface of your ideas, but you have already sunk deeper, into darker regions—so that one only thinks one has been given all you thought, one only imagines you have emptied yourself in that clarity. But there are layers, and layers—you're bottomless, unfathomable. Your clearness is deceptive. You're the thinker who arouses the most confusion in me, most doubts, most disturbances."

Marguerite added quietly, "One feels that she gives you a neat pattern and then slips out of it herself and laughs at you."

"Exactly," said Henry.

I laughed. But the idea that Henry could suddenly attack me, become critical, wounded me. War, war with him, was inevitable.

Henry stayed on after Marguerite was gone. He said, "Now I've acted in my usual way. I've said things I did not mean. The truth is, I was carried away by your speech. I've never seen you go to the bottom of anything like that, but it made me jealous of Allendy's achievement. I have a strong, perverse hatred of the person who can tell me something new. You opened worlds to me, but it came from Allendy."

His explanation sounded weak to me.

I am myself wrapped in lies which do not penetrate my soul, as if the lies I told were only to lull others, *"mensonge vital,"* which never become a part of me. They are like costumes. But Henry's lies?

He talked about his malevolence, his sudden launching into a role, a part which baffles those who believe in him, who believe they know him. If unity is impossible to the writer, who is a sea of spiritual protoplasm, capable of flowing in all directions, of engulfing every object in its path, of trickling in every crevice, of filling every hole, at least truth is possible in the confession of our insincerities. But at times, what my mind engenders fictionally I enrich with true feeling and I am taken in, in good faith, by my own inventions.

Henry said I had broken him down with my talk of *destinée intérieure,* as if I were working on him the emotional cycle of analysis: confidence, understanding, love, strength, independence. My talk about sincerity, the joys of repose in complete confidence, the human relief of depending on another; all this upset him, hit the mark. I talked emotionally about the flow of confidence developed in analysis such as one cannot have even with the loved one. How the analysis taps hidden and secret sources. How the aim of analysis resembles the old Chinese definition of wisdom: wisdom being the destruction of idealism. The basis of insincerity is the idealized image we hold of ourselves and wish to impose on others—an admirable image. When this is broken down by the analyst's discoveries, it is a relief because this image is always a great strain to live up to. Some consider the loss of it a cause for suicide.

What a lot I had to say about the artist. I only began the other night.

How to defeat this tragedy concealed within each hour, which chokes us unexpectedly and treacherously, springing at us from a melody, an old letter, a book, the colors of a dress, the walk of a stranger? Make literature. Seek new words in the dictionary. Chisel new phrases, pour the tears into a mold, style, form, eloquence. Cut out newspaper clippings carefully. Use cement glue. Have your photograph taken. Tell everyone how much you owe them. Tell Allendy he has cured you. Tell your editor he has discovered a genius, and turn around into your work again, like a scorpion in his fire ring, devouring himself.

If the Chinese had not discovered that wisdom is the absence of ideals, I would have done so tonight.

While I was working, I was in despair. I discovered that I had given away to Henry all my insights into June, and that he is using them. He has taken all my sketches for her portrait. I feel empty-handed, and he knows it, because he writes me that he "feels like a crook." And what have I left to work with? He is deepening his portrait with all the truths I have given him.

What was left for me to do? To go where Henry cannot go, into the Myth, into June's dreams, fantasies, into the poetry of June. To write as a woman, and as a woman only. I begin with dreams, hers and mine. It is taking a symbolic shape, closer to Rimbaud than to a novel.

When life becomes too difficult, I turn to my work. I swim into a new region. I write about June.

Henry has asked the impossible of me. I have to nourish his conception of June and feed his book. As each page of it reaches me, in which he does more and more justice to her, I feel it is my vision he has borrowed. Certainly no woman was ever asked so much. I am a human being, not a goddess. Because I am a woman who understands, I am asked to understand everything, to accept everything.

Today I began to think of an escape. Writing the poem, the myth, was not enough. I began to think of Allendy's teachings. His ideas have been underlying many of my actions. It is he who has taught me the world is vast, that I need not be the slave of a childhood curse, of devotion to whoever plays, in a major or minor way, partly or wholly, the role of a much needed father. I do not need to be a selfless child, or a woman giving to the point of self-annihilation.

Henry came yesterday. A serious, tired Henry. He had not slept for several nights. He was keyed up by his book.

Henry was worn out. I forgot my literary rebellions. "Henry, have some wine. We'll have lunch in the garden. Yes, I have been working too. I have a lot to tell you, but it must wait."

Emilia brought lunch out. Joaquin joined us. And then we were left to talk.

Henry, pale, intense, eyes very blue, innocent.

"While I worked on my book I realized everything between June and me had died three or four years ago. What we lived out together the last time she was here was only an automatic continuation, like a habit, like the prolongation of an impetus which cannot come to a dead stop. Of course it was a tremendous experience. The greatest upheaval. That is why I can write so frenziedly about it. But this is the swan song I am writing now."

Later he added, "Certainly I had to live through all that but, precisely because I have lived it through, I am finished with it. I feel stronger than June; yet if June came back, things might start out again out of a kind of fatality. What I feel is that I want you to save me from June. I do not want to be diminished, humiliated, destroyed again. I know I want to break with her. I dread her return and the destruction of my work. I was thinking how I have absorbed your time and attention. You are always asked to solve problems, to help, to be selfless. And meanwhile there is your writing, deeper and better than anybody's, which nobody gives a damn about and nobody helps you to do."

〜

The work I have done these days amounts to thirty pages of poetic prose, written in absolutely imaginative manner, a lyrical outburst.*

Henry was mystified by my pages. Was it more than brocade, he asked, more than beautiful language? I was upset that he did not understand. I began to explain. Then he said, "Well, you should give a clue; we are thrown into strangeness unexpectedly. This must be read a hundred times."

Henry was writing about June so realistically, so directly. I felt she could not be penetrated that way. I wrote surrealistically. I took her dreams, the myth of June, her fantasies. But certainly myths are not mysterious, undecipherable.

Henry was about to leave on his bicycle, but with characteristic thoroughness he decided he must stay and get to the bottom of what I had written. He walked up and down the garden while I explained my abstractions.

I see the symbolism of our lives. I live on two levels, the human and the poetic. I see the parables, the allegories. I felt that he was doing the realism, and that I could go up in my stratosphere and survey the mythology of June. I sought to describe overtones. All the facts about June are useless to my visionary perception of her unconscious self. This was a distillation. But it was not mere brocade; it was full of meaning.

The more I talked, the more excited Henry became. He began to say that I should continue in that very tone, that I was doing something unique, that if anyone was writing surrealism, it was me. Later he dwelt on this. He could not classify my work. It was not surrealism. There was a deeper intention, direction, a more determined attitude. He discarded all ideas of clues and preparations. He knew I would do something unique. It was on a second reading that he deciphered the meaning.

He stood by the window saying, "How can I go back to Clichy? It is like returning to a prison. This is the place where one grows, expands, deepens."

He has begun to turn his rich experience into writing, to taste more deeply all that he has lived.

* Opening passages of *House of Incest*.

Allendy has lost his objectivity. He is beginning to pass judgments on Henry. I was trying to describe the contrast between Henry drunk, flushed, combative, assertive, destructive, callous, all instinct and animal vitality; and his other self, sober, almost religious in tone, pale, wistful, sentimental, childlike, frail. A complete and amazing transformation. But Allendy has another name for this, a medical name. He says Henry is a dual personality, perhaps schizophrenic.

I quoted Henry's words: "Strange, how blindly I have lived until now."

"You need to be rescued from that milieu," said Allendy. "It is the wrong milieu for you, ma petite Anaïs."

I bow my head so he will not see me smile.

I went to see him again. I asked him to give up analysis and come and visit us in Louveciennes. He said he could not do this until he was sure that I was "cured." We talked about domination. I do feel he has strength, steadfastness. He does guide me. I was particularly distressed about the pages Henry wrote on my thirty pages of poetry. They seemed a parody to me, and not to Henry. A satire. An absurd mockery of it. Why? He is not aware that it is a caricature. If he were, I would accept it as such.

Does he satirize what he does not understand? Was it his way of conquering what eludes him? Allendy could not explain this. Whenever I mention Henry now, he looks severe.

Allendy has written about alchemy; he is an astrologer. He cannot read plays or novels because they seem tame and colorless to him, compared with the lives exposed to him in that small, dimly lit library. I know nothing of his life. Once I accused him of not understanding the artist, of being a scientist. Then he mentioned that I was wrong. He was a friend of many artists, and his own sister-in-law was a painter. She lived in a studio they had built for her on the top floor of his house.

He does have the eyes of a crystal-gazer. His superb teeth gleam in a smile which is rather feminine. He is very proud and sure of himself.

Henry tells me how all his talks with June became great battles. June would say such wounding things that Henry would grow irrational and desperate, but that now he realizes all these superb battles were fruitless, frustrating, puerile, left him broken, incapable of working or living. She had a genius for botching, tangling, aborting, in a blind, instinctive way.

The phrase which fired me and made me begin to write on June was Jung's "To proceed from the dream outward . . ."

Today, as I repeated them to Henry, they affected him strongly. He had been writing down his dreams for me, and then antecedents and associations.

Henry said, in the middle of the dream talk, "I have realized I am a man of value, and it is not believing this which almost led to my self-destruction."

Allendy is mistaken not to take my imagination seriously. Literature, adventure, creativity are not a game with me. I am touched by his paternal protectiveness, but I laugh too. The absolute limited sincerity of men like Allendy is not interesting to me. It is humanly comforting but it is not as interesting as Henry's insincerities, dramatics, lies, literary escapades, excursions, experiments, audacities, rascalities.

I may be basically good, human, loving, but I am also more than that, imaginatively dual, complex, an illusionist.

Allendy talks, perhaps, to ease his own doubts. He stresses my frailness, naïveté; whereas I, with a deeper instinct, choose friends who arouse my energy, who make enormous demands on me, who are capable of enriching me with experience, pain, people who do not doubt my courage, or my toughness, people like Henry and June who do not believe me naïve or innocent, but who challenge my keenest wisdom, who have the courage to treat me like a woman in spite of the fact that they are aware of my vulnerability.

JUNE ARRIVED LAST NIGHT.

Henry telephoned me. He sounded grave, bewildered. "June has come in a decent mood, she is subdued and reasonable."

Henry is disarmed. Will this last?

June telephoned me. She wants to come and see me tomorrow night.

What is going to become of Henry's work? What will June do to him?

"I'm bewildered . . ." He is weak, lost. Will June hurt him again?

I take a walk. The *vigne vierge* is blood-red on the fences and walls. I walk against the wind, while the dog licks my hand.

How far I have moved from June. When I sensed that she was jealous of what I had done for Henry, I said, "I did it all for you." She lies to me, too, when she says, "I wanted to see you before I saw Henry."

Then she came and the madness returned with her. She said, "Anaïs, I am happy with you." Immediately she began to tell me that Henry had "killed her." She had read all he had written about her. "I loved and trusted Henry until he betrayed me. He not only betrayed me with other women, but he distorted my personality. He created a cruel me which is not me. I have such a need of faithfulness, of love, of understanding. I had to set up a barrage of self-protecting lies. I need to protect my real self from Henry. And now you, you give me strength. You are calm and strong, and really know me."

As we walked up the hill, through the dark small streets, I saw a confused and tormented June, seeking protection.

"Henry is not imaginative enough, he is false. He is not simple enough, either. It is Henry who has made me complex, who has devitalized me, killed me. He has introduced literature, a fictitious personage from whom he could suffer torments, whom he could hate; because he can only write when he whips himself by hatred.

I do not believe in him as a writer. He has human moments, of course, but he is a liar, insincere, buffoonish, an actor. It is he who seeks dramas and creates monstrosities. He does not want simplicity. He is an intellectual. He seeks simplicity and then begins to distort it, to invent monsters, pain, etc. It is all false, false, false."

I was stunned. I saw a new truth. I saw a gigantic tangle. I am mystified and strangely lucid at the same time. I am not vacillating between Henry and June, but between two truths I see with clarity. I believe in Henry as a human being, although I am fully aware of the literary monster. I believe in June, although I am fully aware of her destructive power.

At first, she said she feared that I now believed Henry's version of her character. She wanted to land in London instead of Paris, and ask me to join her there. At the first sight of my eyes, she trusted me again. As Henry trusts me. They both need my faith. She shatters all my protection of Henry: "You have achieved nothing. Henry only pretends to understand, only to turn around later and destroy."

Has not Henry been more human with me, and June more sincere? I who partake of the nature of both, will I fail to destroy their poses, to reach the true essence of both?

I remember being struck with great pity when I read in Henry's notes that when she was working for both Henry and Jean, she exclaimed once, in a frenzy of fatigue and revolt: "You both say you love me but you do nothing for me."

June has become sane. She is no longer hysterical or confused. I realized this change in her today. Her sanity, her humanity is what Henry wanted. They can now talk together. He may understand her better.

June and I, arriving at the house, stand under the light over the front door, the light like a stage light which illumined her the first night I saw her, and we look at each other with lucidity. What has made her clearer about Henry, and clearer about me? What is the fever between us which clarity does not dispel? They are clearer to themselves and to each other. And I? I may suffer from the insanities they left behind. I may pick up their tangles, their insincerities, their complexities.

Will she deprive Henry of his faith in himself? She is seeking to destroy his book. Will she leave him once more dispossessed and reduced? She advises me strongly against helping Henry to get his book published, paying [Jack] Kahane.*

"Anaïs, you are giving me life. You are giving me what Henry has taken away from me."

Our hands are locked, and while I answer her with loving words, I ask myself how will I save Henry.

Who is the liar? Who the human being? Who is the cleverest? Who the strongest? Who is the least selfish? The most devoted? Or are all these elements mixed in each one of us? I feel most human because my anxiety is protective, towards both of them.

June, who is older than I am, yet sees me as the teacher in *"Jeunes Filles en Uniformes."* † She sees herself as Manuela taking refuge in my serenity.

And then a letter from Henry:

Anaïs, thanks to you I am not being crushed this time. Don't lose faith in me, I beg you. I hate to put in writing what I wish to tell you about the first two nights with June, but when I see you and tell you, you will realize the absolute sincerity of my words. At the same time, oddly enough, I am not quarreling with June. It is as though I had more patience, more understanding and sympathy than ever before. June has come to me in her very best guise, when there should be more hope than ever, if I wanted hope. But I see it all coming too late, I have passed on. And now, no doubt, I must live some sad, beautiful lie with her for a while. And perhaps you will see more in June than ever, which would be right.

Each one has found in me an intact image of himself, his potential self. Henry sees in me the great man he might be, and June sees the superb personality. Each one clings to this image of himself in me. For life and for strength.

June, having no core of strength, can only prove it by her power to destroy others. Henry, until he knew me, could only assert his strength by attacking June. He caricatured her; she weakened him

* Kahane, the proprietor of the Obelisk Press in Paris, had read the manuscript of *Tropic of Cancer,* and wanted to publish the book.
† The German film, *"Mädchen in Uniform."*

by protecting him. They devoured each other. And when they succeed in destroying each other, they weep. June wanted Henry to be a Dostoevsky, but she did all she could to make it impossible. She really wanted him to sing her praises, to paint her as an admirable character. It is only in the light of this that she judges Henry's book a failure. It failed to aggrandize June.

But when I thought June complained because she was not portrayed poetically, I find that she also quarrels with my description of her in my prose poem! She overlooks its strength and beauty, and says it is not an exact portrait. I did not want to say to June that a writer is not a portrait painter. But I could see by this that she had an image of herself which corresponds to no one else's image, and that she cannot judge writing objectively.

We sat in the Poisson d'Or.

June had told Henry that he was a failure as a writer, that he was a child, dependent on woman. That he could do nothing without woman.

We were drinking.

I said I thought Henry was a powerful writer.

"Let's go and tell him that he's great. You make me believe in him, Anaïs."

"You want to believe. What will you live for, if you lose your faith in Henry?"

"You, Anaïs."

"But loving me is only loving yourself. We are sisters."

"You believe in Henry, don't you?"

"Yes, I do."

"Then he must be good, he must be worthy of it."

I am giving Henry and June to each other. I am the impersonal revealer.

June said wistfully, "I used to be like you, Anaïs. I did not need to drink. I was already over-stimulated. But now I want to make you drunk and drugged. I want to be drunk, because I am intimidated by you, and I want to feel free to say anything, and to feel that you will forgive me. You don't need experience, Anaïs. You were born knowing. I don't want to see you stumbling through experience now—like watching someone learning to walk. I have done the vilest things, foulest things, but I have done them superbly, and I feel I have passed through them, I feel intact, I feel innocent. Do you believe that, Anaïs?"

"I could do the same. I want experience to catch up with you and Henry. I want to catch up with my understanding. I don't want to disappoint you, fail you."

"But you have all I need, an understanding without need of facts, realities. You don't ask questions, as Henry does. You have intuition. What does it matter what I do, it is what I *am* that matters."

True. What matters is the essence of June, and it is this essence which Henry has not grasped. He is too literal.

Henry and I at a café table. Henry confessing: "June has become a stranger to me. The first two nights with her I could not feel any passion. I cannot even get used to her body again."

I read his last pages on her return, and they are empty of emotion. She has exhausted his emotions, overplayed them. Then the whole thing becomes unreal to me, and it seems as if Henry were the sincerest of the three.

He asks me if June does not bore me. He finds that she talks too much. He would like her to be silent at times, to read.

As I leave June in a taxi, she looks at me like a child. As I walk away, I see her face blurred behind the taxi window, a tormented, hungry face, unsure of love, frightened, struggling desperately to wield power through mystery. She is under a great strain. Every gesture is a gesture of frenzied singularity, to compel attention, love. Strain. When she creates disturbances, hatreds, conflicts, jealousies, she believes she is living dramatically. She feels that when she is not there, Henry is not living. She has to make the atmosphere boil. She feels that Henry is dead when he is not raging and fuming.

Beautiful June, who talked to me for three hours, sometimes wise, sometimes boring and empty. Her anxious self, anxious about Henry, believing only in the moment of vertigo, in ecstasy, in war, in fever. And then when she leaves me, she struggles against her distortions. She talks with Henry warily. We always begin by talking clearly and then she ends up confused.

A moment before, she had said, "I see myself in you, as I was before Henry. You have that same strange mixture of utter femininity and masculinity."

I said, "That is wrong, June. As soon as a woman has creativity, imagination, or plays an active role in life, people say: masculinity. Allendy does not call it that. You are active. Henry is passive."

Henry talked to June about my love of truth, my calm. June said, "Henry never wanted those things. I tried to give them to him."

The rain was falling, rolling over the taxi window. As I saw June's pale face through the glass, she looked like a woman drowning. I felt such pity for her. How can I rescue her?

I am suffering from their conflicting image of each other. They seem distorted to each other, and it makes me wonder if they see me as distortedly as they see each other. I wonder whether I can succeed in making them see each other without distortion, love each other again. I see her making efforts to regain her power. She wants to get Henry's books published, does not approve our plan. She complains that Henry does not take her advice.

"Only four persons have really disturbed me in my life: Henry, Jean, you and another person you don't know."

Is this other person the lover Henry suspects she has, the one who made it possible for Henry to get to Paris?

I was amazed to see Henry showing a new protectiveness. For him June is now a pathological child.

I was amazed to hear from June that Henry was hurt that people should think he can only write "cunt portraits." Is this why he has been so intense about his Lawrence book?

I told him that it was true he had sacrificed June to a "fiction," made use of her as a character he needed to create (creation of a cruel woman because he needs pain and violence to create at all, or because he enjoys being the "victim" of woman, I don't know). He says he is fascinated with evil, yet all he does is chastise June for living as freely as he does.

How glad I am to be a writer, making my own portrait, concerned with his work as writing and not as a portrait of anyone I care about.

Superimpositions. The impish face of Henry. A sudden flash into his multilateral nature. Behind him I see a severe Dr. Allendy, condemning him. Then I see June's face falling away behind the taxi window, and the whole world confuses me.

Henry writes: "Because I am a monster. A monster, you understand! A necessary monster. A divine monster. A hero. A conqueror. A holy destroyer. A destroyer of dying rhythms. A maker of living rhythms."

The important thing is to set the passions free. The drama is everything, the cause of the drama nothing. Élie Faure: "The hero is the artist."

For the first time, Henry fixed upon his interior life with poignant attention.

Will Allendy's wisdom block my desire to move on, to disperse myself; or will he hold my hand as I travel through hell?

Henry is writing about Proust and Joyce. He sends for me, asks me to roll up my sleeves, give him help and criticism. June is a hindrance, and suddenly I feel her as a hindrance too. Henry exclaims, "If only June would go back to New York. I need freedom!"

Last night I went to Clichy. Henry and June tried to use me as a referee to one of their battles.

I sat silent. I said quietly that whatever I had to say I would say to each one separately. Henry was impatient with June's flood of talk. And June was saying: "He is like a steel wall."

Henry was in a high-powered writing mood. He was working on two books at the same time. I read what he had written on Joyce and on D. H. Lawrence. We discussed it. Henry told June that she did not let him work.

I understood his abstract mood. His eyes were hard and bright. June's beauty was suddenly submerged in a wave of creation.

Instead of spending the night out, as she did whenever they quarreled, June returned that night meekly, to tell Henry that she now understood him. The next day she reported this reconciliation to me. "I've got Henry working and happy."

Does June really love Henry? This is impossible to find out because of June's lies.

That night, too, she was ill. She awoke in the middle of the night shivering with fever. Henry said: "I knew why she was being ill. I felt sorry for her, but that's all. I was more annoyed than anything." June could not arouse his pity. The brutality of their life together frightens and appals me.

It is a barbaric jungle.

I think that is why I return to Allendy. His window is open, like a haven. I see the bookcases. I stand in the street imagining his quiet voice, his gentle laughter, his compassion. I feel a yearning for peace, as if the world of Henry and June were a glimpse of hell.

A half of me escapes Allendy, rebels against him. I rebel against wisdom, against sublimation. The conflict is all the greater because each man is strong within his own role and symbolic value. Allendy is truly a kingly man, an intrepid scientist, a scholar, a man who is seeking to relate science and mysticism; he is a leader, a teacher, a healer. And Henry is his opposite. Henry is a sensualist, an anarchist, an adventurer, a pimp, a crazy genius. I feel despair before the austerity of Allendy's life. I walk up and down before his house as other people might walk up and down before a church. I am smoking. My face is pale. *I feel like June.* He is in there talking from higher spheres, cooler spheres, shedding compassion and clairvoyance. He is there bottling dramas into alchemist's bottles, distilling, annotating.

I must let myself flow unilaterally.

"J'ai été bon quelquefois. Je ne m'en félicite pas. J'ai été méchant souvent; je ne m'en repens pas," writes Gauguin.

Clichy. June, Henry and I. June and I are sitting on Henry's bed. Henry is sitting before his table, which is covered with paper, books, and notebooks. We are discussing the financial problem of his book's publication. Kahane wants to be paid. I promise to raise the money. June makes pointless and illogical remarks. The talk breaks down, becomes irrational and confused. As I suspect that June may be jealous of my backing Henry's book, I suggest she try and raise the money in New York. Henry begins patiently, "Now, June, listen. You are confused about this."

June says, "It is you who are confused."

When they have thoroughly irritated each other, we drop the subject. Then Henry asked very quietly, and gently, "June, I can't work here. I want to go to Louveciennes for a few days. You understand. This is the most important period of my life as a writer."

"You don't have to leave, Henry, I'll leave. I'll go back to New York as soon as I can get the money. Tonight I will go and stay with friends." There are tears in her eyes.

Henry said, "It is not a question of that. I am not asking you to leave, only to leave me alone. I can't work when you are around. I can't work, June. And at this moment, I must be hard in self-protection. To finish this book I could commit a crime."

After this the thread was lost again. June was weeping hysterically, her whole body shaking, raving wildly about Henry not being a human being, that she must fight him to protect herself against him, that if she stayed, she would kill herself or do something mad.

I console June. I stroke her arm. Henry is weeping too, sentimentally. Suddenly June's intuition flashes, terrifyingly acute. "Henry, you are better in some ways that I cannot understand, and worse in some ways which affect me. There is something in you I cannot seize. I can't be a slave to your ideas, you're too spiritual a man. I'm the wrong woman for you."

She is sobbing uncontrollably. She leaves the room. I follow her. In the dark, windowless bathroom she is convulsed with sobs. I take her in my arms. I caress her hair as if she were a child. Her tears are falling on my neck. I am overwhelmed with pity. She clings to me. I caress her until she grows quiet. I leave her to wash her face. I return to Henry and we take up the talk about his work. June returns, quiet. I prepare to leave. She asks Henry to buy some food and to take me to a taxi stand. Henry and I walk for ten blocks talking about June the child, and how to protect her. I offer to take her out often to give Henry peace. He now knows that June's talk bores me. He tells me how he would have given his life before to hear and see a submissive June begging for his love, and that now it means nothing to him. All she says to please him only reveals how confused she is, in her own mind, about his significance and value, how she misses the point whether she is praising or cursing him. He tells me how she came home the other evening and said, "I believe you are the sincerest man on earth."

I cannot forget how beautiful June looked, sitting on Henry's bed with her blonde hair tumbled about her shoulders, and I felt that it was a curse that such beauty could utter words Henry would answer with: "That is stupid of you, yes, and that is why I cannot take it seriously."

June and I were walking together over dead leaves crackling like paper. She was weeping over the end of a cycle. How one must be thrust out of a finished cycle in life, and that leap the most difficult to make—to part with one's faith, one's love, when one would prefer to renew the faith and re-create the passion. The struggle to emerge out of the past, clean of memories; the inadequacy of our hearts to cut life into separate and final portions; the pain of this constant ambivalence and interrelation of emotions; the hunger for frontiers against which we might lean as upon closed doors before we proceed forward; the struggle against diffusion, new beginnings, against finality in acts without finality or end, in our cursedly repercussive being . . .

I could see the crumbling of her love for Henry.

It tormented me to see June unequal to life, and watch her pitiful efforts to rationalize it, to set her emotions in order, to understand. She talked feverishly. She told me, "One night I went to Henry intending to confess to him as to a priest. I was in a holy mood. I saw him as a saint. His attitude silenced me. From that moment on, if he had been brought back to me dead on a stretcher, I would not have cared. He cannot hurt me any more."

As we walked, she became more alive and less submerged by pain. "I feel such harmony with you, Anaïs," she said, using Henry's own words. Am I only a medium of clarity and harmony through which others find themselves, each one finding his potential self, his vision? June added, "It is not I who am shrewd, but Henry. He talks about my shrewdness, but it is he who is shrewd and baffling."

Then I saw the ravages which Henry's literary inventions have caused in June's poor vacillating mind. Everything he has written, said, distorted, exaggerated, has confused her, disintegrated her personality, her own sincerity. Now she stands before the bulk of Henry's writing and cannot tell whether she is a prostitute, a goddess, a criminal, a saint.

Henry has buried himself in his work; he has no time for June. I fall back into my own work. Henry telephones me. Mails me the bulk of his work, and I try to follow his ideas, but what a tremendous arc he is making. D. H. Lawrence, Joyce, Élie Faure, Dostoevsky, criticism, nudism, his creed, his attitude, Michael Fraenkel, Keyserling. He is asserting himself as a thinker; he is asserting his seriousness. He is tired of being considered a mere "cunt painter," an experimentalist, a revolutionary. Fred tells him his books would mean nothing but for the obscenities.

I feel sadness when I look at Allendy's photograph. I am always between two worlds, always in conflict. I would like sometimes to rest, to be at peace, to choose a nook, make a final choice, but I can't. Some nameless, undescribable fear and anxiety keeps me on the move. On certain evenings like this, I would like to feel whole. Only a half of me is sitting by the fire, only my hands are sewing. I am concerned with the sorrow of June, and yet I am aware that June does Henry more harm than good.

A bar. June in a gay mood, making fun of Henry's abstract mood, of his passivity in life, of his writer's *esprit d'escalier.* "He is quite dead, you know, Anaïs, dead emotionally and dead sexually," How they love to contemplate their mutual murder of each other! I have to interest June each time in other things, to take her mind off drugs. I tell her my whole life, and she tells hers. What stories! She is amazed that I could have been staying near where D. H. Lawrence was, in the south of France, and that I never dared to call on him. "But who am I? What did I have to bring him?" I asked June. And at the house of René Lalou I met André Gide for a moment, clad in his dark cape. And June tells me about Ossip Zadkine and his strange statues, and how he desired her, and gave her a statue to sell in America.

We are dancing on our irony as upon the top of glowing sparks.

"I love you in your simple raincoat and your felt hat, Anaïs." She kissed my neck in front of Allendy's house. And always, when we part, she gives me that look of a drowning woman.

June said, "I am now looking for someone to bow to, now that I can no longer bow to Henry."

As I bow to Allendy? A daughter's respect? I tell her about Allendy. "I don't want to give up my madness."

I try to explain to her that the writer is the duelist who never fights at the stated hour, who gathers up an insult, like another curious object, a collector's item, spreads it out on his desk later, and then engages in a duel with it verbally. Some people call it weakness. I call it postponement. What is a weakness in the man becomes a quality in the writer. For he preserves, collects what will explode later in his work. That is why the writer is the loneliest man in the world; because he lives, fights, dies, is reborn always alone; all his roles are played behind a curtain. In life he is an incongruous figure.

To judge a writer it is necessary to have an equal love for writing as for the man. Most women only love the man.

When I talk like this, I know June will rush to Henry and say all this to him (unsigned work of art, for I am sure she tells it as a thought of her own).

A flippant evening. Ideas exposed tonight to June, not to be considered tomorrow. Influence of jazz. When I step into a bar or a cabaret, before I have handed my coat to the waiter, I assimilate such a draught of sensations, wonder at the beauty of women, the magnetism of men, the starriness of the lights, that I am ready to slip under the table like a drunkard. How quickly I slide down the slope of a snowy voice, plunge into smoky eyes, diffuse into music.

June and I sink into this need of warmth and love. Gifts, praise, words, admiration, incense, flowers, perfume.

We entered a dance hall. Found an unexpected chicness and formality. Evening dresses, champagne in pails, white-coated waiters, a mellow jazz. Should we leave? I saw defiance in June's eyes. She wanted to defy the world, insult society, because Henry had given himself to a book, turned away from both of us.

We forgot the formality of the place. We talked, leaning over the small table. June luminous, prophetic, and eloquent. A match, a beautiful match for each other. I want to know if she has a lover in New York.

We need each other. We do not know, at times, which one is the child, which one the mother; which one the sister, which one the older wiser friend; which one dependent, which one protective. We maintain a maddening oscillation, and we do not know what we want of each other. Tonight it is June who says, "I want to dance with you." It is June who leads me, she heavy and I light and willowy. We glide on the last beat of a jazz piece which is descending and gasping and dying. The men, in stiff evening shirts, stiffen even more in their chairs. The women close their lips tightly. The musicians smile, benign and malicious, rejoicing in the spectacle, which has the effect of a slap in the face of the pompous diners. They cannot help exclaiming that we are beautiful together. June dark, secret under the brim of her Greta Garbo felt hat, heavy-caped, tragic and pale, and I a contrast to her in every way. The musicians grin. The men feel insulted. At the table a waiter is waiting to tell us we cannot dance again. Then I call for the bill like a grand seigneur and we leave. I have the acrid taste of rebellion on my lips. We go to the Cabaret Fétiche. There the men and women are unmasked, at ease. We are not outcasts. Men struggle to catch our attention. June responds. I bristle with jealousy. June talks. She tells me each story Henry has told me, but the reverse of the story. They never fit together at any point. Every scene is reconstructed differently. It is Henry who vulgarizes her and toughens her. She is delicate and sensitive. It is Henry who was unfaithful, and made love to women right before her eyes. It is Henry who wanted to think of her as a femme fatale, incited her to do her worst. It is Henry who taught her how to speak in slang. "Henry does not want a human life, Anaïs, a human happiness. I know he does not want it. He wants performances, wildness, fever, fermentations. I had to do all that Henry did not dare to do. He was timid. He was meek. I had to bring him his Dostoevsky characters. But he is no Dostoevsky. He could not *see* them. Henry is nothing as a human being; he is disloyal. He hates me because of all he owes me; he has made a bad use of all I have given him. He has been neither realistic enough, nor fantastic enough."

Her fortune-teller's eyes, and that forward, eager thrust of her profile.

Both of us drunk now, and she is talking about someone in New York. An exceedingly handsome man. Does she love him? She is so uneasy every moment, as if each word she utters were a surrender to the enemy. Does she fear that I will use this knowledge to detach her from Henry?

She complains of having found no great love, but great egotists, seeking only an expansion of themselves through her.

It seems to me, through the fumes and incoherence, that she is talking about a past Henry, that I know another Henry.

"I expected Henry to do wonderful things with my life, my stories, my friends, to heighten them, add to them. But instead he reduced it all, vulgarized it, made it shabby and ugly . . ."

She had wanted to be restored to literature as a character, in all her magnificence and abundance and wildness.

"I will make a great character out of you, June, I will make a portrait you will like."

"But not like the poem, *House of Incest,* I didn't understand that. It was not me."

Henry cannot impose a pattern on me, because I make my own. And I can make my own portrait too.

June said suddenly, "When I first came from New York, I thought that you had certainly become Henry's friend and that you would pretend love for me in order to find out everything for Henry."

I remembered saying to Henry: "If I ever find out that June does not love you . . ."

"And now?" I ask, looking into her eyes, and my own fill with tears of guilt. June takes them for a sign of love, and is moved, and clasps my hand.

"I trust you."

Later she talks ramblingly about her two years with George, who is as beautiful as a god, but not deep. "I wanted to love him madly, but I can't. And anyway, Henry needs me so very much. Without me he stagnates."

I cannot tell if I am witnessing the echoes of a great love, or a living, incurable obsession on the part of both of them.

"Henry was talking to me the other day and he seemed like a puppet making absurd and meaningless gestures. He couldn't move me."

Henry tells June that the sacrifices she makes add to her greatness and that, therefore, there is no debt.

"What did you feel when you gave him your typewriter and wrote by hand, and he pawned it to buy drinks for all of us? Did you mind?"

Is there malice behind these questions which stress Henry's thoughtlessness? I remembered Henry's warnings: "She will try to turn you against me."

Clichy. June, Fred, Henry, and I are eating in the kitchen. Henry attacks one of my phrases as one which cannot be said in English.

I defend it. I report a dream in which I was covered with mushrooms.

"That is not surprising," Henry said, "as you are an esoteric substance."

June said, "And Henry hates intelligent and exotic women."

"*Le fiancé des bonnes,*" said Fred maliciously.

As this reminds me of my father's entanglements with maids, I bristle.

The talk continued with play on words, banter, teasing, sallies, duels, allusions. Abstract intoxicants. June began to lose her footing, so she drank more often from the bottle of Pernod.

It seems to me that everyone became cruel.

At some point in the interplay, Henry said, "Don't turn against me, Anaïs," so humbly, meekly, that he sounded like a child. June talked confusedly, Fred waspishly. Henry was drunk too. He shook his head and looked like a bear which anyone could lead and command to dance. He would dance and grunt. June was fermenting with an inexplicable savagery.

The talk ended because Henry felt dizzy and had to lie down. June was restless. Henry was lying on his bed and she had not been able to persuade him to drink something which would help his drunkenness. She gave me the glass and asked me to take it to him. I thought that she wanted to test my power over him, but I think now that she wanted to be alone with Fred; for after I gave Henry the drink and I returned to the kitchen, I saw their heads joined together through the frosted glass door, and when I opened the door I heard the rustle of separation. The lipstick was smeared on June's mouth. She sat with her legs wide apart, her skirt up to her knees, and her shoulders slumped. I could not bear the way she looked, disheveled, unkempt, her face coarsened by drink. I looked at her reproachfully. She felt my misery. She raved, "Anaïs, I love you, you are cruel and clever, you are all cruel and clever, that is why I got drunk. I'm terribly drunk." She lurched forward, towards me, and almost fell on me. I held her up. Her eyes watered. I led her to bed. She was too heavy for me. (Oh, someone could laugh at the picture we make, June leaning on me.) We totter into Henry's room. He awakens. He helps me to put June on the bed. She laughs. Then she weeps. And then she begins to vomit. I place a wet towel on her forehead. She tears it off and throws it at me. She raves, "I always wanted to be drunk, Henry, as drunk as you. Now I am. I've taken your drunkenness away from you." But in reality, she is not drunk enough to stop thinking. And what rises to the surface are her fears, her doubts, her suspicions, her childish calls for protection, her self-condemnation. "Oh, Henry, Anaïs, you are both cruel and clever. Clever and cruel. I am afraid of both of you. Where is George? George. I am not afraid of you. I am so sick, I'm putrid. Leave me alone. Anaïs, don't come near me. This is terrible, I'm so terribly sick, and tired. I want rest. Won't you give me peace? I want peace. Anaïs. I love you. Wipe my face. Give me a cold, cold towel. Go away. Foul. Foul smell."

Henry is totteringly wiping up the floor, rinsing towels. Diffuse, bewildered, not sober yet.

I feel a sickness of the soul: I wish I could rid myself of my whole life, of all I have heard, seen, illusions, fantasies, adventures, drink, orgies, sensations.

June believes my seriousness is a reproach, a moral judgment. But it is not that. It is a repudiation of ugliness. Of June rolling in her vomit in her black satin dress. Ugliness and emptiness. The sorrow of emptiness. It is June who vomits, and I who feel I have vomited my whole life. The real wine, the real bodies, the real kisses, the real cafés, the real kitchen, external ecstasies. I yearn for the ecstasies of writing, reading, music, philosophy, contemplation; I yearn for that room I saw through an open window, lined with books, suspended over life, where nothing ever turns to dregs, where landings are not crash landings. June sees in my sorrow a severity, and it is not that. I place the cool towels over her forehead. I soothe her. I say, I am not cruel, I love you, June. June is snoring. I lie beside her, all dressed, coat and all. Henry brings coffee for both of us. June drinks it slowly. It is dawn. She asks me, "You will come back tonight?"

I want my solitude, my peace, the beauty of my house; I want to find my lightness and my joy again. Ecstasies without hangovers, without vomit. June comes with me to the station. She buys me violets. I throw them under the seat in the train.

June retracted the story of George. She said she had only invented him because so many interesting things were happening to me, and nothing was happening to her.

She taunted me when I said I could not return to Clichy the next night, saying it was because I did not have the energy. I could not explain that I came home to the diary, to note my last image of June and me walking towards the station, our two sandaled feet in unison: I could not explain the breaking away, the withdrawal that took place in me.

Tomorrow I return to Clichy. I return to Clichy but I will not stay there. It will not swallow me. The image of Henry's passivity, watching June act, avoiding the scenes made by June, matched her image of him. I wanted them in my life, but I don't want to live their life. I can no longer watch them actively destroying each other. They negate each other. Henry says June was a promiscuous woman who tormented him and destroyed his romantic faith and love. He describes her boldness, hardness, callousness and his illusions. He describes a June whom he initiated to literature, raised away from Broadway and dance halls, a converted sinner. June asserts that she was romantic and intact when she met Henry, that she was impregnable towards men, that it was she who introduced him to Strindberg, Dostoevsky, Nietzsche, Élie Faure. June insists that what she learned from Henry she quickly surpassed him in, growing quickly ahead of him; that Henry wished to see her as a child, a woman, a whore, and refused to acknowledge her mind. That she took refuge from his cynical sex talk and whoring in stories of fantastic adventures. That it was his realism and literalness which drove her into invention, to escape from his vulgarizations. June says Henry took from her and never acknowledged her influence. That she served him a rich experience rarely equaled and which, for the most part, he failed to understand, to seize. It is true that Henry's descriptions of their life in the Village, the speak-easies, the friends they had, June's multiple stories, are recorded entirely from the outside and that Henry never looked for their significance. But he is doing that now. It is also true that when June read the poetic descriptions I made of her in my long prose poem, she did not understand them. It is also true that she cannot understand either Henry or herself, that they are both unconscious beings, acting instinctively and blindly. It is also true that June has intermittent intuitions which are acute and deep, but that her mind also goes into eclipses, that her acts need to be translated with a knowledge of symbolism, and that symbolism is something unknown to Henry. They need a translator!

I was sitting on Henry's bed in Clichy, and doing just that, translating them to each other. June was in a lucid mood, talking quietly. I was telling Henry that he knew very little about himself and that this was the root of his lack of understanding of the world. I quoted June. Henry said, "Now you are telling me something." June applauded when I spoke of his egocentricity, his over self-assertion in his books, his absence of core; so that he lived always guided by his reaction against another person's attitude, never out of a deep self-guidance; lived negatively, I said, and always either over-estimated or depreciated himself. Self-knowledge was the root of understanding and wisdom. Henry distorted June because of his neurotic love of his mother and his hatred of her, his need and repudiation of woman. Would he save himself through his work? Would his work have the same ultimate weakness of Joyce, Lawrence, and Proust, a monstrous growth of the ego? I attacked everything, but more tactfully than I write it here. I acted Allendy to Henry, pointed to his dependence on the criticism and opinion of others; to his measuring of himself always not from within but against something; his need of constant experience and no time for digesting it; his need of much talk instead of a struggle for significance. It all had begun with a talk on the confusion of his style. He was, as he said, the man always ahead of himself. He was always going back to his finished books and adding to them, altering them, for each day revealed a new tone, a new accent. I felt he accumulated too many facts and was hampered with the weight of them, that they *concealed* reality. He was full of dissonances.

Then Henry left us to get food for dinner, and June and I were left alone. She told me I had been wonderful, that it was the first time she had heard someone talk to Henry, not missing him, striking neither too high nor too low; and that I had done wonderful things for her too. All the fragments of our talks, short encounters, fused into a monologue such as I had always dreamed of hearing June utter, a June no longer hysterical or merely spilling over, but quiet, supple, flexible, aware, clear and wise.

"Anaïs, I am sexually dead. I have burned myself out, all into a great faith and a great illusion. Henry is losing even his manhood. I see it by his embrace. I sense that it is not because he does not want me, but that he does not want any woman."

"Perhaps it is because he is writing so much. When I was writing my book on Lawrence, for two weeks my body was dead."

"Oh, it isn't that. I have seen him in that mood too. This is different. But I don't want to tell him. He is so crushed with complexes, I don't want to add another."

Whenever June laments, however, I am aware that she is weeping over a dead Henry, that there is another Henry alive and happy. She complains that Henry has never given her any credit for anything. He is inhuman, perhaps, out of self-defense against her will.

The absence of muscular structure in woman's mind makes Henry suspicious. But just before June came back, he was beginning to trust my intuitions. It is this kind of feminine thinking which psychoanalysis makes clear, and I am better able now to explain what I feel.

June has a curious way of jumbling values, of mentioning in the same breath Dostoevsky and Greta Garbo, Proust and some Village character like Max Bodenheim. Literature for her is an adornment. Henry wrote: "She wore it like plumage." But this knowledge I derived from Allendy she understands.

At one moment, when she had spoken movingly of her faith and the wholeness of her love for Henry, I laid my head on her knees and said, "June, I worship you."

She answered, "I don't want worship. I want understanding."

Henry's cry, too: "I want understanding!" There is a shortage of understanding. It is as if I had lived my whole life, from childhood on, cultivating the one thing they needed, living within the meaning of everything, in preparation to receive this bulk of facts and experience and be able to understand it, and to clarify it for them.

Then I became aware of the atmosphere of her talk. It sounded like a testament, an abdication. Why? She was telling me what to do for Henry, and what not to do. What intuition did she reach while she watched me talking to Henry? How little she understood Henry and herself, the hopelessness of their ever understanding each other? Did she become aware of the depth of my friendship with Henry, and was she relinquishing him because their discords had become more and more violent? She mixed perfidious remarks with her generous ones, always in an effort to destroy Henry the writer for me as well as for herself. Was it protectiveness towards me which made her say, "Tonight you showed yourself wiser than Henry. Don't let him destroy your mind and your work. Remember that your work comes first."

Was it feminine loyalty? Was it prophecy? Did she mean that Henry had destroyed her? But this was different. They were lovers.

"But he can harm you as a writer, as he harmed me as a woman, by taking and never giving."

I will never be able to write down all of that night, all of the words we said. It seemed to me that June was climbing into more impersonal spheres, that she was eliminating all personal jealousies, that she was accepting my friendship for Henry and his for me.

June was wearing her hair loose. She sat on the edge of the bed and smoked.

"You are so young and so full of faith. Your body is so young, so slim, so white."

Every statement that night carried a strange weight, a sadness, an admission, a defeat. I could sense a symbolic image haunting her: her own lost youth and freshness reappearing in me. I remember one of her phrases, uttered with desperation: "Why do I have such a coarse, earthy body, Anaïs, I am not earthy and coarse."

"But June, Henry loves your earthy body. And I love you as you are. I want to be like you."

She wanted as much to escape from herself as I wanted to inhabit her body, become her. We were both denying our own selves and wishing to be the other.

We talked until dawn, smoking, June pacing up and down at times.

Henry said: "I have always thought a great deal, but there was a hub missing. And what was the missing hub? It was, as you said, an understanding of myself. It is your vision of me which keeps me powerfully together. You reject all the unimportant details. You never get confused as June does, and you give my acts and my experiences the correct proportion."

When I saw him again, he was working on a synthesis, "Form and Language," and I read the pages as he unwound them from the typewriter. We talked endlessly about his work, always in the same manner, Henry flowing, gushing, spilling, spreading, scattering, and I weaving together tenaciously. He ends by laughing at my tenacity. Until I reach a clear finality of some sort, I can't stop. I am always seeking the core, the hub, the center of all his chaotic and abundant ideas. I struggle to coordinate, to tie up loose ends.

Henry is a mold breaker. He obeys the rhythms, as Lawrence said, and all clear patterns can be damned.

At any moment he can begin to rant, rave, fume, drink, and the continuity of his thinking is broken by the fermentations of his body. And this is good. It gives a mobility to everything, the mobility of life itself. He accepts absurdities.

I walked through the streets which Henry taught me to love. Water is being thrown on the sidewalks and swept by an old man with a broom. Dirt is floating down the gutter, windows are being opened, meat hung on hooks, vegetables poured in baskets for display, wheels are rolling, bread is baking, children are skipping rope, dogs are carrying the weight of downtrodden tails, cats are licking off bistro sawdust, wine bottles are being carried up from the cellar. I love the streets I did not know as a child. I always played in houses in Neuilly, Brussels, Germany, Cuba. Henry played in the streets. His world was filled with ordinary people, mine with artists.

Henry's recollections of the past, in contrast to Proust, are done while in movement. He may remember his first wife while making love to a whore, or he may remember his very first love while walking the streets, traveling to see a friend; and life does not stop while he remembers. Analysis in movement. No static vivisection. Henry's daily and continuous flow of life, his sexual activity, his talks with everyone, his café life, his conversations with people in the street, which I once considered an interruption to writing, I now believe to be a quality which distinguishes him from other writers. He never writes in cold blood: he is always writing in white heat.

It is what I do with the journal, carrying it everywhere, writing on café tables while waiting for a friend, on the train, on the bus, in waiting rooms at the station, while my hair is washed, at the Sorbonne when the lectures get tedious, on journeys, trips, almost while people are talking.

It is while cooking, gardening, walking, or love-making that I remember my childhood, and not while reading Freud's "Preface to a Little Girl's Journal."

Henry teases me about my memory for conversation. Every now and then he says: "Put this down in your diary." He never says, as others do: "Do not put this down in your diary."

Even his face is changing. I was looking at him in amazement while he explained Spengler. No trace of the gnome or the sensualist. A gravity. An intentness.

Talk about his work. I feel sometimes I have to hang on to the significance of it while he tosses about, fumbling, stumbling.

Fred criticizes Henry's reading, his efforts to think, attacks his knowledge of science, interest in movies, in theatre, in philosophy, criticism, biography. A big enough artist, I say, can eat anything, must eat everything and then alchemize it. Only the feeble writer is afraid of expansion. Henry is fulfilling a deep necessity: to situate himself, to adopt values, to seek a basis for what he is to build.

I laugh at my old fear of analysis. The possession of knowledge does not kill the sense of wonder and mystery. There is always more mystery.

I have no fear of clarity.

Henry is lost in a labyrinth of ideas, like an ostrich who has buried its head in a mountain of papers.

He said, "I crumbled at the end of my six-year war with June, like a man unaccustomed to peace."

Allendy said: *"La fatalité se déplace: plus l'homme prend conscience de lui-même, plus il là découvre intérieure."*

I let Henry and June take care of my tough-minded self. Jung said:

We must include both the tender-minded and the tough-minded within ourselves because we cannot permanently allow one part of our personality to be cared for symbolically by another . . .

And it is Jung, too, who observes that it is usual for a patient to endow the physician with uncanny powers, somewhat like a magician, or a demoniacal criminal, or as the corresponding personification of goodness, a savior.

Jung also said:

Since we cannot develop backwards to animal consciousness, there remains nothing for us to do but advance into the more difficult pathway to higher consciousness.

Pauvre de nous!

Henry writes me:

Had a frightful night. Went to bed exhausted about midnight. At one o'clock woke up and lay in a half-dream state till 5 A.M., then fell into a stupor until one today. Dreamed the most horrible dreams, among them that I saw my own grave with a tombstone and a light shining on it. Am trembling. Don't know what ails me. Tried phoning you just now, but you were out. Feel terrible. Another night of this and I'd go completely mad. Jesus! I feel like Richard Osborn before he went mad.

[December, 1932]

I never imagined when I gave Henry the money to escape to London, that June would come the night before he left, take it all away from him. He writes me a weak letter:

I'm angry, furious at myself, I'm leaving for London tonight. Fred came to the rescue. I'm leaving so it won't happen again. I hate June. After a bitter, nauseating conversation, I feel humiliated, deeply ashamed. It was agony, what I endured. And why I stood it, I don't know, unless it is that I have a feeling of guilt. June is beyond reason. She has become a madwoman. The vilest threats and recriminations. That is why I broke down and wept. She is capable of anything. She is terrifying in her violence.

Henry can only fight in his books. In life he runs away. Now he is in London. I am raising money for June's ticket to New York, as she asked me for it. I am to leave it at the American Express.

June is leaving a parting impression which is not beautiful. Emptying Henry's wallet, frightening Henry.

Henry was stopped at the English frontier for carrying too little money. Questioned. Deported. He was wearing his shabbiest clothes. He told the authorities he was running away from his wife!

In the café where we met, he broke out in talk about June. And two things stood out: his goodness, his real feelings. The weakness of the man, his listening to June to the very end of all she had to say, becomes, in the case of the writer, the passivity of the artist as spectator of life. Listening to June he ceased to be a man who should have silenced her; he became an investigator listening to what a normal man would not have wanted to observe. "I discovered the baseness of June. Through her anger, what was thrown into relief was her enormous egotism. Worse than that. Tawdry. When she left me, she turned to say at the door: 'And now you have your last chapter for your book!' "

Henry had tears in his eyes when he described this last scene. Tawdry. What an unexpected word to brand June with.

At this moment Henry looked careworn, sad, profound.

Then he began to talk about D. H. Lawrence and Dr. Otto Rank's *Art and Artist*. His mind makes immense detours. Then he gets lost. And then I am able to bring him back, not because I know any more than he does, or because I am more whole, but because I have a sense of direction in the world of ideas.

Much that I am reading in *Art and Artist* helps me to confirm the intimations I have had about the artist. What efforts I am making to understand. There are moments in Henry's talk when I feel truly tired, like a woman reaching for knowledge beyond her capacity. I stretch my mind to follow the curves and sweeps of man's mind. It is always the big, impersonal spaces which frighten me, the vast deserts, universe, cosmologies. How small my guiding lantern, how vast man's universe. It seems to me that what I hang on to is the human, and personal. I do not want to enter impersonal, non-human worlds.

Is Henry right? He does not want me to write a diary any more. He thinks it is a malady, an outgrowth of loneliness. I don't know. It has also become the notebook of my extroversion, a travel sketchbook: it is full of others. It has changed its aspect. I cannot abandon it, definitely. Henry says: "Lock up the journal, and swim. What I would like you to do is to live without the journal, you would write other things."

I would feel like a snail without its shell. Everyone has always stood in the way of the journal. My mother always urged me to go out and play. My brothers teased me, stole it, and made fun of it. It was a secret from my girl friends in school. Everyone said I would outgrow it. In Havana my aunt said it would spoil my eyes, frighten the boys away.

Henry is sorting his numerous notebooks so that I may have them bound. His desk is covered with manuscripts. His books of reference are lined up before him. He is in his shirt sleeves. I bring a number of the surrealist publication *This Quarter*. Fred is typing too. Someone else is cooking in the kitchen.

[January, 1933]

In the Sorbonne lecture hall. A classroom atmosphere, chastity, seriousness. Madame Allendy is there, white-haired, blue-eyed, maternal, solid.

(In 1928 Allendy and his wife incited the surrealists to produce a film of a dream for *Études des Idées et Tendences Nouvelles*. They found the money and director, Germaine Dulac. She ruined the film. *L'Âge d'Or* contains some pieces of this film. From this incident Allendy inferred that the surrealists were insincere. It was for this group that he invited Adler, Einstein, Fernandez, Milhaud, Satie, Honegger, and Gris to speak. Maurice Sachs in his later memoirs was to describe Madame Allendy thus: *"Un beau visage de révolutionnaire de 89, grave, sûr, bon et intelligent. Son regard est superbe."*)

Allendy comes out on the platform, serious, austere. It is the first time I see him from a distance. He looks more furtive, more timid than in his office. He stoops a little, like a scholar bent too long over books. One only sees his high brow and his crystal-gazer eyes. His sensual mouth is hidden in his beard. I can hardly hear what he is saying. It is a conference on the Metamorphosis of Poetry. The words of a doctor, a professor, a scientist. He is dissecting poetry. It has become a cadaver.

I carried a muff. I was all in fur, fur hat, face in a high fur collar. It was winter. I was sitting on a hard bench of the Sorbonne. I heard words: *science reductible, éléments, fusions, pensée métaphysique, altitude poétique, antinomie proviennent de la pensée statique, le poète inspire plus qu'il n'est inspiré.*

I am but a silky fragment of a woman.

It is freezing outside. There is an orange butterfly on my quilt. My diary lies there. If it too had wings, they would have stuck to the wine stains on café tables, but the only scar it bears of its expeditions into the world is the trembling handwriting when I write in the train.

Note to Allendy:

It is not only the cure of the individual, but that in curing it, you reveal the worlds which lie beyond the ego. This liberation from the ego is what seems to me your most precious gift to me. And it is only *then* one begins to love . . .

It was after the shock of June's ugly behavior that I went to see Allendy again. I felt overwhelmed by reality. I told Allendy about my preoccupation with reality. When I collide with it (it was the behavior of June which I called collision), I seem to experience a sudden break, I feel I swing in space, I go up in the air, I create enormous distance. Then after the collision, I feel submerged into dreams. The realism of June. Ugliness. And then I cease to live in reality. I feel that I miss it, always. I am living either in a dream or in pure sensuality. No intermediate life. The overtones or the undertones. And Allendy understands.

Instead of seeking to help me, as I am talking in generalities, he begins to talk about his own madness. But his madness is on a different level. He tells me that at times he feels his house is haunted, that his *dead father is always there.* He believes that when he wants news of a friend who is far away, he needs only to open a book and read a phrase at random. He opened the manuscript of a friend and found: *"Il avait de la fièvre,"* which turned out to be true of his friend. Allendy believes in the tarot cards, in alchemy, in astrology. But then he added, "Don't tell anyone, as they will think I am mad."

This touched me. Underlying the cautious doctor, the wise analyst, this occultism . . . He had a curious way of remaining silent, suspended, of never answering direct questions. How far does he go into these realms, I asked myself. There are times when he does not understand me, as when he said that I wanted to take drugs out of snobbism, instead of out of a real curiosity of my imagination.

Yesterday I was trying to see him clearly, from behind my shroud of heavy dreams. I liked his face when he talked about the book he was writing and his desire to find time to go to the Bibliothèque Nationale to look up data on alchemy; wonderful books there were, there. I liked him when he got up to investigate some noises and opened the door, saying: "This is a house full of mysteries."

That he should mention all these intuitive, disquieting elements just when I looked upon him and his study, his books, his work, as a solid anchor in the middle of Dostoevskian instabilities and hysterias, troubled me. The brutality of June had exiled me from my own world, and this one I had taken refuge in was not familiar to me.

When I left Allendy, I met Henry and his friends at a café. As we sat down, I heard the street accordion music which pursues me everywhere.

Henry began to talk about *Bubu de Montparnasse,* and his own Bubu life, his bumming life, relation to whores, starvations, etc. He described his worn shoes, his desperations.

Even though I am not familiar with this life, I understand it. If there was a distance between the world of Allendy and myself, and less between Henry's life and mine, what was there between me and the formal dinner at a stately house to which I had to go afterwards? Like the distance between planets. I had to struggle against the opium smoke of my dream to look at a ceiling doubly high, at candles doubly long, at the lace pattern of the tablecloth. The concert of crystal glasses on trays was like that of bells heard in far-off Swiss mountains early in the morning. I could not see the people; they seemed like engravings or paintings. I could feel my evening dress dragging on the gravel path, I saw a faceless chauffeur opening the well-oiled door of a car, the starched aprons of the maids like the sails of small boats. When the fur rug was placed over my knees, I wondered what drug I take which makes ordinary superficial life invisible to me.

I was still examining some of the stories I had told Allendy, examining them for loopholes, defects. For he had demanded I never see Henry or his friends or June again.

I said I had broken with them.

Could I deceive a professional analyst?

The secret of my lies must be that which makes for good acting. I never plunge into a lie carelessly, without first telling myself: "How would I feel if this were true?" (How would I feel if I had broken with Henry's world?) I start feeling and believing the situation. Also I have learned transpositions. I borrow from the distress caused me by June's behavior and transfer this to the present. I am distraught, I am shocked by June. But it is simple to include in this a break with Henry for having submitted to June's attacks. I have sometimes wished I could break with Henry's world. My hands are cold. I show symptoms of distress. Allendy can check that, but they have a different cause. However, by this time, I have entered my own story. I feel as if I had broken my friendship with Henry and his friends, and his café life. (And I have, for the space of an hour.) And it is true I need Allendy. It touched me humanly that Allendy could no longer be objective.

Allendy said, "You had to do this, you were in great danger. I can tell you now that when I saw Henry at your brother's concert, he seemed a monster to me. It's your neurosis which made you associate with June and Henry and their friends. You, such an extraordinary woman . . . like a *fleur sur du fumier* . . ."

I laughed. Allendy thought I was laughing at the idea of a neurosis being the cause of my Bohemian life. Alas, it was not that. Allendy's phrase, "a flower on a dung pile," belonged so much to the dime novels read by servant girls that the poet I am was offended by that, as another woman might be by a man talking with his cigar in his mouth and his hat on his head.

The absurdity of the image, the phrase, concealed from my eyes the complete absurdity of Allendy's statement because this was made with so much sincerity and devotion; but as soon as I left him, I thought, "An analyst in love is as blind as anyone else in love!"

But to finish with my lies to Allendy. "Was he violent?" he asked me. "No, of course not," I said, wanting to laugh again at the idea of Henry's violence. "Dr. Allendy, you are being taken in by literature. Henry's violent writing deceived you."

"You imagined Henry just as you imagined June," said Allendy.

"Oh, no, I knew Henry very well." (Be careful, Anaïs, always use the past tense.)

"He was a lucky man. He will never again have a friend like you."

I could not help enjoying his post-mortem on my friendship with Henry. Allendy really believes that Henry was an illusion (was!).

Allendy asked me about the diary. Is he uneasy? He wants to see it. I tell him I have written much less in it.

"That's a good sign. You are able to tell me everything."

When I left Allendy after my web of lies, I was happy. I felt that Allendy was a wonderful personage. For a moment I felt that I had really broken with my Bohemian world because I was unwilling to accept their way of life, and I walked carefree, lightly. It was only later that I regretted the lies, for lies create solitude. I needed someone to talk to openly, and by lying to Allendy I forced myself back into a terrible solitude. What could Allendy have done if he had known the truth? Withdrawn, been angry. He is so proud.

He always said that one could feel lies. Yet he cannot feel mine. He must think I am a superficial person, who can surrender an artist's life so easily.

I think it's humorous that I should have gone to Allendy to get cured of a lack of confidence in my womanly charms, and that it should be those very charms he has succumbed to.

What is most touching about Allendy is his *"mon petit."*

He is not a poet. What a pity. It is just what I need. His supply of imagery and symbolism is limited. What am I asking for? Literature. Literature, my bread and wine.

But I do know I am surrounded by children and that I go to Allendy because I need someone to help me take care of my children.

At the Sorbonne, Allendy talked eloquently about surrealism. Antonin Artaud, he tells me, is like his son. But he is still anxious about June, about my being in danger.

He is pale and very tired. When he was eighteen, he went to war and was "gassed." It affected his lungs permanently. When he was four or five, he lost the nurse he adored.

He looks very human, very sincere.

But he does not understand the artist, so I am reading Rank's *Art and Artist*.

He believes that my affection for him is only due to "transfer." "One always loves the person who understands you."

I asked him if he was not suffering from excessive doubts of others' affections!

He admitted that he suffered from a lack of affection, and the need of it since childhood. The love he receives from his patients is not for him, the man, but for the healer.

He wanted me not to need him any more, to be weaned from him.

Suddenly I realized the tragedy of an analyst's life. It is that the control he exerts over life gives him the tantalizing power to enter others' lives, to share in their secrets, in their intimacy, knowing more than the husband, the lover, the parents, taken into the patient's very heart and body. But then he is only allowed to look, to be the "voyeur," not to touch, not to be loved, desired, or hated. My whole life was offered to him but did not belong to him.

When he first saw me, he thought, "How happy I would be with a woman like that!"

Today he said, "You are full of precious qualities."

But he knows all the time that what creates this sense of a bond is his understanding.

I felt that if I surrendered him, or lost him by confessing I had not cut myself from Henry's world and friends, I would be losing the last of the idealistic men, the heroes, the protective, scholarly, learned, dedicated men. Because Henry is no hero, he is the rebel, the warrior, he is made to inflict wounds, not to heal, protect or to love.

Henry writes me a note: "Read nearly all the Nietzsche—you will like it. You will see what a great thinker you are. It fits marvelously with Rank, and Spengler."

I would be rudderless without Allendy.

And who is to say whether the analyst is as much a victim of an illusory affection as the patient?

Who is to say that if the patient loves the doctor because he feels understood, therefore known, therefore loved, perhaps the doctor only falls in love with the patient because he is allowed this intimacy with a human being; he is allowed to peer at a body making love, into beds, into weeping fits, into cries of hunger, of fear, of sorrow; he is allowed to live another's life, to rescue him, to feel the weight of his guilts, his confessions, to know his needs. He feels wanted, indispensable, intermingled and interwoven with another. He can almost touch the body whose every quiver and vibration he is permitted to know

Why should this love be any more illusory than the others?

I have a feeling that the masochism of woman is different from that of man. Hers comes from her maternal instinct. A mother . . . suffers, gives, feeds. A woman is taught not to think of herself, to be selfless, to serve, help. This masochism is almost natural to woman. She is brought up in it. (Example set in the family by my Spanish grandmother.) It is like the masochism of people brought up in the Catholic religion.

It is my maternal instinct which places me in danger.

If only I could be freed of this quest for the father. Father? Savior? God?

Each contact with a human being is so rare, so precious, one should preserve it. Allendy is now convinced it is illusory; and I, since he has confessed his insecurities, anxieties, need of love, feel I must convince him of the reality of my affection.

So I telephoned him this morning: "Have any of your patients got the flu, so I may come instead?"

Henry, like D. H. Lawrence, had a healthy, troublesome, joyous father who liked drinking, and a mother who was sharper-tempered, cleverer. [Saul] Colin says in his book on Lawrence [*Naturalisme et Mysticisme chez D. H. Lawrence*] that Lawrence sought to return to the father by divinizing him as God, as a way to escape from woman and the worship of the mother. Henry does this by his cult of men of ideas, and his work is a struggle to triumph over woman, over the mother, over the woman in himself.

I began our session by making Allendy sit in the patient's arm-chair and by analyzing his "omens" as expressions of his lack of confidence in life and in love. I pointed out that he carried in him a projection of defeat which creates defeat. He laughed.

I used all his formulas and his lingo on him.

He said, "I always wanted to be a magician. When I was young I used to imagine I was a magician."

"Perhaps becoming an analyst was the modern expression of this need."

"I have missed all the joys and pleasures of life. There was always a veil between me and reality. I have never been happy with a woman."

I was taking care of him, not he of me.

"It is a malady in me, perhaps, but I have never been a passionate man, never knew anything but tenderness for women."

Henry is sitting revising his novel. I see so clearly the aim, the mood, the temper of his work, that I am able to help him cut out extraneous material, change the order of chapters. I told him my theory of skipping meaningless details, as the dream skips them, which produces not only intensity but power. He begins, "Wednesday morning I stood at the corner . . ." I say, drop "Wednesday"; drop the extra weight to achieve speed, the essential . . . a literature of "cuts." His pages on ecstasy are the most fiery pages I have ever read. A climax in ecstatic writing. I bow before them. There are times when he produces gigantic dissonances: at other times, a kind of Dadaism. He will make one assertion on one page and on the next page he cancels out what he said and asserts the opposite. His pages on "seismographic shock" are marvelous. He runs from extremes of sentimentality to cold, monstrous madness. There are humorous scenes as we work, particularly when we proofread. Once I read aloud in a mechanical tone, looking for proof errors: "Before and after the erection . . . the genital banquet." I read it as if it were "Thursday the sun was shining . . ."

We laughed.

Henry thinks only of his work [*Self-Portrait,* later called *Black Spring*]. No more whoring and vagabonding.

The first half of his novel is all incident; the second is all ecstasy, rivers of poetry and surrealism issuing from the adventures, explorations, a fascinating completion. When I praise his writing for its power and explosiveness, he says he thinks the same of mine. A feminine revolution.

We have much influence over each other's work, I on the artistry and insight, on the going beyond realism, he on the matter, substance, and vitality of mine. I have given him depth, and he gives me concreteness.

Yesterday I suggested a change in the order of the last two chapters because one was slow, human, sentimental, not too well written, the other mad, brilliant, and I felt this one was the climax. Henry often produces without any artistic consciousness. He also refuses to evaluate, or throw out, as I do. He is uncritical. I believe in impulse and naturalness, but followed by discipline in the cutting.

I am merciless on his childish rantings (he has a folder of pages I have extracted because they were just tantrums, as I said), everything petty, over-realistic (his fights with June over the value of Greta Garbo). I say: "Have bigger fights." When he is irritated he produces a petty literalness. He stops to rave against June's coldcreaming. He describes this as an attack upon American women! It is all cheap, like a newspaper report on what do you think about platinum blondes. I will not let him make the faults of bad taste which marred Lawrence's work. Bad taste and bad temper.

I only act as an analyst, helping him discover himself, revealing to him only his own nature, desires, aspirations.

He helps me by always asking me to say more, to write more assertively, to clarify, expand, to be strong.

The first time Jeanne came to Louveciennes all I noticed were her eyes, the distress in them, the wild swimming of the pupils in their orbit. She was tall, blonde; she looked like Danielle Darrieux with less softness of contour, a more austere quality. She limped. She dragged her leg and she talked continuously.

"I hate to see my brothers as bodies, to see them growing old. Once I sat writing a letter in a room and the two of them were playing cards. I looked at them and thought: What a crime that we should be alive, it is a simulacrum, everything was finished long ago, we have lived already, we are far away from our husbands, wives, children, friends. I have tried so hard to love, and I can, up to a certain point, and then no further."

We were sitting in the back of the garden, where trees, bushes, flowers, ivy, all grow wildly, and a small trickle of water runs under a small Japanese bridge. Her husband was visiting the house and talking with other friends. Jeanne was so restless, her eyes tossing like miniature ships at sea, that I offered to walk through the forest. We walked over a thick carpet of pine needles, and she talked:

"I have no human sympathy, I suffer neither pain nor feel joy either. I am only aware of my brothers. I know only fear, a great fear which makes me stay away from the theatre, from reading, from analysis, from any avenue of realization, of clarification. I want to preserve my divorce from reality, and yet I know that at times this divorce is so absolute that I step into madness. I reach moments when I become deaf to the world. I stand in the street and see the automobiles passing and I hear nothing. I stamp my feet and hear nothing. I ran into a bar and asked the woman serving drinks a question. I saw her lips moving but I could not hear the words. I was terrified. I may be lying on my bed and this great fear invades me. I begin to knock on the floor or the wall, to break the silence; I knock and I sing until the fear passes."

As we walk, she breaks off branches, and listens to the dry sound of the break. She said: *"Passons à une nouvelle forme d'exercice."*

She became aware of the quality of my listening. "You listen in silence, yet one feels you never pass judgment. What do you do when you are defeated?"

But she did not wait for my answer.

She stops on the path to catch her breath. "I may be shaking hands, and suddenly the person recedes into the other room and I see my hand miles away. I am in my own room, amused." The word "amused" is the key word to her social world. In her world everything must be amusing, piquant.

The stability, the gravity of her husband is also amusing, his dependency on clocks, his methodical reading of newspapers, his unbreakable engagements, his important business trips.

"What made him venture into the esoteric, mysterious, impregnable, inhuman citadel of my brothers and me? Tragic marriages for the women who married my brothers too: they feel like outsiders. We do not feel their sorrows, for who are they? Merely human beings, banal little human beings, baffled and defeated by emotions, by our lack of sympathy, unable to share our anachronistic exaltations, our search for ecstasy."

She said, as she left: "Come and see me. We will practice rhabdomancy."

Jeanne's house was a castle where one might have spent years exploring all the rooms filled with antiques. She whisked me through

them as if she did not want my attention caught by furniture, bro-
cades, candelabras, screens, rugs. She took me to her room, which
was all white, curtains, rugs, bedspread, uncluttered, shuttered, with
the only note of color coming from Orient-blue bottles. Her room
did not seem part of the castle. Next to it was the children's room,
the room they occupied as children, with the small beds, small chairs,
small table she had described, where they came in time of trouble.
The toys were still there, scattered. Stamp collections, circus horses,
dolls, trains, colored balls.

"You don't turn away from your fears," said Jeanne, "you don't
laugh at them."

"I'm a writer, Jeanne, I don't want to frighten away any of the
ghosts, I want to know them well, intimately. I have to be able to
describe them."

"I write too." I read her writing. It was so light, so frivolous, so
shallow, it was like her life in society, a masquerade. She does not
write as she talks.

I saw the lightness and the masks, the leaps into space, even
into madness, as ways to out-distance the unutterable incest. Nuptials
in space, like some insects, while in flight. Faithful to the first bonds,
the first cell and the first unity of childhood passions. To the poets,
insanity seems closer to divinity than sanity. The madman arrives
at death not by human progression, the disintegration of cells, but
by a series of holocausts. Joan of Arc roasting at the stake was perhaps
in no greater pain than Jeanne seeking to live in the romantic world
of Byron which no longer existed.

This family had exhausted, in five generations, the ordinary joys
of fame, fortune, beauty, intelligence, voyages, honors, genius, debauch, power, leaving four heirs who could only love each other.

As we walked swiftly through the rooms, a servant rushed towards
Jeanne to intercept her: "Monsieur de Saint-Exupéry is waiting
for Madame."

She led me into the salon. He sat by the fire. He had a round, pale
face, dark but soft eyes, and a body not too tall and rather plump.
He had a calm manner, and spoke gently to Jeanne. He seemed to be
dreaming.

The car which had brought me was waiting and I had to leave.

As I sat in the car, Jeanne's brother came out. He leaned over formally and kissed my hand. *"Mes hommages, Madame."*

As the car drove me away, I caught a glimpse of the stately house, concealed gradually by enormous old trees.

I remembered Jeanne's words: "I love to feel in unfamiliar worlds, disoriented, uprooted. I love to go out with an ordinary man who says banalities, who wants to offer me a silver fox and makes me feel like a kept woman."

Her house reminded me of the house in *The Wanderer* of Alain Fournier.

Poisson d'Or. Tziganes. Three aristocratic Russian women, beautiful, with two wealthy men. Seven bottles of champagne. Ordering gypsy singer to sing for them at their table. Russian painter seated in front of me. Stares at me. When I dance with my escort, we collide and he kisses my neck. Orgy of singing and dancing. The three Russian women weep, quietly, with enjoyment, voluptuous satisfaction. The painter and the host almost fight because a man breaks lumps of sugar while the gypsy sings. Musicians sing and dance for the angry man as if to soothe him. The painter smiles subtly at me. Lady in white also begins to dance in front of him. The painter is whisked away by his partner who makes a scene. Irony, with the deep emotional music going on. The feeling that when I handed my coat at the check room, I handed over my identity. I become dissolved in the atmosphere, into red curtains, champagne, ice, music, singing, the weeping which the Russians love to do, the caress of the painter's eyes. Everything sparkles and exudes a warmth and a flowering. I am not like Jeanne, fragmented into a thousand pieces. I am at one with a sea of sensations, glitter, silk, skin, eyes, mouths, desire.

I wanted to be back in Henry's kitchen: Henry in his shirt sleeves, salting the pâté de foie gras (what a faux pas), steam on the windows, the smell of cauliflower, the warmth, Henry's voice filling the room with resonance, elbows on the table, the cigarette holes in the oilcloth.

I stand before each new world, new person, new country, hesitant, unsure, hating new obstacles, new mysteries, new possibilities of pain, of blunders from lack of courage. Fear, lack of confidence, has narrowed my world, limited the people I have known intimately. The difficulty of communion. *Je vous présente mes hommages, Madame.* Politeness like a shield. Culture is a shield. The world of my father. With Henry it is the world of my mother.

I read Jeanne's manuscript, which is touching, but thin, shallow, vague. A fairy tale. In dreams too, there is maturity, growth, depth, power. A long travail. I would like to take her by the hand and lead her. Her hair, her long Mélisande hair loose, her mouth open, her eyes dilated, her skin fair and pale. *"Elle vivait d'elle même,"* she writes. I hear her deep voice singing Brazilian songs, accompanied by her guitar.

A Georgian prince, Mahreb, fell in love with Jeanne. Lucie and I urged her to give herself. I analyzed her lyrically, poetically, fantastically.

Jeanne sits curled up on the couch and looks unreal. She talks about wanting to give Mahreb magic gifts. When she complains that he utters only perfectly ordinary phrases, then I experience the strange pain and jealousy of not being a man; for I would know what to say to Jeanne, how to court her dreaming heart. But I sit very still now.

Jeanne looks mysterious, elusive, unseizable. She went out one Christmas morning with the Christmas tree tinsel rolled around her neck many times, and carrying a glass bird perched on her little finger. Of course, she met a White Russian taxi driver and, of course, he understood and would not charge her for the trip and, of course, she wrapped the tinsel necklace around his neck, clasped the bird on his meter, and gave him fifty francs.

We planned an "accidental" meeting with Prince Mahreb. Jeanne, her husband, and I would go to the Hermitage Moscovite. We would let the Prince know and he would happen to be there with a friend.

But when the Prince came to our table, acting surprise, I saw the eyes of Jeanne's husband flare green with jealousy and suspicion. He suspected us all, rightly, of treachery. Wild music, champagne, Jeanne breaking three glasses of champagne as she would break her marriage. I danced with Prince Mahreb, a very dark, tall, quiet, stupid man, but sensual in every motion he made, dancing, or lighting a cigarette, or drinking champagne as if he were drinking you. Using his fiery eyes like a hypnotist, resting them on you. The black long hairs on the wrist, the bronze skin, and saying little, never dispelling the mystery, the suspense of what his eyes were saying. I saw the eyes of Jeanne's husband on us (she had told him it was I who was interested in him) and I felt uneasy. Eyes of the world. Jeanne's eyes floating like water lilies on a cloudy pond. She is drunk with defiance, hatred, destruction, the joy of destruction. Eyes of her brother caressing me, eyes of Jeanne's husband ransacking my conscience: "You betrayed me." He watches Jeanne, who is exalted, breaking more and more glasses. We dance. I am stricken with compassion, for I know Jeanne is trying to break out of a prison; but I fear it is not Prince Mahreb who will help her. The Georgian prince is dancing a folk dance alone on the floor, wild, like the Cossack dances, and he utters chilling battle cries. One can well imagine him on horseback, with sword and fur hat, and I remembered, at this moment, Jeanne's children explaining to a stranger why their mother went out so much. "Father is very boring. He reads his papers all the time."

We are alone in the night club, at two in the morning, and the musicians are tired; but Jeanne is demanding, "A Georgian dance! A rhumba! A waltz! More champagne!" The eyes are revealed in the flare of matches lighting cigarettes. Eyes of Jeanne full of drunkenness; the Prince's eyes heavy, torpid, without dreams, waiting like a banked fire only for the moment of love-making to burn; eyes of Jeanne's husband suspicious; eyes of her brother mocking. I sit between them and I feel the union of their minds, the synchronization of all their gestures, pride, affectation, arrogance; and while he says to her, "Take a lover," and she pushes me into his arms, I know we are but understudies, the Prince and I. Eyes like brimming glasses, foaming. The love of others an intrusion, but necessary, to divert the attention of the world away from their unbreakable child marriage. A union without organs, members, roots, like those of fishes. Promiscuity of eyes, of language, twinship. They were married long ago, in their children's room, at some children's game and ceremony, as the *Enfants Terribles* of Cocteau.

Henry writes me:

Yesterday I bought you *À Rebours,* and afterwards had a great attack of conscience. What have I ever bought you? Why, when I got that check from [Dr.] Conason, didn't I cash it and get you something? I am always thinking of myself. I am, as June said, probably the most selfish person in the world. I am amazed at my own selfishness. When I bought the book I felt like a worm. So little. I could have bought you the book store and handed it to you, and it would be nothing.

I want to live only for ecstasy. Small doses, moderate loves, all half-shades, leave me cold. I like extravagance. Letters which give the postman a stiff back to carry, books which overflow from their covers, sexuality which bursts the thermometers. I am aware also that I am becoming June.

Allendy tells me about the research I can do for him at the Bibliothèque Nationale. He said, "You see everything as a poet." Was it a reproach? He said, "You remind me of Antonin Artaud, only he is fierce and angry, and I cannot help him."

The man who is only half a magician is coming Thursday night. As I could not, or would not, picture him taking a taxi, going to the Gare Saint-Lazare. buying a railroad ticket to Louveciennes, landing at the small shabby station like an ordinary man, I told him that a friend had loaned me a car and chauffeur and he would be driven from his house to my house, magically. I told him it was the car of the Countess Lucie because he had been fascinated with my description of her. I wanted to create a journey like the journey of *The Wanderer* to the house in the forest where there was a masquerade going on. Poetry. Then I took almost all of my month's allowance and hired a car for the evening.

Allendy came. He was enchanted with the house, the garden. We sat downstairs by the fire, in the small salon.

In this setting of sensuous colors and textures, he seemed out of place. A leaping, joyous fire glowed in the fireplace which I had found at the Arts Décoratifs, and was made of Moroccan mosaics in a rich design of blues with a few touches of gold. Allendy admired it like something exotic. The reflections of the fire played upon it, on the peach-colored walls, on the dark wood, on the wine bottles from Spain.

The two hundred years of the house had given it a look of sinking into the ground comfortably. It was not an illusion. It had settled, and the angles of the ceilings and walls were slightly askew. The bedroom, particularly, had a slant to the ceiling so marked that, at times, looking out of the window, the tilted frame gave one the sensation of being at sea.

Allendy admired everything. He was amazed at the solidity of the setting I had created: outside, I gave the impression of an ephemeral, fleeting creature not at home in the world and about to vanish.

The house made him see me as a human being.

"At eighteen," he confessed, "I wanted to commit suicide. My mother gave me a distorted idea of women."

Just as my father gave me the idea that all men were selfish, incapable of love, unfaithful.

Then, to prove the exactness of the image, one seeks people who match this image, corroborate this assumption, this generalization.

But how wonderful it is to acquire an objective knowledge of others.

When Allendy says, "I am cold and grey," I sense the obscure, buried, sunken, eclipsed man who was stifled by his mother.

No one was ever born without that light or flame of life. Some event, some person stifles or drowns it altogether. I was always tempted to resuscitate such men by my own joyousness or luminosity.

When I break glasses in a night club, as the Russians do, when my unconscious breaks out in wild rebellions, it is against life which has crippled these idealistic, romantic men. I respect these men, cold, pure, faithful, devoted, moral, delicate, sensitive, and unequal to life, more than I respect the tough-minded ones who return three blows to one received, who kill those who hurt them.

Yet I would have loved D. H. Lawrence rather than intellectual Huxley.

But each time I take the side of the primitive men, I turn my back on half of myself.

Allendy can see with his seer's eyes. He lacks poetry, extravagance, the power of ecstasy.

But he has won as an analyst, because he made me understand something very important. Whether because I am a Latin, or because I am a neurotic, I have a need of gestures. I am myself expressive, demonstrative; every feeling I have takes on expression: words, gestures, signs, letters, articulateness or action. I need this in others.

But Allendy says the need of gestures, of proofs of friendship, love, devotion, comes from lack of confidence. I should not need them. I should be able to dispense with them.

Proofs of love and friendship are what I give to others all the time. And everyone seems to need them.

He admired my aquarium, with its fish and plants made of glass. I asked him if I could give him one for his birthday on the nineteenth. And he accepted.

When Allendy left, I could not sleep. I was retracing the entire course of my life in the light of his words, and discovering new interpretations. I had always seen my father as cold, sadistic, cynical, faultfinding. Perhaps there was another image I had missed. The day he was about to beat me after beating my two brothers, because of the look on my face, he let me alone, almost tenderly, actually moved. Was he really moved? Did he beat us because Spanish fathers believe in beating their children? Because he himself was severely beaten by his father, a military man? Another day, when I was gravely ill, he bought me a compass, and brought his work to do by my bedside. His letters from France when I lived in New York, age twelve, thirteen, were loving.

I could not tell Allendy that Henry had bought me a present, because he has said, "I hate Henry because he is a barbarian. The barbarian is the type of man I most hate."

The barbarian bought me a present, yet a friend of his put him in a novel as a callous, anarchic, destructive drunkard and adventurer.

"I was badly analyzed," said Allendy, "and I tried all these years to finish the job myself."

I plied him with questions. He said, "I always thought that one had to *deserve* love, I worked so hard to merit it."

This phrase was so much like what I often wrote in my diary. The idea of deserving love. And then watching love being given to people who did nothing to deserve it.

Les Criminels by Ferdinand Bruckner, done by the Pitoëffs. The play shows a complete house of three floors and what happens on each floor, each room, simultaneously. When the action is strong, the spotlight is on that one room, while the others are in semidarkness and the actors whisper. I was immensely moved by it. Not so much by the theme of the blindness of justice (a very different kind of crime takes place on each floor, and all of them are judged by the same law, as the same crime) as by the simultaneity of life being lived in various rooms (levels) at the same time.

The same process takes place in life constantly. Layers, levels. I come down from the studio where I have been fixing the aquarium for Allendy's birthday to answer a telephone call from Jeanne about our evening, and I return to my opened Nietzsche marked by Henry while the radio plays on, and I open another of Marguerite's cramped, timorous letters (like a man walking on stilts) while Emilia brings me the electrician's bills to pay and asks me to telephone for coal and all this time I am remembering Madame Allendy trying to charm me last night by her artistry in her home. She designed a gigantic pearl in the center of the dining room table, which gave off a planetary light. She forces the tulips open until they look like exotic flowers (whose name I asked). But she complained that the armchairs had not lasted ten years as the upholsterer had promised and asked me if I did not think that too short a period. I answered that I had never been able to test the life span of an armchair that long because I had traveled and changed home constantly, and that, *entre nous,* I did not want an armchair to last that long!

The dinner was for the purpose of my meeting Bernard Steele, the publisher of Antonin Artaud. He wanted to meet me because he liked my book on D. H. Lawrence. But he made mocking remarks about Lawrence: "A man who never saw the sunshine in life," to which I retorted, "He was a miner's son!"

"You are terribly interested in Lawrence?"

"Not so much now. He does not need defending any more."

Steele gave me a small book by Artaud, *Letters to Rivière.*

The next day I arrived with the aquarium, the creation of a glass blower, everything of glass, the colored stones at the bottom, the fishes, the plants, the coral, the caves. I unpacked the pieces and set it up for him. How Allendy loved the glass ship, the stones the color of his eyes, the lights placed so that one could not see them, only as radiance from the fishes themselves. His eyes. They were humid with pleasure. The ship had foundered on the semiprecious rocks.

Allendy said, "I always wanted so much to travel . . . I liked hearing your description of Deya, in Mallorca."

"And now . . . ?"

"Oh, now there is nothing new to see. We are familiar with every place, with the movies and with books. There only remains the moon to be explored. Have you ever thought of the moon?"

"It is too far away. I am still interested in so many places right here, all around me. And it is not the places one wants to explore, but one's joys, surprises, responses to a rich world. I am not satisfied with Blaise Cendrars' descriptions of South America, or Siberia, or with films either. I want to see for myself. I want my own feelings and visions."

Allendy's detachment from life frightens me. He is dying. I don't want him to die, I said to myself. It is dangerous to hold men back from death. I feel it is unhappiness which drives him to meditate on the moon. I want to give him life and adventure, but I cannot convey to him that it is the mood, not the places, the relationships which can light up shabby hotel rooms, stained café tables, brimming noisy streets, sour wine.

I met Zadkine, the sculptor of wood figures. We went to his little house behind an apartment house on the Rue d'Assas. There are two small houses with a garden between them. In one he lives with his Russian wife; in the other are his sculptures. There are so many of them they look like a forest, as if so many trees had been growing there and he had carved them into a forest of bodies, faces, animals. The different qualities of the woods, the grains showing, the various tones, weights, make one feel there is much of the tree left in them. Women carved out of bamboo, slaves in joyless slavery, faces cut in two by the sculptor's knife, showing two sides forever separate, eternally two-faced. Truncated undecagonal figures, in veined and vulnerable woods, fragments of bodies, bodies armless and headless. At night, when he is out of the studio, do the trees bend, weep, shiver, nostalgic for the leaves? Wailing at the transmutations?

In the center of these figures, Zadkine, small, rosy-skinned, with a round face like a boy, hair tousled, always laughing, joking, mischievous.

His small, quick gestures, his ironic, mischievous expression, his red cheeks, give him something of a handsome clown, a handsome monkey. His humor and joy are so strong, tinted with philosophy, he says gaily such profound things, his sculptures so ponderous and haunting, that one seeks in vain for the affiliation between his carving and his delight, his boyish pranks and his wood contortions. For he carves prisons, man in bondage, yet he himself laughs within them, as if they were part of a game.

He wears corduroy suits, an orange wool tie; one might meet him at the gate of a farm, flushed with wine. How did abstract art ever capture this playful Russian who should be braving the snows, with a fur hat to cover his red ears, and shouting to his horses as he shouts for his dinner at the restaurant.

"I want to see more of you," he says, as I leave.

Allendy tells me of the incident which took his confidence away. The person he loved the most in the world, as a child, was his nurse. She adored him and pampered him. Always baked him cakes and pastry which he ate with great pleasure. But she left him to get married. The child Allendy erases her from his memory. He does not want her name mentioned. But he refuses ever to eat pastry or cakes again. At her leaving he has his first serious illness, pneumonia, and remains in weak health until eighteen. Last November, while walking through the Trocadéro Gardens, he saw a nurse feeding pastry to a little boy. The whole incident was revived in his memory; he became excited and felt relieved of a great secret weight. He blames this loss for his reluctance to install himself in life.

I tell him it is too early for him to prepare for death; accepting separation is a step towards death (as he has told me). He answers that now he is afraid to become too attached to life. I feel that I am sitting by the bedside of a dying man. I feel the load of his sadness. Can I help him? He is basking in my warmth, he is rejuvenated by my presence. He is anxious about my lies, doubtful, confused. He knows he cannot tell when I lie. "You lie so well," he says sadly. But I retort, "I only lie as doctors do, for the good of their patients." Which made him laugh uproariously, as I have never heard him laugh.

How much in need of love he is! How he expands when I show concern over him. And the wiser, more objective I become, the closer he thinks I am coming to him. And what a rascal I am! Yet I did not feel treacherous. I felt like myself at thirteen when I first felt the ugliness of life and began mothering my brothers. That Allendy has completely given his life to others is a point of resemblance between us. When Henry says, "Life is foul," he makes it more so. When I say to Henry, "I have to go and see my mother," he says, "Why?" What I really want is to abandon all my duties and responsibilities for adventure. And that I will never do, leave my mother and Joaquin helpless. I will not do to others what was done to me.

There is a great continuity in my relations and devotions to people. For example, I remember what Allendy and I talked about the last time, and if a thread remained loose I pick it up and set about untangling it and placing it where it belongs. It is a work of minute cellular construction which all life constantly strives to destroy. The entire mechanism of practical life obstructs such a construction. The telephone rings; the patients are waiting; the conference has to be written, prescriptions, and my own mass of cares, duties, the house, the friends, the garden, the needs of others. All this brutally submerges the pattern, the web of profound correlations. I fight hasty, casual, careless contacts. Just a patient, subterranean, delicate effort to destroy the solitude of human beings, to build bridges. To achieve this in relationship and in writing takes much time. Proust had to retire from life to do it in writing.

I give to this creation a care I give to none other. When we are interrupted, it is characteristic of me that my thread remains unbroken. I stand in the room possessed by the theme, and I do not let go. While Allendy is finishing his telephone call, in my mind I continue our talk until it is completed, only superficially disturbed by the realistic intrusion, deeply untouched by it, independent of it.

This continuity Henry has felt: it is like a catalyzer, a *point de rallie-ment,* a magnetic centralizer of scattered and disconnected elements.

A friend of Joaquin's has just seen my father in the south of France and he tells me, "Your father has suffered from your abandonment. I believe him. He does lie occasionally but I always know when he is lying. He is very sensitive, very effeminate, and extremely selfish, of course. Needs to be loved and pampered. He came to see me the other day and talked for several hours about the sorrow of having lost his children. Said he sometimes reread your letters, which he adored, and he could not understand why you abandoned him. He has suffered very much from this."

I said, "Write to him that I will see him when he comes to Paris."

When I came home I sat by the fire and, staring at it so long, I became hallucinated. I thought I was standing inside a glass bell such as I have as a paperweight, a ball of glass which I shake and then the flurries of snow dance inside of it and cover a diminutive castle.

This castle resembled "Les Ruines" in Arcachon where my father left us. It was a copy of a medieval castle built for D'Annunzio and which my father had rented for the summer. It was a gloomy place, covered with ivy, completely overshadowed by old trees. A fine haunted-castle setting for the drama which was to take place there. It could have served as a setting for the stories of Edgar Allan Poe. The windows were of colored glass, as in churches.

The town itself was a gay sea town, full of summer visitors, but we did not seem to be a part of that life. I had just come out of the hospital after a near-fatal operation on a burst appendix, and after three months of a slow recovery, I was weak and terribly thin. My mother thought the seashore would be good for me. When we arived, I saw him watching us from the window. He did not seem happy to see us. (I learned later that the parents of Maruca, one of his piano pupils, had rented the place for him so she could continue her studies.)

But there was a garden, a tangled and wild garden one could get lost in. And there were colored glass windows, and through the core of the designs, a button of multicolored glass, one could see a prismatic, colored world in oranges, blues, water-greens, rubies. I kept my eye glued to those stones for hours, looking at this prismatic world. Another world. It was my first sight of another world. Colors. Ruby-colored trees and a sky of orange. Faces elongated like dirigibles, swollen like balloons.

Gabriele D'Annunzio lived near us, the man who wrote that, at any time, he preferred to keep a rendezvous with music rather than with a woman. He had a mistress who loved her dogs better than her children, who sent her children to the hospital but nursed her dogs.

I decided to become a painter. I was ten years old and wrote poetry. I made plans for the future. I planned to have an orphanage and take care of orphans. I would give my fortune to the poor. I would have no children of my own.

We spent a great deal of time with my father's wealthy patrons. I was instinctively jealous of Maruca, who was sixteen and seemed almost like a playmate to us. She was small and childlike, with tiny hands and feet. She was officially engaged to a young painter, yet I had an intuition she was loved by my father, an intuition which was confirmed when he married her many years later.

It was there my father deserted us forever. It was there that, when he announced he was leaving on a concert tour, I did not believe him, and I clung to his coat saying, "Don't leave us, Papa, don't leave us." I knew he was leaving permanently and not, as my mother thought, on another concert tour.

Years later, when I returned to Europe after ten years in America, my father was at Le Havre to meet me. I was returning to France for the first time. Life in America had changed me.

We talk in the train for three hours, all the way to Paris.

I see before me a stranger. He is a dandy. He smokes his cigarettes in a gold cigarette holder. He is dressed with utmost chic. He wears cream spats and a pearl pin on his tie and brilliantine in his hair, which is long but perfectly controlled. He carries a cane, and cream-colored gloves. This would not disturb me. But his talk . . .

There is something wrong with his talk.

It is artificial.

Perhaps living in America, with my mother, I had become more sincere.

He was preparing me for his marriage to Maruca.

Why could he not say: "I love her," and that is all. He was making an elaborate apologia, based on worldly reasons: a man could not live alone; she was wealthy, and would help "Grandmother" in Spain; his health would be better with a wife; his mistresses wasted too much of his time; etc. It sounded frivolous and trivial, mundane and superficial. It may have been that I expected too much, at least not salon talk.

In Paris I met Maruca, grand-couturier dress, a wave of perfume, a light girlish voice, an anxiety to please. She had been almost a playmate of ours! She was small, sweet, devoted. But I felt absolutely estranged, and more so when my father began to criticize my mother. The years of poverty, life in America, had created an abyss, and my father felt that this is what my mother had wanted. To estrange us from him. I had forgotten how to speak Spanish, remembered only half of my French. I gradually withdrew from the relationship.

Taxis are my wings. I cannot wait for anything. Wonderful to step off the little train at 3:25 in the smoke and noise and crowd of the city, to run downstairs, to ride dreaming through the city, to arrive at Allendy's just when he is about to pull open the black Chinese curtain. To run out again to the café where Henry is sitting with friends. The taxi is the magic chariot, passing without pain from one plane to another, a smooth course through the pearl-grey city, the opal that is Paris, answering my mother about the dyed sheets while I am still, on another line of the musical score, repeating in myself the fragments of my talk with Allendy. My mother is saying, "Fifille, do you like the binding for your last journal? It only cost twenty francs." I love my mother deeply now, her humanity, her goodness, her energy, her buoyancy. Joaquin says, "You are so quiet, are you ill?" He catches me smiling at myself, at the overfullness of my life: the music holder filled with books I have no time to read, George Grosz's caricatures, a book by Antonin Artaud, unanswered letters, a wealth of stuff; wishing I were like June, divinely indifferent to details, allowing safety pins on my dresses; but I am not. My closets are in beautiful Japanese order, everything in order, but all subordinate to a higher order, and at the moment of life, thrust into the background. The same dress can be crumpled and worn in bed, the same brushed hair thrown to the winds, safety pins and hairpins can fall, heels of shoes can break. When a higher moment comes, all details recede into the background. I never lose sight of the whole. An impeccable dress is made to be lived in, to be torn, wet, stained, crumpled.

Talking with Henry I experience the sensation that there will come a time when we will both understand everything, because our masculine and feminine minds are trying to meet, not to fight each other. June could only be perceived by way of madness. The territory of woman is that which lies untouched by the direct desire of man. Man attacks the vital center. Woman fills out the circumference.

By telephone from Henry: interview with Dr. Otto Rank 100 per cent successful. Rank has made a friend of him. Admires Henry. Says *Tropic of Cancer* does not represent all that he is, only an exaggerated aspect of him.

"I owe all this to you," says Henry.

I answer, "You owe it to what you are yourself."

I had told Henry that Rank would appreciate him. Henry was a little uneasy, but he trusted me. He needed the confidence that this challenge would give him.*

The Countess Lucie, who appears all the time in the pages of *Vogue,* shell-rose skin, pale gold hair, as slender as one can be without loss of voluptuous outline, green-eyed, resembling Brigitte Helm. *Très frileuse.* A big fire in the fireplace in the spring. White satin armchairs and divans. Wearing a negligee which recalls all the negligees of Odette. Her talk is strange, brittle, sharp-focused. She is starting a magazine with Edmond Jaloux; she will translate some of my writing for it. I look at the tall, tall windows covered with lace. Pillows under your feet, and life tasteless. She is so eager, so eager that I should accomplish a miracle. It is Lucie who has sought me out, who said, "I like so much your great calm, you have conquered life. I am at a stupid, vacillating period of my life. I would like to have your sureness. I am waiting for love, the core of a woman's life."

"Don't wait for it," I said. "Create a world, your world. Alone. Stand alone. Create. And then the love will come to you, then it comes to you. It was only when I wrote my first book that the world I wanted to live in opened to me."

"I feel doomed to being a spectator. I am a spectator of Jeanne's life. I adore Jeanne. But I want to find my own world. I can usually imagine people's surroundings. I cannot imagine yours."

"I can only tell you that my surroundings are *me*. Everything is

* For a detailed account see *Henry Miller: Letters to Anaïs Nin,* pp. 80–86, Putnam, 1965.

me, because I have rejected all conventions, the opinion of the world, all its laws. I am not obliged, as you and Jeanne are, to play a social role."

Lucie is floundering between art and society, Bohemianism and aristocracy, conventions and perversions. Because she is an artist she speaks glowingly of my walk, my hands, my gestures. I watch her opening her tulips so that they look less prim and more like exotic flowers. Would all this beauty have to be swept away for Lucie to find a life that tastes of life? What is the difference between us? I lived out my dreams. The dreams were only a beginning. They indicated the path to follow. This world which fascinated Proust, seduced him, I do not wish to live in. Lucie can come into mine.

I walk out lightly in the germinating, blossoming spring, hearing new sounds, the joyous new breathing of the earth, anticipating meeting Antonin Artaud tonight with the Allendys .

Allendy, by his wisdom, has dissolved my friendship. How can I tell him this, when he has begun to suffer from jealousy, and has begun to demand. The truth is, I find it impossible to resist the tremendous pleasure of charming, flirting, even when I am not in love. What a confession! It must resemble the elation ski champions feel before a beautiful, endless, white slope, or the swimmer faced with a mountainous wave, or the mountain climber looking at the highest peak. Ascensions, leaps, swift descents. But Allendy's wisdom has saved him from greater pain. I have begun to play, as he tried to teach me, to yield to caprices, whims, fancies. If, as Allendy wished in his fantasy, he had married me when he was young, what a life I would have led him!

The visitors have left. I am sitting alone in the studio. The Allendys came with Antonin Artaud. Antonin looked at the crystals. We walked through the moon-drenched garden and Antonin was strongly moved and in a romantic mood: "The beauty we think lost in the world is here. The house is magic, the garden is magic. It is all a fairy tale."

Artaud. Lean, taut. A gaunt face, with visionary eyes. A sardonic manner. Now weary, now fiery and malicious.

The theatre, for him, is a place to shout pain, anger, hatred, to enact the violence in us. The most violent life can burst from terror and death.

He talked about the ancient rituals of blood. The power of contagion. How we have lost the magic of contagion. Ancient religion knew how to enact rituals which made faith and ecstasy contagious. The power of ritual was gone. He wanted to give this to the theatre. Today nobody could share a feeling with anybody else. And Antonin Artaud wanted the theatre to accomplish this, to be at the center, a ritual which would awaken us all. He wanted to shout so people would be roused to fervor again, to ecstasy. No talking. No analysis. Contagion by acting ecstatic states. No objective stage, but a ritual in the center of the audience.

As he talked, I wondered whether he was right that it was the rituals we had lost, or whether it was that people had lost the power to feel, and that no ritual would give it to them.

Artaud is the surrealist whom the surrealists disavowed, the lean, ghostly figure who haunts the cafés but who is never seen at the counter, drinking or sitting among people, laughing. He is the drugged, contracted being who walks always alone, who is seeking to produce plays which are like scenes of torture.

His eyes are blue with languor, black with pain. He is all nerves. Yet he was beautiful acting the monk in love with Joan of Arc in the Carl Dreyer film. The deep-set eyes of the mystic, as if shining from caverns. Deep-set, shadowy, mysterious.

For Artaud, writing is painful too. It comes spasmodically and with a great strain. He is poor. He is in conflict with a world he imagines mocking and threatening. His intensity is brooding, rather terrifying.

In the garden, as we stood behind the others, he had cursed hallucinations and I had said, "In my world of hallucinations I am happy."

"I cannot even say that. It is torture for me. I make superhuman efforts to awake."

Allendy had told me that he had tried to free Artaud of the drug habit which was destroying him. All I could see that evening was his revolt against interpretations. He was impatient with their presence, as if they prevented him from exaltation. He talked with fire about the kabala, magic, myths, legends.

Allendy had told me that Artaud had talked with him several times, but had finally refused analysis. It was a formula, and yet he admitted it had helped him.

When Allendy first came to Louveciennes, he said, "I feel here as in a very distant country."

And Artaud had said, "Not at all, I feel at home here."

As I predicted, Henry is getting stimulated by Walter Lowenfels while I am being stimulated by Artaud, and it is only because I too am living multilaterally that I can understand Henry's new enthusiasm. His extravagant pages on Lowenfels are the counterpart of my extravagant pages on Artaud.

Artaud had written about his frightening solitude, so after reading his *L'Art et le Mort,* I gave him *House of Incest* and wrote this for him:

Dear Antonin Artaud:

You who have used the language of nerves and the perception of the nerves, who have known what it is to lie down and feel that it is not a body which is lying down, flesh, blood, muscles, but a hammock suspended in space swarming with hallucinations, may find here an answer to the constellations your words create, and the fragmentation of your feelings, an interweaving, a parallelism, an accompaniment, an echo, an equal speed in vertigoes, a resonance. A resonance to your *"grande ferveur pensante,"* to your *"fatigue du commencement du monde."* What is essential is not to feel that one's words fall into a void. Not one of your words in *L'Art et le Mort* has fallen into a void. And you can see, perhaps, in these pages how I prepared a world to receive you, by an absence of walls, absorbent lighting, reflecting crystals, drugged nerves, visionary eyes, dreaming fevers. This book, though written before I knew you, was written to synchronize with your vision of the world.

Letter from Artaud:

I had intended to write you at great length about the manuscript which you gave me to read, and in which I feel a spiritual tension, a sharp selection of language and expression similar to my ways of thinking. But these days I am literally obsessed, haunted, and uniquely preoccupied by a conference I must give on Thursday on The Theatre and the Plague, a hard and elusive theme, and one which forces my thoughts into a movement completely contrary to my usual mode of thinking. Besides, I read English very badly, almost not at all, and you write a particularly difficult English, complex and selective: so my problem is doubled and tripled. Please excuse me for not communicating with you more fully. I will do so as soon as my lecture is over. Meanwhile believe in my most grateful feelings for all you have already done for my Theatre project which I hope you can give your care to actively and as a *"realizatrice."*

The journal as itinerary. Artaud did not understand why I preserved the journal in iron boxes. He is the very opposite. He preserves nothing. He owns nothing. Henry, when I first met him, owned nothing. I have a sense of destiny, of time, of history. Henry says he would no longer have the courage to travel penniless on the open road. He is tired of external adventures. His intense collecting of his notes, binding them, designing charts, proves that.

I am doing research for Allendy on the Black Death, for a book he is writing.

Henry talks about schizophrenia, the universe of death, the Hamlet-Faust cycle, Destiny, the Soul, macromicrocosm, megalopolitan civilization, surrender to biology. I feel he should be writing only about his life, not ideas. Why does he want to appear to be a thinker, a philosopher? Or is he seeking to put his world in order so he can make a place for himself? Or is he under the influence of Lowenfels and Fraenkel? Henry is at his desk, wrestling with D. H. Lawrence, delving into hills of notes, sighing, smoking, cursing, typing, drinking red wine. But he hears me tell Fred about the research I have been doing for Allendy, *Chronicles of the Plague,* and of the violent life which suddenly burst from the terror of death. It was evidently a rich and fecund period. Henry began to listen, thought this fitted into his scheme, too, and so fired questions at me, very pleased with the data, the information which strengthened his thesis. He uses everything.

His new phase is philosophic. Henry talks about his Bohemian life with June, chaos, as a phase, not as his true nature. He likes order. He says all great artists like order. A profound order. So Henry is now trying to master chaos.

"Joyce," says Henry, "stands for the soul of the big city, dynamics, atheism, gigantism, frustration, an archeologist of dead souls."

We talked about Lawrence and death. I read Henry my comments. "Did you write that? Did you write that?" In amazement. "Why, that's the last word that can be said . . ."

Feminine vision is usually myopic. I do not think mine is. But I do not understand abstract ideas.

Before our talk we had been to see a movie with Lil Dagover, one of Henry's enthusiasms. A bad movie, but her statuesque, voluptuous body makes him dream. After the movie she appeared in person, mincing, attenuated, artificial, slick, and disillusioned him completely. Perhaps in a fury against the disillusion, he began to talk wildly. We were sitting in a Russian café. Women in evening dress, ugly, but Henry was tempted to bite their bare shoulders.

Henry believes he is passing through a great transition from romantic interest in life to classical interest in ideas. A year ago, when Fraenkel said to Henry, "People are ideas," Henry had asked: "Why ideas? Why symbols?"

He has become a philosopher. We sit in cafés and drink, but he continues to talk about Spengler. I wonder why. Is he trying to organize his experience, to situate it? I am proud of his activity, yet I feel cheated of the adventurous Henry. Of his underworld, his gaudy tribulations, bawdy nights, of his search for pleasure, curiosities, his life in the streets, his contact with everyone, anyone.

I do not miss Allendy at all. How wise he was to doubt my affection. The transfer is ended, the dependency. What remains is gratitude, and an acknowledgment of his wisdom. But wisdom is a swifter way of reaching death. I postpone death by living, by suffering, by error, by risking, by giving, by losing. Allendy has chosen to die quickly, early, for the sake of dominating life. The romantic submits to life, the classicist dominates it.

He saved himself from pain. He is dead now, living only through others, the voyeur sitting behind the chaise longue, behind the upholstered back which muffles his presence, and I can still hear his pencil noting down the life of others. One can live the life of others, too, but only if one is living one's own; because when we are alive we are able to see, hear, sense, understand more, penetrate other lives. His indirect participation . . . watching alcoves, night clubs, dance halls, bars, cafés, night life, love affairs of others . . .

He gave me courage to go on living. To this I bring tributes. But I only gave him sadness and regrets, yearnings, a few moments of madness. Pride in his insight and his skill, for he recreated me.

Schoolroom of the Sorbonne.

Allendy and Artaud were sitting at the big desk. Allendy introduced Artaud. The room was crowded. The blackboard made a strange backdrop. People of all ages, followers of Allendy's lectures on New Ideas.

The light was crude. It made Artaud's eyes shrink into darkness, as they are deep-set. This brought into relief the intensity of his gestures. He looked tormented. His hair, rather long, fell at times over his forehead. He has the actor's nimbleness and quickness of gestures. His face is lean, as if ravaged by fevers. His eyes do not seem to see the people. They are the eyes of a visionary. His hands are long, long-fingered.

Beside him Allendy looks earthy, heavy, grey. He sits at the desk, massive, brooding. Artaud steps out on the platform, and begins to talk about "The Theatre and the Plague."

He asked me to sit in the front row. It seems to me that all he is asking for is intensity, a more heightened form of feeling and living. Is he trying to remind us that it was during the Plague that so many marvelous works of art and theatre came to be, because, whipped by the fear of death, man seeks immortality, or to escape, or to surpass himself? But then, imperceptibly almost, he let go of the thread we were following and began to act out dying by plague. No one quite knew when it began. To illustrate his conference, he was acting out an agony. *"La Peste"* in French is so much more terrible than "The Plague" in English. But no word could describe what Artaud acted on the platform of the Sorbonne. He forgot about his conference, the theatre, his ideas, Dr. Allendy sitting there, the public, the young students, his wife, professors, and directors.

His face was contorted with anguish, one could see the perspiration dampening his hair. His eyes dilated, his muscles became cramped, his fingers struggled to retain their flexibility. He made one feel the parched and burning throat, the pains, the fever, the fire in the guts. He was in agony. He was screaming. He was delirious. He was enacting his own death, his own crucifixion.

At first people gasped. And then they began to laugh. Everyone was laughing! They hissed. Then one by one, they began to leave, noisily, talking, protesting. They banged the door as they left. The only ones who did not move were Allendy, his wife, the Lalous, Marguerite. More protestations. More jeering. But Artaud went on, until the last gasp. And stayed on the floor. Then when the hall had emptied of all but his small group of friends, he walked straight up to me and kissed my hand. He asked me to go to the café with him.

Everyone else had something to do. We all parted at the door of the Sorbonne, and Artaud and I walked out in a fine mist. We walked, walked through the dark streets. He was hurt, wounded, baffled by the jeering. He spat out his anger. "They always want to hear *about;* they want to hear an objective conference on 'The Theatre and the Plague,' and I want to give them the experience itself, the plague itself, so they will be terrified, and awaken. I want to awaken them. They do not realize *they are dead.* Their death is total, like deafness, blindness. This is agony I portrayed. Mine, yes, and everyone who is alive."

The mist fell on his face, he pushed his hair away from his forehead. He looked taut and obsessed, but now he spoke quietly. We sat in the Coupole. He forgot the conference. "I have never found anyone who felt as I did. I have been an opium addict for fifteen years. It was first given to me when I was very young, to calm some terrible pains in my head. I feel sometimes that I am not writing, but describing the struggles with writing, the struggles of birth."

He recited poetry. We talked about form, the theatre, his work.

"You have green, and sometimes violet eyes."

He grew gentle and calm. We walked again, in the rain.

For him, the plague was no worse than death by mediocrity, death by commercialism, death by corruption which surrounded us. He wanted to make people aware that they were dying. To force them into a poetic state.

"The hostility only proved that you disturbed them," I said.

But what a shock to see a sensitive poet confronting a hostile public. What brutality, what ugliness in the public!

It makes me sad that Allendy helped me to live and that I have not been able to help him. I hate to abandon him to his narrow, constricted world. I would have liked him to know joy. He once described his feeling that between him and life there was always a veil. Last night I hated to see his magic fading. It is as if, between his appearance at Joaquin's concert and today, he had taken several more leaps away from life. Perhaps last night at the Sorbonne he realized he was dying; that he will continue to send forth from his small book-lined room timid neurotics to live and love in the world; and that he will be left sitting behind his chaise longue, taking notes, while everything he wanted will pass him by: adventure, eroticism, travel, ecstasy, high living.

So last night at the Sorbonne, his magic wavered, flickered, paled, and sank.

My father's letter: "My daughter Anaïs, my darling . . ." I can laugh at the theatrical D'Annunzio phrases. My theatrical father. Didn't he and D'Annunzio hunt the same mistresses, singers and actresses, although D'Annunzio was older and more cynical and, according to my father, not always able to carry out his fervent promises as my father was. And yet, according to the stories told, too, so capable of talking enchantingly to women that they forgave him, and often words and poetry were substituted for action without their noticing. I still remember his leaning over me when I was a child, in Arcachon, and observing with a flowery bow: "What passionate eyes she has, watch out!"

But I do miss Allendy. I let him guide my life, judge it, balance it. The period of dependence was sweet. He was God, conscience, absolver, priest, sage. He freed me of guilt and fear. But when he became human, he used his power to separate me from my artist life, to thrust me again into the stifling, narrow bourgeois life.

Now he warns me against Artaud. He tells me Artaud is a drug addict and a homosexual.

I have no guide. My father? I think of him as someone my own age. All the others are my children. It saddens me to have become again an independent woman. It was a deep joy to depend on Allendy's insight, his guidance.

Today Bernard Steele came, Artaud's young publisher. He is also the publisher of Dr. Otto Rank. He brought Rank's *Don Juan and His Double*. The night I met him at the Allendys, he had been so ironic and flippant that I had disliked him. Today, sitting in the garden, he looked tender, alive, exposed, his eyes wide open and drinking in everything with a tremor. He had mocked D. H. Lawrence and had been ironic about Artaud. The wind is warm. The little brook rustles through the old ivy. The wild strawberries are perfuming the air. We are sitting in the sun. The bottle of sherry gleams like a jewel.

Bernard Steele plays the guitar. He is intelligent but paradoxical, full of contrasts and contradictions. He is a musician seeking to appear as an intellectual. As an intellectual he is not logical. He is refined and unhappy. He does not deceive me. He is not interested in publishing, or in literature, but in living his own life.

Marguerite and I are completely open with each other. Our confidences have taken the place of talks with Allendy.

She made me laugh today.

She wanted to free herself from Allendy without hurting his feelings. She did not know how. To arouse her jealousy, perhaps, he told her that he had a "legitimate" mistress who would be very angry if she knew about Marguerite.

"There had never been, in all of Allendy's confidences, any question of a mistress. He had told me that his life was empty because of his last experience with a neurotic woman, which had frightened him. I sensed him free. I know his relation to his wife is purely fraternal. I was putting on my stockings when he said this. I stopped to make some gay remark. But later this statement returned to me and inspired my psychoanalytical way out of my situation.

"When I began to invent the 'schema' by which I was going to free myself of meeting Allendy on Thursday without harming him, I was making an abstract play. But by the time I told Allendy all this, I began so vividly to imagine how I would feel if I loved Allendy and discovered that he was dividing his love between me and another woman, that I became very emotional and thoroughly sincere.

"Allendy's eyes became soft. 'I understand too well. You need absolutism.' Then I was moved by his goodness. He said he knew all this before, he knew I was not a woman who could play with love, but then he lost his insight, lost his head. I could not hold that against him. He would be my friend for life. He would give up the pleasure he took with me.

"I became aware that I had moved Allendy with a most fraudulent case, which I was beginning to believe in! It was becoming increasingly difficult to remember that Allendy had no mistress, because I was moved by my own story, and Allendy's compassionate interpretation of it.

"Then he begged for Thursday's meeting as a good-bye meeting, promising me a big scene, a drama, promising me violence, since I liked drama. His humor and sense of play came to the surface. He was almost joyous, almost radiant. His eyes flashed in a dangerous manner and he said: 'I'll beat you, as your father did. You deserve it. You have played with my feelings.' Now the theme of beating recurred so often in Allendy's talk that when he mentioned it today with his eyes flashing, I was impressed. My curiosity was aroused. Thursday promises to be interesting."

Marguerite did meet Allendy at the Métro Cadet. She was late and Allendy thought she was not coming.

"I said I would like a drink but Allendy did not approve of this. He said he never took anything in the afternoon. It would upset his habits. The room this time was all in blue, the style of Madame de Pompadour, the alcove lined with sky-blue velvet. Allendy did not kiss me. He sat on the edge of the bed and said: 'Now you will be punished for everything, for enslaving me and then wanting to abandon me.' And he took out of his pocket a whip!

"Now I had not counted on a real whip. My father used his hands. I didn't know how to react to it. I liked Allendy's fierceness, his angry eyes, his will. But when I saw the whip I felt like laughing. He ordered me to undress. I undressed slowly. I had to control an irresistible desire to laugh!

"Oh, Anaïs, it was such bad theatre! It was Grand Guignol. A dime novel. What does one do when one is suddenly in the middle of a dime novel? *La Vie Scandaleuse de Sacher-Masoch*. When Allendy tried a few lashes, I laughed. It was not exciting. It was only my pride which was offended. I was laughing at the absurdity, the unreality. When my father beat me it was real. My mother would sit sobbing in the next room. I refused to cry.

"Allendy said he would reduce me to a rag, that I would beg and crawl and do everything he told me. He used the whip only once, and I stood where he could not touch me again. He thought I was playing the game.

"And then he said this, which was right out of the cheap books they sell on the quays: 'You can scream your head off, nobody pays any attention to screams in this house,' and at this classic line I began to laugh uncontrollably, and Allendy thought I was laughing to tantalize him, egg him on.

"Just before we met, Allendy had said to me that his work was growing monotonous; that it was sad to see how human beings were all alike—reacted the same way at the same moment; that it was always the same pattern. I remembered this when I felt the whip lashes warming my body, *faute de mieux*. Allendy looked satisfied. He kept saying that he felt good, that he felt wonderful, that he knew I would like it, that it *brought out the savage* in him. *Un sauvage pour rire!* The wise man who must arouse the savage in himself with a whip!

"But I acted well so that, in the taxi, he had a recurrence of 'passion' (I speak relatively) and he was joyous. He said that no one would ever imagine such a scene possible, nobody. Not even my novelist father! This idea delighted him. Poor Allendy did not understand that all I craved were the flagellations of real passion and enslavement by authentic savages only. Allendy said: 'This way you reach a kind of vertigo.' "

After we laughed, we became serious. I said to Marguerite: "The question is, have men died today because they have tampered with the sources of life, or do they tamper with the sources of life because they are dead and wish to find its springs again, to create an artificial control of the sources of life?"

The other day Henry came with William Bradley, the literary agent and friend of many writers.

Immediate sympathy.

Bradley was enthusiastic about me. Talked to Henry in the train back. Fervently.

Today he telephoned me. Has read my childhood journal. Says it is remarkable—naïveté—charm and depths. Amazing child. Quaintness. Everything. I was upset and cannot remember all he said. His voice was warm and expressive. He and his wife had laughed and wept over the journal.

Artaud wrote me:

I have thought a great deal about all you said on my conference. I did come away with a feeling of total failure, but I do not feel the same way today. I have, since then, heard many reactions to it and I believe that it was effective. But I also know what I intended to do and what fantastic concept I had wished to reach when I first planned it. And summing it all, it inspired anxiety, it disturbed without satisfying and without taking people's intelligence where I wanted to take them. You knew, but *beyond* my words, and not because of them.

One thing amazes me, judging from the manuscript which you gave me, *House of Incest,* you seem to have an awareness of subtle states, almost secret ones, which I have only felt at the cost of enormous nervous suffering which I did not seek out. I am very curious to know by what science you reach the core of psychic states.

Forgive me for writing you so late, but I have work to do for my publisher on a book on Heliogabalus which I have just decided to write. I work at it all day and have also to do much research in libraries. That is why I have not yet telephoned you.

For this work on Heliogabalus I seek knowledge of Chaldean astrology (the true one) and it would make me happy to talk about all this with you.

I have holes in my shoes. I do not pay my bills. I try to finish *House of Incest*.

Henry on my writing:

Elaborate! That is the only way out of these watertight abstractions of yours. Break through them, divest them of their mystery and allow them to flow. Now and then you break them and rush out with convincing power and eloquence. But it is as if you had first to break diamonds inside of you, powder them to dust, and then liquefy them, a terrific piece of alchemy. I think again that one of the reasons you have lodged yourself so firmly in the diary is because you fear to test your tangible self with the world. You are producing gems.

I think Henry is right about elaborating. But I think he does not understand that it is because I have a natural flow in the diary: what I produce outside is a distillation, the myth, the poem. The elaboration is here. It is the gem made out of this natural outpouring. Shouldn't people prefer the gems?

"I've gone beyond Lawrence," Henry said.

Henry retracts the criticism of "abstraction" as applying only to the beginning of *House of Incest*. He attacks the extreme reserve and mystery of the phrases, asking for more explicitness. But that is poetry, I protest. Poetry is an abstraction. I am not sure Henry understands *House of Incest*. Soon I will see a parody of it. There is a paradox between the seriousness of his attitude towards his writing and the burlesque quality of it, and I puzzle about this. At times, parts of his writing I find of the highest buffoonery; he is surprised that I laugh.

Artaud a tortured being. Irritable. Stutters at times. Always sits in some hidden corner of the room, sunk into the deepest chair, as into a cavern, as if on the defensive.

He relaxed slowly as we talked. He began to talk flowingly. His talk so tenuous. It gives a strange feeling, as if one were witnessing the very process of a birth of a thought, a feeling. One can see the nebula, the unformed mass moving, struggling for shape, the careful, precise, meticulous, scrupulous effort made not to betray its meaning by a careless word. He doubts all explicitness. Thought has to be surrounded, spied upon, captured, like some elusive matter.

"I have never been able to talk as I think, to anyone. With most people you can only talk about ideas, not the channel through which these ideas pass, the atmosphere in which they bathe, the subtle essence which escapes as one clothes them."

I said, "They are not ideas at all, they are sensations. It is sensation no one can describe, the perception of the senses."

I was so moved when he explained his difficulties and struggles to write, his excessive sensitivity, impressionability, his incapacity to enjoy. Everything filtered through pain, exacerbated nerves. It was not inertia, or death, or insensibility, but an excess of every faculty, of every sense. The weight he must lift, the sunrise seen through fog, a bilious fog. The walls of the absolute against which he breaks his head. He cannot live within the relative, the everyday, it is always the extreme, a tearing of the being.

I am not sure I understand the excess of his torments.

"In my self-created world of dreams, nightmares, hallucinations, I am at ease," I said. "I am glad to be in it. The most terrifying images which haunt me, once I have written them, no longer frighten me."

"I do not have even that relief," said Artaud. "Those regions you say I reach, I get no satisfaction from reaching them. It is all torture. I make superhuman efforts to awake . . ."

"But why awake?" I asked. "Why? I prefer my dreaming world, my nightmares, to reality. I love those houses which fall into the river."

"Yes," said Artaud. "I observed you were satisfied in your world. That is rare. I sense great abstractions in *House of Incest,* an orchestration in writing, a force, an intensity. Translate a few parts of it for me, I don't read English very well."

We talked about our fears, listed them. His were of madness, of being unable to write, or to talk, or to communicate with others (he wrote that no one had ever felt more keenly the inadequacy of language). Was it that what he wanted to tell was so difficult? Or that he had an impediment to writing itself? Or that he did not know when he had succeeded in saying it? But that is the struggle of every writer, I said. Every writer feels he is struggling with an inchoate, formless mass, fails to say the greater part of what he feels.

He is in great need of sympathy.

We are born under the same sign.

He left me to have his Wednesday evening dinner with the Allendys.

Dr. Otto Rank on *Art and Artist:*

The neurotic, no matter whether productive or obstructed, suffers fundamentally from the fact that he cannot or will not accept himself, his own individuality, his own personality. On one hand he criticizes himself to excess, on the other he idealizes himself to excess, which means that he makes too great demands on himself and his completeness, so that failing to attain leads only to more self-criticism. If we take this thwarted type, as we may do for our purpose, and compare him to the artist, it is at once clear that the artist is, in a sense, the antithesis to the self-critical neurotic type. Not that the artist does not criticize himself, but by accepting his personality he not only fulfils that for which the neurotic is striving in vain, but goes far beyond it. The precondition, then, of the creative personality is not only acceptance, but its actual glorification of itself.

Cannot or will not accept himself. How can I accept a limited definable self when I feel, in me, all possibilities? Allendy may have said: "This is the core," but I never feel the four walls around the substance of the self, the core. I feel only space. Illimitable space. The effect of analysis is wearing off in this way. The clear, stark vision I had of myself is getting lost again by my obedience to the life of the imagination in which I chose to believe. The veil was sundered, and soon after, I covered the truth again. Eddies of illusion engulf reality again. I have accepted a self which is unlimited. What I imagine is as true as what is. I want to get lost in mystery again. Wisdom engulfed by life.

The artist goes beyond the neurotic. He glorifies his personality.

Henry has done that. I do it through June, portrayed in *House of Incest*.

Henry has an intuition about this. He said, "The first day I saw you, I felt and believed you perverse, decadent, as June was. I still feel in you an immense yieldingness, I feel there is no limit to you, to what you might be or do. An absence of boundary, a yielding that is limitless in experience."

But why call this perverse? Henry has it too.

What interests me is not the core but the potentialities of this core to multiply and expand infinitely. The diffusion of the core, its suppleness and elasticity, rebound, ramifications. Spanning, encompassing, space-devouring, star-trodden journeys, everything around and between the core.

My father writes me a beautiful letter:

Your letter, your beautiful letter, and the reading of your child diary (a marvelous gift) were for me not a revelation but a justification of the faith I had in you, my hopes and illusions for you, of my attachment to you, and this is the same period during which you mourned for me around a Christmas tree. You are not only my daughter, you are my daughter doubly, through flesh, and through the spirit. You are like me, a dreamer, excessively idealistic and exalted. The inevitable catastrophe of my departure. Oh, how you clung to me that day, how you kissed me. How you wept. You must have had a presentiment that it would be a separation of many years, of the great sorrow which would from now on weigh down our life.

He stresses harmony, beauty, love. I am overjoyed at our coming meeting, meeting the one I called my double, my twin. Which one, in this case, is the conscience of the other, the haunting double of the unfulfilled ideal? I have found my father again, lost many years ago when my mother took us first to Spain to our grandparents, to my father's mother and father. The father was an old general and a teacher, director of the first non-Catholic school in Spain, a man who wrote pamphlets against bullfighting; the mother an angelic, sacrificing, sad wife, the one who had spoiled my father as much as she could (sewing all night to pay for his rental of a bicycle). She was the model for the wife he wanted, abnegation, adoration, respect, selflessness.

There, in a typically Spanish apartment opening on a courtyard, all tiles, with short swinging doors between the rooms to allow the air to blow through, to keep the place fresh, with shutters closed against the sun, pictures of the Virgin, rubber plants in the corners, lace doilies on the chairs, we stayed, where my father felt he could raise us by remote control, and where letters began to arrive telling my mother how to bring us up.

We did not stay with them very long. Grandfather was a tyrant, and a miser. He counted the *garbanzos* (the big yellow beans which were our daily fare) and worried about us and my mother's independence.

We moved to a small apartment of our own, clean and new. Barcelona was gay and lively. From the balcony I could look at the sea and at people walking by, hear the music from the cafés. I began to write, poems, memories. I went to a convent and learned Catalan. Letters of instructions came. In Barcelona I did not feel my father's absence as final. He might come any moment, and we saw his family, his parents, his sister, my cousins. It was his native land. I was learning his language.

I never knew whether it was my mother who wanted to leave, whether she wanted to take us far away from his influence. The story told was that my aunts came to visit and, with a Cuban prejudice against Spain, criticized everything and said my mother would be better off in America where they could watch over her and she would be near her sisters. America was a better country for a woman alone with three children. She could obtain free schooling for us. And soon we were off, uprooted from a place I liked, friends, family, school, a smiling happy city of sun and sea and music and cafés open all night.

The diary began as a diary of a journey, to record everything for my father. It was written for him, and I had intended to send it to him. It was really a letter, so he could follow us into a strange land, know about us. It was also to be an island, in which I could take refuge in an alien land, write French, think my thoughts, hold on to my soul, to myself.

I find my father again when I am a woman. When he comes to me, he who marked my childhood so deeply, I am a full-blown woman. I understand my father as a human being. He is again the man who is also a child.

The father I imagined cruel, strong, hero, famous musician, lover of women, triumphant, is soft, feminine, vulnerable, imperfect. I lose my terror and my pain. I meet him again when I know that there is no possibility of fusion between father and daughter, only between man and woman.

Henry says this will reconcile me to God.

My father comes when I no longer need a father.

I am walking into a Coney Island trick house. The ground gives way under my feet. It is the ironies which swallow the ground and leave one dizzy and stranded. Irony of loves never properly timed, of tragedies that should not be tragedies, of passions which miss each other as if aimed by blind men, of blind cruelties and even blinder loves, of incongruities and deceptive fulfillments. Every realization is not a culmination but a delusion. The pattern seems to come to an end and it is only another knot.

My father comes when I have gone beyond him; he is given to me when I no longer need him, when I am free of him. In every fulfillment there is a mockery which runs ahead of me like a gust of wind, always ahead. My father comes when I have an artist writer to write with, a guide I wept for in Allendy, a protector, brother, symbolic children, friends, a world, books written. Yet the child in me could not die as it should have died, because according to legends it must find its father again. The old legends knew, perhaps, that in absence the father becomes glorified, deified, eroticized, and this outrage against God the Father has to be atoned for. The human father has to be confronted and recognized as human, as a man who created a child and then, by his absence, left the child fatherless and then Godless. The absurd disorder in time, in answering of needs, in fulfillment, must not be revealed to human beings except in this book, intended to be hidden, on a night when a child died from the excess of its expectancies and the circuitous, delayed, mortally mistimed way life has of answering its demands.

Allendy once said: "Each book I write is a compensation for something I have not had, and I am so keen on the achievement, *pour arriver au but,* that when the book is written I do not enjoy the victory, I do not stop to enjoy my victory. I have never enjoyed my achievement."

Allendy, with his watch chain across his dark grey vest, his noble bearing, looking tall and impressive among his books, talking wisely, restored to his atmosphere, his kingdom.

His words affect me, and I felt they applied to me on the eve of my father's return. My life has been one long strain to create, to make myself interesting, to develop my gifts, to make my father proud of me, a desperate and anxious ascension to efface and destroy a haunting insecurity created by the conviction that my father left because he was disappointed in me, because he did not love me; and that the woman he loved was Maruca. Always aiming higher, accumulating loves to compensate for the first loss. Loves, books, creations. Shedding yesterday's woman to pursue a new vision.

I forget to enjoy all I have—incredible treasures. I am traveling again, emotionally, restless while there is land to discover, lives un-lived, men not known. What madness. I want to enjoy. I want to stop and enjoy. This will be the journal of my enjoyment.

Letter to Henry:

Long talk with Bradley. The secret of Bradley is that when he was young, he wrote a book of poems (thought daring at the time) and that behind his work lies a wistful interest in writing. He loves to help, direct, criticize and influence writers. He is really fine. Dreams of playing the role X played with Conrad. Supported and sustained Conrad. That is his vision of his role. He loves to handle and work on manuscripts and really participates in all that is done with a great secret satisfaction. The type of man that every non-artist should aspire to become if he has enough humility and the power to abdicate and serve. I admire Bradley for that. . . .

Bradley was curious about my life. Imagines me sheltered, preciously unknown, discovered by him. His face fell when I said my life was eventful. He did not want it to be so. Nobody wants me to live, to get known. Like a guitar for chamber music only. You are the only one who said: "Get out, get a little tougher." You dared me. It is you who are right. The damned journal should end Wednesday when my father comes to Louveciennes. But my life is only beginning. I love the idea of anonymity for the journal. It fits my earlier desire to remain unknown. It is wonderful, the secrecy again and always.

It is all so incredible, this interest in my journal, the presentation to Alfred Knopf (who rejected my book on Lawrence). Bradley concerned about my health because of the mention of handicaps in the early journals. Asking if his visit tired me. The concern of the world. I am frightened by his praise, and highly nervous. Moved by his kindness, generosity, thoughtfulness. Bradley looked at June's face in the photograph and said she looked fictitious, unreal, false. Her personality was all acting and pretending and empty of core. "I'm against moral make-up," he said, cannily.

Before such people as Bradley, I begin to imagine that I am also a fake—that maybe all my journals, books, and personality are fakes. When I'm admired I think I am duping the world. I begin to add my lies and to tremble. I have to say to myself: "Either I am just a cleverer liar and actress than June, or I'm real." So many people believe in me instinctively, suspicious and intuitive people. Simple people who hate artificiality above all, severe, moral people. And now Bradley.

And I see the question of my sincerity could easily drive me insane if I studied it continuously. My imagination entangles me hopelessly. I lose myself. What distresses me is that I seem to play on the feelings of people. June reproached Henry for playing the role of the "victim" in their relationship. I have often wondered whether June was not the sincerest one of all because so easily discovered.

[May, 1933]

My father came.

I expected the man of the photographs, a more transparent face. A face less furrowed, less carved, less masklike, and at the same time I liked the new face, the depth of the lines, the firmness of the jaw, the femininity and charm of the smile, all the more startling in contrast to the tanned, almost parchment-toned skin. A smile with a forceful dimple which was not a dimple but a scar from sliding down a stairway banister and piercing his cheek with an ornament when he was a child. The neatness and compactness of the figure, grace, vital gestures, ease, youthfulness. A gust of imponderable charm. A supreme, open egotism. Webs of talk, defenses against unuttered accusations, justifying his life, his love of the sun, of the south of France, of luxury, preoccupation with the opinion of others, fear of criticism, susceptibility, continuous play-acting, wit and articulateness, violence of images, the lusty and vivid imagery of the Spanish language transposed into French.

He had come to France, had studied with Vincent d'Indy, had been made the youngest professor at the Schola Cantorum, when I was born. A childlike, disarming smile. Always charm. The predominance of charm. Undercurrents of puerility, unreality. A man who had pampered himself (or been pampered by women?), cottoned himself against the deep pains of living by luxury, by salon life, by aesthetics, yet preoccupied with the fear of destructiveness, compelled to expand, obeying his quest of sensuality, of pleasure, having found no other way to obtain his desires but by deception. A passion for aesthetics and for creation. Concerts, composition, books, articles. Research into lost and rare music, discovery of talented people, introducing them to the public (The Aguilar Quartet, La Argentina).

Was the source of feeling dried up by pretenses, play-acting, by egotism? Would my double be my evil double? He incarnated all the dangers of my illusory life, my inventing of situations, my deceptions, my faults. In some way they seemed a caricature of me, because mine seemed motivated by deep feelings, and his by more superficial and worldly aims. The public played a major role in his life, the concert stage, the critics, fashionable and titled friends, salons, and manners. Something very human and warm in me (my mother?) lived by truer values in people. He cared about display, dress, money. There was an unawareness of others. Almost a cynicism.

"And now you write and speak a language I do not know. I don't know what life in America has done to you. Your mother was very clever in taking you so far away, trying to estrange us. She knew I did not like America, feared it, even. That I did not know English. *Le pays du 'bluff'*."

"But you could have come to see us, you could have come on a concert tour. Many people told me that you had been invited."

"Yes, it is true, I could have come when you were still children. America intimidated me. Too different from all I cared about."

I know that he is looking for resemblances.

"Do you like to dress well?"

"I like to dress with originality, to suit myself, not the fashion."

"Do you like gardening?"

"With gloves on!" We laughed.

When he describes himself, I see that he draws an idealized image. He wants to believe himself kind, altruistic, charitable, generous. Yet so many people have commented on his selfishness, his not sending money to his mother in Spain, and talking about not being able to send it, while smoking gold-tipped cigarettes, wearing silk shirts, driving an American de luxe car, and living in the fashionable quarter of Paris in a private house.

We are both looking into mirrors, to catch reflections of blood twinship.

We are punctual, a stressed, marked characteristic. We need order around us, in the house, in the life, although we live by irresistible impulses, as if the order in the closets, in our papers, in our books, in our photographs, in our souvenirs, in our clothes could preserve us from chaos in our feelings, loves, in our work.

Indifference to food, sobriety; but this, we admit, is part of the war against a threatening fragility.

"*Will*," says my father, drawing himself up. The will to counterbalance the sudden abandonment to sensations, lyrical flights and fantasies. He, too, suffers from romanticism, quixotism, cynicism, naïveté, cruelty, schizophrenia, multiplicity of selves, *dédoublement,* and is bewildered as to how to make a synthesis.

We smile with sympathy at each other.

As a Spanish man, demanding of women only blind devotion, submission, warmth, love, protection, he is amazed to find in a woman a spirit like his own, adventurous, rebellious, explorative, unconventional. Amazed, and at first delighted, for every narcissist dreams of a twin. No Dorian Gray in a painting, but a father like myself, a daughter like myself. The double who will answer questions. Do you feel this way, or that way? You too? Well, we are not so strange, or so lonely. There are two of us. The fragments of our life which do not fit into a desired image, we discard. But I cull them in the diary, and I cannot forget them. My father forgets them.

My father clings to the woman who holds him together by her faith—innocent and wholehearted Maruca.

But he is not guiltless. He spent an hour explaining why he had had to go to the south of France for four months. I had not asked him to justify his trip! Long explanations on the state of his health, the hard Paris winter, the exhaustion. Why should he not go to the south of France if he wishes to? There must be something else behind this which he is covering up. He probably went to meet a mistress.

When he walked up to me, talking and laughing, he does not seem like a father, but a youthful man of infinite charm and fascination, labyrinthian, fluid, uncapturable as water.

"We must always tell each other the truth."

What an unusual request, my dear Father.

"We are both very proud," he says.

We are gay, playful. We do not reveal our anxieties, our fears, our weaknesses.

"I wondered which side won in you, before I saw you, the French or the Spanish. You have never looked more Spanish than right now."

Why did he seem so severe to me as a child? To his children, at home, he showed an over-critical, ever-dissatisfied self. Displeased, discontented. No sign of feeling, no demonstrations of tenderness. This smiling, radiant, charming father was for visitors. So I am a visitor now. I see no sign of the criticalness which seemed always at work to detect and underline the flaw, the error, the weakness.

I had always lived not to be my father.

Through the years I had made a portrait of him which I had sought to destroy in myself. On the basis of a few resemblances, one fears total resemblance. I did not want to be him. That may be why I sought a more sincere life, real values, disregarded the outer forms, took flight from society, wealthy or aristocratic people.

We love music.

We love the sea.

We dread squalor. (But I never pursued money to avoid it.) I was unflinchingly poor many times. I can make real sacrifices. I never calculated. I am capable of immense devotions. I set about scrupulously to destroy in myself any over-attachment to luxury, beauty. Frivolity. Grand hotels. Cars. Salons.

My father is a dandy. When we were children, his cologne, and his luxurious shirts, were more important than a toy for us, or clothes for my mother.

When he left, I felt as if I had seen the Anaïs I never wanted to be.

Antonin Artaud. We talked with passion about our habit of condensation, rigorous sifting, our quest of the essential, love of essence, and distillations, in life, in literature. And not a premeditated effort, simply faithfulness to our way of thought and feeling. We do not consciously try to condense. It is a natural tendency. When we condense and extract essences, we are approximating the true and normal functioning of our minds. I never saw as clearly as with Artaud what the meaning of poetry is: it is an abstraction, to match allegorical patterns.

We discussed analysis. Artaud was bitter about the pragmatic use of it, said it only serves to liberate people sexually; whereas it should be used only as a metaphysical discipline, to reach wholeness, etc.

Artaud said, "I have never needed it because I have never entirely lost my equilibrium. I can remain lucid and objective about my states of being, describe them. We are born in the same sign, but I feel you are more elusive. I do not believe you are *good,* in the strict sense of the word. I think you do good out of a voluptuous joy in creation."

He talked fluently, easily. He had lost some of that hard, taut bitterness, his suspicion, his persecution mania. He has a deep lack of self-confidence. He always thinks people do not want him, that he is interrupting my work when he calls me. He was touched by my interest.

When Henry the prose writer says, "Expand," it is because he is not writing, as a poet, the pattern of symbolism: he is giving the entire substance. Poetry is the description of an intangible state.

I sit waiting for my father, fully aware of his superficiality. The gate bell tinkles, as in the cow fields of Switzerland. The big green iron gate is opened by Emilia. My father's American car, the one he wanted all his life, rolls in. My father is loaded with flowers which hide his face, and with a box containing a Lalique vase. He is in a sincere mood, and no longer performing.

He is still trying to discover our sameness. We create harmony, security, a shelter, a home, and then we chafe for adventure, like restless tigers. Restless, vital, fearing to hurt others, to destroy others, but avid for life, renewals, evolutions. We are cowards before the goodness or loyalty of others. People think we are tyrants, but my father and I know how enslaved we are by tenderness, devotion, pity, the goodness of others. Enchained. Renewal, said my father, could come from anyone, from a nobody.

Like a parlor game in which questions are asked—what is your favorite flower? your favorite piece of music? My father was pacing up and down the long, red-tiled floor of the studio, firing questions at me: What about religion? What about politics? What are your ideas on morals? And so exultant because I answered them as he wished me to. It is as if he had educated me. He says, "We do not need to lie to each other." Always the same wish, not to have to lie, but we will, of course, at the first sign of danger, of vulnerability, of jealousy, of withdrawal; we will lie to make an illusory relationship, a perfect one, without wounds.

He tells me, "You have become beautiful. Lovely, that black hair, green eyes, red mouth. One sees that you have suffered, yet the face is smooth, placid. It was made beautiful by suffering." I was standing against the mantelpiece. He was looking at my hands: "You have the same long, tapered hands of your grandmother. These hands run in the family. When your ancestor, the court painter, who painted portraits of the kings and queens, of the aristocrats, the famous people, needed a model for refined hands, he painted in the hands of your great-grandmother." I pulled away my hand brusquely, hit the glass bowl with the crystal fish and stones, and it broke, and the water ran down the mantelpiece to the floor.

He had been saying, "In June you must come to the Riviera with me. They will take you for my mistress. That will be delightful. I will say: 'This is my daughter,' and they will not believe me."

I tease him. I call him my "old oak," to make fun of the sentimental letter he wrote me about my being the Sun which will shine on the Old Oak. I tell him it's scandalous to have such a young-looking father. At fifty he looks like a man of thirty-nine or forty. His hair is luxuriant (and tinted), his figure trim, his gestures lively and quick. He seems, at times, gentle and clever, fair and logical.

His ideal was the *"homme complet"* of Leonardo da Vinci. He knows medicine, architecture, decorating; he composes music, gives concerts, writes books on art; and he was often ahead of his time, for he took sun baths when people covered themselves at the beach, he made us wear sandals so our feet would grow free, and he invented a machine to copy music before it was invented in America. Alert, curious, explorative. Like Oscar Wilde, he put his genius in his life, his talent in music. He has created a personality. There is also a Spartan quality in him; he abstains from drink and overeating to remain slender. He lives with great discipline. He has a passion for perfection. Even his lies are to embellish, to improve on reality. There is no vice or decadence, a great luminosity, a wisdom and joyousness. His only indulgence is love-making.

Strange how, living under my mother's totally opposite nature, I discovered by myself that same discipline, that Spartanism, wisdom, that love of harmony. How I spent my life developing myself, training myself, tutoring myself, setting myself difficult things to do, critical of my conduct, from childhood on, as if I had taken on my absent father's role which was that of a perfectionist. Self-appointed tasks, self-created goals.

The immense pride in my father. True, he did not love us humanly, for ourselves, just this reflection of himself in three human beings reproducing him, continuing his attitudes. He loved us as his creations. It must have been painful for so willful a man to see this domination superseded by my mother, his children alienated by a different background, foreign language, influenced by America. He was overjoyed that, although he was prevented from training us, our blood obeyed him. Thorvald carried on my father's scientific interests, Joaquin his musicianship, and I his talent for living.

He talks about our illnesses as proudly as if they were heirlooms, jewels, possessions. He injects pride even into our humiliations. This pride is softened in me by my femininity. I choose to express it by humility. But the more humble the form, the prouder the core. I suffered from poverty, and only great pride can explain the depth of the wounds. If I were not proud I would not be so mortally offended.

I am proud of my father. I understand in him the artist's egotistical quest for protection, like the woman's quest for male protection so as to attend to the bearing of children. Pregnant women are helpless. The artist while he is at work is helpless too. He too seeks a nest. I understand in him, as I do in Henry, the need for independence, for stimulants, for love affairs.

The same gaiety in us. Gravity, earnestness, intensity, passion, joyousness. We are disconcerted by our faults, distressed, surprised by our weaknesses. The intentions are noble. The lies cover the flaws.

When I spend hours on manual details, covering nail holes with putty, painting the laundry basket, washing stains off the walls, painting trays, etc., I am ashamed of this and invent more important occupations. I am translating for Allendy, or working on my prose poem. My father inflates the number of singers who come to work with him, the number of lessons he gives, of concerts he gives. He is ashamed of the hours he spends cutting newspaper clippings, filing the latest discoveries on hormones, remedies for damp walls, reports on spiritism.

Henry never feels shame for anything he does. He accepts everything, shabby, small, petty, ugly, or empty. He is all-inclusive. Uncritical. I wonder whether I admired Henry's uncriticalness as a respite from the perfectionism I was cursed with.

When I broke the crystal bowl and the water gushed out, was I shattering artificial, contained life and letting life break through and flow? Catastrophe and flow. No control. Nature, not crystal.

Father, who loves crystal, had said tenderly, "And we had taken such pleasure in looking at it together. We love crystal because it is transparent, luminous, and yet solid. It has weight. Feel the weight of the Lalique vase."

Later he said, "I wasn't worried about being old—I know I am not old. But I was anxious that you might come back to me too late, when I would be old. Anxious that you might not see me vivid and laughing and able to make you laugh."

A great gusto for life. I felt a surge of admiration for my double. I regretted the years I had not known him, learned from him.

Henry often says, "I'm tired of war. I must get rid of hatred. I need peace." He believes Lawrence would have done more if he had had peace with Frieda. It was Lawrence's cry too. It was my father's cry against my mother. Such a distance between my mother and me tonight. We are only bound to each other by similar maternal instincts. Henry understands me when I say: "I have known motherhood. I have experienced childbearing. I have known a motherhood beyond biological motherhood—the bearing of artists, and life, hope, and creation." It was Lawrence who had said: Give up bearing children and bear hope and love and devotion to those already born.

Awoke this morning to read this letter from my father:

Anaïs, *cherie, ma plus grande amie!* I owe you the most beautiful, the most profound, the most complete day of my life. I leave very moved and full of you. I rediscovered you whole, sensitive, vibrating. Yesterday as I lifted the veils accumulated by the years, I rediscovered your radiance. I see it, I feel it, I divine all of it, secret but strong, penetrating, human, all charm. Thank you, Anaïs. We sealed a pact between the best of friends. I send you all my thoughts and my fervor.

I was shattered with happiness.

Then he telephoned: "I must come to see you, even if it is only for an hour."

And Father comes, resplendent, and we understand each other miraculously. He believes in polarity, man very masculine, woman very feminine. He hates violence, as I do. Great possibilities for both good and evil, but great control. The mold we give to our lives is so that there will be no cataclysms. The order we seek we are willing to surrender to the flow of life at any time, but it is there as a brake on a car, and our health is a brake. We put brakes on, against our temperament. He said, "Even a room, arranged in a certain manner, prevents certain things from taking place in it."

As he talks I see the effort at equilibrium which is at the basis of our natures. But is it possible that I should become Father's bad double instead of the opposite? Which one is going to disturb the other's control? If my father is going to try to keep me from breaking loose, then I will hurt him too. He will not tolerate perversity, homosexuality. My father understands that when I seem to be most yielding, I am still selective. A friend told him I was in danger from psychoanalysis, which removes all the brakes. My father understands that my willingness to explore everything is a sign of strength. The weak ones have prejudices. Prejudices are a protection. We agree on this.

My father and I elaborated on this, taking joy in discovering each other. He sat admiring the design of the bookcase and advised me to have my gate oiled. (I liked the long flute chant of its rusty hinges.) He has a passion for perfection which frightened me as a child. I felt I could never live up to it.

He understands the strength in me. And I know that I can lean on him. I am less concerned than he is with a cleanliness that goes so far as to sterilize the silverware, and wash his hands every ten minutes. (It may be the doctor in him.) I am more human, more neurotic. But we are both enslaved by sensations. How we ever extricate ourselves is a miracle. Certain lapses of wisdom seem divinely wise to me . . . I plan less than he does. My father likes to guide, to play the teacher, the judge in quarrels: he loves to form lives. Father, too, is jealous of my journal. "My only rival," he says. (All of them would slay the journal if they could.)

My father laments my use of English, which he cannot read. Using English, he says, is doing violence to my own nature, to Spanish vehemence and French incisiveness. But I say to him I can give English these things, I can break molds for my own use, I can transcend a language. And I do love English: it is rich, fertile, subtle, airy, fluid, all-sufficient to expression.

I write to Artaud, sending him a little help. And, above all, a letter which may give him relief from the feeling that the world is against him.

I remember Allendy's words: "Do not play with Artaud. He is too miserable, too poor."

"I am only interested in his genius."

"But then be a friend, not a coquette."

"In literary relationships I am very masculine," I said.

"But your silhouette is decidedly not masculine," said Allendy.

Long walk with Joaquin around the lake, talking, talking, about Father. I am begging Joaquin not to judge his father without first knowing him. I say, "If you judge my father, you are also judging me, because we are alike."

Joaquin protests violently, saying there are no resemblances in the essentials, only in details. "Father lives in a non-human world." And Joaquin praises my mother for being "human."

I say, "My mother's possessiveness and violence are real, human enough. But primitive."

"Better than Father's artificiality."

Joaquin's defense of my mother is always: "She loved her children."

"As lions do. Biologically, yes. But she was just as selfish as my father, in the end. She fed us, protected us, worked for us, but would not allow us to be ourselves. Father and his pride, his narcissistic creative love for his children—I almost prefer his intellectual love for ideas, for his children as creations, than my mother's great possessiveness. She loved without understanding, and what good is that?"

"I understand and pity Mother," said Joaquin.

"Why don't you give Father the same pity?"

"Because he is not human, and I do not approve his life. And he wants my approval. He has got to win everybody. It is all selfish and vainglorious." He added, "He never gave himself, Mother did. Mother loved Father."

"To love is to forgive, to understand, to wish the other's happiness. That is not Mother's love. Just blind, blind possessiveness . . ."

I was weeping as I walked, haunted again by the old fear of resembling my father (for which my mother would reproach me whenever I did not behave as she wished me to). Fearing Joaquin's condemnation. I asked him not to abandon me, begged him to understand my life. Had he lost faith in me?

"No," said Joaquin.

"Don't turn against me, Joaquin. If you turn against me as my mother has, you drive me into my father's arms."

"But I'm not, I'm not. There is a pact between us. I have a feeling for you which I will never have for Father. I am the bridge between Father's other world and the human, *and I will not let you go into the other.*"

He took my hand, locked it in his. It was the end of the walk. He was relaxing. He said playfully, "Father has had enough joy with your return to him, your allegiance. I want to be economical and keep some joys for the future."

"Father is at his worst in the world," I said. "When he felt that I believed him, he dropped all his poses and talked for a whole afternoon truthfully, without a single false note."

What would he think of Joaquin, who is austere, does not care about externals, only for his music, and for his religion?

"Father is still trying to justify his abandonment of Mother, he has a bad conscience."

"But that may be merely an over-scrupulous one. If he were non-human as you say, he would not feel he had to explain his actions to anyone."

Knowing about the original sin, the old burden of guilt which applies to all one does, I wondered how far back my father's sense of guilt was born? What was the crime?

Reawakening to joy and livingness. The sun. Warmth. Euphoria. Bath. The joys of water. Powder. Perfume, Italian dress. Who is there? Open the doors. The house is festive, singing, with the odor of mock orange and honeysuckle filling it.

I sit absolutely still, inundated in joy. And so I am loved and can love my father. He needs me. I have gifts for my father. And all the lifelong feeling I had of not being loved by him, of it being my fault, all annihilated in one day. He said in front of everybody, "Nobody, nobody has given me the feeling Anaïs gives me." Deep accents. Everybody knows the man has become real. Real feelings. My poor father. In one moment I understood so much that it overwhelmed me. I talked about faith, and faith creating miracles.

Letter from Father:

I dream of my flight to the south of France, and to have you alone for a few days. We deserve this after such a long separation. We must spend hours to know each other intimately. Bless you, Anaïs.

How often I have traced my course back to a beginning. Where is the beginning? The beginning of memory or the beginning of pain?

Memory. A French house in Saint-Cloud. A garden. I loved to get dressed up and go out in the street to invite everyone to come in for tea. I stopped carriages as I had seen my mother do. This is a rosy, plump, festive Anaïs, before the typhoid fever in Cuba. But there is already tragedy. Quarrels between my parents.

My father is gay and charming for visitors. In the house, alone, there is always war. Great battles. War at mealtimes. Over our heads at night when we are in bed. In other rooms when we are playing. I am continually aware of the battles. But I do not understand them.

In the closed study there is much mysterious activity. Much music, quartets, quintets, singing. My father played with Pablo Casals. The violinists were Manén and Ysaye. Casals was older and did not mind staying with me while my father and mother went to a concert. I used to fall asleep listening to chamber music.

Visitors. Laughter. My father always moving, alert, tense, passionately laughing or passionately angry. When a door opened and my father appeared, it was a radiation. It was dazzling. A vital passage, even if only for a short moment, passing from one room to another. A gust. A mystery. The three of us felt included in his anger. We were overshadowed by the war. There was no serenity, no time for caresses. Always tension. A life pulled and ripped by dissension. While I played, I heard, I sensed. It hurt me. The uneasiness, the mystery, the scenes. No peace. No complete joy because of a subterranean awareness. One day the violence was so tremendous that it frightened me. An immense, irrational fear. Fear of catastrophe. Fear that my father and mother would kill each other. Mother's face red, my father's dead-white. Hatred. I began to scream, to scream. The intensity of my outburst frightened and silenced them. There was stillness. Or a pretense of stillness. Broodings. Suspicion. The neighbor woman writes me fairy tales in the form of letters and gives them to me across the hedge of our small garden: it seems that the letters were for my father, to charm my father. Suspicion. Jealousies.

I stole into my father's library when he was out and read books I did not understand. I knew Bach and Beethoven almost by heart. I went to sleep on Chopin.

There was a storm in the Bay of New York. The Spaniards on the ship are terrorized. They kneel on the deck and they pray. The lightning strikes the bow of the ship. It was our arrival in New York with wicker trunks, bird cages, a violin case, and no money. Aunts and uncles and cousins on the docks. Negro porters who throw themselves on our belongings. I was obstinately holding on to my brother's violin case. *I wanted people to know I was an artist.*

It is a strange country, America, where the staircases move up and down and the people stand still. Everything is speeded up. In the subway a hundred mouths masticating; and Thorvald asks, "Are they ruminants?" It is a place of immensely tall buildings.

I make notes to report to my father. They eat oatmeal and bacon for breakfast. There is a remarkable shop called the Five and Ten Cent Store, and a library where you can borrow books for nothing. Men rub their hands and spit in them as they stand waiting for the elevators. The elevators travel so fast it is as if they were falling. I see no one dressed as my father dressed. He wore a velvet lining on his coat collar, or black beaver fur. Well-pressed clothes, and Guerlin cologne.

The new life did not appeal to me. A brutal climate, and school in a language I did not know.

Occasionally there was an echo of the old life. When a musician came to New York to perform, and it was someone we knew, we were feted with the celebrity. We would be invited to a box, or to visit the reception room after the concerts, and there was talk, laughter, brilliancy. Echoes of another life. In New York my mother's struggles became heroic. She was not trained in any profession but singing classical music. Soon she abandoned the idea of becoming a concert singer. Poverty, and all the drabness of it. Much work. Housework. Care of my brothers while my mother worked. Meals in the kitchen. Every day, plainer and homelier friends. My mother's friends were less interesting than my father's. But I am making another world, out of reading, out of the diary. I write stories to amuse my brothers. I publish monthly magazines, with serial stories, puzzle games, drawings.

My mother does not tell us directly what reproaches she has against my father, but each flare of temper, each lie, each theatrical attitude, or dramatization, or willfulness, is condemned by her with: "You are just like your father." Joaquin's temper, his destructiveness, or Thorvald's secretiveness, or my fantasies.

But I became aware that she had a great burden, and I dedicated myself to helping her. I became my brothers' second mother.

Mother leaned on me. She shared her anxieties with me.

The features, the form, the voice of my father blurred. The image was buried deep into my being. The yearning spent itself. We corresponded. He sent books, and tried to teach me French by letters. I was not very disciplined. In one letter I wrote two pages without accents and then added one hundred accents at the bottom and said: "For you to distribute correctly."

But although he seems submerged in my memory, he is magically ineffaceable. Unconsciously he guides my actions. Consciously I become what my mother wanted, hard-working, helpful, devoted, a housekeeper, a mother, practice bourgeois sobriety, purity, simplicity. Our life is altogether human, a struggle for existence, good-hearted friends, laboriousness. I become a devoted daughter. I mend, sew, embroider, knit. But I also read voraciously, and put on plays (improvisations, an innovation at the time, which distressed my brothers). I refused to write scripts, so it would be spontaneous; but once in costume, they stood and waited: "What shall we say?"

In school I made friends. An Irish girl, a Jewish girl. I spent my afternoons with them; we skated in Central Park. We wrote for the school magazine. I went to dancing school, had infatuations.

My mother, with the help of her sisters, had bought a brownstone house, and she rented rooms. In the rooming house there were artists, the Madrigueras, etc. I loved the Catalonian violinist. My mother said, "Beware of artists, beware of Catalonians." I was sixteen but my mother treated me like a child. I was timid, and naïve.

I read avidly, drunkenly, by alphabetical order in the library. I had no guidance, as I rebelled against the rowdy, brutal Public School Number 9.

My father invited me to come and stay with him and with Maruca in Paris for a visit. My mother dictated a letter which I wrote obediently. The sum of it was that if he had not loved me all these years enough to worry about my existence, my eating, schooling, dressing, that I would not now (when I was beginning to give no trouble) leave my mother to stay with him. My mother convinced me that he did not really love me, that now it was a matter of pride to show off his pretty daughter.

Today I accepted a dinner invitation at Bernard Steele's house in the suburbs. I took the train with Artaud, and Steele met us at the station. I was bringing *Tropic of Cancer* to show Steele. I had been invited to stay overnight. But the entire evening, the dinner was so flippant, so artificial, so cynical, that both Artaud and I looked at each other and recognized the same distress, the same uneasiness. It was false, false. Instead of staying, I said I had to leave and I took the train back with Artaud.

In the cold, harsh light of the train, on the hard, bare, wooden benches, Artaud sat brooding. I said I could not stand flippancy, bantering, mockery. Artaud said he felt the same.

"But I saw how deeply disappointed Steele was that you did not stay all night." Artaud had noticed that, and I thought he was a thousand miles away from the whole evening.

"And I heard you promise you would dance for him."

"He plays the guitar, that was natural."

Was Artaud pointing out an inconsistency in me? Did he doubt that I was in the same mood, cut off from the artificial gaiety of the evening?

He sat brooding, as if suspicious of me.

The next day he wrote to me:

Last night I was extremely preoccupied, obsessed rather, by a few ideas which only manifested themselves in me by a void. I did not thank you enough, nor tell you once more how precious your friendship is to me. You once said that no revelations about the intimate life of a human being ever offended you, but there are things even more difficult to confess in such a state of mind as mine, and which may justify amply my being absent to the point of being barely courteous.

This short note, special delivery, was soon followed by a letter:

A few pages of *Heliogabalus*, which I expect to read you Thursday and which I finished last night, will explain to you, and justify, my attitude last night, which may have disturbed you. You must surely know similar mental obsessions, but you cannot have lived—I hope you have never experienced —such horrible states of mental constriction, of exacerbation, of emptiness which, in me, manifest themselves outwardly by a constant role-playing, a lie. The work and suffering of my spirit cause a lie on several levels of which the most revealing is the creation of an attitude, a frozen attitude, static, formal: the smile on the face corresponds to a secret rictus, extremely secret. I know I do not need to say more, or dwell longer on this. Water is very close to fire. But I imagine an attitude like mine is not quite believable, and yet it is real. I do not need to tell you that I was not what I was, I did not feel what I pretended to feel, that my stiffness did not correspond to what I would have liked to be, and yet I was absolutely incapable of modifying my external behavior. You understand, I am sure, but I will explain personally and more clearly—with details which the written word cannot convey, I mean that the written word is not able to convey such states. My external behavior created itself in spite of myself, against my own wishes, and yet I was temporarily satisfied with this external self: my organism could not dream of another modality, could not compose a different attitude. The best of myself was reduced to non-existence. Excuse this spontaneous correspondence, tempestuous; a kind of guilt and shame incites me to send this letter anyway . . .

Such scrupulousness. How many of us have been guilty of not being ourselves, yet none of us would have taken such care to confess it, to atone for it. He could not be himself in the unnatural atmosphere of the Steeles. I realized that he was irritated and humiliated by his inability to participate in the tone of the evening. But in the train I was unable to make him understand that I had sensed all this, that to assume a false role was a natural way of protecting one's true self from some inimical places. Such disguises are necessary, particularly if the true interior state is grave, at work, creating.

I wrote him this. And added:

One cannot expose the true self everywhere, at any time. It was the Steeles who were in dissonance with us. I tried to tell you in the train that the conversation at that dinner was impossible, and that we both felt *"dépaysé."*

You can play a thousand roles, and never deceive me about the true Artaud. It is no crime to play roles. I am too aware of the basic self. And once I have seen it, known it, I believe in it, no matter what appearances say. One evening of false tones, a false atmosphere, is only a detail without importance. You feel humiliated by vulgarity, banality. I understand that. When one is truly rich, inwardly, ordinary life becomes a form of torture. I divined the malaise you felt all night. And that is why, to show you on whose side I was, I left with you and offended Steele.

Such an immense pity I have for Artaud, because he is always suffering. It is the darkness, the bitterness in Artaud I want to heal. Physically I could not touch him, but the flame and genius in him I love.

[June, 1933]

Visit from Bradley, who understands a great deal. He takes the role of adviser, director, asks me for a direct narrative. He wants to bring me out of my secret caves. He said many interesting things on art, music, writing, artists. Acute things.

He said the influence of literature on a writer was bad, that Henry was hampered by too much reading. Said my theme of love of my father was big and obsessional like that of Henry's with June. Must write it out. Sometimes when people talk to me, I feel that I have done all they ask of me here, in the journal, when they ask me to be authentic, passionate, explosive, etc.

He fought the poetry of *House of Incest*. Objects to stylization. Said I had come under the influence of American idealism, which I denied because I feel the puritanism, idealism, came from my mother, the Dane, the Northern influence. Bradley said, "Your father remains the great love of your life—it is hard on other men. I speak for my sex."

Bradley was humorous, quick, and stubborn too. Urging me to become more egotistic. Said my humanity was my weakness. Urged me to live for myself, write for myself, work for myself only.

"But I feel alive only when I am living for or with others! And I'll be a great artist in spite of that. And if I am not a great artist, I don't care. I will have been good to the artist, the mother and muse and servant and inspiration. It's right for a woman to be, above all, human. I am a woman first of all. At the core of my work was a journal written for the father I lost, loved and wanted to keep. I am personal. I am essentially human, not intellectual. I do not understand abstract art. Only art born of love, passion, pain."

My father writes me:

MA GRANDE CHÉRIE:
Your letter brought me one of the facets of your innumerable faces. An aspect of goodness and grace which reveals all the capacity for compassion of woman. Do not regret your efforts to win Joaquin over to me, nor your

failure. You have planted a seed; it will grow. Anaïs, your image, your hands, your eyes, your voice, all of YOU I love, are such a great happiness for me, a happiness so new and profound, of such a rare quality that I am incapable of receiving another love. You cannot imagine how you have fulfilled my life with a new sense of intimacy and penetration of woman I have never known before. A false religion, false and narrow—a false morality turns us away every moment from all the forms of happiness possible to us. The entire world suffers from this lack of intimacy, of fusion, of interrelation and (I insist on the word) interpenetration.

Remember that afternoon when, at the risk of losing you, I began by talking about my faults (and I am not through yet) and I tried to know yours? And this was the beginning of a real bond. Qualities I consider taken for granted and, anyway, most of them are acquired; whereas faults neither our logic nor our will were able to modify or correct—they are the real expression of our primitive selves, natural selves, in the state of absolute purity. Spontaneous ideas, lightning thoughts, resonances of the inner self, new obscure vibrations, hereditary echoes, deformations acquired in the contractions imposed on us by our society—physical, moral, psychic—feelings good or bad, generous or selfish, sweet or bitter, cynical or absurd, monstrous or normal (oh, these useless, poor words, so inadequate when one enters the psychic world): all this is us. To seek to understand one another and to love one another while concealing this double self, the only one which is really us, and of which we are neither the creators nor the responsible inventors; it means not to understand, not to love life.

I regret nothing. I only regret that everybody wants to deprive me of the journal, which is the only steadfast friend I have, the only one which makes my life bearable; because my happiness with human beings is so precarious, my confiding moods rare, and the least sign of non-interest is enough to silence me. In the journal I am at ease.

We had a very important talk on dreams. Henry has followed my ideas and has been recording them. Now he begins to see the book it might become, to see its authentic surrealism. He is beginning to wonder what the quality of dreams is, and how to render it, to ask himself questions I have asked myself. In *House of Incest* there was a development *from* the dream, because I have, so often, the dream mood in life, about life, while living. But Henry is sticking closely to the actual night dreams.

I talked about light and atmosphere and fluidity; he about the tone and absence of inhibition, body and feelings acting in absolute unison, a wonderful feeling of ease. I was excited that he should enter and possess the dream world. When he began, he only wrote them down to please me. Henry laughed about it. I said, "Hold on to them, they will make a new kind of work, of book." This is my territory, to which Henry, as usual, brings a new power.

After all, I did not understand what happened to Artaud the other night. He came yesterday and explained that his stiffness was not caused by Steele's mockery but because he was suspicious of me. He was resisting me and was suspicious of my sympathy. He was afraid.

"I don't understand," I said.

We were sitting in the garden. There were books on the table, manuscripts from which Artaud had been reading to me. Just before he spoke of this, he had been talking about his book *Heliogabalus*, about his life. He was born in Turkey. He stopped suddenly and asked, "Are you really interested in my life?" Later he added, "I want to dedicate my book to you. But do you realize what that means? It won't be a conventional dedication. It will reveal a subtle understanding between us."

"There *is* a subtle understanding between us," I said.

"But is it an ephemeral one? Is it just a whim on your part, or is it an essential, fundamental connection? I see you as a woman who plays with men. You have so much warmth and sympathy, one can get deluded. You appear to be fond of everybody, you scatter your affections. I am afraid you are fickle, changeable. I imagine you interested in me today, and dropping me tomorrow."

"You must trust your intuition. All my agreeableness is superficial. In reality I care for a few people very deeply, thoroughly and enduringly. Certain connections cannot change like that. I have not based my interest in you on any worldly discovery of you. I read your work carefully, thoroughly, and I feel I understand you, that is all. I was open and frank about it."

"But do you often write letters like that to writers? Are you in the habit of doing that?"

I laughed. "No, I have not written to many writers. It is not a habit. I am very selective. I can only think of two writers I have written to besides yourself—Djuna Barnes and Henry Miller. I wrote to you on the basis of a correlation between your work and mine. I started on a certain plane, I met you on this plane. It is a plane on which one does not play a superficial game."

"You did a thing which was magnificently unconventional. I could not believe in it. If it were done with that disregard of the world, out of an impulse such as you describe, then it is too beautiful to believe in."

"I would not write to Bernard Steele like that. If you misunderstood what I wrote, that I was addressing the Antonin Artaud revealed in his writing, if you had answered on an ordinary plane, then you would not be Artaud at all. I live constantly in a certain world where things happen not at all as they happen in Steele's world, for example. I am aware that Steele would put a different interpretation on my letter, but not you."

"I could not believe this possible," said Artaud. "I never believed such an attitude possible in this world. I feared to understand. I feared to deceive myself, that it all should turn out to be ordinary, that you should be a sociable woman who enjoyed writing letters to writers, acting sympathy, etc. You see, *I take things so seriously.*"

"So do I," I said, in a tone of gravity he could no longer misread. "I am warm towards people, hospitable and friendly, but it is on the surface. But when it comes down to basic feelings, to meaning, connections are very rare, and it is to the seriousness in you, the mystical poet, that I addressed myself directly, unconventionally, because my insights are swift, and I trust them. I also take things very seriously. I have already told you, I live in another world, and I thought you would have an insight into it, as I had of yours."

Artaud added, "The other night, in the train, when you talked so gently, I felt I hurt you by my withdrawn mood."

"No, I attributed it to your work. I know that when one is doing a work of imagination, one becomes completely absorbed in it, and that it becomes difficult to come out into the world and participate in it, particularly if it is a flippant world."

"It was all too wonderful. It frightens me. I have lived too long in the most absolute moral solitude, spiritual solitude. It is easy to people one's world, but that does not satisfy me."

Artaud put his hand on my knee. I was startled that he should make a physical gesture. I made no gesture. I said, "You won't feel such a spiritual solitude any more.' Defining it, I thought, would postpone the question I saw in his eyes, and which hangs over us, puzzling, as to the nature of our bond. He withdrew his hand. We sat very still. His eyes looked very beautiful, filled with seriousness, mystery, wonder, the *Poète Maudit* for a moment out of his inferno. I asked him to read to me from his book.

He said Steele had tried to make him appear gauche and ridiculous at his house, out of jealousy. I know that is true. I also realized that Steele had watched my growing interest in Artaud with irritation. Again it was clear that the only route to me is by way of the imagination. Steele is handsome, magnetic, but ordinary. Artaud is tormented and inspired.

He embroidered on the meaning of my name. Anaïs, Anahita, the Persian goddess of the moon. Anaïs, the Grecian external me, lovely, luminous, not the somber me. Where is the somber me who matches Artaud's despairs? In the diary. Secret.

The night after Artaud's visit, I dreamed that he possessed me and that I was surprised by his passionateness. But awake, I did not feel that this was the nature of my bond with Artaud. In my dreams I sleep with everybody. The twelve rooms in the dream? Past, present, and future? I ought to be able to capture the atmosphere of the dream better than anyone. I live so much in it, following sensations, impressions, intuitions, trusting in them.

Tropical weather. Bliss. Well-being.

I did not describe well the exaltation which accompanied my talk with Artaud, the overflow of feeling, a transparent openness, those terrific moments of expansiveness, of emotion. Artaud's own intensity so exposed, his eyes so revelatory. But those moments when I feel carried away are so intimate that others may take for love what is a kind of passionate friendship. Too much warmth.

Loving loving loving as the artist can love, the poet in love with the world, with all his senses, adoring all that is alive, courting the whole world with songs, dancing, poetry, music, a huge passion for life, a passion for all its faces, phases, contents, aspects, for man, woman, child, the sun, nerves, pain, the perspiration of nervous agony on Artaud's face. Artaud watches the vessels of the clouds and stammers as he tells his early poems.

The fear of Artaud, the dream I have of lulling and consoling the men I tantalize during the day, loving the creations, the poems, the dreams of men . . . loving.

I meet Artaud in a café, and he greets me with a tormented face. "I'm clairvoyant. I see you did not mean anything you said the other day. Right after our talk in the garden, you became aloof, your face impenetrable. You eluded my touch. You took flight."

"But there was no question of a human love . . . as soon as I spoke, I felt you had given my words a human interpretation."

"Then what was it a question of?"

"Affinities, friendship, understanding, imaginative ties."

"But we are human beings!"

I forget the order of our phrases. All I knew was that I did not want a physical tie with Artaud. We walked. When he said, "We walk in step. It is heavenly to walk with someone who walks with the same rhythm . . . it makes walking euphoric," then I began to feel it all to be unreal. I was no longer within my own body. I had stepped out of myself. I felt and saw Artaud watching me with delight. I saw him looking at my sandals; I saw my light summer dress trembling, ebbing back and forth to every breeze; I saw my bare arm and Artaud's hand on it; and I saw the momentary joy on his face, and felt a terrible pity for the sick, tormented madman, morbid, hypersensitive.

At the Coupole, we kissed, and I invented for him the story that I was a divided being, could not love humanly and imaginatively both at the same time. I expanded the story of my split. "I love the poet in you."

This touched him, and did not hurt his pride. "That is like mine, like me," he said. "Human beings appear to me as spectral, and I doubt and fear life, it all seems unreal to me; I try to enter it, to be a part of it. But you, I thought you were more earthy than I, your glidingness, your vibrancy. I have never seen a woman look so much like a spirit, yet you are warm. Everything about you frightened me, the enormous eyes, exaggerated eyes, impossible eyes, impossibly clear, transparent; there seemed to be no mystery in them, one thought one could look through them, through you immediately, and yet there are endless mysteries under that clarity, behind those naked, fairy-tale eyes . . ."

I was stirred, and Artaud pleaded: "Whom do you love? I know Allendy loves you, Steele, and many others, but whom do you love?

"Soft, and frail, and treacherous," he said. "People think I am mad. Do you think I am mad? Is that what frightens you?"

I knew at that moment, by his eyes, that he was, and that I loved his madness. I looked at his mouth, with the edges darkened by laudanum, a mouth I did not want to kiss. To be kissed by Artaud was to be drawn towards death, towards insanity; and I knew he wanted to be returned to life by the love of woman, reincarnated, reborn, warmed, but that the unreality of his life would make a human love impossible. Not to hurt him, I had invented the myth of my divided love, spirit and flesh never uniting. He said, "I never thought to find in you my madness."

Artaud sat in the Coupole pouring out poetry, talking of magic, "I am Heliogabalus, the mad Roman emperor," because he becomes everything he writes about. In the taxi he pushed back his hair from a ravaged face. The beauty of the summer day did not touch him. He stood up in the taxi and, stretching out his arms, he pointed to the crowded streets: "The revolution will come soon. All this will be destroyed. The world must be destroyed. It is corrupt, and full of ugliness. It is full of mummies, I tell you. Roman decadence. Death. I wanted a theatre that would be like a shock treatment, galvanize, shock people into feeling."

For the first time it seemed to me that Artaud was living in such a fantasy world that it was for himself that he wanted a violent shock, to feel the reality of it, or the incarnating power of a great passion. But as he stood and shouted, and spat with fury, the crowd stared at him and the taxi driver became nervous. I thought he would forget where we were, on our way to the Gare Saint-Lazare, to my train home, and that he would become violent. I realized that he wanted a revolution, he wanted a catastrophe, a disaster that would put an end to his intolerable life.

Henry amalgamated his *Self-Portrait* [*Black Spring*] and the dream book. He does a gigantic bulk of writing, but it has to be torn apart and placed, piece by piece, in its right setting. He confuses the critic, the philosopher, the novelist, the confessor, the poet, the reporter, the scientist, and the note-maker. There is always a big task of creative synthesis of his fragments, a struggle for unity. His work is chaotic, diversified, uneven, like a torrent that has to be contained at some point or it inundates, engulfs, drowns him. He appears to yield, is washed over, engulfed by his impressionability, responsiveness, expansiveness. But later he extricates himself. If he is jealous he can become cruel; if he feels secure he becomes human.

He was in a reminiscent mood, recalling his life with June and with his first wife. The music over the radio made him sob. "All literature does not make up to one for the tragedy of life, the struggles. They make literature pale." He was recalling his great concessions to sex, how divided he always was between the sexual hunger for a woman and a hatred of her, of her imperfections, limitations. "The humiliating abdication of one's integrity, the terrible haunting dissatisfaction . . ."

When Henry writes insane pages, it is the insanity produced by life, and not by the absence of life. The insanity of the surrealists, Breton and *transition* is in a void; whereas that of Henry is caused by the absurdities, ironies, pains of a surcharged over-full life. His life never ends in a crystallization, but in a fantastic spiral ecstasy, the motions of a top, turning forever.

When I meet Artaud, he stands nobly, proudly, with eyes mad with joy, the eyes of a fanatic, a madman. The triumph in his face, the lightning flash of joy and pride because I have come. The heaviness, the clutchingness, the strange despotism of his gestures. His hands only hover over me, over my shoulders, yet I feel the magnetic weight of them.

I have come dressed in black, red, and steel, like a warrior, to defend myself against possession. His room is bare like a monk's cell. A bed, a desk, a chair. I look at the photographs of his amazing face, an actor's changeful face, bitter, dark, or sometimes radiant with a spiritual ecstasy. He is of the Middle Ages, so intense, so grave.

He is Savonarola burning pagan books, burning pleasures. His humor is almost satanic, no clear joy, just a diabolical mirth. His presence is powerful; he is all tautness and white flames. In his movements there is a setness, an intensity, a fierceness, a fever which breaks out in perspiration over his face.

He shows me his manuscripts, talks about his plans, he talks darkly, he woos me, kneeling before me. I repeat all I have said before. Everything is whirling around us. He rises, his face twisted, set, stony.

"Allendy has told you that I take too much opium . . . that sooner or later, you will despise me anyway. I am not made for sensual love. And this has so much importance for women."

"Not for me."

"I didn't want to lose you."

"You won't lose me."

"Drugs are killing me. And I will never be able to make you love me . . . to hold you. You are a human being. You want a whole love."

"Gestures mean nothing. I did not want that kind of bond with you, but another, on another plane."

"You won't run away from me? You won't vanish? You are everything to me. I have never seen a woman like you before. You are rare. I can't believe it. I am in terror that it should be a dream. That you should vanish." And his arm, so taut, clutched at me like a man drowning.

"You are the plumed serpent," he said. "You glide over the earth but your plume stirs the air, the mind. That small detail, of your coming dressed as Mars, that a woman should live thus in symbols, that alone is amazing to me. And your ecstasy, too, is strange and different. It does not come in spurts; it is continuous. You live continuously on one level, you use a certain tone and never depart from it. Your talk is unreal."

He identifies with Heliogabalus, the mad prince. But Artaud is more beautiful, a dolorous, contracted, tragic, and not cynical or perverse human being.

"I love your silences," he said, "they are like mine. You spoke of self-destruction as a holocaust. Then you were dying for a god?"

"For the absolute, one dies if one wants the absolute."

"I am proud and vain," he said.

"All creators are. You cannot create without pride and self-love."

Then he offered to burn everything else for me, to dedicate himself to me. I deserved a holocaust. What would Artaud burn for me? I did not ask. And I knew that, just as Allendy's magic was too white, Artaud's was black, poisonous, dangerous.

"Write to me. Every day of waiting will be torture. Don't torture me. I am terrifically faithful and terribly serious. I dread that you should forget me, abandon me."

Artaud's letter:

I have brought many people, men and women, to see the marvelous painting ["Lot and His Daughter"] but it is the first time I have seen an artistic reaction move a being and make it vibrate like love. Your senses trembled, and I realized that, in you, the body and the spirit are completely welded, if a pure spiritual impression can stir up such a storm in you. But in this incongruous marriage, it is the spirit which leads the body and dominates it, and must end by dominating it completely. I feel in you a world which waits to be born to find its exorcist. You yourself are not aware of this but you are calling for it with all your senses, your feminine senses, which in you are also spirit.

Being what you are, you must understand the great painful joy I feel at having met you, joy and amazement. I find filled, in all ways, my infinite solitude, filled in a way which frightens me. Destiny has granted me more than I ever dreamed of demanding. And like all things given by destiny, all that is inevitable, designed in heaven, it comes without hesitation, spontaneously, so beautiful it terrifies me. To make me believe in miracles, as if miracles could happen in this world; but I do not think that either you or I am quite of this world, and it is this, this too-perfect encounter, which affects me like a sorrow.

My own spirit and life are made up of a series of illuminations and eclipses which play constantly inside of me and, therefore, around me and upon all that I love. For those who love me, I can only be a continuous disappointment. You have already observed that, at times, I have swift intuitions, swift divinations, and, at other times, I am absolutely blind. The simplest truths elude me then, and one has to possess a rare understanding, an unusual subtlety, to accept this mixture of darkness and light when this affects emotions one has a right to expect from me.

Another thing binds us closely: your silences. Your silences are like mine. You are the only one before whom I am not ashamed of my silences. You have a vehement silence: one feels it is surcharged with essences, it is strangely alive, like a trap open upon an abyss from which one might hear the secret murmur of the earth itself. There is no fabricated poetry in what I tell you, you know it well. I want to express these powerful impressions, the real impressions I had. When we stood at the station and I said to you: "We are like two lost souls in infinite space," I had felt this silence, this moving silence speaking to me and it made me want to weep with joy.

You make me confront the best and the worst in myself, but before you, I feel I do not need to be ashamed. You inhabit the same domain as I do, but you can give me all that I lack, you are my complement. It is true that our imagination loves the same images, desires the same forms, the same creations; but physically, organically, you are warmth, whereas I am cold. You are supple, voluptuous, fluid, whereas I am hard like flint, calcined, fossilized. A fatality which is beyond us has thrown us together: you were aware of it, you saw the resemblances, you felt the good we could do to each other.

What I fear most is that you too should be blinded by destiny, that you too might lose contact with all these truths. I am afraid that during one of those periods when half of me is cut off from the other, you may feel such a disappointment and no longer recognize me, and that I may lose you then. Something marvelous has barely begun which might fill an entire life. I divine you with all the sincerity of my soul, all the gravity and depth I am capable of. In eight days my life has been totally transformed. I have a name which my mother gave me when I was four years old and which people call me when they are very close to me: "Nanaqui."

Artaud said:

With you I might return from the abysses in which I have lived. I have struggled to reveal the working of the soul behind life, beyond life, in its deaths. I have only transcribed abortions. I am myself an absolute abyss. I can only imagine my self as being phosphorescent from all its encounters with darkness. I am the man who has felt most deeply the stutterings of the tongue in its relation to thought. I am the one who has best caught its slipperiness, the corners of the lost. I am the one who has reached states one never dares to name, states of the soul of the damned. I have known those abortions of the spirit, the awareness of the failures, the knowledge of the times when the spirit falls into darkness, is lost. These have been the daily bread of my days, my constant obsessional quest for the irretrievable.

Before his eyelids come down, the pupils of the eyes swim upward, and I can see only the whites. The heavy eyelids fall on the white and I wonder where his eyes have gone. I fear that when he opens them again the sockets will be empty like those of Heliogabalus's statue.

To be touched by Artaud means to be poisoned by the poison which is destroying him. With his hands he was imprisoning my dreams, because they were like his. I have a love for the poet who walks inside of my dreams, for his pain and the flame in him, but not for the man. I cannot be physically bound to him.

Artaud and I walked along the Seine, pursued by the grotesque and riotous students of the Quatz Art Ball. The night I met them with Henry, they seemed like clowns, jesters, and we laughed at them. But tonight, around Artaud, they seemed like gargoyles grimacing and mocking us. We walked in a dream, Artaud torturing himself with doubts, questions, talk about God and eternity, wanting my sensual love; and, for the first time, I asked myself if his madness was not really like a Way of the Cross, in which each step, each torment, was described to make one feel guilt; and whether Artaud was desperate because he could not find anyone to share his madness.

Artaud said, "What a divine joy it would be to crucify a being like you, who are so evanescent, so elusive."

We sat in a café and he poured out endless phrases, like the phrases in his books, descriptions of his states, moods, visions.

"When you say 'Nanaqui' it sounds natural."

"It sounds Oriental."

As we walked along the Seine again, all the books and manuscripts we were carrying fell on the pavement and I felt a relief, as if this web of poetry, of the magic of words, would cease to enclose me. I was frightened by his fervor when he said, "Between us, there could be a murder." We were by the parapet and his books fell to the ground as he said this.

He had written: "I have chosen the domain of pain and shadows as others choose the radiance and weight of matter." The beauty and softness of the summer does not touch him. He disregards it, or fights against it. He said, "I have only known painful emotions."

But how little he knows me when he says, "Why do you make an impression of evil, cruelty, of seductiveness, trickery, superficiality? Is it an appearance? I hated you at first as one hates the all-powerful temptress, I hated you as one hates evil."

My father and I had agreed to meet at Valescure, but I left ahead of time to have a few days of quiet and meditation.

In the hotel, by the sea, I can add small touches to the portrait of my father. The hotel keeper says, "He is so gay." The hairdresser, "He is very vain. He has his hair tinted not to reveal his grey hair." The manicurist, "He loves beautiful women." He is extravagant, sent a telegram and flowers to greet me, telephones orders, preparations for his coming, a special room, a special bed, no noise. He was delayed by a serious lumbago. But he took the train just the same. "This carcass must be subjugated." He arrived at the station stiff, limping. He would not let me unpack his bag. He suffered in his pride. He immediately orders special fruit, special biscuits, special drinking water. For the *garçon* to come with the Flytox and exterminate every fly. "A fly can keep me awake." He organizes his surroundings, his day, his care of his health. The doctor is called. He ordains his world, must have everything immediately, at any cost.

We have meals in his room. We talk. He says, "We have constructed our own system of living. We cannot be true to human beings, but to ourselves. We have lived like civilized barbarians because we are primitive, you know, and highly civilized too."

Later: "The two men who have done the greatest harm to the world are Christ and Columbus. Christ taught us guilt and sacrifice, to live only in the other world, and Columbus discovered America and materialism."

Later still: "You have created yourself, by your own efforts. You developed the blood cells I gave you. I consider that you owe me nothing."

He is pale. He appears, at first, cold and formal. His face is a mask. We set out for a slow walk. He says, "We have a world of our own. We have a peculiar way of looking at things. By current standards we are amoral, but we are true to an inner development. But we have given much to others, enriched their lives."

We are not talking, merely corroborating certain theories.

He says, "My obsession was to be a complete man, which was the ideal of Da Vinci. That is, civilized, but primitive too, strong but sensitive. I had to learn to balance the elements of the greatest unbalance, a masterpiece of equilibrium." He is older. He has found a way to balance this nature full of contradictions, as I have not.

At lunch he was sober and played the doctor, obsessed with certain diets, uncompromising. Would not let me eat bread or tomatoes. Again cold in appearance. He told the *maître d'hôtel* I was his "fiancée." I realized how this "mask" had terrified me. The taut will, the criticalness, the severity. He watched the waiter and winced at a few drops of water spilled on the tablecloth. As a child I had the obscure feeling that this man could never be satisfied.

He bore his illness with dignity and grace. Though it hurt him extremely to move, he took his bath, he shaved, his nails were immaculate, he dressed with care.

After lunch he rested. Then he met me, looking immaculate, dressed with subtle elegance. Walking stiffly with a cane, but head held high, joking about his infirmity. The people of the hotel leaped to serve him, adored him, catered to his every whim. He took me out in his beautiful car. I could see in him far more rigid patterns. I am more flexible, more easygoing. We sped out towards the sea, reveling in the opaline colors, the changing light, the smells of heather, flowers. We sat on a rock facing the sea.

And then he talked about his love affairs, and they did not seem as casual, as indifferent as legend had described them. Not the Don Juan who conquers, and the next day is gone. He mixed his pleasures with creativity; he was interested in the creation of human beings. He tells me the story of the humble and rather homely little governess no one paid attention to. "Without me she would never have known love. I used to cover her homely little face to be able to make love to her. It transformed her. She became almost beautiful."

He said, "I only abandoned a woman when she ceased to have a meaning for me. Or when there was a danger of my falling in love.

Usually, after the third or fourth night, I sent a big bunch of red roses, and they knew what it meant."

The next morning he could not move from his bed. He was in despair. I surrounded him with gaiety and tenderness. I finally unpacked his bag while he talked to me. And he continued the story of his life. Meals were brought to the room. I told him stories too, my whole life.

"You are the synthesis of all the women I have loved. What a pity that you are my daughter!"

He sat in a chair the next day and read me an article on his musical opinions and sketches.

The mistral was blowing. This gave to the summer days an enervating, feverish quality.

He was getting better. We were able to go to the dining room for lunch. He dressed to perfection and, with his alabaster skin, his neat trim figure, his soft hat, he looked like a Spanish grandee. We walked slowly under a tropical sun, he teaching me the life of insects, the names of birds, and the distinctions between their cries, so that the world became filled with new sounds and everywhere I go now, I hear voices of birds that I was not aware of before.

He talked about his life with my mother. The greatest cause of conflict between them was his passion for aesthetics and her lack of it. She did not care about dress, about grooming, about illusion. The very day of their wedding they had a quarrel, and his disillusions began. She had a high temper, and was jealous and possessive. She was primitive, natural, and hated "illusion," which she conjugated with "lie." If my father made harmless inventions, such as saying it was she who had made the *marrons glacés,* my mother had to confront him with the gravity of his lie, and force him to acknowledge it before people. If he hung a painting on one wall, she moved it to another.

He told me ribald stories. The Spanish earthiness mingled, in him, with the romantic illusionist. He showed me a thousand faces, a thousand aspects. Could I have heard this coarse earthy language from him as a child, and so be less surprised by Henry's use of it, almost familiar with it?

237

We both started out with the desire to be devoted, complete, human, noble, faithful; but our passions broke the dam, and forced us into lies. We were never reconciled to our treacheries, to the impetuosity of our nature, to our evolutions and transitions, which made us humanly unreliable. As D. H. Lawrence said: "Every human being is treacherous to every other human being. Because he has to be true to his own soul."

But we dream of union, faithfulness.

One night we walked on the terrace of the hotel in the moonlight. He looked twenty-five years old, like Joaquin.

He talked a great deal about the importance of balance. "Such a tenuous balance," he said, "we could easily become unbalanced. Our balance hangs on a tenuous thread. Look for the light, for clarity, be more and more Latin." When Samba the Negro brought the mail on a silver platter, my father said, "Take them away. We have no need of anyone in the world."

And then I felt the need to leave, the need I always have, to leave. Fear of breaking down? Fear of disillusioning him? Fear of discovering we did not agree? Of the flaws in the harmony? He stressed the harmony. But if I stayed, we might discover contrasts. Flight. I always look for the exit. After nine days . . .

My father said I angered him as a child because he felt I had a whole world of secret thoughts which I would not, or could not express, that I lied like an Arab, and that I was high-tempered. But I explained to him that the feeling I had was that no one was interested, and also that what I invented constantly was *fantasy,* and that when I tried to tell of it, people always said: "You are lying." It was an invented world I lived in, and I was afraid to have it destroyed. He should have understood that. Perhaps because it was like his world, he fought it in his own child. "And now," he said, "the discovery of each other brings a kind of peace, because it brings the certitude that we are right. We are stronger together . . . we will have less doubts."

This seemed deeply true, yet I wonder if it is good to ally similarities, one agreeing with the other, as twins might, so that this might give an illusion of balance, reassure us about our orientation, or whether we should seek this by contrast with others, in extreme opposites as Henry is to me? I did find my way alone out of Catholicism, out of the bourgeois life created by my mother, out of the emptiness of my life in Richmond Hill. I found D. H. Lawrence alone.

Is it possible my father should love me more than I love him? Perfection paralyzes me.

In Valescure, the day when we found our new relationship, it was the day of San Juan. In Spain, on the feast of San Juan, people pile up all the old furniture from their attics, anything which might burn, old beds, old mattresses, and make bonfires in the street. I do not know the meaning of the ritual; but, for my father and me, it seemed to me appropriate, to make a bonfire of the past, of memories, of everything and to start anew. I left my father and continued on my trip.

Father writes me now:

All my life I have hated Sundays [just as I do.—A.N.]. The Sunday of your departure was particularly hateful. The train took away clarity, luminosity, fire. My room seemed cold, shrunken, somber. Where were the sparks, the *charbons ardents*? A subtle perfume floated in the air, yours. Wherever there is light, look for the shadow. The shadow is me. You are an inexhaustible flow of precious stones, a rare soul, proud and ardent, your radiance is inner, and full of beauty and clarity.

And again my father writes:

I received a letter from my mother. Joaquin has been to see her every day. He was tender and charming. Everyone liked him. She writes: "He is handsome and charming, but does not have your elegance. When I asked him if he had seen you, he said to me very emotionally: 'No, I haven't, because of my mother. Not to hurt her. I prefer to sacrifice myself. It is a double sacrifice because my father will think that I judge him, condemn him, and that is so far from the truth, first of all because I have no right to judge, and secondly because tomorrow I might behave exactly as he did or worse. But my mother dedicated her life to me, and I owe her my total devotion to make her happy. Even at the cost of a sacrifice such as seeing my father only from afar.' He is always pleased when any resemblance to you is observed by anyone, in way of speaking or acting!" But he did add that he would not say this to anyone but Grandmother or to me, to the only ones concerned.

I have just finished reading Lawrence's *Plumed Serpent*. A great disappointment. I was absolutely bored . . ."

Letter to Henry:

You do not have a philosophy. You have feelings about living. Your ideology woven into the Lawrence book is really a protest against ideology. Your discontent, windmill attacks, are a protest against opinions, judgments, prophecies, conclusions. Your letters to me have been a protest against ideas. You are at war with yourself, with the intellectual you.

I say, let the intellectual alone, the savant, the philosopher. Enjoy life. Intoxicate yourself with life. Describe it. Do not comment on it, or draw false conclusions. You have had your cerebral winter—your mental fervors. You were not happy. *Black Spring* will make you happier. I beg you, give up cerebration. You are in rebellion without knowing why.

I dislike Henry's blind attacks on everything, like Lawrence's. When he is unhappy he is ready to destroy the world.

Women are so much more honest than men. A woman says: "I am jealous." A man covers it up with a system of philosophy, a book of literary criticism, a study of psychology. Henry is so often confused, irrational, formless, like D. H. Lawrence.

Henry has nothing to be bitter about. Why does he continue to fight the world? He loves war for its own sake. He lives in an animal world, in which life is full but without directive power or a fully awakened self-consciousness.

Note from Artaud:

We have a world of things to stir up together, we will concern ourselves with them when you return, face to face. All this is too important and too vital for us, and I cannot, in a letter, answer your multitude of questions and, above all, the great question which your multiformed attitude presents to me.

NANAQUI

You will understand my silence in suspense and my brief note when you return.

Letter to my father:

I almost wept when I opened your letter at Aix les Bains at the very moment when I was packing my bags. This detail—of thinking to write me on the day of my departure—a detail so thoughtful, so delicate, a thing I weary of doing for others and which I had dreamed of being done to me, but others love in such a different way. One has to know how to love, how to think in love, as well as in other arts. As you know. It seems to me that you have come to reward me for all the art and ingenuity I have wasted on others, on loving, the rest of my life.

Louveciennes. Home again. Evening: to walk into my house is to walk into down, into color, into music, into perfume, into magic, into harmony. I stood on the threshold and re-experienced the miracle, forgetting I had made it all, painted the walls Chinese red, turquoise, and peach, laid the dark carpets, selected the mosaic fireplace, the lamps, the curtains. I was ensorcelled, as by the work of another. A caress of color, warmth, a hammock of suave harmonies, a honeyed womb, a palanquin of silk.

My joy and energy overflowed. I love living, moving. I began to ordain my kingdom. I swam through a Sargasso Sea of mail; the telephone rang, Allendy, Artaud, Henry, Joaquin. Work. Engagements. Letters. To give each one the illusion of being the chosen one, the favorite, the only one. If all my letters were put together they would reveal startling contradictions. Because I imagine people need those lies as much as I need them. Truth is coarse and unfruitful. I tell Allendy I have just arrived as if he were the first one I called.

My father tells me benign lies such as: "This is the first time I have wanted a lot of money," (to make me gifts) when I know he has always needed a lot of money, that he loves luxury, American cars, silk shirts, gold-tipped cigarettes, and lavish bouquets for his mistresses. I smile. All the incense I gave others is blown back to me, under my nose. All my own tricks and lies and deceptions are offered to me out of my father's magician's box. The same box I use for my illusionist practice.

While he is writing me, Delia, or some other woman, is lying two feet away; her perfume can reach me; and he may be saying to her:

"I must write to my daughter that she is now the only woman in my life, for that is a proper romantic end to an aging Don Juan's life: he must surrender all and become his daughter's *chevalier servant.*" The treachery of illusion. Creating illusion and delusion. Improving on reality. Who is going to wring the truth from the other? Who lied first? Once when my father was reading me aloud a letter from Maruca, he read me a whole paragraph of affectionate greetings to me from her. Then he left the letter on the table and when I reread it, there were no such messages, just a conventional: "Give my love to Anaïs."

Henry has these Saturnian eclipses, as Artaud has. Cold, inexpressive, somber, lost. Artaud warned me against them because he is fully aware of them, aware of the self separated from the self. Henry does not know what he suffers from. I say the word "eclipse" and that word is enough to illumine the chaos of Henry, and he begins to coalesce. I pull his scattered mind together. I make him focus on his direction, self-knowledge. He makes me taste the streets, cafés, movies, food and drink, and he tastes the joys of awareness. "So true, so true," he cries. And he begins to work almost immediately.

This diary proves a tremendous, all engulfing craving for truth since, to write it, I risk destroying the whole edifice of my illusions, all the gifts I made, all that I created and protected, everyone whom I saved from truth.

What does the world need, the illusion I gave in life, or the truth I give in writing? When I went about dreaming of satisfying people's dreams, satisfying their hunger for illusion, didn't I know that this was the most painful and the most insatiable hunger? What impels me to offer now, truth in place of illusion?

I was going to continue to pick up the threads of an early narrative and superimpose them upon the present, which reveals their synchronization.

I thought that the image of my father had become blurred with time; yet at thirteen I describe in the diary the man I am going to marry:

A very pale and mysterious face, with very white teeth, a slow noble walk, an aloof smile. He will have a sweet and clear voice. He will tell me about his life filled with tragic adventures. I would like him proud and haughty, that he should love to read and write, and to play some instrument.

This is a portrait of my father. An image engraved indelibly in mysterious regions of my being, sunk in sand, yet reappearing persistently, in fragments, in other men.

The sky was full of dark clouds, which saddened me, for it seemed to me that these clouds were there expressly for me, to announce the dark clouds which would weigh down my future life.

My mother allowed me to read a few novels by George Sand, and when I returned from this realm I contemplated the deep waters of the lake with a new feeling, for I had just learned what love was.

My dear Diary, it is Anaïs who is speaking to you, and not someone who thinks as everybody should think. Dear Diary, pity me, but listen to me.

Even then, I had literary preoccupations. This event, I sensed, was important, decisive:

I should rewrite my arrival in New York [age thirteen]. It seems to me that my briefness does not do justice to the occasion.

I did not know that this trip to America was, deep down, my mother's effort to estrange us from my father, not only by distance, but by immersing us in a contrasting culture, the opposite of the Latin, and teaching us a language he did not know. It was a gesture made against all that he represented.

In America, my mother hoped we would learn idealism, purity, as she understood it. Her own Nordic ancestry asserted itself against the Latin. Her Danish blood against her French blood (her mother was a New Orleans beauty—had lovers, abandoned her children). My mother was puritanical, or my father's behavior had turned her against sex, against man. She was secretive about sex, yet florid, natural, warm, fond of eating, earthy in other ways. But she became all Mother, sexless, all maternity, a devouring maternity enveloping us; heroic, yes, battling for her children, working, sacrificing. Accumulating in us a sense of debt, a sense that she had given her life to us, in contrast to the selfishness of my father. She upheld bourgeois virtues, thrift, domestic talents, honesty, sense of duty, self-sacrifice, etc. She battled against all "resemblances" to my father. But she did let Joaquin be a musician, and she encouraged my intellectual pursuits.

Scene with Artaud. "Before you say anything," he said, "I must tell you that I sensed from your letters that you had ceased to love me, or rather, that you had never loved me at all. Some other love has taken hold of you. Yes, I know, I guess, it is your father. So all my doubts of you were right. Your feelings are unstable, changeable. And this love of yours for your father, I must tell you, is an abomination."

A venomous, bitter Artaud, all fury and rancor. I had received him with a wistful tenderness, but it did not touch him. "You give everyone the illusion of maximum love. Furthermore, I do not believe I am the only one you have deceived. I sense that you love many men. I feel you hurt Allendy, and perhaps others."

I was silent. I denied nothing. But I felt he was wrong to interpret it as premeditated. He sees impurity everywhere.

"I believe in your absolute impurity."

Like a monk with his gods, purities, and impurities. Such accusations did not move me. They reminded me of a priest shouting from a pulpit, and I felt I would rather have him think me a Beatrice Cenci than one who had pretended to love him. He loved Beatrice enough to present her on stage, but in life he would set a bonfire for her and burn her. He was acting not like a poet, but like a vulgar mistress with a gun in her pocket. Apocalyptic condemnations. There was nothing beautiful about his anger. I seemed to take pleasure in his misunderstanding of me. Because he did not believe me when I tried to say "I do not want you as a lover" and now he was blaming me for my weakness. I let him. I did not seek to make him understand himself or me. I let him describe me as one "tenebrous oscillation." I let him pronounce his anathemas, curses, as a malefic, dangerous being, black magic, and he seemed more and more like an outraged castrated monk.

He accused me of literary living. This has always amused me. Men can be in love with literary figures, with poetic and mythological figures, but let them meet with Artemis, with Venus, with any of the goddesses of love, and then they start hurling moral judgments.

At thirteen I wrote: "Is there anyone who will understand me? I do not understand myself."

But I know I am not what Artaud believes me to be.

From my childhood diary:

Time does nothing to my companions in school. For me each day is a novelty, and it seems to me that my character changes every day. If I do rise at the same time, I have different impressions each day. Even if I wear the same dress, it seems to me that I am not the same girl. Even if I repeat the same prayers during one year, each time they appear different to my interpretation, and I understand them differently.

Today I began a new story called "Heart of Gold" and I am mixing a great deal of mystery with it.

In front of me there is a deep abyss, and if I continue to fall into it, deeper and deeper, how long will it take me to reach the bottom? I imagine that life is such an abyss, and that the day I strike bottom will be the day I cease to suffer. One of these days I will say to my journal: "Dear Diary, I have touched bottom."

The question is: am I like everyone else?

I say to Henry: "I am not going to lie any more. Nobody is grateful for my lies. Now they will know the truth. And do you think Allendy will like what I have written about him better than what I said to him or implied by my evasions? Do you think Marguerite will prefer to know what I think of her in place of what I have told her? Truth is death-dealing, as your truths are death-dealing, Henry. You killed June psychically with your brutal honesty, as you would kill anyone you wrote about. People may not appear to be injured, but they are, irretrievably so, by a certain knowledge.

"I have always believed in Bergson's *'mensonge vital.'* The trouble is not with my lies; the trouble is that we were all brought up on fairy tales. We were poisoned with fairy tales. Women expected love to always take a lyrical form, a romantic expression. We have all expected wonder, the marvelous. You yourself wrote me a few days ago: 'I expected so much, so much of the world and it all fell short.' I was more poisoned by fairy tales than anyone.

"*Only I decided to work miracles. I decided that when somebody said: 'I want' that I would fulfill this want.* I decided to be the fairy godmother who made things come true. And to some degree I succeeded. My faith in you has strengthened you miraculously. Only don't forget, fairy tales are based on lies. I wanted *everybody* to have everything they wanted! The mistake I made was to encompass too much. I could not make everyone happy, take care of everyone. I had to let some down, and they hate me for it. I over-estimated my strength. When I told a lie it was a lie which gives life."

"I admit that your faith nourished me," said Henry. "I could not have done anything if you had been unbelieving, and without enthusiasm."

"And to my faith I add perception. My faith in you was no illusion. Look at the work you have done. Today Lowenfels praised you, and Cummings."

"You may be lying to me."

"Don't forget I have always let you read the diary until you yourself stopped."

"Most of the time," said Henry, with his usual candor, "I am just an egoist, too full with my own ideas to take in any more."

From my childhood diary, at age thirteen:

At times I have sensations which I cannot explain, impulses I cannot control, impressions I cannot shake off, dreams and thoughts contrary to the usual dreams and thoughts of others. When I read a book I discuss it with myself, I judge it, I find its qualities or its faults, I begin to think such deep thoughts that I get lost, weary, I no longer understand myself . . .

And after a visit to a woman writer who encouraged me:

I am not mad, I do not think of impossible things. I am not stupid, I may be good for something one day.

And if I do get easily saddened, it is because, as my mother says, I have inherited a dramatic soul, more easily given to sadness than to joy.

I tell Joaquin and Thorvald so many stories that my mother said my imagination is like Niagara Falls in its richness and continuous movement.

↶

In my eyes, my father has the beauty, the proud and magnificent beauty of my dreams . . .

So that my dreams may be my own, so that they may never become real, so that I may always call them back to keep me company, to help me live, I keep them in the deepest part of my being or in the most secret pages of my diary.

To my father:

There is an emptiness, a void in our life which only you could fill.

Alas, why must I change so much? I feel nothing today. I am cold and do not understand religion at this moment and I know, I understand, that it is my exalted nature which also causes these sudden coldnesses for what I adored and into which I poured all the strength of my passion . . .

Yes, I am light, I am not persevering, I am passionate . . .

My father asked me to come down to Valescure for a few days and drive back to Paris with him. When I arrived in Valescure my father met me alone, but it was impossible to detect on his face what his feelings were. Always the same impenetrable mask, the cold mask. When he takes his glasses off, the myopic blue eyes have a yearning, clinging look. It is only later that I discover he has not slept the night before.

At the hotel Maruca is waiting for us. This time I see her more clearly and I appreciate her. Small, plump, beautifully formed, a Tanagra with a boyish face, a humorous small uptilted nose, a little girl's light voice, frankness and directness. The quick, determined gestures, the simplicity. She was warm and I responded to her.

She took me to my room. She watched me with affectionate curiosity, to see what had become of the little girl she knew at Arcachon who had slept in her bed while my mother went to close the house at Uccle after my father's departure. I gave her the perfume I brought. We have a talk later, while my father takes his siesta. She is expansive, natural, feminine, a Japanese wife. Paderewski invites us to dinner. Father demanded that we dress up. Delia, a friend, said it was absolutely ridiculous to dress up in the summer, in a hotel which was half deserted. But we dressed up.

Paderewski seems to be standing in a spotlight, because he is all in white, and the light touches up his white hair. He bowed over our hands like a king. Charm. A noble face. Gentle blue eyes which are keen and aware. He was accompanied by his doctor and his secretary, who were furious because my father had dressed in full regalia while they wore Riviera open shirts. I mention this because it was characteristic of my father. When he first came to Paris, married, poor, to play for Vincent d'Indy, he dressed up. D'Indy was displeased, because all the other pianists were so ragged, shabby, and soiled. But, all dressed up like a window mannequin, my father could still play Bach as d'Indy had never imagined. "Where did you learn?" asked d'Indy. "Out of old manuscripts and my own logic," answered my father.

And now he was talking with Paderewski, enchanting him with grace, wit, and erudition. He was under the spell of my father's charm, he himself being a man of enormous romantic charm. It was a beautiful encounter. Paderewski looked like the man of the legends, like the many photographs of him at the piano, playing, with his long hair floating. The courtliness, the romantic attitude, the individualism: they shone from his white hair, his radiant rosy skin, his long fingers.

He has an amazing memory for details. When talking of the cities where he had given concerts, he mentioned the exact number of inhabitants. Speaking of my father he said, "He is *l'homme complet*." He said, "Anaïs is your most successful creation." He has dignity, pride, wisdom. A romantic figure.

I describe him fully because this is a vanishing race. He embraced my father at the end of the dinner as if he were decorating him, thanked him for the red roses my father had ordered to be scattered all over the table. As I went up in the slow cagelike elevator, he looked up at me warmly and gallantly and said: "You have a beauty of other times."

The next day we are packing. My father is marking road maps. We are driving alone to Paris. Delia is looking at me. She has the brilliant shining eyes of a little girl in the body of a fifty-year-old woman. Maruca gives me instructions as to how to take care of my father. "He must have his siesta after lunch. He must rest."

The car is ready. Lunch in Saint-Canna. Heat. Flies. Night in Arles. There is a noisy fair under my window, and I hear the "Habañera." The water of the bath runs so slowly that I begin to do other things, and I forget about it when my father knocks at the door to come and have breakfast. As we are sitting in the dining room, I see the water of the overflowing bath coming down the tile stairs like a Versailles fountain.

My father gives me another Herr Professor lesson. "When you travel, you must give up all your exigencies. Accept and laugh at everything. Abandon all your habits." He has not noticed that I have none! He laughs, tolerates and accepts everything but dirt. Extreme dirt angers him. So he writes in the *Livre d'Or* of the hotel, following many distinguished signatures: "This place is full of shit."

Over dinner it is he who talked. He was urging me to live for myself, to give up the parasites, the Bohemians, the failures. "Believe me, I have done all that. Just like you. The failures are not due to any injustice, but to an inner defect. It is always caused by the person himself. Yes, I know, you think you are doing an act of justice. But they will only suck you dry, wear out your energy, nourish themselves on your ideas. After being the most compassionate man in the world, I say to you today: Let the weak ones die, let them commit suicide. You have explored many dark regions. They are dangerous for a woman."

He talked in a general way.

"I didn't tell you at first, but I was terribly concerned about your life and your friends. What dangers you have skirted!"

At the table he observed the manias, tics, idiosyncrasies of people, their ridiculous or absurd ways. Yet he will caress a mangy cat or overtip the waiter.

On the balcony, where he was taking a sunbath, I discovered the beauty of his feet. Small and fine, so delicate, like a woman's. They seemed to be treading space, not earth. His feet were the most vulnerable, most revealingly delicate fragment of an otherwise steely, taut body. Like an intimate revelation. Achilles heel, the reason, perhaps, for the mask. The reason for the tense will, the imperious tyranny, the erect bearing. The armor of his will. When I saw his feet he became a human being and I felt less in awe of him. I was glad to wipe the perspiration from his face while he was driving. Perfection has precious-stone incandescence which frightens. I am less afraid of his cold, death-dealing criticalness.

Under the superficial surface, there are mysteries, never-ending depths, unknown regions, extending infinitely, unseizable because of his need to create an ideal figure. He has to see, in the eyes of others, an idealized figure. He cannot bear a true mirror. I see him as a sensual, burning flame in bowls of Lalique crystal.

I wore an organdie blouse of salmon rose with a black costume. The organdie fluttered and perked gaily in frills, like fluttering feathers, transparent and blooming. My father said, "You look as if you would fly away."

My father picks up a scarab on the road so it will not be run over. He talks to me as we walk in the sun the next morning.

Two aspects: one of severity, one of sudden tenderness. Pride makes him silent. But he is full of wit and inventiveness. He is sad at my mother's unjust descriptions of him. His father did not love him. His mother loved him too well. His first love betrayed him. Isolina. Unforgiven. She had red hair, and was vivid and beautiful. But while he was in Cuba she married suddenly, did not wait for him. He talked at length on his disillusion with rescue work. He devoted himself to the talent of La Argentina, discovered her, pushed her, composed music for her. Devoted himself to Andres Segovia, to the Aguilar Quartet. He culled only ingratitude. He begs me to live only for myself. The failures. They are an incubus. They feed on your mind, weigh you down, cheat you.

There must be an accord between his writing, his music, his life. He regrets not having been mercenary. He spends too much time helping others.

The rigid forms of his life. Tact. Politeness. Promptness at meetings. On time always. "If I had transgressed in money matters, my music would not have been as pure. I could not have upheld such severe standards in music, philosophy, life. Every detail is important to the whole."

He caused me a great shock by saying, "Henry is a weakling who is living off your virility." He judged Henry's weakness from his love of ugliness, bad smells, strong odors, strong excitations. He says it is a sign of impotence, of perversity. Real sensuality has no need of stimulants.

After a few days we started on the journey back in his car. Saint-Canna was as hot as a tropical town. There were walls of blue stucco in the hotel, as in Cuba, and this reminded him of life there. "I could never wear espadrilles as fashionable people are wearing here in the south, because I associated them with poor Spaniards who came to Cuba seeking work." "He came in *alpargatas*" was a derogatory phrase often used to describe the first Spaniards who came to Cuba seeking their fortune.

He is kind to animals. But he is full of will. "You have to twist events to your desire." He has all the stoicisms and forcefulness, heroisms, except the one which impelled him to marry my mother for her strength, her faith and devotion and sustenance. His walk supple, erect, royal.

My father organizes life, interprets it, controls it. His passion for criticism and perfection paralyzed me. Henry's absence of criticalness liberated me. But when it goes too far, it becomes a disintegrating force, and one cannot build with it.

The rigid walls of my father's constructions terrified me. What a horror of walls, discipline, confinements, controls. When I was telling my father, amusingly and gaily, my experiences as an artist's model at sixteen in New York, and painting in the liveliest colors my first appearance at the Model's Club in Watteau dress, my father interrupts me to say, "Why do you say Watteau? In French it is Vateau." When I first met him I feared he would not like my house at Louveciennes. When he said, "*C'est bien*. It has charm," I was relieved. Yet under the severity there was a well of love.

I would have liked my love for my father to be relaxed. The seventh day, I called it, asking him to rest from this effort at perfection. We both struggled so hard to recreate ourselves, to grow, aiming always higher, rejecting yesterday's self. If today my father could only say to himself and to me, "*C'est bien*," how enjoyable it would be.

Sadness. My maid Emilia leaves me to get married. We kiss weeping. Emilia, who passed unnoticed, yet whose faithfulness, loyalty, devotion have served me deeply and helped to make a difficult life possible. Emilia, disorderly, absent-minded, sympathetic, understanding, indefatigable, with a strange, blind approval of my life and of me.

Service with idolatry and uncanny insight. I repaid her with the same affection and she was happy with me. Her secrecy, her unquestioning attitude. Her blind acceptance of me, her enjoyment of the life in my house, of what the artists brought to the house, of my inventions, the colored stones or the painted horoscopes on the attic's slanting walls, the copper mobile of the astrologic changes in the sky which I kept up to date, as one keeps a clock. Emilia, with her Goya face, an asymmetrical face, the forehead bulging out, the black hair oily, straggly, the big Spanish eyes heavily lidded, the sweet voice, the orphan smile, her singing while she worked.

Her only romance before that of her present fiancée had been the courtship by a young Japanese valet when we lived on the Boulevard Suchet. He had come to see me and had made me a ceremonious speech: Emilia had saved so much, and he had saved so much, and he thought it would be a good marriage of convenience. He did not seem to love her at all, and I had misgivings. He seemed to be planning for a little café in Japan, in his home town.

I felt unsure that Emilia would be happy. "She is such a hard worker," he repeated admiringly. As if Emilia had been my daughter, I worried, but did not want to oppose the marriage. I suggested that he wait until Emilia had the proper trousseau: hand-sewn underwear, dresses, sheets and pillow cases in the old-fashioned Spanish tradition. I bought Emilia materials, and a beautiful wooden wedding chest and encouraged her to sew, embroider, crochet, petit-point all her clothes for a bride. She was adept at all this, patient, and worked at it during spare moments and in the evening. The Japanese valet was invited to come and visit the treasure chest. But this took time. And before Emilia had terminated the trousseau, she had discovered that he did not love her. The trousseau was now going to be used for a devoted Spanish husband who adored her.

I dream that I am in a train. My journals are in a black valise. I am walking through the cars. Someone comes and tells me the valise with the journals has disappeared. Terrible anxiety. I hear that a man has burned the journals. I am furious and I have a great sense of injustice. I ask to have the case brought before a court; the man who has burned my journals is there. I expect the lawyer to defend me. The judge sees immediately that the man has committed a crime, that he had no right to burn the journals. But the lawyers do not talk or defend me. The judge becomes apathetic. Nobody says anything. I have a feeling that the world is against me, that I have to make my own defense. I get up and make a very eloquent speech. "In those journals you can see I was brought up in Spanish Catholicism, that my actions later are not evil; just a struggle to react against a prison." I talk, I talk. I am aware that everybody is aware of my eloquence, but they say nothing. One of the judges interrupts me to correct my language. I say: "Of course I am aware that I cannot talk pure legal French. I beg you to forgive my inaccuracies." But this does not deter me from continuing a passionate defense and accusation. But everybody remains inert. The extent of my despair awakens me.

[September, 1933]

Maruca took me to Father's house. The neatest, the most spotless street of Paris, where the gardeners were occupied in clipping and trimming a few rare potted bushes in small, still, front gardens; where butlers were occupied in polishing doorknobs; where low cars rolled up silently and caught one by surprise; where stone lions watched fur-trimmed women kissing little dogs. On winter evenings the luxurious home was heated like a hothouse. The windows were of amber stained glass, the rugs deep.

Maruca gave me a photograph of my father taken when he had just left us. I fell in love with this image of his inner self, the one before he donned a mask. The face before the will asserted itself. Mouth soft and half open, full, not yet thinned out by tightness. No furrows between the eyes, no hardness, no setness. This was the face I had expected to see the first day, the face I probably carried away with me as a child, the face of exposed sensibility, vulnerability, emotion. The years had built a mask. Will. Will. Will. I was shocked and sad. I placed this photograph on my desk. And then I realized that I had loved a face which was disappearing, a young father; and the full horror of my father's aging struck me, chilled me. His age. I felt nostalgia for a soft face which no longer exists, who might have been, then, the lover of my dreams. Today I see the crystallization. The mask of wisdom, control, aging, death.

Henry and I met at the Trocadéro. I was waiting, standing against a big old tree reading *M. de Phocas* of Jean Lorrain, an echo of *À Rebours*—morbid and sulphurous. All Paris was tinted the color of the eyes of Astarte which haunted the man. All Paris smoked with opium, murder, insanity. I felt all the hells described by Artaud, by the maddest poets, even while walking with a healthy and blooming body after horseback-riding in the Forest at seven in the morning. I am like a person walking through a mirror broken in two. I see the plot. One woman, stylish, fresh, blooming, is walking towards the Trocadéro; and the other walks into nightmares which haunt the imagination, and which I described in *House of Incest*. The nightmare always. Am I in love with the nightmare, as Kafka was, as so many poets? In the forest, air and sun and dappled leaves, dancing blood, flying on a horse, leaping over white gates.

"Le bouc noir passe au fond des ténèbres malsaines."

Henry thinks as he approaches me, "I don't recognize the hat but it can only be Anaïs who reads while she waits."

And together we visit Abyssinia, the Sudan, East Africa, etc. We look at masks, wooden figures, grass huts, instruments for magic ceremonies, weavings, paintings on stones, pottery, idols, the mother of the dead, costumes for ceremonies of circumcision; we gloat over the rolls of manuscripts and the drawings to be carried as talisman against the devil and which must be as long as the person is tall. All eyes. Eyes. No heads. But squares pierced with eyes. Book of Magic Recipes. Books of magic. Monsters of hair, of cord, fish teeth, burnt wood, breasts like funnels, vulvas carved open, scrawls, lace-patterned chairs. I am vibrating from head to toes. Artaud was right when he said artistic sensations were perceived by me through my senses. I felt intoxicated.

We sat in a café afterwards. I was still laughing about a huge necklace of bones which was put around the necks of the women who lied. Henry was talking about his books, his ideas, his notes. So fertile, so rich. His book *Black Spring*, his scenario, his book on the movies, his book on June. He became lost.

"I am coming now to my China . . ."

"What does China mean to you?"

Henry's explanation is vague at first. China seems to stand for a certain condition of existence . . . the universe of mere being. Where one lives like a plant, instinctively. No will. The great indifference, like that of the Hindu who lets himself be passive in order to let the seeds in him flower. Something between the will of the European and the karma of the Oriental.

But I have not entirely seized Henry's idea of China. At the moment I sensed what he meant, but it was fragile and tenuous. His life has been one long opposition to will—but that was not difficult for him: he was born without a will, he was born passive. It is a philosophy created out of a temperament. He has practiced letting things happen. Now he wants to express in literature the effectiveness of relaxing the will for the sake of enjoyment. He is the man who dodged jobs, responsibilities, ties. He freed himself of all tasks but one: to write, perhaps at the expense of others, at the expense of smaller men and lesser artists.

But among the forces behind Henry's work, aren't there others' wills? Henry talks about the need to organize his notes—his mountains of notes. Organization. I have, so many times, plunged into his chaos with two hands, to organize first the man, and then the work. To be consistent with himself, he should not have sought this from me: a unification, a wholeness, a drawing together, a core.

For, at bottom, what he is is Dada.

Manifesto of Dadaism.

Dada, c'est tout, ce n'est rien, c'est oui en Russe, c'est quelque chose en Roumain, c'est quelque chose en presque toutes les langues et qui n'a pas son dada, c'est l'absurde absolu, l'absolu du fou, du non, c'est l'art pour l'art, c'est Dada.

I love the darkness. I love walking through the streets of Paris with the image of Sacher-Masoch as he appears on a paperbook cover, dragging himself at the feet of a beautiful naked woman who is half-covered with furs, wearing boots and whipping him. She deceives him because he asks her to deceive him. His eyes glisten when he sees a strong servant girl, because he thinks perhaps she can whip him much harder than Wanda.

The figure of a cringing Masoch does not appeal to me. What appeals to me is this violent tasting of life's most fearful cruelties. No evasions of pain. That day I could not talk to the doorman or to the hairdresser, who needed sympathy, because I wanted to ask them why I had such a passion for fur, a real passion, so that if I had money I would carpet a room with fur, cover the walls with it, and cover myself with it. Is it possible, I wanted to ask, that we remember having once been an animal? That this incapacity to destroy, which Henry accuses me of, may soon be reversed? That my cruelty wears a velvet mask and velvet gloves?

Sacher-Masoch's book is gaudy, but how can one ever forget the

Hungarian peasant dancers who, on warm days, took off their chemises and danced in big voluminous skirts, turning until the skirts lifted and showed all the brown hot bodies? And the African maidens who wore little belts of beads and fish teeth with bells. Bells dancing around their hips. And the motion of the horse this morning, the sweat and smell of the horse between my legs, the turmoil of smell and heat and motion between the legs so that I wanted to lie on the grass and be made love to.

Without his writing, I don't know what Henry would be. It completes him. People who know him as gentle, wonder at the writing. Yet sometimes I have the feeling that this gentleness is not entirely genuine. It is his way of charming. Of disarming. It allows his entry anywhere, he is trusted. It is like a disguise of the observant, the critical, the accusing man within. His severity is disguised. His hatreds and his rebellions. They are not apparent, or acted out. It is always a shock to others. I am aware at times, while he speaks in a mellow way to others, of that small, round, hard photographic lens in his blue eyes. The writer is a coward. He does not fight his battles *sur place*, openly, in the presence of others. Later. Later. Alone.

I began my letter to Father: "*Quelle triste heures . . .*" and realized I was going to write *heureuse* instead of *heure*. Revelatory. For I was to tell him how sad I was that I could not come to Valescure. Why? Why?

I remember a whimsical moment when he was reading from Journal Three, Mother's description of Father's proposal. "I looked at his beautiful blue eyes, his long dark hair, his patched pants . . . and said yes . . ."

Father, who was resting after his treatment, almost leaped out of bed. Leonine indignation. Half humorous, half serious: "Patched pants! *Quel blasphème! Me,* me in patched pants! Why, if I had ever worn such mended trousers I would not have left the house. I would have cloistered myself. Can't you see how unlike me that is?" And it was, it was absolutely incongruous, impossible to imagine my father wearing mended trousers!

He has a touching trick of being hurt easily but of rising out of it quickly by humor, mocking himself, ironic, whimsical. Subjugating his vulnerability, covering it, disguising it. Later he wrote to me, commenting on a gift I sent him: "Crime of extravagance. Where do you get such extravagance? No wonder. You issued from a pair of patched pants!"

Humor. Humor on the brink of a desolate, tragic secret, as mine is, a gaiety always for others, like a bouquet in silver paper, on the periphery, while inside . . .

The only tender and stirring part of his rigid forms. I felt the form of his life, his instrumentation of it, as if he were a conductor. Musical intricacies and development. Each word, each feeling, each gesture composed, the synthesis of an élan, but an élan of art. At this hour, it is right. The moment is right. The lights. The room. Life orchestrated, molded by his will. When we walk together, don't take my arm. Movement subjugated, movement molded. Life contained, shaped, improved upon. No sloppiness, slovenliness, abandon, casualness. Style. Form. Now you can come. Wear your evening dress. Orchestration. Instrumentation. No disorder, no whims, no fantasies.

Henry breaks all the molds, all the forms, all the shells, all the edifices of art, and what is born is warm and imperfect. It is human.

My revolt against my father died. I was looking at the photograph of him when he was twenty. I thought of his stoicism, the will with which he dominates his moods, his chaos, his melancholia. My father and I give only our best to the world. I was thinking of his whimsicality and gaiety when he is saddest. I did not want this plaster cast of stoicism over my face and body. I wanted to get out of my own shell. Overcome this terrific timidity which encloses me. At Lowenfels', I barely talked, and envied him his drunkenness. I must expand, live out, love, so as to evade obsession. I must think of others, spread out.

How deeply jealous is my father, I wonder. He is so enigmatic, so secretive. Is there as much darkness in him as in me? How desperately he seeks the sun, beauty, harmony. To heal himself, to keep his balance.

I must learn to stand alone. Nobody can really follow me all the way, understand me completely. My father encourages a restricted life. He is driving Maruca's mother around, to movies, a bourgeois life, bourgeois ideals. Henry is the egotistical artist. He is a better example.

Dear diary, you have hampered me as an artist. But at the same time you have kept me alive as a human being. I created you because I needed a friend. And talking to this friend, I have, perhaps, wasted my life.

Today I begin to work. Writing for a hostile world discouraged me. Writing for you gave me the illusion of a warm ambiance I needed to flower in. But I must divorce you from my work. Not abandon you. No, I need your companionship. Even after I have worked, I look around me, and who can my soul talk to without fear of incomprehension? Here breathes my love of peace, here I breathe peace.

Dropped the diary and wrote first twenty pages of June story objectively.* Conscious order. Excision of irrelevant details.

My father writes me:

My only real failure in life was my marriage to your mother. But then I was so young, and your mother was, consciously or unconsciously, playing a role: she deceived me, and took her mask off the day of our marriage.

He was shocked by Artaud's *Théâtre de La Cruauté*.

Sick, neurotic, unbalanced, drug addict. I do not believe in exposing one's sickness to the world. In dramatizing one's madness.

Dissonances with my father. I wrote him two letters, with news of Thorvald, and my talk with Joaquin; and the interest of the news is marred for him because our letters crossed and there was confusion. That was the essential point: that I, having written him

* Intended as part of *Winter of Artifice*, these pages were later taken out.

without waiting for an answer, caused a disorder which was painful to him. I wrote him ironically, mocking myself for having disregarded the conductor's directions, for having played impulsively and disorganized the symphony. Deep down, I felt that an inhuman order which kills spontaneity and naturalness is wrong.

But the real tragedy in our relationship is that we both set up an ideal and romantic image: we were both going to dedicate ourselves exclusively to each other. We were not going to lie to each other. We were going to be confidants and friends. But, inevitably, being so much alike, I was going to conceal my Bohemian life, and he his mistresses. I could read transparently through his hypocritical excuses for sending Maruca back to Paris ten days earlier, and coming back alone on the thirtieth. I could visualize him entertaining a mistress at Valescure in the same hotel. Nor was he going to travel back alone. It offends me that he should tell me the same lies as he tells his wife.

Forget this pestering female, lamenting that her men have not the courage to kill the dragons, and that the only men who are capable of killing dragons are Telephone Kings, Oil Kings, Boxing Champions, Horse-smelling Generals, none of whom I could have loved.

Nail carpet in the hall.

Buy my father's favorite cigarettes.

Organize and clean the house.

And as for the dragons . . .

Somehow or other I always lose my guide halfway up the mountain, and he becomes my child. Even my father.

I do not think I am looking for a man, but for a God. I am beginning to feel a void which must be the absence of God. I have called for a father, a guide, a leader, a protector, a friend, a lover, but I still miss something: it must be God. But I want a god in the flesh, not an abstraction, an incarnated god, with strength, two arms, and a sex.

Perhaps I have loved the artist because creation is the nearest we come to divinity.

My father's emphasis on non-human perfection, for a while,

seemed to indicate he might play the role of God the Father. He has no love of human imperfection.

My father says: do not look at me, look at all that I am attempting to be, look at my ideal intentions.

The death of Antonio Francisco Miralles in a hotel room, alone, of asthma. Miralles, my Spanish dancing teacher.

Whenever I stepped off the bus at Montmartre, I could hear the music of the merry-go-rounds at the fair, and I would feel my mood, my walk, my whole body transformed by its gaiety. I walked to a side street, knocked on a dark doorway opened by a disheveled concierge, and ran down the stairway to a vast room below street level, a vast cellar room with its walls covered with mirrors. It was the place where the little girls from the Opéra Ballet rehearsed. When I came down the stairway I could hear the piano, feet stamping, and the ballet master's voice. When the piano stopped, there was always his voice scolding, and the whispering of smaller voices. As I entered, the class was dissolving and a flurry of little girls brushed by me in their moth ballet costumes, laughing and whispering, fluttering like moths on their dusty ballet slippers, flurries of snow in the darkness of the vast room, with drops of dew from exertion. I went down with them along the corridors to the dressing rooms. These looked like gardens, with so many ballet skirts, Spanish costumes hanging on pegs. It overflowed with the smell of cold cream, face powder, cheap cologne.

While they dressed for the street, I dressed for my Spanish dances. Miralles would already be rehearsing his own castanets. The piano, slightly out of tune, was beginning the dance of Granados. The floor was beginning to vibrate as other Spanish dancers tried out their heel work. Tap tap tap tap tap. Miralles was about forty, slender, erect, not handsome in face but graceful when dancing. His face was undefined, his features blurred.

I was the favorite.

He was like a gentle Svengali, and by his eyes, his voice, his hands, he had the power to make me dance as well as by his ordinary lessons. He ruled my body with a magnetic rule, master of my dancing.

One day he waited for me at the door, neat and trim. "Will you come and sit at the café with me?"

I followed him. Not far from there was the Place Clichy, always animated, but more so now, as the site of a permanent fair. The merry-go-rounds were turning swiftly. The gypsies were reading fortunes in little booths hung with Arabian rugs. Workmen were shooting clay pigeons and winning cut glass for their wives. The prostitutes were enjoying their loitering, and the men were watching them.

My dancing teacher was saying to me: "Anaïs, I am a simple man. My parents were shoemakers in a little village in the south of Spain. I was put to work in an iron factory where I handled heavy things and was on the way to becoming deformed by big muscles. But during my lunch hour, I danced. I wanted to be a dancer and I practiced every day, every night. At night I went to the gypsies' caverns, and learned from them. I began to dance in cabarets. And today, look!" He took out a cigarette case engraved with the names of all the famous Spanish dancers. "Today I have been the partner of all these women. If you would come with me, we could be happy. I am a simple man, but we could dance in all the cities of Europe. I am no longer young but I have a lot of dancing in me yet. We could be happy."

The merry-go-round turned and sang, and I imagined myself embarking on a dancing career with Miralles, dancing, which was so much like flying, from city to city, receiving bouquets, praise in newspapers, with joyous music at the center always, pleasure as colorful as the Spanish dresses, all red, orange, black and gold, gold and purple, and red and white.

Imagining . . . like amnesia. Forgetting who I was, and where I was, and why I could not do it. Not knowing how to answer so I would not hurt him, I said, "I am not strong enough."

"That's what I thought when I first saw you. I thought you couldn't take the discipline of a dancer's life. But it isn't so. You look fragile and all that, but you're healthy. I can tell healthy women by their skin. Yours is shining and clear. No, I don't think you have the strength of a horse, you're what we call a *petite na-*

ture. But you have energy and guts. And we'll take it easy on the road."

Many afternoons, after hard work, we sat at this little café and imagined what a dancer's life might be.

Miralles and I danced in several places together, at a *haute couture* opening, at a millionaire Brazilian's open house, at a night club; but when I auditioned for the Opéra, *Amor Brujo*, and was accepted and would have traveled all over the world, I gave up dancing [1928].

And Miralles died alone in his hotel room, of asthma. He had been saving his money to retire to his home town, Valencia. He was good, homely, and would say to me: "You know, I have no vices like the others. I would be good to you." Just because I listened to his gaudy stories of a gaudy past, he glowed, he went at his dancing with renewed vigor, he was rejuvenated, he bought himself a new suit.

For a while, it was as if I had lived in his shabby hotel room, with photographs of Spanish dancers pinned to the walls. I knew how it was in Russia, in music halls all over the world. The odor of the dancers, of dressing rooms, the pungent atmosphere of rehearsals. Lola, Alma Viva, L'Argentinita. I would wear bedroom slippers and flowered kimonos, big Spanish flowered cottons. I would open the door and my father would be standing there, saying: "Have you forgotten who you are? You are my daughter, you have forgotten your class, your name, your true stature in life."

One day I awakened from my amnesia. No longer a dancer. Miralles turned ashen and grey, was snuffed out. He became again an old, weary dancing teacher.

How often I tried to kill the "ideal" self, assassinate the critical self. Lose myself. That is, one of them.

The ideal self is slowly becoming a ridiculous figure. I laugh at it.

My books are splitting, too: the dream on one side, the human reality on the other. I took passages out of *House of Incest* which belong in *Winter of Artifice*. The mood is human, not hallucinated.

About *House of Incest*, when I read Mirbeau's *Jardin des Supplices*, I remember being struck with the limitations of physical cruelty and pain. I also remember that I felt obsessions and anxieties were just as cruel and painful, only no one had described them vividly, as vividly as physical tortures. I wanted to do, in *House of Incest*, the counterpart to physical torture in the psychic world, in the psychological realm. (June, Jeanne, Artaud, Marguerite, their very real suffering.)

Henry very pleased with his "portrait" in *Winter of Artifice*. "Such a full portrait, so human, so warm."

I saw my father in one of his out-of-the-world, out-of-reality moods. He was reading as he walked from the gate to the door of the house. He launched into a discourse, a monologue: "Why don't they have first-class smokers on the train? I went to the station master and complained. I said to him: 'It is a loss for French revenues because I smoke French cigarettes, etc.'"

Like June. A torrent of words. To cover what? I tried to tune myself to his mood. I urged him to continue his life as before, to enjoy his mistresses, that his love for me must expand his life rather than narrow it.

He answered, "No, I could never live like that again. I want this love to be the apotheosis of my life. It is too great a thing to spoil with ordinary love affairs. It must remain clean, single, unique."

As I can only judge my double from myself, I can see that he would like to make our love an ideal finish to his Don Juan career, that he confuses the wish with reality. I know he cannot live up to this, and I do not ask him to. It was not my suggestion at all. But when he questions me about my life, I feel I have to make the same romantic promises. We will both lie to each other, and for the same reason: to create an impossible ideal world.

The frightening thing about men aging is how they count their love-making. My father says, "I should only make love once a week at my age."

Is my father tired of his one-night affairs, lonely, loveless? Does he want understanding in place of sexual diversions?

His narcissism is much stronger than mine. He has never loved his *opposite*. My mother was his opposite and they immediately began to battle. The greatest crime, it seems, that she ever committed (aside from her strong will and bad temper) was a crime against romantic aesthetics: on their wedding night (at that time, women wore half-wigs and much stuffing in their hair) she laid all the false hair pieces on the night table.

As he can only love what is like himself, he will love, in me, only what resembles him, not our differences.

He always says: "How natural you are, how real."

In Louveciennes he relaxed finally. I took him to see the bird nest in the garden.

It is like looking into a mirror. I know that when he leaves me, he will ride back to Paris meditating on his errors, what he should not have said, what went wrong.

He may have regretted the opportunity I gave him to be open and truthful about his life, which he did not take advantage of.

When Henry returned the copy of *House of Incest*, it was annotated. I found he had made this note: "All pictorial passages wonderful. Would make a film script. Begin with scene of gigantic fish bowl."

When he came, we launched into a vigorous talk. He presented me with some of Brassai's photographs and told me of the talk they had together. I introduced him to Joseph Delteil. We began to compose a scenario. Henry would compose a scene, I another. We enlarge, expand, probe my sketchy material. He wants to pour into it his notes on a scenario. He would create the universe of the dream, I the details. He drags in cosmic symbology, and I the individual. We get intoxicated with our inventions. It is like a drug. We talk about the dream—return to my original statement that most dreamwriting is false and intellectually composed, that the real dream has an authenticity and can be recognized. The intellectually composed or fabricated dream does not arouse the dream sensation in others (like Cocteau's film, for instance).

Talking on the dream, I am always fertile and voluble. It is my favorite realm, and I am so familiar with its technical aspects. Henry gets excited, and he invents, collaborates, extends. All that the movie could do with *House of Incest*. "Go and see Germaine Dulac," he says. "She will like you."

We get drunk with images, words, scenes, possibilities. We are in such a mood that Henry says, "This is what I enjoy—a talk like this —I don't enjoy myself going out for a spree—it's all dead, the cabarets, the cafés, most of the people. I go out expecting fun and I come back spitting with anger and disgust." He gets up to show me how he walks, spitting crossly, and it makes me laugh.

He reads the last pages of *Winter of Artifice*, criticizes and praises. I am ironic about French literature which he praises and in which I find, at present, no great figure—no D. H. Lawrence. We agree that the French bring more perfection—Duhamel, Delteil, etc.; but that the others, less perfect, are greater. Impossible to say why. They are great with the greatness of human imperfection. One loves them. One admires the French writers. They are like Bach, compared with more lyrical musicians. I love the romantics. Henry tries me out, tests me in this, by playing records I don't know. Immediately I catch the elements I do not like, which leave me cold. Logic, order, construction, classicism, equilibrium, control. I wanted to shout: I admire imperfections, Dostoevsky, Lawrence, and Henry. There is a power there.

Henry tries to restrain my extravagance in writing, while yet allowing himself complete exuberance. Why? It may be I am not good at my craft yet. My style suffers when I seek freedom, when I feel too strongly. My writing will have to learn to support the weight of my vitality. I guess I'm still a little young, in writing. But window-breaking brings in oxygen and I am full of oxygen just now.

I should caricature my weakness. I want to master my tragic sense of life and achieve a comic spirit. I want to be less emotional and more humorous.

Certain events happen very close to me, others are dim. Some are vital and warm, some have a dreamlike quality. With my father the relationship is unreal, like something happening in a dream state.

I awakened in a courageous mood. I had on my list three difficult things to do, three ordeals to face. Visit to Rank. Reconciliation with Bernard Steele. Visit to Edward Titus to ask for the money he owes me. I wondered which one I would tackle. Decided first to bring Steele out of his jealous sulking, his anger that I did not stay at his home for the weekend but left with Artaud, his jealousy of Artaud and Henry.

He was out.

Edward Titus was in the south of France.

When you know someone from his writings you think he will live forever. I considered Otto Rank a legend even after Henry visited him. He was a legendary character until I came across a list of his works in the Psychoanalytical Library and saw on the card, on the left-hand corner, the date of his birth, and on the right-hand corner, a blank left for the date of his death. This shocked me into awareness of his temporary presence. His life span was already over half spent, and I must talk to him now. He was not eternal. On the right-hand corner of a library card lay the inescapable proof of his inescapable fate. His books, big, heavy, and substantial, would always be there, but I felt I must talk to him now.

The library card also gave his address. He lived overlooking the park.

There were other reasons. I felt torn apart by my multiple relationships, and I would have been able to live fully in each one, had enough love and devotion for all of them, but they conflicted with each other. All of my father's values negated Henry's: all his exhortations and his influence were spent on eliminating from my life Artaud, Allendy, psychoanalysis.

I felt confused, and lost.

It was not a father I had found, in the true sense of the word.

It was a foggy afternoon when I decided to call on Dr. Rank. At the subway station near his home, there was a small park with benches. I sat down on one of them to prepare myself for the visit. I felt that from such an abundance of life, I must make a selection of what might interest him. He had made a specialty of the "artist." He was interested in the artist. Would he be interested in a woman who had lived out all the themes he wrote about, the Double, Illusion and Reality, Incestuous Loves Through Literature, Creation and Play. All the myths (return to the father after many adventures and obstacles), all the dreams. I had lived out the entire contents of his profound studies so impetuously that I had

269

had no time to understand them, to sift them. I was confused and lost. In trying to live out all of my selves . . .

There were always, in me, two women at least, one woman desperate and bewildered, who felt she was drowning, and another who only wanted to bring beauty, grace, and aliveness to people and who would leap into a scene, as upon a stage, conceal her true emotions because they were weaknesses, helplessness, despair, and present to the world only a smile, an eagerness, curiosity, enthusiasm, interest.

Should I come and say, Dr. Rank, I feel like a shattered mirror, or mention my book on D. H. Lawrence and the other books I was writing?

He considered neurosis a failed work of art, the neurotic a failed artist. Neurosis, he had written, was a manifestation of imagination and energy gone wrong. Instead of a fruit or a flower, I had borne obsessions and anxieties. It was this concept which appealed to me, that he did not call it an illness, but, as in nature, a misbegotten object which might have equal beauty and fascination as the relatives of more legitimate and noble birth. Neurosis was Spanish moss on a tree.

Which self should I bring him? The Anaïs who could be swept off her feet in the middle of a busy street and experience an emotional levitation? Street, people, incidents, words: all acquired a poetic diffusion, dissolving all sense of obstacle, fatality, crystallization, finite conclusions. It was an abstract drunkenness, druggedness, like the illuminations of the poets.

Or should I tell him about my crash landings?

I had no in-between existence: only flights, mobility, euphoria; and despair, depression, disillusion, paralysis, shock, and a shattering of the mirror.

"I am one of the artists you are writing about, Dr. Rank."

It was Dr. Rank who opened the door.

"Yes?" he said, in his harsh Viennese accent, wrapping the incisive, clear French words in a German crunch, as if the words had been chewed like the end of his cigar instead of liberated out of his mouth like a bird out of a cage. French words were sent out to fly in the air like messenger doves, but Dr. Rank's words were chewed, spewed.

He was short, dark-skinned, round-faced; but what stood out were his eyes, which were large, fiery, and dark. I singled out his eyes to eclipse the short Dr. Caligari body, the uneven teeth.

"Come in," he said, smiling, and led the way to his office, which was a library, with bookcases reaching to the ceiling, and one large window overlooking the park.

I felt at home among the books. I chose a deep chair and he sat across from me.

"So," he said, "it was you who sent Henry Miller to see me. Did you perhaps wish you could come yourself?"

"Perhaps. I felt that Dr. Allendy's formulas did not fit my life. I have read all your books. I felt that there is *more* in my relation to my father than the desire of a victory over my mother."

By his smile I knew he understood the *more* and my objection to oversimplifications.

He asked me for a clear, full outline of my life and work. I gave it to him.

"I know the artist can make good use of his conflicts but I feel that, at the present time, I am expending too much energy trying to master a confusion of desires which I cannot solve. I need your help."

Immediately I knew that we talked the same language. He said, "I go beyond the psychoanalytical. Psychoanalysis emphasizes the resemblance between people; I emphasize the differences between people. They try to bring everybody to a certain normal level. I try to adapt each person to his own kind of universe. The creative instinct is apart."

"Perhaps it is because I am a poet, but I have always felt that there *is something beyond* Lesbianism, narcissism, masochism, etc."

"Yes, there is creation," said Dr. Rank.

When I mentioned the brief psychoanalytical formulas he smiled again, ironically, as if agreeing with me as to their insufficiency. I felt the expansion of his thought beyond medicine into metaphysical and philosophical universes. We understood each other quickly.

"What I want to know is what you created during periods of extreme neurosis. That will be interesting to me. The stories you wrote as a child, which all began with: 'I am an orphan,' are not to be explained, as Allendy did, merely as criminal desire to do away with the mother out of jealousy of the father, out of an inordinate love of the father. *You wanted to create yourself, you did not want to be born of human parents.*"

He was neither solemn nor grave. He was agile, quick, as if each word I uttered were a precious object he had excavated and was delighted to find. He acted as if I were unique, as if this were a unique adventure, not a phenomenon to be categorized.

"You tried to live your life like a myth. Everything you dreamed or fantasied, you carried out. You are a myth-maker."

"I am tired of lies and deformities. I need absolution. I must confess to you the mood which preceded my talk with you. I made this note on the train: 'On my way to see Dr. Rank I am planning impostures, cheatings, tricks.' I begin to invent what I will tell Dr. Rank, instead of coordinating truths. I begin to rehearse speeches, attitudes, gestures, inflections, expressions. I see myself talking and I am sitting within Rank, judging me. What should I say to create such and such effect? I meditate lies as others meditate confessions. Yet I am going to him to confess, to get help in the solution of my conflicts, which are too numerous, and which I do not succeed in mastering by writing. I prepare myself for a false comedy, as I did with Allendy. Preparing to deform, and all to interest Rank."

"Your inventions are you, too," said Dr. Rank. "They all stem from you."

"Perhaps I came not to *solve* anything, but for another adventure, to dramatize, to enlarge upon my conflicts, to discover all that they contain, to seize upon them in full. My experience with Allendy was a new conflict added to my life, added to the old. Perhaps I want to go on juggling. I am again at an impasse. So I shift my ground, displace my objective. Conflict insoluble, so I will interest myself in my talks with you."

I had been afraid he would rush into a definition, a formula, but not at all. What predominated was his curiosity, not the impulse to classify. He was not like a scientist intent on fitting a human being into a theory. He was not practicing mental surgery. He was relying on his intuition, intent on discovering a woman neither one of us knew. A new specimen. He improvised. I felt that my lost identity was already being reconstructed with his recognition and vision of me. He had not thrown me back upon a vague ocean of generalities, a cell among a million cells.

"What you call your lies are fiction and myths. The art of creating a disguise can be as beautiful as the creation of a painting."

"Are you saying I created a woman for my artist life, bold, gay, courageous, generous, fearless; and another to please my father, a clear-sighted woman with a love of beauty, harmony, and self-discipline, critical and selective; and still another who lives in chaos, embraces the weak and the stumbling, the confused?"

No judgment from Dr. Rank.

"What brought you here?"

"I felt like a shattered mirror."

"Why a mirror? A mirror for others? To reflect others, or yourself living behind a mirror and unable to touch real life?"

"Allendy called me a *petite fille littéraire*. This did not dispose of my passion for writing, my vital preoccupation with orientations, awareness of the deviations of my creative instincts. But he was the saving diversion. I need to be diverted from my anxieties."

"There is nothing wrong with a desire for intellectual adventure."

"But now, as I sit here, I am as truthful as I am with my journal."

"Confusion creates art. Too much confusion creates unbalance."

He seemed to have such a love of creation, of invention, to understand my motivations coming from dreams. When I talked about my father, he related it immediately to the various myths in literature which stemmed from dreams. He said:

"In folk tradition, handed down through fairy tales, there exists a type of story, similar all over the world, which contains the same elements. They are the mythological motifs which we see now guiding your life. In these stories the father leaves for twenty years, returns and finds his daughter a woman. In an early book of mine on the Father and Daughter love in literature, I collected all these stories and analyzed carefully the classical representation of them. One of them was the well-known Pericles legend, popular throughout the Middle Ages and dramatized by Shakespeare.

"While the details of this universal legend change according to time and custom, the essential plot always remains the same: the girl is abandoned as an infant but is miraculously rescued and, after many adventures, finds her father whom she does not know or recognize. This meeting takes place after some legendary twenty years. A lapse of time which can be explained on the simple ground that, at this time, the daughter is mature and ready to become a woman. The father, not knowing that he has found his abandoned daughter, falls in love with her; but in the traditional story they recognize each other before incest is committed.

"These elaborate stories with their dreamlike quality have been explained, mythologically that is, as symbolic representations of cosmic cycles, as myths of the Sun and the Moon which flee and meet each other alternatively. It must be admitted that such a cosmic explanation, provided it is not carried too far into astronomic details, fits these adventurous happenings much better than the realistic interpretation of the psychoanalysts, who claim that these stories prove the human desire for incestuous union between parent and children. The fact that, in tradition, they do not know or recognize each other when they finally meet, does not bother these psychological interpreters, who see in that motif a reflection of the repression of the desire for incest, a desire which has to remain unconscious, unknown to the self.

"The question was whether, in a literary sense, these stories were created or written from the point of view of the girl or the father? Because the corresponding tradition of the hero (which I studied in a separate essay wherein the hero is exposed as an infant, miraculously rescued, and usually married his mother, like the famous Oedipus of the Greek saga) is evidently created from the son's point of view. Naturally his story glorified the superhuman deeds of his heroic self; whereas the feminine heroine, in the other kind of tradition, seems to be seen through the eyes of the father and pictured the way he wants her to be.

"Another difference between the cosmic hero and the cosmic heroine, as depicted in these sources of tradition, is equally puzzling. Although the myth of the hero glorifies his godlike achievements, it sounds, to me, more human and less cosmic than the adventurous life of the daughter, whose main achievement seems to be the finding of the man in the lost father by simply following her love inspirations. And yet this human, all too human motif is expressed in a wealth of cosmic symbolism which is lacking in the presentation of the hero, whose life and achievement have an earthy quality.

"This seeming paradox may be due to the fact that the man was able to carry out some of his ambitious dreams in reality by cultural creations; whereas the woman, being closer to the cosmic forces, had to express even human motifs in universal symbols. In the Arabian Nights, for example, which grew out of old mythical traditions, the woman not only is constantly compared to the moon, but she *is* the moon, she acts like the moon. She always disappears for a certain amount of time and has to be pursued and found by her true lover, as the day meets the night at dawn, just for a kiss, in order to separate again.

"The humanized tradition of this 'incestuous' cycle, as we find it in the literature of all times and all people, might very well have been written down by man. He has always been keen to usurp all creation; and the proverbial passivity of the woman, who always appears as waiting or pursued, might have enabled him to depict her as he wanted her, *in her life story written by him*. And now I am glad to hear the woman's side of the story."

This was the substance of our first talk. As we talked, he showed me the books in his bookcase. Then, as I left, he looked at the diary volume I was carrying and said, "Leave that with me."

I was startled. It was true I had brought it, as I often carried it about, to write in it while I waited here and there. But I had also written in it the fabrications I had intended to tell Dr. Rank. And to suddenly expose it all to someone frightened me. What would he think? Would he lose interest in me? Would he be shocked, startled? It was a bold stroke. He interpreted my carrying it as a wish to share it. He challenged my "offer." I hesitated, and then I placed it on the low table between the two armchairs. And I left.

˷

The second talk. Dr. Rank said:

"We know very little about woman. In the first place, it was man who invented 'the soul.' Man was the philosopher and the psychologist, the historian and the biographer. Woman could only accept man's classifications and interpretations. The women who played important roles thought like men, and wrote like men.

"It was only while delving into the subconscious that we began to understand that the feminine way of acting, woman's motivations, more often came from that mixture of intuition, instinct, personal experience, personal relation to all things, which men deny having. It was through psychology that we discovered that man's illusion about his objectivity was a fiction, a fiction he needed to believe in. The most objective systems of thought can be exposed as having a subjective base. Now, the way a woman feels is closer to three forms of life: the child, the artist, the primitive. They act by their instant vision, feeling, and instinct. They remained in touch with that mysterious region we are now opening up. They were inarticulate except in terms of symbols, through dreams and myths."

As he talked, I thought of my difficulties with writing, my struggles to articulate feelings not easily expressed. Of my struggles to find a language for intuition, feelings, instincts which are, in themselves, elusive, subtle, and wordless.

Wasn't it D. H. Lawrence who wrote of how women took their pattern from man, and proceeded to be what man invented? Few writers have had a direct vision into woman. Few women had vision into themselves! And when they did, they were revolted at what they saw, just as people were revolted by what Freud exposed.

Man must fear the effort woman is making to create herself, not to be born of Adam's rib. It revives his old fears of her power. What he forgets is that dependency does not create love, and to control nature is not a greater achievement than to control woman, for there will always be the revolts of instinct, the earthquakes and the tidal waves. With control one also killed the rich natural resources of both nature and woman. It was woman who reacted against the great dehumanization of man by industry, the machine. Man reacted by mutiny, or crime. Woman sought other ways. Mutiny is not in her nature.

Dr. Rank said: "I do not believe in long-drawn-out psychoanalysis. I do not believe in spending too much time exploring the past, delving into it. I believe neurosis is like a virulent abscess, or infection. It has to be attacked powerfully in the present. Of course, the origin of the illness may be in the past, but the virulent crisis must be dynamically tackled. I believe in attacking the core of the illness, through its present symptoms, quickly, directly. The past is a labyrinth. One does not have to step into it and move step by step through every turn and twist. The past reveals itself instantly, in today's fever or abscess of the soul.

"I believe analysis has become the worst enemy of the soul. It killed what it analyzed. I saw too much psychoanalysis with Freud and his disciples which became pontifical, dogmatic. That was why I was ostracized from the original group. I became interested in the artist. I became interested in literature, in the magic of language. I disliked medical language, which was sterile. I studied mythology, archeology, drama, painting, sculpture, history. What restitutes to scientific phenomenon its life, is art."

This was the substance of our second talk.

He knew that it was a shock to me, his asking for the diary.

"But why did you bring it, if it was not to offer it to me, to wish someone would read it? Whom was it written for, originally?"

"For my father."

"Did your father ever read it?"

"Only the first few volumes, which were in French. He cannot read English."

"Here in your diary we have the story written by the woman herself, and yet it is essentially the same story we find in tradition. It may well be that you thought yourself at fault when your father left you, that you felt you had disappointed or failed him in some way, as your mother did. So you tried to win him back by telling him 'stories' which would distract, please him (Scheherazade). It was the story of your faithfulness to his image. Revealing yourself to your father, you thought he would grow to know you, love you. You told him everything, but with charm and humor. And in this way you were reunited with him long before you found him again, in fact, from the moment you began to write the diary, probably with this compelling motivation, of making a link, a bridge to him."

"But then when I found him, the first time, why did I abandon him?"

"You had to abandon him first, to complete the cycle. You had to fulfill the obsession to be reunited with him, but also to liberate yourself from the fatalistic determinism of your whole life, of being the abandoned one. When you lost him as a child, you lost in him the personification of your ideal self. He was the artist, musician, writer, builder, socially fascinating personage. When you found him, you were a young woman in search of your real self. This your father could not give you, because the relationship was only a reflection of the past, of child and father love. This had to be broken so you might find a man independently of this image. Your father, as far as I can make out, is still trying to create you to his own image."

After a while, he added: "Man is always trying to create a woman who will fill his needs, and that makes her untrue to herself. Many of your 'roles' came out of this desire to fulfill man's needs."

One day Dr. Rank told me about his childhood. He was born in 1884 in Vienna, Austria. At an early age he was put to work in a glass blower's factory because his mother was a widow. But he was a great reader. He spent all his evenings at the library. He came across the books of Freud. He adopted his interpretations.

Then he became ill. His lungs were not very strong. A friend took him to Dr. Alfred Adler. During his physical examination they talked, and Dr. Rank expounded some of his opinions of Dr. Freud's work. He also expressed some dissensions. He was already exploring the possibility of a memory of the body, a visceral memory in the blood, in the muscles, long before consciousness, as a child's first awareness of pain or pleasure, a memory of actual birth. A memory which started with birth itself. The experience of birth. Emotions formed like geological strata, from purely animal experiences. Birth, warmth, cold, pain.

Adler was so impressed with Rank that he introduced him to

Freud. Freud offered him a secretarial job and the possibility of study. He became a pupil of Freud's in 1905 and for twenty years was his assistant and collaborator. From their first talk, Freud recognized in Rank a fecund and original mind. The men who surrounded Freud were awed and acquiescent. Not Rank. Freud enjoyed the disparities and the clashes of opinions. Rank learned, but he also questioned. Rank was surrounded by older, more scholarly and disciplined disciples of Freud. But he became his research worker, his proofreader, his adopted son. Freud made him editor of the *Psychoanalytical Review*. He gave Rank a ring (which Rank showed me and was wearing) and wanted him to marry his daughter, to be his heir, and continue his work.

Freud tried to analyze Rank, but this was a failure. Perhaps because they were too closely bound, perhaps because Rank was the rebel son and he was beginning to disagree with Rank's ideas. Freud did not like the concept of the Birth Trauma, nor Rank's ideas on illusion and reality. Like all fathers he wanted a duplicate of himself. But he understood Rank's explorative mind, and he was objective. Even their disagreements on theories would not have separated them. The real cleavage was achieved by the others, who wanted a group united by a rigid acceptance of Freud's theories. In 1919 Rank founded a publishing organization to concentrate psychoanalytical literature in one enterprise. While in Vienna, Rank was chairman of the Viennese Psychoanalytical Society, and general secretary of the International Psychoanalytical Association.

This closeness caused much jealousy among Freud's collaborators. They hoped for a fissure. Even though Rank's discoveries were dedicated to Freud, Freud could never quite forgive him for differing from his established concepts. He began to consider Rank's explorations a threat to his own work. The other disciples worked actively to point up the estrangement, to add to it. Dr. Rank was made to feel so alienated from the group that he finally went to practice in France. This was the break in the father and son relationship. In 1926 he resigned from his Vienna offices and moved definitely to Paris, feeling he could no longer adhere to the old psychoanalytical school. After twenty years they had succeeded in banishing him. He not only lost a father but a master, a world, a universe. In Paris he worked alone. His book had placed him on the periphery of academic psychology.

In earlier writings Rank had applied a Freudian theory to literary and cultural studies, but in 1924 he published a volume entitled *Trauma of Birth,* laying the foundation for a new philosophy of life. This contribution of his own he has developed, since then, in a number of books. His last three works have been translated into English under the titles, *Modern Education, a Critique of Its Fundamental Ideas*; *Art and Artist*; and *Creative Urge and Personality Development.*

He became the director of the Psychological Center in Paris.

Rank had begun to consider the neurotic as a failed artist, as a creative personality gone wrong. Neurosis was a *malfunction of the imagination.* Rank did not treat neurotics with the contempt that some doctors did, as the old doctors treated insanity. There was also, in neurotic guilt, a symptom of the religious spirit, the negative expression of religiousness, and the negative aspect of creation.

His saying this reminded me that while I had been reading the lives of the romantics, I had been struck by the analogy between neurosis and romanticism. Romanticism was truly a parallel to neurosis. It demanded of reality an illusory world, love, an absolute which it could never obtain, and thus destroyed itself by the dream (in other centuries by tuberculosis and all the other romantic illnesses).

And now I could see that Dr. Rank had become himself a father, had written his own books, evolved his own theories.

First, he seized upon the diary as a shell, and as a defense. Then he asked me not to write it any more, and this was as difficult as asking a drug addict to do without his drugs. Not content with that, he asked me to live alone for a while, to disentangle my real self from all my "roles," to free myself of the constellation of relationships and identifications.

I started from a complete acceptance of Dr. Rank's definition of the neurotic: the failed artist, the one in whom the creative spark exists but is deformed, arrested, feeble, hindered in some way, by some disorder of the creative faculties which finally succeeds in creating only neurosis. Therefore it is by a re-enacting of the process of creation that the analyst can arrive at a liberation of it. This miracle of contagion which the analyst must perform can only be done by the closest approximation of creation itself.

I was watching Dr. Rank in action. First of all, he took the image of today, the pattern of my life in the present. To come close to others I had surrendered many of my beliefs and attitudes. But closeness achieved by such compromises and abdications is not genuine.

When my father appeared, I realized how many things I had been in rebellion against, in open mutiny, I should say, which had been merely a way to blaspheme, to desecrate, to repudiate his values, order, harmony, balance, and classical lucidity.

Dr. Rank immediately clarified my relationship to June. It was not Lesbianism. I was imitating my father, courting women.

"You replace the lost object of your love by imitating him. It was also an act of fear of man's sensuality which had caused you so much sorrow as a child." (I knew all the storms and wars at home were due to my father's interest in women.)

I *became* my father. I was the intellectual adviser of my mother. I wrote. I read books.

"And what about music?" asked Rank.

"No, music I repudiated. I don't know why. I love it, I have a strong emotional response to it, but I refused to become a musician."

Mental surgery, liberation of the instincts, the pure knowledge of deformation is not sufficient, as Allendy carried it out. It is a process of creation. The analyst has to communicate, to impart the capacity to create, and for self-creation. He has in his favor the power to arouse faith, but no matter how profound his perception, the final effort had to be made by me.

Now, with Allendy, I felt that certain definite categorizations, overlooking the creative, the metaphysical, were reductions, in order to fit me into a general pattern.

Dr. Rank, on the contrary, expanded his insight.

With Allendy, I was an ordinary woman, a full human being, a simple and naïve one; and he would exorcise my disquietudes, vague aspirations, my creations which sent me out into dangerous realms.

Allendy took pains to delineate my character, my true nature, my human attitudes, but it was by a process of oversimplification. The mold into which he tried to fit me came to a climax the day he suggested I should take love more lightly, give it less importance, to evade tragedy. That I should take a playful attitude towards it. It should be sweet and casual, easygoing and interchangeable. "I will teach you to play, not to take it tragically, not to pay too heavy a price for it, to make it pleasant."

This was the natural conclusion to the formation of my human self, to normalcy; and if he was right about overcoming tragedy, *par contre*, he overlooked the deeper cravings of an artist, for whom deep full love is the only possible form, no simmering life but a boiling one, no small compromise with reality. He saw me as a Creole in a white negligee, New Orleans style, sitting on a rocking chair with a fan, feminine, awaiting light-footed lovers.

This conclusion put an end to my faith in Allendy. Whatever magic I had been able to find in analysis, whatever beneficial influence, was defeated by the kind of Anaïs this naturalness was leading me into. Rather than enter this ordinary life, which was death to my imagination (my grandmother's life!) and my creativity, I chose to retrogress into my neurosis and obsessions. Disease was, in this case, more inspiring and more fertile to poetry.

Dr. Rank agreed with me.

"You sought to preserve your creative instincts and what would nourish them. But neurosis itself does not nourish the artist, you know; he creates in spite of it, out of anything, any material given to him. But the torments of Artaud, or the hells of Rimbaud, are not for you."

"As an ordinary woman I might have been serenely happy with such a miniature life, but I am not that woman."

It was in this vast, amorphous, restless realm that Dr. Rank sought the key. A human being lies there at the center, but the core of this human being is an artist, not just a human being. This revelation of the artist and the creative process runs through all of Dr. Rank's questionings, and it is by being able to lay his hands on the invisible, the "soul," that he travels so much further than Allendy.

It is by the expansion of his imagination that he can penetrate the artist, and it was in the realm of the imagination that the disease concealed itself, and alone could be reached and operated upon. And it was this imagination which Allendy discarded as "delusion."

Allendy would say: "You must separate these games of your fantasy. They are just games." But in the fantasy lay the secret desires and the seed of positive creation. Allendy was trying to peel them away. Rank was trying to bring on a transition from game to art. Art began in play. Allendy did not consider some of my games as creations.

Rank spoke of the influence of dreams, literature, and myths upon life:

"In other words, one must learn the language of the other and not force upon him a familiar idiom. Allendy separated you from your diary, your early stories, your novels. He thought he could cure you by prying you away from them. I admit the tragic end to all absolutism, and I do fight the tendency to extremes; extremes in life, debauchery because it defeats its own quest for pleasure; extremes of love because they defeat love; extremes of pain which defeat aliveness.

"But there is a vast difference between the solution offered by Allendy, and mine. He was trying to replace your love of the absolute, and your search for the marvelous, by an adaptation to ordinary life. I place the emphasis on adaptation to an individual world. I want to increase your power of creation in order to sustain and balance the power of emotion which you have. The flow of life and the flow of writing must be simultaneous so that they may nourish each other. It is the revelation of creative activity which becomes a channel of redemption for the neurotic obsessions. Life alone cannot satisfy the imagination.

"In Allendy's analysis he tried to adapt you to the social ideal. Not enough emphasis has been put on the differentiations, because the object of the 'cure' has been adaptation. The error here is that there is an individual solution for each case, a varied and individual form of adaptation, and that it is the adaptation to the self that is important, not the adaptation to the average. To bring about, as he tried to do, the possibility of happiness through ordinary definitions of happiness can never satisfy you because your desires are not on the average level. The identification with the WHOLE can only come when the individual has lived out the utmost of his aspirations and is at peace with himself."

The happiness described by Rank, then, is the one of positive, creative assertion of the will through the consciousness of creation; and that, by this highest of efforts, I can arrive at a self-abnegation or forgetting of myself to a greater whole. An artistic enthusiasm for a variety of manifestations is the basis of creative exuberance.

I had thought I would have to endure his compassion for an illness, but when I spread before him the rich events of my life, he said, "The new hero, still unknown, is the one who can live and love in spite of our *mal du siècle*. The romantics accelerated their suicide. The neurotic is the modern romantic who refuses to die because his illusions and fantasies prevent him from living. He enters a combat to live. We once admired those who did not compromise, who destroyed themselves. We will come to admire those who fight the enemies of life.

"What did you feel when I asked you to leave your diary?"

"First of all, I was afraid of what you would think of the lies I was going to tell. Then I felt a feminine elation, like that of a woman who is asked to give all her possessions, all of herself. You demanded everything in one blow. I felt an elation due to a recognition of power, of mastery. Was it not power and mastery I was looking for? Did I not come to you because I felt lost, confused, disturbed. You realized that the diary was the key. I always kept an island, inviolate, to analyze the analyst. I had never submitted. If I did look for a leader in Henry, a man of experience, he very soon became like a child, or at least an artist I must take care of, and who could not guide me."

"The diary is your last defense against analysis. It is like a traffic island you want to stand on. If I am going to help you, I do not want you to have a traffic island from which you will survey the analysis, keep control of it. I do not want you to analyze the analysis. Do you understand?"

I felt I had chosen a wise and courageous guide.

"Did you make arrangements to live alone for a few weeks? I can't help you unless you break away from all of them, until you are calm and integrated again. There is too much pressure on you."

This was even more difficult than giving up the diary. Rank's eyes were shining. He sounded so certain, and I said I would try.

I felt deprived of my opium. In the evenings when I would be habitually writing in the diary, I paced back and forth in my bedroom.

I chose a very well-known hotel near Rank, which seemed cheerful, a studio room they called it, with kitchenette and bathroom and a bedroom which had the appearance of a living room. It was all in cream-whites and orange, and modern. It turned out to be a very well-known hotel for temporary alliances, well-kept mistresses, weekend lovers, intended to give an "illusion" of home! My choice was right for the situation, but it shocked my father (who had, possibly, very good reasons for being familiar with the place).

All this I have had to write in retrospect. From sketchy notes. Memory.

Dr. Rank would talk, at times, about the evenings in Vienna cafés where he and other young writers discussed Freud, and the motivation of character, fully and endlessly. Rank wanted to write plays. They dissected Bruckner's plays. Because his friends laughed at Rank's divergences of opinion with Freud, he wrote an article about his ideas; but he was certain then that Freud would never hear of it.

I feel equal now to writing a sketchbook with only the human essences which are always evaporating, with the material left out of novels, with that which the woman in me sees, not what the artist must wrestle with. A sketchbook, without compulsion, or continuity.

I will never write anything here which can be situated in either *House of Incest* or *Winter of Artifice*. I will not give my all to the sketchbook. Is this what Rank wanted, to throw me into my novels, books, out of the intimacy of the diary?

Yet, in no other book can I situate the portrait of Dr. Rank, and this portrait haunts me, disturbs me while I am working on the novel. This portrait of Rank must be written.

Background: Books, shining and colorful books, many of them bound, in many languages. They form the wall against which I see him. Impression of keenness, alertness, curiosity. The opposite of the automatic, ready formula and filing-away. The fire he brings to it, as if he felt a great exhilaration in these adventures and explorations. He gets a joy from it. It is no wonder he has evolved what he calls a dynamic analysis, swift, like an emotional shock treatment. Direct, short-cut, and outrageous, according to the old methods. His joyousness and activity immediately relieve one's pain, the neurotic knot which ties up one's faculties in a vicious circle of conflict, paralysis, more conflict, guilt, atonement, punishment, and more guilt. Immediately I felt air and space, movement, vitality, joy of detecting, divining. The spaciousness of his mind. The fine dexterity and muscular power. The swift-changing colors of his own moods. The swiftness of his rhythm, because intuitive and subtle.

I trust him.

We are far from the banalities and clichés of orthodox psychoanalysis.

I sense an intelligence rendered clairvoyant by feeling. I sense an artist.

I tell him everything. He does not separate me from my work. He seizes me through my work.

He has understood the role of the diary. Playing so many roles, dutiful daughter, devoted sister, mistress, protector, my father's new-found illusion, Henry's needed all-purpose friend, I had to find one place of truth, one dialogue without falsity.

When others asked the truth of me, I was convinced it was not the truth they wanted, but an illusion they could bear to live with. I was convinced of people's need of illusion. My father had to believe that, after rediscovering each other, we would abandon all our other relationships and devote our lives to each other. When he returned to Paris after the relaxation of the summer, his social life began, and he began to try and fit me into it. He wanted me to dress conventionally and discreetly, at the best of the *couturiers,* as Maruca did

. . . neutral colors, English tailored suits in the morning, neatly cut and trimmed hair, every hair in place . . . and appear at his house, where the life resembled that of Jeanne, completely artificial, insincere, snobbish. My artist life was just the opposite. My artist friends liked slovenliness, even shabbiness. They were at ease, and would have been more so if *I* could have dressed indifferenly, sloppily, casually, if my hair had been in disorder, my skirt pinned up, etc.

Somewhere in between lies Anaïs, who wants a free life but not a shabby one.

Rank immediately touched upon a vital point, the connection between the diary and my father. He had always been interested in the Double. He wrote a book about it. Don Juan and his valet. Don Quixote and Sancho Panza. (Henry and clown Fred.) The need of the Double.

"Isn't this a narcissistic fantasy, that the Double is one's twin?" I asked.

"Not always. The Double, or the shadow, was often the self one did not want to live out, the twin, but in the sense of the dark self, and the self which one repudiated. If Don Quixote was a dreamer, why did he annex to himself his opposite, the good, earthy Sancho Panza; and if Don Juan liked to mirror himself in the eyes of adoring women, why did he need a valet-servant-disciple-devotee-shadow?

"You are right when you feel your father was trying to stress and reinforce the resemblances so that you would become duplicates, and then he could love his feminine self in you as you could love your male self in him. He was also the one who dared to be Don Juan. Didn't you tell me that he set out to possess more women than Don Juan, to surpass the legendary figure of a thousand mistresses? This, your double was doing for *you*, while you were loved by the men he might have wanted to be loved by, and so you could have been the perfect Androgyne.

"There is so much more in all this than the simple fact of incestuous longings. It is only one of the many variations upon the effort we make to unite with others; and when, for one reason or another, fusion with others has become difficult, one falls back again into the easiest one, the ready-made one, of blood affinities. It is only one of the millions of ways to palliate loneliness."

A scientific formula acts as a reduction of the experience. With Allendy I became aware that each thing I did fell into its expected place; I became aware of the monotony of the design. I experienced a kind of discouragement with the banality of life and character, the logical chain reaction of clichés. He discovered only the skeleton which resembled other skeletons. He left out the quality of the personages, the intricacies, complexities, surprises, which Rank uncovers.

Rank said, "A man can never have the indulgence for a woman's behavior which a woman has towards man's behavior, because a woman's maternal instinct makes her perceive the child within the man. And it is when she becomes aware of this that she cannot judge. It may be that a paternal man may get the same protective perception about a woman. And this may explain these excessive indulgences no one from the outside can find a justification for."

I was trying to find the root of my indulgence towards Henry. I was trying to explain to Rank that I did not see him as a mature man who is aware of what he is doing. He did not deny this possibility.

I could not go on. I felt Rank's influence, his sureness that the diary was bad for me. I knew immediately that I would show him all this, that everything is transparent to him because I wish it to be so. This is my fourth attempt at a truthful relationship. It failed with Henry because there is so much he does not understand; it failed with my father because he wants a world of illusion; it failed with Allendy because he lost his objectivity. Rank explained to me today that the reason why I had written about him was because the analysis was coming to an end, and I felt I was going to lose him. I felt impelled to recreate Rank for myself, by making a portrait of him.

As soon as I knew I was going to see Rank Monday, I had no more desire to write.

At the same time, I am still a romantic. Not that I am contemplating Werther's suicide. No. I have outgrown the religion of suffering fatally. But I still need the personal expression, the direct personal expression. When I have finished ten pages of the very human, simple, sincere novel, when I have written a few pages of the corrosive *House of Incest*, my season in hell, when I have done ten pages of the painstaking, minute "Double" (*Winter of Artifice*), I am not yet satisfied. I still have something to say.

And what I have to say is really distinct from the artist and art. *It is the woman who has to speak.* And it is not only the woman Anaïs who has to speak, but I who have to speak for many women. As I discover myself, I feel I am merely one of many, a symbol. I begin to understand June, Jeanne, and many others. George Sand, Georgette Leblanc, Eleonora Duse, women of yesterday and to-day. The mute ones of the past, the inarticulate, who took refuge behind wordless intuitions; and the women of today, all action, and copies of men. And I, in between. Here lies the personal overflow, the personal and feminine overfulness. Feelings that are not for books, not for fiction, not for art. All that I want to enjoy, not transform. My life has been one long series of efforts, self-discipline, will. Here I can sketch, improvise, be free, and myself.

Rank wants to see if I can keep a sketchbook, instead of being kept by a diary. It is the compulsion of the diary he fights. I began with a portrait of Rank because it did not fit anywhere else. Let us try again.

Rank. I have a blurred memory of vigorousness, of muscular talks. Of sharpness. The contents alone are indistinct. Impossible to analyze his way of analyzing, because of its spontaneity, its unexpectedness, its darting, nimble opportunism. I have no feeling that he knows what I will say next, nor that he awaits this statement. There is no "suggestion" or guidance. He does not put any ideas in my mind as the priests in the confessional put sin in my mind by their devious questions: "You have not been impure, my daughter? You have not enjoyed the sight of your own body? You have not touched your body with intent to enjoy, my daughter?"

Rank waits, free, ready to leap, but not holding a little trap door in readiness which will click at the cliché phrase. He awaits free. You are a new human being. Unique. He detours the obvious, and begins a vast expansion into the greater, the vaster, the beyond. Art and imagination. With joyousness and alertness.

I stopped for a moment to search for the order and progression of our talks, but these talks follow a capricious, associative pattern which is elusive. The order made in reality, chronological, is another matter entirely. Rank does not believe in that "construction" by logic and reason. The truth lies elsewhere. In what one connects to one's self, by emotion (as in Proust). I began to perceive a new order which lies in the choice of events made by memory. This selection is made by the power of the emotion. No more calendars!

That also meant a death blow to the rigorous sequences of the diary calendars.

A nonchalant perspective.

Yes, everything is changed. There is a pre-Rank vision, and there is an after-Rank perspective. Perhaps he has the secret of mobility and change. Other patterns, such as my father's, bring on a static "frieze" or "freeze."

And so we go on. There is courage in these disorders, these skips of memory, these seemingly erratic or devious explorations.

I do remember the day he discovered two important facts: one, my love of exact truth; and two, my lies in life, my artistic and imaginative deformations.

There was a great change in me, but no change around me. Beyond a certain limit, there was little I could do for my father or with him. Maruca was his wife, devoted and complete; and she was also secretary, music-copier, letter-writer, social assistant, manager, accountant, etc. Henry, beyond a certain point, needs independence, and no care. Rank divined that this would happen: the woman could not find a total role for all her energies. But then Rank began to show me how my concept of woman was *mother*. To protect, serve, mother, care for. So it was the mother in me which found uses for her talents, but the woman? It was being such a mother that made me feel I was a woman.

We left that in suspense, and he went into another problem: my excessive need of truth to balance my facility for imagining, my fear of this imagination, the fear of what happens to the truth in my mind, so fertile with inventions. *A great passion for accuracy because I know what is lost by the perspective or objectivity of art.* My desire to be true to the immediate moment, the immediate mood.

Dr. Rank questioned the validity of this. The artist, he said, is the deformer, and inventor. We do not know which is the truth, the immediate vision or the later one.

We talked about how Henry "deformed" and never understood people. Rank said that was the true nature of the artist. Genius is invention.

Then we talked about the realism of women, and Rank said that perhaps that was why women had never been great artists. They invented nothing. It was a man, not a woman, who invented the soul.

I asked Rank whether the artists whose art was a false growth, an artificial excrescence, bearing no relation to their personal truth, insincere artists, were greater than sincere ones. Rank said this was a question which he had not yet answered for himself. "I may have to write a book for you, to answer it," he said.

This statement gave me great pleasure. I said, "That would please me more than if I finished my own novel."

"There's the woman in you speaking," said Dr. Rank. "When the neurotic woman gets cured, she becomes a woman. When the neurotic man gets cured, he becomes an artist. Let us see whether the woman or the artist will win out. For the moment, you need to become a woman."

This was the most joyous moment of the analysis. I feel that what restitutes to scientific phenomena their *life* is the naïve, emotional rediscovery of each problem as an individual miracle, the faith in the uniqueness of it which leads to enthusiastic unraveling. What kills life is the absence of mystery. But even the scientists today, however advanced their inroads into significance, admit a final and even more interesting ultimate mystery. Nothing is lost to the lover of shadows and darkness. Mystery remains.

But what is living is the constant motion towards unraveling, a dynamic movement from mystery to mystery; otherwise one remains faced with a single one (mystery of the origin of fire, for instance). And such a static mystery becomes a restriction. Mystery born of ignorance, of taboos, fear, ignorance.

But today, in digging deeper, the universe of our character has become greatly enlarged, unlimited in space. It exists in depth and is far more reaching. We do not strike walls or obstacles by discovery, by tampering with the soul, the unconscious, but are tapping new sources of mystery, new realms. We are relinquishing second-rate mysteries for greater and deeper ones. We are no longer frightened by lightning, or storms, but are discovering these dangers lie in our own nature. We are discovering the symbolic significance of fact, even of a sexual act, which is not always a physical act.

The fear that truth should prove uninteresting is known only to weak-stomached artists. Respect the mysteries, they say. Do not open Pandora's box. Poetic vision is not the outcome of blindness but of a force which can transcend the ugliest face of reality, swallow and dissolve it by its strength, not evasion.

Dr. Rank said, "Too limited a meaning has been placed upon the sexual experience, and although it is wrong to say that psychoanalysis brings merely a sexual liberation, this is only a phase, a step in the progress. Sexual liberation does not make a man or a woman, does not bring on maturity. The gesture, which some analysts take as a sufficient sign of liberation, is, in itself, empty of power and effect if it does not correspond to a complete inner transformation and preparedness for an exteriorization of maturity."

He added, "This true maturity comes from far deeper sources, and is far more inner than is supposed by the scientific analyst when he pronounces himself satisfied after the patient has won a physical victory, or a sexual victory. In psychoanalysis we still see the consequences of this, in the fallacy that because sexuality is obviously biologically fundamental, it must also play the leading role."

He also said, "Thus psychology has become the worst enemy of the soul."

It is not necessarily a shock received in childhood which may have turned a woman away from thoughts of sex. It is not alone that she may have been offended by her father's infidelities to her mother and that this may have created a resentment against the cause of this attitude and neglect. There may be another cause, Rank suggested. There is an existing creative urge which makes certain demands on the nature, and orders a certain deviation of energies into other channels. Not all flights of mysticism or imagination are escapes from life. Creation, too, whose importance Rank alone recognizes (for it's a noticeable weakness of psychoanalysis that it has overlooked the artist as a separate entity), is a source of action, a directive which alters the course of human life.

And then we came to my playing of roles. I wanted to be the woman Artaud needed, to feed his poetry, and rescue him from madness. I wanted to be the decorative and charming "salon" writer and classically decorous artist my father wanted. I wanted to be the woman not born of Adam's rib but of his needs, his invention, his images, his patterns.

"The capacity of the artist, through the imagination, to lose himself in a hundred roles, is the same imaginative process of self-dissolution described as identification. It is not only the human parents. (You wanted to be both like your father in brilliance, talent, and like your self-effacing, saintly grandmother who was your ideal of a woman.) It is also the fiction heroines, the literary models you sought to emulate."

"Yes, there was a time when June, Henry, and I were all Dostoevskian characters."

"Psychoanalysis sometimes overlooks the importance of the imagination, the production of an artist, while I see the revelatory character of it, as well as its value for a 'cure'; for it is by an expansion and satisfactory expression in art that the balance alone can be readjusted."

"Henry once wrote: 'I must either go mad immediately or write another book.' "

"What you lose, you re-create. When you lost Europe, Spain, music, your atmosphere, you wrote a diary to carry your world with you, build another."

Once, as I arrived, I caught a glimpse of a small, rather thin woman dressed all in black like a widow. I asked Rank who she was. He told me, "It is my wife. A short time before we married, she lost her father. I thought, then, that her wearing black and mourning was rather natural. But she has remained bereaved and grieving; she remained a widow. Compare this permanent mourning with your immediate efforts to create something in place of what you lost. That is the artist."

Dr. Rank seemed to be saying that there is a metaphysics of the artist. Viewing everything from the creative angle, that is, the activity which transcends our human life, the artist enlarges the boundaries of our whole life. Compare Rank's interpretation of guilt with the interpretation of the average psychoanalyst. He feels that guilt comes from a far deeper source than a child's offense against moral laws. There is the sense of guilt of the creator. The artist (or the failed artist, the neurotic) takes from the world. He receives impressions, he absorbs colors, pleasurable sensations, he is a witness or a part of experiences of all kinds, he travels, he enjoys beauty, he relaxes in nature; and he feels committed to love this in return, to emulate creation, to celebrate, to worship, to admire, to preserve. There is, according to Rank, a guilt about not creating, as well as a guilt for destroying.

When I wrote so many stories beginning, "I am an orphan," the obvious interpretation first touched upon, even by Rank himself, was that this was a fantasy of a desire to get rid of the parents in order to be able to assert my own individuality; but in looking further, he interpreted this as the creator's desire to be born a hero, self-born, a mythical birth.

For a moment I felt or divined the man behind the analyst Rank. A warm, compassionate, divinatory, gentle, expansive man. Behind the eyes, which appeared at first analytical, I saw now the eyes of a man who had known great pain, great dissatisfactions, and who understood the abysms, the darkest and the deepest, the saddest . . .

It was only a flash. It was as if he, too, were enjoying the soft human moment. He knew, perhaps, that the woman would soon fade because there was no role for her; that the woman's role to live for a man, for *one* man, was denied to me by my neurosis; and that to live fragmented was a negation of the wholeness of woman. And he knew that I would be driven back to art.

I feel that I am missing the overtones. For me, the adventures of the mind, each inflection of thought, each movement, nuance, growth, discovery, is a source of exhilaration.

When we were talking again about June, he said, "To explain homosexuality by identification with the mother for the man, or with the father for the woman, is not enough. There is in it a trespassing beyond boundaries by which creation is expressed: a dominating energy which expands to fecundate on a plane which is difficult to apprehend and which bears a small relation to ordinary sexual activity."

Dr. Rank has an agile, leaping quality of mind. I see him always as the man with very open eyes and I hear his favorite phrase which he repeats with elation: "You see? You see, eh?" And there is more, there is always more. He is inexhaustible. When he shrugs his shoulders, then I know that he has dismissed the unessential. He has a sense of the essential, the vital. His mind is always focused. His understanding never wavers. Expansion. A joyous fertility of ideas. The gift for elevating incident into destiny.

It is said that the process of psychoanalysis is the one by which we are made to relive the drama of the obstacle against which we always repetitiously stumble, but this re-enacting, for Rank, cannot be limited to the event in the life which caused the "stuttering" (my word, for neurosis to me always seems like a stuttering of the soul in life). It must include an *exercise in creation*.

My father left: love means abandonment and tragedy, either be abandoned or abandon first, etc. Not only the leap over the obstacle of fatality, but a complete artistic rehearsal of the creative instinct which is a leap beyond the human through a complete rebirth, or perhaps being born truly for the first time. To accomplish this it was not sufficient that I should relive the childhood which accustomed me to pain. I must find a realm as strong as the realm of my bondage to sorrow, by the discovery of my positive, active individuality. Such as my power to write, which Rank seized upon as the most vital core of my true maturity.

To heal or release, alone, is not enough; but to teach the creation of a world in which one can live, on what plane, by what pattern, this can only be done by a vision into potentials, a vision into the capacities of the neurotic.

Dr. Rank's soul-seeking man, the artist, seeks not only a victory over his nightmares or weaknesses, but a positive creation.

I still wonder if it is not the presence of the man Rank which imparts the wisdom he gives. I find it difficult to retain exact phrases. His presence, his being, conveys all kinds of subtle teachings. He defeats the past, its obsessive clutching hold, more by the fact of his enthusiasm, his interest, his adventurousness, his war against conventions than by any simple statement. It is his aliveness which sings the funeral rites of dead emotions, dead memories.

"In conventional analysis there comes that well-known moment of inflation of the ego, in which one feels the power of release, the sheer power of being able to advance, to move, to act, to decide, to desire, and to realize. But the inflation cannot last. The analyst here, in his role of god or devil, has released a power without properly hinging it, canalizing it. Thus, without the support of the positive creation awaiting the released one, as it were, we find the lamentable man who is dispersing his newborn energies, and only experiences a momentary joy in movement."

Every idea of his could give birth to a book. Yet he regrets not having written a novel, and this amazed me. He may be more of an artist than a scientist. When he was young, he had written plays. In Vienna they thought his pen name was Bruckner, that he had written Bruckner's plays. This may be what prevented him from getting the recognition he deserves. He is considered a rebel, a desecrator of the conventions of Vienna analysts.

More and more, it seems to me, the generative, fruitful principles of analysis which lay in the reconstitution and re-enacting of the individual's drama, were overshadowed by the eagerness to find the diagnosis and classifiableness, in order to maintain an intellectual control over them. Each time the artificial process of the drama's reconstruction was done with less respect for the drama, and a greater respect for the pattern of the drama, then the fruitful elements were diminished.

One might say that it is natural that a mechanical feeling should arise in the analyst who is confronted, say, a hundred times a year with a drama of incest; but if he had not hastened to the conclusion that all dramas of incest resemble each other, he would not have lost the vital interest in how or why the incest drama developed. It is very much like demanding a sincere participation on the part of the analyst; and no such participation would be possible if we did not refer back to the feelings of an artist when he is about to paint, for the thousandth time, the portrait of the Virgin and Child. The real artist is never concerned with the fact that the story has been told, but in the experience of reliving it; and he cannot do this if he is not convinced of the opportunity for individual expression which it permits.

Otto Rank should not be confused with the other psychoanalysts. He uses the same language, the same method, but he transcends the psychoanalytical theories and writes more as a philosopher, as a metaphysician.

The axis of psychoanalysis is displaced by Rank, and the preoccupation becomes a metaphysical or creative one. It is this emphasis I want to make clear, for a great popular confusion tends to classify all psychoanalysts more or less in the same pragmatic category: as doctors and not as seers, as healers and not as philosophers. Even though they deal with psychic illness, illness of the soul, the cure they offer is vaguely understood to be a sexual one.

Rank's creative attitude situates the drama on an emotional plane, saving it from mere mental surgery. The acceptance of life as drama is art, not science.

The scientific attitude skeletonizes the personality and produces a contraction, a reduction to phenomena. Otto Rank emphasizes the difference between individualities and produces the expansion of it. The stressing of differences enlarges his universe. Rank seeks and delineates the individual mold into which each one is helped to enter, *his own mold,* as against the general mold imposed by scientific analysis.

Scientific analysis, in its effort to simplify, in order to conclude, restricts the outline of the personality and slowly creates a kind of disillusion, or impoverishment. The emphasis is laid on the explanation, not on the *expression of the drama.* Rank's artistic interest in the drama has an incalculable effect on the living experience of the neurotic.

It is his artistic, creative attitude which is contagious and which differentiates him from the scientific analysts. The average Freudian analyst is a purely analytical type, bored by the variations on eternal themes. Rank prizes the variations as precious indications of the character, color, nature of the neurotic's imagination, a key to be used later in helping him to construct his own world.

The scientific rigidity acts very much like a trap, the trap of rationalization. The patient who is a hypersensitive person cannot help being influenced by what he is expected to say, by the quick classification baring the structure too obviously. The neurotic feels his next statement is expected to fit into a logical continuity whose pressure he finally succumbs to.

The more this process becomes clear to him, the more he experiences a kind of discouragement with the banality of it. The "naming" of his trouble, being in itself so prosaic, links it to his physical diseases, and deprives him of that very illusion and creative halo which is necessary to the re-creation of a human being. Instead of discovering the poetic, imaginative, creative potentialities of his disease (since every neurotic fantasy is really a twisted, aborted work of art), he discovers the de-poetization of it, which makes of him a cripple instead of a potential artist.

With Rank he discovers the contrary: his affinity with history, with the myth, with philosophy, with art and religion. He is restored to the flow of life and his disease is discovered to be a manifestation of imagination, the very stuff of creation itself, only deformed and perverted. Reality is not merely the realism he could not face, but a reality he has the power to transform and shape to his needs.

The generative, fruitful principle of analysis lies in the reconstruction and reconstitution of the individual drama as an artist achieves it—with enthusiasm for its development, a passion for its expression, color, and ramifications. It is this attitude which is necessary to his salvation.

To raise the drama instead of diminishing it, by linking it to the past, to collective history, to literature, achieves two things: one, to remove it from the too-near, personal realm where it causes pain; the other, to place the neurotic as a part of a collective drama, recurrent through the ages, so that he may cease regarding himself as a cripple, as a degenerate type. Such a wide participation in human experience, coming from the analyst, is only possible if he takes the attitude of the artist, who is not so much concerned with the pure ideological structure of his book as with the lyrical or dramatic expression of it.

It is in this difference between individual expression that we find a new dimension, a new climate, a new vision. To reduce a fantasy is only a means of dredging the neurotic imagination, of diminishing the stage on which the neurotic must live out his drama with the maximum of intensity, for the sake of catharsis.

Rank has given the neurotic his full importance as a potentially creative human being. The world of false inner reality which he has constructed, like the one constructed by the madman, can easily be transmuted into a truer inner reality with the power of affecting its surroundings rather than being destroyed by them.

Dr. Rank opposes the concept that all struggle in the neurotic is merely a perverse resistance to an infallible teacher. He apparently diminishes the supreme oracular role of the analyst in order to equalize the relationship. He encourages the individual creation which sustains the power of self-creation. The act of self-creation which the neurotic must make with the analyst is only possible *if he is convinced that the invention of his illness is a symptom of the power to create,* and not a symptom of impotence.

It is in the realm of imagination that the disease lies, and it is with imagination that it can be reached. It is this imagination which the scientist regards as a purely negative, destructive, illusory element.

Dr. Rank differs, too, in his concept of adaptation. The cause of discord in the personality is usually the tragic disparity between the ideal goal of the individual, the image he creates of himself, and his actual self. It is this which he projects on the world, on his relationships with others. Most analysts immediately seek to reconcile the individual to the world without realizing the deeper, inner discord, or considering what world it is the individual should be adapted to.

It is only when the disparities between his desires and his capacity to fulfill them are removed that a harmony becomes possible. Rank does not offer the ordinary solution of adaptation to the outer reality, but rather a power to create an inner reality which will mold the outer one to one's needs, which will act upon the outer one (creating a climate, a language, a level of life one is in harmony with), and so will make fulfillment possible.

The creative activity becomes the true channel of redemption for the neurotic who is paralyzed by analysis, or by his obsessions with perfection or the absolute. It is when he applies to human life those obsessions which should only be applied to creation that he fails. It is not adaptation he is taught by Rank, but transmutation and mobility. That element in human life which he cannot adjust himself to if he is intent on the fulfillment of a mental pattern, caprice, paradox, contradiction, treachery, evanescence, he will accept when he begins to live by the mobility of his own emotions and not by premeditation or intentions.

Deprived of religious beliefs, and of the power to create, man finds himself projecting into relationships his need of God, and his need for perfection. There is, in reality, nothing wrong with his nature except a great confusion. That is why the real doctor today must be the philosopher, and Rank is among those who know most deeply man's needs and the origin of his suffering today.

A sorrow made me create a protective cave, the journal. And now I am preparing to abandon this sorrow, this cave. I can stand without crutches (or without my snail shell). I face the world without the diary. I am losing my great, dissolving, disintegrating pity for others, in which I saw deflected the compassion I wanted for myself. I no longer give compassion, which means I no longer need to receive it.

I think of a self-portrait today in order to disengage the self from dissolution. But I am not interested in it, or perhaps the old selves are beyond resuscitation. It is the old selves Rank is scattering, and I feel strange without them. I feel spent, lost, given, empty. I wrote the portrait of Rank and I gave it to him.

Turmoil. I regretted the diary which held my body and soul together, and held together all of my many selves. But it is dead.

The dependence on Rank, learning from Rank, became the desire to give Rank a gift. More important, the moment of his understanding of me was the moment when he said: "I like what you wrote about me immensely, immensely." And his expression was full of gratitude, the eyes seemed almost as if about to dissolve in tears. He ruled the empty space between my first visit to him and these notes on him . . . November 8th, when the journal died, and today.

Rank wanted to free me of the compulsion to write everything in the diary, and so little in the novels. He encouraged an intermittent notebook, not the need of describing everything. Yet when I gave him what I wrote about him, he was pleased. As Henry was. Kill the diary, they say; write novels; but when they look at their portrait, they say: "That is wonderful."

Rank wanted me to describe the present, enter the present, never look back. So I enter the present and I find Henry at work upon his book on Lawrence. He is completely drowned in his notebooks, sketches, plans, schemas, projects, lists; and so I suggested: "Let us draw a tree." A struggle against chaos. Henry adds details, details, a massive construction, thick with substance, solidities, facts, but chaotic, dense and without clarity. He drowns in gigantism. I try to throw the unessentials overboard, to travel light. So things will become transparent. Henry said, "I will dedicate it to you. I will say, 'To Anaïs, who opened the world of Lawrence to me.'"

And I am happy. My novel lies gathering dust. I am reading Knut Hamsun's *Mysteries*, and I am filled with the hushed, mute beauty of mystery, of no explanations. Henry thinks he is like Knut Hamsun. But he is not as pure or as simple. He is tainted with intellectualism.

To be in Paris during the cold winter, nearer to Rank, I rented a pompous, furnished apartment on the Avenue Victor Hugo, belonging to an old-fashioned painter. It is full of fireplaces, coal stoves, cold studio windows, furniture. I thought the tall, high-ceilinged studio would be beautiful, but it is so cold we can never stay in it. As Emilia got married, I have no maid, and I thought this would be easier to take care of. Teresa comes with her husband, and takes one of the small rooms. At night the stove, like old Russian stoves in Dostoevskian novels, goes out. I freeze. I get up and do not want to awaken Teresa, so I am always carrying coal and shaking the fire. Then Teresa has to leave, and I rescue a starving Spaniard with a pregnant wife. He waits on me devotedly, but as she is pregnant, I end up by taking care of her while he takes care of the stoves, the window cleaning, etc.

Life. Literature. I am sitting here with a fever, and a desire not to explain. Has this notebook a new accent? Has the diary truly died? I am like an opium addict, lost without my drug. Donald, the young Scotchman Elsie loved and betrayed, is staying here too. I have to watch him every moment, for he gets up out of bed to jump out of the window. Fortunately, the French windows are rusty, creaky, and take time to open, and I hear him and hold him back.

He raves and rants. "It is not the betrayal which I can't take, Anaïs. I expected that from Elsie, somehow. In our most passionate moments, she would say: 'Donald, you are too young, too young.' I knew there was another man because she would never stay with me all night. But why did she not tell me? She came to Paris with me, we were very happy together, she gave herself with such abandon, and then when I became suspicious of her life in London, and when she refused to marry me, I went to London and I found out about Justin, and that they were planning to marry. But none of this really matters, none of this would make me want to die."

He sobbed for a while. I held his hand. He was so young, about twenty, dark-haired and violent, with burning eyes.

"What made you want to die, Donald?"

"I will tell you what, if I can, if I can. I am not sure I can describe it. But when I went to London and found out . . . found out that Elsie was about to marry Justin and not me, and when I faced her with my discovery, and begged her to tell me the truth, and to free me, to let me go, not to hang on to me, and tell me lies, when I wept and pleaded, and made a scene, she stood there, and instead of show-ing some feeling, even a little pity for me who loved her with my body and soul, instead of being warm, and helping me, consoling me, saying something, asking for forgiveness, explaining, justify-ing herself, she *smiled*. She gave me a long, cool, satanic smile."

As he told me this, he made one wild leap out of bed and rushed to the studio. I called the Spaniard and ran after Donald. He fum-bled with the heavy and rusty studio windows, and I pulled him away with the help of the Spaniard.

Elsie broke the only law, the only law I respect: don't inflict un-necessary pain. That smile!

The fever gives a strange rhythm to my thoughts. Now, at last, I understand the plain chant of the neurotics. When I hear the la-ments of the neurotic-romantic, I recognize the tone. It is not a com-plaint born of what is happening; it is born of what they had im-agined, expected, dreamed; and the lament seems out of proportion. Elsie's smile! To Donald it was the smile of cruelty. Donald had dreamed of a woman feeling with him, with him against the cruel-ties of life, of destiny; he had not dreamed cruelties of her own do-ing. She signed the cruelty with her own name. Did she enjoy it? Was it a smile of triumph at her power to hurt? Donald's accusing tone, reproaches. One thinks: he is a coward. He cannot take the blows. But consider for a moment what Donald had "imagined." The greatest love of the century! Passion an absolute. He was a full-fledged romantic, who had been dashed from the top of the highest mountain, Olympus. So call the doctor and ask for a sedative, and explain to the French doctor why he wants to die, and watch him shrug philosophical shoulders. "One does not die of love."

"I am going to kill her," said Donald, with fists clenched, as he awakened from the effects of the sedative.

He has to abolish that smile.

So I coax him into dressing, into a taxi, and I take him to Allendv, who had been analyzing Elsie.

There is an end to my giving. A point at which I feel I must rescue myself. I reached this point today. Henry is immersed in a work I admire. We have talked over every page. Today he brought me twenty-five pages of an apotheosis of his philosophy. He said, "People will say I could formulate such a philosophy (quietism, non-willing, being, passivity) because you took care of me."

I close my eyes to the immense web of ideologies. They weary me, this gigantic juggling of systems, orders, prophecies. I am a woman. I let my vision fall short. I understand everything, Spengler, Rank, Lawrence, Henry; but I get tired of those glacial regions. I feel their coldness, too high, too far from life. I am not happy there. I think of myself: I am tired of ideas. I feel myself pulling downward, growing more and more earthy. Yet I owe some of my greatest joys to that world, joys almost akin to the joys of love.

Other demands pull on me, the house in Louveciennes, repairs, care, Elsie's tragedies and conflicts, servants' lives and problems, family, my father. A litany of weariness. To the lost self.

My father, when he returned to Paris, was no longer the father of the south of France. He became once more a dandy, a man of the world and of the salon, a public figure, a virtuoso, a concert pianist, a frequenter of countesses. He was on stage. I would not have minded this, but he wanted to mold me into it. He wanted Maruca to take me to her dressmaker, to conventionalize me; he wanted me to go to all the soirees, concerts, to share in his frivolities, to shop with him for a special cane, to use the most expensive perfumes; and I am at an austere self-sacrificing moment of my life, seeking the *dépouillé* (bare) life of the artist, seeking to strip myself of externals.

I was far now from my symbolic dress, my inventions. Father Momus, I called him. Momus, in Greek fables, was the god of mockery and censure, and delighted in finding fault with gods and men. When Neptune, Minerva, and Vulcan strove to prove which was the most skillful artist, Momus was chosen as judge to decide among them. Neptune made a bull; Minerva, a house; and Vulcan, a man. Momus declared that Neptune should have put the horns of the bull nearer the front, that he might fight better; Minerva should have made her house movable, so that she could remove it in case she had troublesome neighbors; Vulcan should have made a window in the man's breast, so that his thoughts could be seen. All were so disgusted with his criticism that they turned him out of heaven; and he died of grief because he could find no imperfection in Venus.

The artificiality of his life repelled me.

There is no objectivity. There is only instinct.

Blind instinct.

I have changed, but nothing around me has changed. I became more woman.

I am full of bitterness to see that my father, Henry, D. H. Lawrence, and other men gave the best of themselves to primitive women, endured them, while I, being the woman whom men associate with their creation, I get treated in a superior, elevated, mature way and so much is expected of me that I cannot always live up to.

I seek more truthfulness. I told the truth to Allendy, but I send him relatives and friends to analyze so he does not feel I lost faith in him as an analyst, only that his analysis of me is now impossible.

I would like to live in the realm of Knut Hamsun's books, that which lies either deep in the earth, homeliness, work, coarseness and simplicity of living, or at night, in dreams, madness and fantasy and mystery. No awareness. No explanations.

Clocks ticking. It is an apartment of clocks: chiming, swinging, ringing, cuckooing, cooing. Red-hot stoves, cold drafts. Waiting. Waiting for what? Rank is waiting to see how I live without him, without crutches.

Could write a comedy about psychoanalysis, beginning with Allendy's remark about his kissing Elsie: "I kissed her so she would not have a feeling of inferiority." The magic of Allendy has died. He has failed. Elsie does not face herself, but escapes into marriage to an older man, very much like her father. Marguerite did not get well. She escaped into astrology. I escaped to Rank, who could help the writer to be born.

Allendy said wistfully, "I have been too soft. *J'ai été trop mou.*"

You have to take into account the human element.

Quietism always reached by immolation. That was always my cure for anxiety. I have rejoiced inwardly when I have taken my revenge, but for myself only. I have no need to exteriorize or celebrate my cruelties. It is a game for myself only, for a secret, inner equilibrium. It is my own private, little, malicious world, with secret laughter and ironies, no need of spectacular manifestations. The pain I give is only like homeopathy, to heal the pain given me, but it is not a blow to be given. Insidious and subtle.

Each time I return from a visit to my father, I add a few pages to the novel (*Winter of Artifice*).

The inner hatreds of men are now projected outside. There are fights in the streets. Revolution in France, they say. Men did not seek to resolve their own personal revolutions, so now they act them out collectively.

Henry's keeping of a dream book for me became a small book (fifty pages) which he rewrote in a particularly chaotic style.* We arrived at a new conclusion about the dream language. One night we clarified it well. If the films are the most successful expression of surrealism, then the scenario is what suits the surrealist stories and the dreams best. Henry sensed this when he suggested a scenario be made out of *House of Incest*. Now I advised him to do the same for his dreams, because they were, as yet, too explicit. (I did not object to obscenity or realism but to explicitness.) It all needed to be blurred, the outline must be less definite, one image must run into another like water colors.

We argued over the question of the dialogue. I said talk in the dream was only a phrase issuing from a million thoughts and feelings, only a phrase, now and then, formed out of a swift and enormous flow of ideas. Henry agreed that the verbalization of thought in dreams was short and rare. Therefore, we agreed, there must be a telescoping, a condensation in words. (Psychoanalysis describes the great condensation in dreams.)

I said there was a need of giving scenes without logical, conscious explanations. I questioned, in his dream book, the discussion in the café before the operation of the child. I gave as an example of the silent mystery, the feeling of the dream scenes from the *Chien Andalou,* where nothing is mentioned or verbalized. A hand is lying in

* "Into the Night Life," later used as material in *Black Spring.*

the street. The woman leans out of the window. The bicycle falls on the sidewalk. There is a wound in the hand. The eyes are sliced by a razor. There is no dialogue. It is a silent movie of images, as in a dream. One phrase now and then, out of a sea of sensation.

We analyzed the feeling one has in a dream of having made a long and wonderful speech, yet only a few phrases remain. It is like the state described by drug addicts. They imagine themselves utterly eloquent, and say very little. It is like the process of creation, when, for a whole day, we carry in us a tumultuous sea of ideas, and when we reach home it can be stated in one page.

The period without the diary remains an ordeal. Every evening I wanted my diary as one wants opium. I wanted nothing else but the diary, to rest upon, to confide in. But I also wanted to write a novel. I went to my typewriter and I worked on *House of Incest* and *Winter of Artifice*. A deep struggle. A month later I began the portrait of Rank in a diary volume, and Rank did not feel it was the diary I had resuscitated but a notebook, perhaps.

The difference is subtle and difficult to seize. But I sense it. The difference may be that I poured everything into the diary. It channeled away from invention and creation and fiction. Rank also wanted me to be free of it, to write when I felt like it, but not compulsively. "Get out in the world!" Rank said. "Leave your house at Louveciennes! That is isolation, too. Leave the diary; that is withdrawing from the world."

How to separate from my father without hurting him? Rank said, "Hurt him. You will deliver him of his sense of guilt for leaving you as a child. He will feel delivered because he will have been punished. Abandon him as he abandoned you. Revenge is necessary. To reestablish equilibrium in the emotional life. It rules us, deep down. It is at the root of Greek tragedies."

"But I have to do this in my own way."

My own way is always to do so very gradually, drop by drop, so that the abandonment is hardly felt, as I did with Allendy. My father's attitude is: "Let us live this external life, and next summer we will have a real intimate feast of talk in Valescure."

Rank asked, "How did you talk to your father?"

I answered, "As you talk to me. I analyzed him subtly. I imitated you."

But my father escaped from this truth as he escapes from all vital issues, from all delving and probing. We see each other gaily, meet only in sophisticated, civilized, trivial spheres. Wit, *racontages, conversation de salon,* anecdotes. There is no connection. It is all false and airy. He makes a screen for himself out of his eloquence, wit, smartness. Is there a deeper man? There is a man who weeps, but that's sensitiveness, not depth. My father is a will-of-the-wisp, a vibration, a nuance, a minuet. And he thinks the same of me. I see how he watches me when I am ready to leave, and I am always ready to leave. Unreality. Flight. Delusion. The kiss that is not a kiss. The talk that is not a talk. He and I should not have tried to meet in life, but in some strange region of dreamlike frozenness. We were punished for trying to materialize a myth.

I would like to say to him: "We are too old and wise to go on pretending. Let us enjoy our maturity and not romanticize ourselves. You will continue to be a Don Juan until you die, because you thrive on the foam of conquest. You are made for mobility, fluidity, not the absolute. Between us there is only narcissism, and I have grown beyond that. I will continue my Bohemian life. Let us pay each other the compliment of not lying to each other."

But I know he is not as courageous as I am. He wants to continue to admire himself. Don Juan, who possessed more than a thousand women, gave up his life for his daughter. His daughter gave up all her friends for her father. A legend! I have grown beyond this. When I arrive at his house it is Maruca who tells me, weeping, that while counting the laundry with the maid she found a shirt all covered with lipstick.

See *Winter of Artifice* for development of theme.

During my struggle against the diary "opium habit" I had many misgivings. Should the diary disappear altogether? Was concerned with its value as a document, its usefulness to my work. Thought of the scenes I had extracted from the diary, the dreams and moods I used in *House of Incest.* Would it reappear in a more objective form? I studied Da Vinci's notebooks. Rank had said that Da Vinci's notebooks were often more interesting than his actual work. Rank could not answer this question from my past work. He awaits the new novel. I stopped writing for two weeks because I felt the need of a reorganization. I wanted to live.

Women, said Rank, when cured of neurosis, enter life. Man enters art. Woman is too close to life, too human. The feminine quality is necessary to the male artist, but Rank questioned whether masculinity is equally necessary to the woman artist.

At this point, when I became a woman, I glowed with womanliness; I was expansive, relaxed, happy.

Rank said, looking at me admiringly, "You look entirely different today." I felt as soft as a summer day, all bloom and scent, all joy of being.

"Perhaps," he said, "you may discover now what you want—to be a woman or an artist."

I had one evening of hysteria. A choice between standing in the middle of the room and breaking out into hysterical weeping, or writing. I felt that I would break out in some wild, disruptive fit of blind, furious rebellion against my life, against the domination of man, my desire for a free artist life, my fear of not being physically strong enough for it, my desire to run amuck and my distrust of my judgment of people, of my trusts and faiths, of my impulses. A fear of the wildness of my fever and despair, of the excessiveness of my melancholy. Then I sat at my typewriter, saying to myself, "Write, you neurotic, you weakling, you; rebellion is a negative form of living. Write!"

Henry said: "You must let things accumulate, not use everything immediately. Let things accumulate, rest, ferment: then explode. Not cover all the ground." He talked like Rank, with tears in his eyes, when he realized that I used the notebook to disentangle myself from human bondages. Pleaded with me to think only of my work.

Lunch at my father's. Talk about trivialities. Comtesse X. Was she the one my father talked about while we walked through the Bois?

He told me, "We met at Notre Dame. She began with the most vulgar cross-examination, reproaching me for not loving her. So I proceeded with a slow analysis of her, telling her she had fallen in love with me in the way women usually fall in love with an artist who is handsome and who plays with vehemence and elegance; telling her that it had been a literary and imaginary affair kindled by reading of my books, that our affair had no substantial basis, what with meetings interrupted by intervals of two years. I told her that no love could survive such thin nourishment and that, besides, she was too pretty a woman to have remained two years without a lover, especially in view of the fact that she cordially detested her husband. She said that my heart was not in it. I answered that I did not know whether or not my heart was in it when we had only twenty minutes together in a taxi without curtains in an overlit city."

"Did you talk to her in that ironic tone?" I asked.

"It was even more cutting than that. I was annoyed that she had been able to give me only twenty minutes."

And then he added, "She slashed her face in order to justify her tardiness to her husband, saying she had been in an automobile accident."

This part of the story seemed highly improbable to me, as no woman in love will endanger her beauty. And here was the countess, with a face fair and flawless, where no knife had ever made the slightest scratch.

My father was curious about Henry. He invited him to lunch. When Henry arrived, my father said, "He looks like Prokofiev." He was formal, and watched Henry serve his dessert in the finger bowl, and watched him playing his naïve Knut Hamsun role. It was Maruca who enjoyed Henry's naturalness and laughed with him, not at him. After lunch she wanted Henry to go with her to the zoo, where she was taking the neighbor's children, and Henry was delighted. My father let them go, as if all of them were children. I was relieved that Henry had not turned into an infuriated giant in a miniature salon, which he does on such occasions. He was sincerely awed by my father. A little later he did explode at the house of Charpentier, the literary critic of the *Mercure de France*. He insulted everybody.

I read the *Jardin des Supplices* of Mirbeau and wondered why it left me cold. Realized it was because the description of physical torture was, for me, so much less potent than mental tortures. Physical tortures are banal and familiar. Mental tortures we are only now beginning to delve into. Each one of these physical tortures, transposed into a psychological plane, would be novel. Interpreting each physical torture as having its correlation, analogy, in the psychic. Take, for instance, the peeling of the skin. That could become a symbol for hypersensitiveness. The death by the loudness of the church bells could be the sounds of hallucinations. This became the theme of *House of Incest* and it helped to coordinate the descriptions of anxieties.

Henry kept my pages on the theory of the dream, atmosphere, etc., at the head of his *Book of Dreams*. He wrote an imaginative page and then said, "I feel I have not done what you have done all through *House of Incest*. The abuse of language, the dislocation of it." Struck by my pages on the water life, Atlantide, pre-conscious, prenatal; and then he wrote a paragraph on "everything born of water." A few days later, still inspired by the liquid writing, he writes: "The buildings and the ships are entangled, the beasts rise out of the sea . . . slippery motion which is no motion . . . downy joy," etc. This time I feel distressed. It is too imitative and not superior. It materializes what I wrote, de-subtilizes it. What can I say? It is a satire. He does not seem to be conscious of it.

This has baffled me for a long time. Henry is the humorist, not I. Yet very often Henry writes, in all seriousness, things which I consider "take-offs," caricatures. Is he unaware of it? They are like parodies of poetry, parodies of ideologies, parodies of criticism, almost a Dadaist mockery of it, but he does not seem to be aware of it. Is it unconscious parody?

The dream world is becoming my speciality. Henry has gathered together all his dreams and is rewriting them, transforming them, expanding them. He wants to use them as a climax to *Black Spring*. He wants to recapitulate the themes of the book via the dreams. He came to me the first time with two pages which seemed off-tone to me. He wanted the animal realism of his dreams, and he introduced vulgar music-hall dialogue. It was not obscene, as some dreams are, but consciously and wordily vulgar. "The obscenity of the dream," I said, "is different. It is one of erotic images, or sensations, but it has no vocabulary. There is no dialogue in the dream, and very few words. The words are condensed like the phrases of poems. The language must be a kind of non-language. It cannot be everyday language. The dream happens without language, beyond language." Then Henry wrote the third part, or the third batch, and experimented with irrational language, getting better and better as he went along, while I watched for the times when he fell out of the dream.

Dear Doctor Rank: What I wanted to say over the telephone was this: I would like to see you when you are well again. And only then. I felt badly when I left you last time to think you were tired and ill. Everyone comes to you and depends on you, and tires you. I was upset to have been one of them.

My father had promised to be truthful with me, to let me be his confidante, and now he was inventing again, as if I were Maruca and could not understand the truth. We had agreed not to try and create for each other an illusion of an exclusive love. When I arrived the next day, after the frivolous lunch and the story of the countess, he had not slept all night thinking he was going to lose me. "And if I lose you, I cannot live any more. You are everything to me. My life was empty before you came. My life is a failure and a tragedy, anyway."

His life? A devoted, slavish wife. A beautiful home. Concert tours, travel, students, admirers, singers coming from all over the world to learn his songs, friends, social life, the life of Paris. He looked deeply sad. His fingers were wandering over the piano keys, hesitantly. "You make me realize how empty my activity is. In not being able to make you happy, I miss the most vital reason for living."

He was again the man I had known in the south of France. But he could not let me be. If I preferred Dostoevsky to Anatole France, he felt that his whole edifice of ideas was being attacked and endangered. He was offended if I did not smoke his brand of cigarettes, if I did not go to all his concerts, if I did not admire all his friends.

Realizing more and more that I did not love him, I felt a strange joy, as if I were witnessing a just punishment for his coldness as a father when I was a child; and this suffering, which in reality I made no effort to inflict, since I kept it a secret, gave me joy. It made me feel that I was balancing in myself the injustices of life, that I was restoring in my own soul a kind of symmetry to the events of life. A spiritual symmetry. A sorrow here, a sorrow there. Abandon yesterday, abandon today. Betrayal today, betrayal tomorrow. A deception here, a deception there. The arithmetic of the unconscious which impelled the balancing of forces.

Was this what Rank meant when he said, in the unconscious there was a need of revenge? That I should hurt my father? But all my life I prevented acts of destruction arising from my unconscious. I wanted to defeat destructiveness and tragedy. To create only illusion.

I did not mind his philandering, but I was eager for the truth. He was as before, but he hated to admit it to himself because of that ideal image he carried in himself, the image of a man who could be so deeply altered by the recovery of a long-lost daughter that his career as a Don Juan came to an abrupt end.

"I am not asking for anything," I said, "except that you be real."

"Now tell me all that your mother used to tell me. Tell me I don't know how to love, that I am artificial and superficial."

He was quarreling not with me, but with his past! Behind me stood my mother. He had been afraid that his daughter would condemn him too.

I could not see him clearly any more.

In that salon with its stained-glass windows, its highly polished floor, its dark couches rooted into deep Arabian rugs, its soft lights and precious books, there was only a fashionable musician bowing.

Although in reality he had not abandoned me, I felt he had passed into another world I would not follow him into.

I am keeping the house at Louveciennes. To live in it from April to October, to shut it in the winter and live in Paris. The fear of losing Louveciennes was a great torment to me. Home. A hearth.

I finished the novel (*Winter of Artifice*).

Henry read half of it and said it was terribly human and more than human. Depth and sincerity. Accepts my stripped, bare, essence writing, a kind of stylization again due to my great condensations. Said it revealed woman, a feminine attitude, more than any book he had ever read.

It is I who stand for life now, while Henry is entirely possessed by his demon. It is I who make him taste meals, walk, relax, go to movies, sit in cafés. He is writing Part One of the book on Lawrence, after immense, fantastic efforts at synthesis and construction, from notes and quotations and loose fragments, some of them written while June was here, others in Louveciennes, others in Clichy, others in various hotels in Paris. A gigantic task. His philosophy, his criticism, his attitude. All this he asserts now, confronting Murray, Spengler, and encompassing all of Lawrence as Lawrence was never encompassed. I have never seen him so possessed. He lives entirely in a world of ideas. It is I who must play the role of preserver of life and pleasure. He is burning up. What an intense two weeks. A book factory. He is disillusioned with Lowenfels. When I first met him, he did not care if a friend did not fit into his world, because at that time his world had not been born yet.

I break down under criticism. Cannot take it.

Reacted well. Next day broke up the whole book and made a different plan for Part One, which Henry did not like. I tried unsuccessfully to weld the fantastic and the real, the plain and the enameled style. Failed because I castrated the poetry and made the plain writing sound false. Henry sensed the compromise. Great talk, in which he urged me to extremes, to combat the world, to face the resistance to *House of Incest,* the antagonism of Hélène Boussinesq, Joaquin, Bradley, Steele. To obey my own integrity, to fuse the two aspects of myself which I insisted must be kept apart.

It is when I am timid that I am ineffectual. Through timidity I also condense, contract, like a visitor who does not dare to stay very long for fear of boring, and makes speeches quickly.

Once again Henry roused my fighting spirit and my strength. Forced me to write a bigger book. Goaded me.

Music is unformulated; that is why it is such a blessing to hear after a struggle with formulation.

Writing now shows the pains of childbearing. No joy. Just pain, sweat, exhaustion. It saps the blood. It is a curse. Real throes. No one knows this but the true writer. The straining of nerves, the relation between the body's well-being and output, the struggle to escape from the grip of conscious ideas, the rest, to renew one's self. So hard. What a grip on one's soul, one's guts, everything.

I yearn to be delivered of this book. It is devouring me.

As I rode to my father's house, I knew I would explode and that I would not let him go to Spain thinking he had been able to deceive me as he deceives Maruca. Through a series of coincidences, I heard about my father's latest escapades. He was taking a virgin violinist with him on tour but arranged to be alone with her, not traveling with the manager or the cellist.

I wrote the scene straight into the novel, not the diary:

"I wanted the truth between us, Father."

But he refused to admit he had been lying. He was pale with anger. No one ever doubted him before, he said. To be doubted blinded him with anger; he was not concerned with the falsity of the situation. He was concerned with the injury and insult I was guilty of, by doubting him.

"You're demolishing everything," he said.

"What I'm demolishing was not solid," I said. "Let's make a new beginning. We created nothing together except a sand-pile of pretenses into which both of us sink, now and then, with doubts. I am not a child, I cannot believe your stories. We both needed one person to whom we could tell the truth. If we had been real friends, been able to confide in each other, I would not have needed Dr. Rank."

He grew still more pale and angry. What shone out of his eyes was pride in his stories, pride in his ideal self, pride in his delusions. And he was offended, like an actor offended at not having convinced his audience. He did not stop to ask himself if I were right. I could not be right. I could see that, for a moment at any rate, he believed implicitly in the stories he had told me. If he had not believed them so firmly he would have been humiliated to see himself as a poor comedian, a man who could not deceive his own daughter.

"You should not be offended," I said. "Not to be able to deceive your own daughter is no disgrace. It is precisely because I have told you so many lies that I myself cannot be lied to."

"Now you are accusing me of being a Don Juan."

"I accuse you of nothing, I am only asking for the truth."

"What truth? I am a moral being."

"That's too bad. I thought we were above questions of good and evil. I am not saying you are bad. That does not concern me. I am only saying that you are *false* with me. I have too much intuition."

"Go on," he said, "now tell me I have no talent, tell me I do not know how to love, tell me I am an egotist, *tell me all that your mother used to tell me.*"

"I have never believed any of those things."

But suddenly I stopped. I knew my father was not seeing *me* any more, but always that judge, that past which made him so uneasy. I felt as if I were not myself any more, but my mother, with a body tired with giving and serving, rebelling at his selfishness and irresponsibility. I felt my mother's anger and despair. For the first time, my own image of my father fell to the floor. I saw my mother's image. I saw the child in him who demanded all love and did not know how to love in return. I saw the child incapable of an act of protectiveness, or self-denial. I saw the child hiding behind her courage, the same child now hiding behind Maruca's protection. I was my mother telling him that, as a human being and as a father, as a husband, he was a failure. And perhaps she had told him, too, that as a musician he had not given enough to justify his limitations as a human being. All his life he had played with people, with love, played at love, played at being a concert pianist, playing at composing, playing; because to no one or to nothing could he give his entire soul.

I was saying, "I am only asking you to be honest with yourself and with me. I admit when I lie. I am not asking for anything except that we live without a mask."

"Now say I am superficial."

"At this moment, you are. I wanted you to face me and be truthful."

It seemed to me that my father was not quarreling with me, but with his past, that what was coming to light now was his underlying feeling of guilt towards my mother. If he saw in me now an avenger, it was only because of his fear that his daughter might accuse him too. Against my judgment he had erected a huge defense: the approbation of the rest of the world. But, in himself, he had never quite resolved the right and the wrong. He too was driven now by a compulsion to say things he never intended to say, to make me a symbol of the one who had come to punish, to expose his deceptions, to prove his worthlessness. And this was not the meaning of my struggle with him. I had not come to judge him but to dissolve the falsities! He feared so much that I had come to say: "The four persons you deserted in order to live your own life, to save yourself, were crippled," that he did not hear my real words.

We could not understand each other. We were gesticulating in space. Gestures of despair and anger. My father pacing up and down, angry because of my doubts of him.

No more warmth or flow. All communication paralyzed by the falsity.

And I was thinking: perhaps I stopped loving my father long ago. What remained was slavery to a pattern.

Certain gestures made in childhood seem to have eternal repercussions. Such was the gesture I had made to keep my father from leaving, grasping his coat and holding on to it so fiercely that I had to be torn away. This gesture of despair seemed to prolong itself all through life. I repeated it blindly, fearing always that everything I loved would be lost. It was hard for me to believe that this father I was still trying to hold on to was no longer real or important, that the coat I was touching was not warm, that the body of him was not warm, not human, that my tragic desire and quest had come to an end, and that my love had died.

Maruca will take care of him. I am here to bring him to life again, out of his artificial, fake, timorous, marginal life. To taunt and drive him out of his downy shelter, out of his self-deceptions, dishonesties, idealizations. The fakeness in us, the poses, the airs, the vanities, the comedians. As Joaquin put it so well: "You and I quarrel not because we are different, but because when you are human, real, my 'chichi' soul attacks you, and when you are full of 'chichi' then my real, human side wants to show you up."

Dream: A fire, which many men are trying to quench. I see them all battling with it, and I hear their moans as they work, because of the intensity of the fire. I know secretly they should give up the fight because there is something burning there, a fuel of terrifically concentrated power, a condensed, unquenchable liquid. I wonder why the men don't realize it and give up.

My father became ill after our scene. He took refuge in illness. He received me in bed, with great theatrical ritual. Maruca was at his bedside. His voice was weak. In front of her he said, "Anaïs thinks I am running off with a virgin violinist of seventeen."

Maruca smiled benignly. "Your father is a simple, loyal, truthful, honest man."

This comedy was unbearable. The bland, hypocritical angel, who knew that I knew all the details of the "virgin's" downfall. And that they were going to Algeria and Morocco. But I was at the end of my strength, and I left them, sobbing uncontrollably, as if I were parting from all my hopes at once, as if he had died. I parted from my desires for an honest, absolute relationship. He wants gay lies. He is weak and puerile.

Back to the diary, loneliness. Isolation. Writing.

So my father has gone on tour, and I will think of him as one does of a minuet, the Parc de Versailles, a Mozartian sonata.

Rewrote my novel three times.

I end the novel ironically.

Now that there will not be a deep understanding between my father and me, I am weary of life. I seem to have come to a standstill. The only avenue is art. Books and more books.

Henry fights my parables, my sibylline tongue, my hieroglyphs, my telegraphic and stenographic style. It takes great courage to criticize me. I fight like a demon.

Marguerite reads it all and says: "Congratulations. It is really visionary writing. Unique."

I got up singing and wrote pages on June and me walking over dead leaves, weeping. June talking about God. Henry has taught me to linger, to wrestle, to be patient.

I write my father a whimsical letter, all fluff, whipped cream and froth.

Return to Louveciennes for Easter holidays.

Jack Kahane has failed in business as well as in true loyalty to

Henry. Bradley has lost interest in him. Rather than see him frustrated again, I will pay for publication of *Cancer*. None will go all the way with him. We felt free. They all worry about money, fear of risk, etc.

Cleaned the whole house from top to bottom, from attic to cellar. Cooking in earnest. Hands soiled and spoiled. But every closet, every nook and corner, tidy and clean.

Invited Rank to dinner.

A disappointing evening. Mrs. Rank is negative, and spent her evening snipping everybody's wings. We were having dinner in the garden. Henry was there too. Rank talked volubly and fully, like his books. Henry broke down the tensions with his enjoyment of food and wine. Mrs. Rank cold and brittle. Rank put his peaches in his champagne, as they do in Vienna. He became very gay.

Planning a trip to London for Henry's book.

Dinners: for an Egyptian etymologist, a moronic millionaire, a young unborn novelist, Jeanne, etc.

Henry has moved to the heart of Paris in the populous Cadet district. Whores, Arabs, Spaniards, pimps, artists, actors, vaudevillians, night-club singers.

Henry, in the Hôtel Havana, is writing about dung, ulcers, chancres, disease. Why? He is writing the final version of *Tropic of Cancer*.

[April, 1934]

I go to London alone. To see what I can do for *Tropic of Cancer*. Before I left, I also won Kahane by a marvelous speech, and he will publish Henry, only I pay for the printing. I was full of courage and determination.

On the crest of this courage I visited Sylvia Beach, for Henry, Anne Green, Rank.

I sit on a camp stool, second class, on deck, tenderly watched by a young English sailor.

I carry in my music-holder Henry's manuscripts, *Self-Portrait* [*Black Spring*] and study of D. H. Lawrence.

The sun on the deck, dreams.

I had an evening alone in London. I went to the Lyric Theatre to see Lynn Fontanne and Alfred Lunt. Captivated by the beauty of Fontanne, her waxy face and her deep, suggestive acting. Curious woman. With hands like ivy growing around one, choking one in a dream of a mysterious, non-human love. The theme was taken from psychoanalysis. Cured of the past, but one sleeps with it, nevertheless. One goes to bed with one's disillusions, just the same. That was the moral. Life stronger than awareness of the mind. The crutches, the hunchbacks, the multiple cripples of our dreams, the scars on them, all of them create a human passion. It is not in heaven that marriages are made. Only when the dreams die do you get genuine copulation. It is the dreams which make fusion impossible. You marry the day you realize the human defects of your love.

I found myself walking the streets, fascinated with houses, windows, doorways, by the face of a bootblack, by a whore, by the dreary rain, by a gaudy dinner at the Regent's Palace.

A friend took me to see Charles Laughton in *Macbeth*. He was moving, and sensual, with his great contrasts of softness and cockiness, his tousled hair and Negroid lips. He may not have been a proper Macbeth, not a man who would 　　 mental and spiritual disease, but he was a Macbeth who really groaned and made one fear, and his cruelty was convincing.

When we visited him afterwards, he was sitting crushed and limp. He expressed a strong condemnation of himself. "I am just not built to portray Macbeth." I was amazed at his humility. His depreciation of himself.

Paris. I walk the streets. I tease Henry for filling my head with streets, names of streets. I say, "In place of thoughts now, I carry the name of a new street. I think about streets. Riding in the bus, I watch them. I have no ideas. I just watch, and look, and listen. Rue du Faubourg du Temple. Square Montholon. What do you have when you have the name of a street?"

"Nothing," said Henry.

My head is empty now, it is full of streets.

One may have nothing when one has the name of a street, but one possesses a street in place of a thought; and slowly the earth, the street, the rivers, gain ground, fill the mind with noise, odors, pictures, and the inner life recedes, shrinks. This advance of life, this recession of meditation, was my salvation. Every street displaced a futile yearning, a regret, a brooding, a self-devouring meal. The Square Montholon triumphs over the long hours I spent constructing an imaginary, ideal communion with my father. Smells, automobile horns, and the eddies of traffic dispel the ghosts. I am letting myself live, I eat in all the restaurants of Paris. I go to all the movies, to all the theatres, I want to know many people, possess a map of realities as Henry possesses his map of Paris and of Brooklyn.

A devouring passion for reality, because my imaginary world is so immense it can never be annihilated. Only it must not be allowed to devour me.

Out. I am always out. With everybody. Last night, I did get sad in the beautiful Scheherazade night club with the wrong people. I pinch myself. *Allons donc*, streets, you're on the street at last, walking along, along the crowded streets of Henry's crowded books. External and internal, to be balanced, nurturing each other, or else the internal eats me, like rust. Introspection almost devoured me.

Henry saved me. He took me down into the street. It is enough that a few hours ago I was obliged to think about my father in order to write about him. It is enough, enough. Come Square Montholon, Boulevard Jean Jaurès, Rue Saint-Martin, like merry dice dancing in my empty head. It is I who taught Henry that streets in themselves were of no interest. He accumulated descriptions but I felt they needed to be the décor for some drama, some emotion. It is I who awakened the man who walked through the streets. No more anonymous maps, but maps of both form and content, matter and significance, streets and the men who walk through them.

Restless. Looking again for intensity, fever, turmoil. Everything seems to move too slowly . . . slowly.

My life is full. I am translating Volume One of the diary. I wrote about the incident of looking for Russian-style pajamas for my father. I wrote for *House of Incest* the visit to the painting of "Lot and His Daughter" at the Louvre with Artaud. Whenever I feel sadness about my father, I write. When I yearn for him, I write. When I feel regrets, I write.

Bloom. There is a bloom on everything and on everybody. Happiness. The soft bloom of happiness. Soft breezes, talk like summer breezes, love like ripe flowers, new dresses like new grass. The round curves and smells of summer. Idyllic. Inside the happiness, the worm, the worm of imagination, craving, expecting, searching. Has pain made too deep a scar so that I do not feel the gentle touch of happiness? The flesh too scarred, too coarse-grained, to feel the softness of the summer? Only another wound can make it tremble. I am not made for happiness. It is like sleep.

In the mail, a letter with Rank's statement, after reading Henry's book on Lawrence: "But where is Henry in all this?" He found pages in which Henry plagiarized him, but admitted Henry had expressed it better. He found that whatever Henry constructed on one page, he destroyed on the following one. I then realized how Henry had unconsciously escaped beyond my judgment by entering the world of Spengler and Rank and overwhelming me with grandiloquence and gigantism, with enormity and massive constructions, imposing ideas, philosophic systems. I was finally blinded by Henry's long speeches, accumulation of notes, enormous amount of quotations, etc. Has Henry deceived himself as well as me? Have we lived in an immense illusion? He did say once: "I wonder whether I am saying something."

Of course, I am not yet persuaded that Henry has produced nothing in the Lawrence book. I feel there is an uncreated, unformulated writer struggling to be born.

On Tuesday I decided to become an analyst. It would make me financially independent, and express my gift for reading character and desire to help others.

I rushed to get my hyacinth-blue dress from the cleaner's and to Rank to tell him of my decision.

He thought my desire to become a psychoanalyst really meant I was identifying with him, wanted to be him.

He would test my sincerity. I would have to study with him at the Cité Universitaire.

Rank is willful, firm, whole. I feel the dynamite in him, a great depth of emotion unified and concentrated.

[June, 1934]

Just outside the gate of Paris, on a broad boulevard, a new and modern Paris, the Cité Universitaire, clean and white and cubistic.

I did not want to go to the Psychological Center. But I had told Rank I would come, and I went for his sake.

As I walked in the sun, I fell into a Grecian mood—life of the body blossoming full in the fragrance of philosophy.

The conference room, with its schoolroom desks, and Rank standing before the blackboard. There are about fifteen teachers. Two of the women have sagging breasts, and hair on their lips. The men, three of them: one a deadpan; one who looks like an artist, and turned out to be Hilaire Hiler; and the third a European with a sly expression. Rank—black-eyed, small and soft hands moving as he speaks, a dolorous expression. Hilaire Hiler is big, loud, overflowing. Mr. Bone, the cool one, has a high brow, laughing eyes, a stiff poise. The conference is like the droning of a bee. Words. Words. Words. I am looking at a window open on a garden. It is a very low window. I am hungry for the sunlight, the trees, the grass. As soon as the lecture is over I move towards the window. Hilaire Hiler offers me a cigarette. "We'll smoke it outside," I say, and I sit on the window sill, swing my legs over it, and leap out into the garden. A moment after I leap out, out come Rank and Dr. Bone by the same route. We talk, Hilaire Hiler tells me some of his troubles. They have to do with his ears. He was born with huge ears, half the size of his head. They stood out. They were an object of ridicule. They made a monster of him. He did not dare expect love from women. He only trusted prostitutes. Then his ears were operated upon by a specialist who had much practice from plastic surgery on wounded soldiers, the *Gueules Cassées,* after the war. He made his ears look almost normal. They were no longer noticeable. Hilaire Hiler had, all his life, attributed his complexes, inferiorities, difficulties in relationships, to his ears. He felt if he overcame this handicap his life would be changed. When the ears became normal, he expected a total change in his feelings towards people.

But the psychic state did not change as quickly, as radically. He did not become, overnight, a confident man, sure of love, bold in courting, natural, easygoing. The change was external. The inner pattern was set, and as if engraved on his unconscious. He refused then to continue psychoanalytical help. He felt he should not need it, a man with normal ears. Why should a man with normal ears need help to live? He had decided to become an analyst. Painting was not a way to earn a living. He wanted to have a dignified profession. That was why he was here today, following Dr. Rank's courses. He was not sure he understood Dr. Rank's theories. Rank talks much more like a writer, an artist, a poet.

It is time to go in. Someone has placed a chair near the window to make returning easier. Rank helps me down. He whispers to me, "How I loved your doing that, leaping out of the window! You could not return to nature quickly enough!"

The discussions after the lecture are pragmatic, dull, prosaic, factual, all craft and technique. Americans are never interested in abstract thought, never attracted by the idea of exercising the intelligence and the imagination for the pleasure of discovery, of the process itself, as they exercise their bodies for a physical pleasure. No. It must be a practical knowledge, applied immediately, immediately useful. Pure ideas, pure speculation, pure exploration without conclusions do not interest them. Rank looms too big, with his talk about cosmological knowledge, his non-conformism, his subtlety, his paradoxes. Listening to him, I can perceive the brilliant philosopher and the dangerous enemy of Freudism.

There is tragedy at the bottom of his black eyes.

At the end of the talk, Dr. Bone comes up to me, asks me to help him raise the level of the discussions. He looks ironic, amusing, smart. He asks me if I will have lunch with him. But I tell him I am not free. When Rank asks me later, then I accept, to meet him at the Café Zeyer.

He comes scurrying. Orders chicken. It is incongruous, his sitting there among the mirrors, the gilded columns, the red plush seats.

I accept life as it is, the ugliness, the inadequacies, the ironies, for the sake of joy, for the sake of life. It is a comedy. It is slightly ridiculous and full of homeliness. The homeliness which my father repudiated at the cost of naturalness. Today I laughed. I let others care. I shift the burden.

In the very center of the Carnival, I began to think of a Cathedral. An immense Cathedral loomed in the heart of my light joys, the opposite of flow. I used to build cathedrals, cathedrals of sentiment, for love, for love of men, for love as prayer, love as communion, with a great sense of continuity and detail and enduringness. Built against the flux and mobility of life, in defiance of it. Then with Henry, with June, with analysis, with Rank, I began to flow, not to build. Yesterday, flow seemed so easy. Pure flow and enjoyment of life leave me thirsty. I begin to think of Cathedrals. Why? I had the medieval faith needed for great constructions, the fervor and exaltation. I build up human relationships with divine care. With sacrifices, lies, deceptions, I build up continuity, permanence.

I like Rank better serious than laughing. He does not know how to laugh. His pranks are inner pranks of the mind, his humor is paradox, the reversal of ideas, the trickeries and trapeze stunts of thoughts. I like his silent humor, his thought humor, but in life he is inexperienced. To living he brings nothing. The details of life which so fascinate Henry, he overlooks. The comic face of a passer-by, the color of a house, the savor of small things. Physical, visible life. He disregards appearance, color, detail. His life is in abstractions.

When caring ceases, when one no longer struggles to build solidly, indestructibly, no longer erects cathedrals of faithfulness to the past, cathedrals of emotion, when one enters the realms of laxity, areas of ironic indifference and resignation, letting life flow with a certain emotional negligence, one may attain states of nirvana, dreaminess, beatitudes of another kind.

Rank has to proceed immediately to extract the meaning or the essence. Too swift a disposal of the flowers which are to be pressed into perfume. *Il pense sa vie.* His true life may be in the analysis of it. He has no enjoyment of the flower.

∽

I get up with great vivacity, dress in fresh and colorful things, rush in a bus to the Cité Universitaire, walk bareheaded in the sun. I greet Rank before we enter the lecture hall. Hilaire Hiler sits at my side. The intellectual nourishment was null. Everyone interrupted Rank, asked obvious questions, and created such a nursery ambiance that it made me furious.

Hilaire Hiler and I went to lunch at a little bistro. We talked vividly. He is emotional, violent and tough. Talked about his father, who is half American Indian, half Jew. Hiler is six feet tall, his father was small. He was a painter too, he exerted a tremendous tyranny over Hilaire. At the same time, Hilaire admires him. His attitude towards psychoanalysis is that it saved his life and therefore he wants to impart it, spread it, practice it. It is sacerdotal. When we returned, Rank talked well and refused a question-and-answer period. He returned my preface to *Tropic of Cancer*, saying: "Wonderful. Too good, too good for the world."

I saw Bradley. Knopf rejected *Winter of Artifice*, but in flattering terms. Bradley accepts me, but criticizes my condensation. When he asks me for more details I say I believe in Japanese painting. He says my novel is written like a play, at times. I say I believe in condensation. I hate stuffing. Bradley attacks my new profession. He says I must stick to writing. I hold my ground. I want to earn my living by psychoanalysis, so that I may always write as I wish to, never make concessions. And this experience, I say, is valuable to a writer anyway. It is like a doctor's life. It opens up people's secret lives, and what can be more interesting than that to a novelist?

The next morning, the sun, the Grecian order of the Cité Universitaire, at the end of the city, like the ramparts of a new city as yet incomplete, with only the sky beyond. The sun. I meet Rank at the café for a coffee. I have lunch with Hilaire Hiler, who has come all dressed up for me. I meet Dr. Frankenstein, who is delicate, and feminine, and dreamy. I spend four hours on psychoanalytical studies. I hear about the classification of disease, about Bergson from Minkowski. But I am more moved by life, by the stories of Hilaire's life.

I am like a person turned inside out, flowering to the utmost, through my senses, mind, emotions. I wear a big white straw hat at a rakish angle. I discover a whole forest of strange new flowers. No ideologies. The realm of pure senses. Hiler's coarseness, Frankenstein's delicacy, a tropical atmosphere in the coldest possible place, flowering under the eyes of twenty withered schoolteachers. The woman is turned inside out, and all this wealth that was once secret is pouring out. I have an immense hunger for life. I would like to be in so many places. I would like to be traveling and roaming and vagabonding. I would like to be writing. I would like to be dancing somewhere in the South. I would like to go on a drunk with Hiler, I would like to go to Zurich and seduce Jung. I would like to meet the whole world at once.

Rank so alert, brisk, tense, swift, witty. Hiler moody. Seminar yields nothing. There are no answering sparks. Rank exerts himself, but wearies of the deadpan faces, and the monosyllabic questions. A B C D E F.

His talk is disruptive and baffling to the others. He undermines conventional psychoanalysis.

I believe that what he has seen is the ultimate error of all philosophies and systems of ideas. He is afraid of the truth he has discovered. It does not help him to live, to heal, or to teach.

Marguerite says that the analyst has been made to play the role of God. He is imagined to be all-knowing, all-forgiving. But this role is destructive to a man.

I never go to the very end of my experiences; I did not take drugs with June, or rebel destructively as Henry does: I stop somewhere to write the novel. The novel is the *aboutissement*. I did not go to the very end with my father, in an experience of destructive hatred and antagonism. I created a reconciliation and I am writing a novel of hatred.

When a philosopher like Rank begins to doubt ideologies, what can he do? By now, whatever gifts he may have had for life are atrophied.

I write novels, perhaps, to supply the deficiencies of life itself. The novel was better than taking drugs with June and destroying my health. It was my superior drug. When life turns into an arid desert, I stop. Rebellion against my father. War with my father's values. A futile waste of emotions which damage other human beings. Better to write *Winter of Artifice*. Rebellions thought out, instead of wreaked upon others. I let June go to the very end of her perversities.

We love best those who are, or act for us, a self we do not wish to be or act out.

Hiler's big eyes have a heavy way of turning in upon their sockets. He seems to be looking over the rim of his own eyes, chin down. They are heavy and sad. He is a dark animal. How will he fare in the lucid world of analysis?

Analysis is the very thing I did not want now. Just when I have learned not to clutch at the perfume of flowers, not to touch the breath of the dew, not to tear curtains off, not to extract essences from petals, to let exaltation and dew rise, sweep by, vanish. The perfume of hours distilled only in silence, the heavy perfume of mysteries untouched by human fingers. Flesh touching flesh generates a perfume, while the friction of words generates only pain and division. To formulate without destroying with the mind, without tampering, without killing, without withering. That is what I have learned by living, that delicacy and awe of the senses, that respect for the perfume. *It will become my law in writing*. All that was pushed into the laboratory, dissected under a hospital-naked light, pushed into clarity and rationality, withered. The beautiful, living and moving, dark things that I destroyed in passing from the nebulous realms of pure dreaming to a realization of the dream. Because I did not bring into life the same aura of blindness, the silences, the same empty spaces, the shreds, and the iridescence of images as they appear in dreams.

I think it is the poet in me affirming itself because of the struggle against psychoanalysis. I live, I laugh, I dramatize, I love in the very heart of Beaudoin's topography of psychoanalysis, of Rank's theory on the birth trauma, Dr. Frankenstein's classification of mental diseases. I sit next to sensual Hiler who has invited me to be his mistress, and if not his mistress, then would I be his analyst, and if I would not be his analyst, would I smoke kief with him?

Finished translation of Volume One of diary into English.

The life of the unconscious is the life without pattern, continuity, or rigidity. It approximates the dream. It is pure flow. It is what I said in my preface to *Tropic of Cancer*: "It is not a question of heroism but of flow."

Henry has been weeping and laughing over *Winter of Artifice*. Says he would not change anything about me if he could.

The Guicciardis gave my novel to Cornelia Vanderbilt. Horace thought she would like it because she has red hair.

Bradley comments on my preface to *Tropic of Cancer*: "Very good, very good. Perfect. But certainly you intellectualize the book, you see it as your generation sees things. I would have been more simple, talked merely about the gusto and love of life and the fine descriptions of Paris. But you see so much more than I ever saw. Yet one cannot say it is not there. It is certainly a preface which would make one want to read the book."

I begged Rank to let me give up the psychoanalytical school. All he said was, "I will miss you."

I went again just to see that unhappy man's eyes light up with pleasure and gratitude.

While at the Cité Universitaire, I experienced my first knowledge of the monstrous reality *outside*, out in the world, the cause of D. H. Lawrence's and Henry's ravings and railings on the disintegration of the world. Doom! Historical and political. Pessimism. Suicides. The concrete anxieties of men losing power and money. That I learned at the school! I saw the headlines, I saw families broken apart by economic dramas, I saw the exodus of Americans, the changes and havocs brought on by world conditions. Individual lives shaken, poisoned, altered. Rank suddenly ruined financially, losing his home, moving, forced to go to America. The struggle and instability of it all. I was overwhelmed. And then, with greater, more furious, more desperate stubbornness I continued to build my individual life, as if it were a Noah's Ark for the drowning. I refused to share the universal pessimism and inertia.

Rank introduced me to a sculptress he admires, Chana Orloff. She has a vast studio at the Villa Seurat. A dead-end street with colorful small villas like an Italian street. The trees from the small yards overhang balconies and big studio windows. The houses are peaked, with slanting skylight windows.

As he took me to visit her, he told me her story. Chana Orloff was always sculpturing pregnant women. She loved to study what happened to women's bodies. Her feeling about motherhood was entirely confined to the image of carrying, holding, extending, and preserving. She made a wish at the time, that if she ever had a child, *he should need her*. She envisaged motherhood as nursing, protecting, serving. She did not say "need her forever." But she may have thought it. When she did have a child, a son, he was born crippled! He lived in a wheelchair. Chana Orloff was shattered with guilt. She felt it was her wish which had caused this. It was to deliver herself of this haunting guilt that she had visited Rank.

The studio was filled with statues of women. They were larger than nature and in all the various stages of pregnancy. It was oppressive!

Chana Orloff wanted to sculpture my head and Rank promised her I would come.

I thought of all those children Chana Orloff wanted to bring into this despairing world, this world going to pieces under our eyes.

My father says: "Your life is all fireworks."

I make him laugh now, with my letters full of verve. He can no longer stifle me.

The despair of the world. Rank's tragic eyes. His understanding is infinite, like the sea. But I have the sensation of sailing alone on it. He is immense and deep but not personified, not in life. Grand stretches of silence, of the unlived, of the non-human. Suddenly he becomes very distinct, clear, when he formulates an idea about Henry's book on Lawrence (he is writing always about Henry Miller, never about Lawrence) or about woman's psychology (woman has had to conceal her real self in order to survive). Man wanted a double, a twin, a half of himself only, in woman. His thought, then, is sharp and acute.

I see a whole cycle of creation closing upon woman, the study of woman. I see all the roads of philosophy, the history of art, morphology, psychology, all converging to clear up the mystery of woman.

I said good-bye to the psychoanalytical school exactly as I said good-bye to Wadley High School when I was sixteen and I walked out after a few days attendance. What is it I salvage from mediocrity, wholesale ideas, stereotypes? My individual world, in which I grow faster, learn more, and live more deeply. I stay home and copy twenty-five pages of my Double book. But I kept the friends I made. I invited them to dinner. Miss Fleming like a mock-orange flower, Dr. Frankenstein grey-haired, intelligent, Hiler and his clownish moods. An amusing evening, a split evening, Hiler pulling towards idiocy, pranks, and Marguerite towards astrology; Marguerite teaching the women astrology, while Hiler dances with me. Hiler saying while we dance: "Why don't you come and smoke kief with me?" Marguerite looking quite noble, refined, distinct, intact. Hiler so puffed, worn, stained with living, pursuing Miss Fleming the virgin, and me at the same time. Hiler all worn at the edges.

I got a grateful letter from Bradley for the day he spent here in Louveciennes, and a note from Bone asking if he can come.

I put back into the vault two more copies of the diary.

I visit Henry. When I am alone now I am not happy. Anxiety devours me. Outside, with friends, whirling activities, overfull days, I can cure an ineradicable melancholy.

This diary is my kief, hashish, and opium pipe. This is my drug and my vice. Instead of writing a novel, I lie back with this book and a pen, and dream, and indulge in refractions and defractions, I can turn away from reality into the reflections and dreams it projects, and this driving, impelling fever which keeps me tense and wide-awake during the day is dissolved in improvisations, in contemplations. I must relive my life in the dream. The dream is my only life. I see in the echoes and reverberations the transfigurations which alone keep wonder pure. Otherwise all magic is lost. Otherwise life shows its deformities and the homeliness becomes rust. My drug. Covering all things with a mist of smoke, deforming and transforming as the night does. All matter must be fused this way through the lens of my vice or the rust of living would slow down my rhythm to a sob.

Compared with Rank, Henry seems pale and passive. Rank is active and explosive. He takes the lead.

In the climate of his certainties, his leadership, there is a rest from doubt. He has doubts about ideas, but none about the significance of life and character and actions.

I am posing for Chana Orloff every afternoon, and Rank sometimes drops in and talks. The statues are all around us, big, white, pregnant, bulging women, a forest of women. Round white plaster flesh, ripe breasts, maternity, abundance. And sometimes, while we are sitting there, Chana Orloff's son arrives, and we hear the creaking of the wheels of his wheelchair and its bumping against the door.

Rank is talking about his despair. He cannot earn a living in France. He may have to accept an offer from America. He does not want to leave. The French, he says, are not neurotic. They have accepted the separation between love and passion. They maintain their family unit, balanced, and faithfulness to marriage, children, home. But they do not give up passion. They have no conflict. Their interest in psychoanalysis is mild. Rank says, "In France I was beginning to live. My creation is done. I have written enough. I want to live." But the pressure of reality is terrible, his wife, his daughter, his future.

I started to write a letter to my father and I was stopped by sobbing. Frustration and despair. He is no father. I loved an image of him which did not exist. When he is away, this image begins to obsess me. It invades me, and I begin to believe in it again. It is destroyed each time I see him. When I want to write him, I don't know who I am writing to, an imaginary father or a real one.

I began to explore Villa Seurat. It is a charming street. The houses are all small, and in various colors of stucco. Most of them have studio windows. Some are private and some are divided into apartments. Chaim Soutine once lived there. People remember how he walked along the narrow sidewalk, always grazing the walls. Trees grow in the backyards, and sometimes in the front. The street is cobblestone and as the sidewalk is so narrow, one often walks in the middle.

I found a studio there for Henry. It is on the top floor. A big studio room, with skylight windows, and a small bedroom with a balcony. The kitchen is very small, inside of a closet. But the studio is joyous and light. Henry is tremendously excited about the idea of living there.

Café Alésia. Artificial geraniums. Many mirrors. Jazz. All red and white. Rank arrives, so alert and quick, and he comes talking about magic. Psychotherapy is magic. The neurotic is a passive magician. Child is a magician who expects magic. And I had come with the word magic on my lips. I said something later about Allendy having lost his magic.

"Because he put it into astrology and took it out of psychoanalysis."

He told his students, "In America I may be burned for this magic theory."

He was inspired, suddenly illumined, full of ideas, bright.

We talked about social psychology and the Double. I asked him why we only remember Robinson Crusoe on his island, whereas two-thirds of the book was really about Robinson Crusoe's travelings after he left the island. He said it was because all of us would like to live on an island!

Freud called him an *enfant terrible*. He loves to upset and disturb.

What he wants me to consider is this: if I could come to New York for a few months, I could give him the courage to make a new start, and he would train me intensively so that I could practice psychoanalysis, and be independent.

"I denied myself life before, or it was denied me, first by my parents, then Freud, then my wife."

He feels that I pushed him into life.

"Knowing you, everything which was an objective fact before has become alive, animated, embodied."

Henry seeks peace and strength for his work.

Rank seeks the presence of someone who is living out symbolism and ideas and theories, not just talking them.

The current of life is so strong, so powerful, that I accept it and turn my back on writing.

Rank is being pushed to go to New York. He is offered plenty of money and a job. He has debts. But he wants to stay in Paris.

"I never wanted success or money." These conflicts which he helps others to solve, he must solve alone. I cannot help him. It is not a question of six months or a year, but of an indefinite time. Why don't I come to help him at the most difficult time, to assist him and learn from him?

For the first time I know the joy of a solid, reciprocal friendship. I touch an absolute of friendship. I like Rank's sadness, his tenacity, his caring about people. He cares. He cares tremendously about everything, and everything that happens to others. I am growing away from Henry's nonchalance and non-caring.

The strange, erratic designs of destiny. Rank was living a block away from our apartment in Boulevard Suchet, our second home in Paris, at the time when my life was so empty and difficult. I had made, once again, a beautiful home, but aside from Spanish dancing, I had nothing to put into it, or rather, I had friends and occupations which had no meaning for me.

And when I went out to walk in the Bois, I passed Rank's apartment, walking under his balcony, almost, the man who possessed the knowledge I needed to enter life boldly and courageously. If I had met him then, what would have happened? Would he have precipitated me into life as Henry and June did later, but with more wisdom?

Tuesday I saw a doctor who said I was too small to have the child without a Caesarean operation. For the moment everything is alive and normal.

[August, 1934]

Several months later. Began to feel heavy, and tremors inside of my womb.

My breasts are full of milk.

It does not belong in my life, for I have too many people to take care of. I have, already, too many children. As Lawrence said: "Do not bring any more children into the world, bring hope into the world." There are too many men without hope and faith in the world. Too much work to do, too many to serve and care for. Already I have more than I can bear.

I sit in the studio, in the dark, talking to my child. "You should not be thrust into this black world, in which even the greatest joys are tainted with pain, in which we are slaves to material forces."

He kicked and stirred.

"So full of energy, my child. How much better it would be if you had stayed away from earth, in obscurity and unconsciousness, in the paradise of non-being. My little one, not born yet, you are the future. I would prefer to live with men, in the present, not with a future extension of myself into the future.

"I feel your small feet kicking against my womb. It is very dark in the room we are sitting in, just as dark as it must be for you inside of me, but it must be sweeter for you to be lying in the warmth than it is for me to be seeking, in this dark room, the joy of not knowing, not feeling, not seeing, the joy of lying still and quiet in utter warmth and darkness. All of us forever seeking again this warmth and this darkness, this being alive without pain, this being alive without anxiety or fear or aloneness.

"You are impatient to live, you kick with your small feet, my little one not born yet. You ought to die in warmth and darkness. You ought to die because in the world there are no real fathers, not in heaven or on earth."

The German doctor has been here. While he examines me, we talk about the persecution of the Jews in Berlin.

Life is full of terror and wonder.

"You were not built for maternity."

I sit in the dark studio and talk to the child: "You can see by what is happening in the world that there is no father taking care of us. We are all orphans. You will be a child without a father as I was a child without a father. That is why I did all the caring; I nursed the whole world. When there was war and persecution, I wept for all the wounds inflicted; and where there were injustices, I struggled to return life, to re-create hope. The woman loved and cared too much.

"But inside of this woman there is still a child; there is still the ghost of a little girl forever wailing inside, wailing the loss of a father. Will you go about, as I did, knocking on windows, watching every caress and protective love given to other children? For as soon as you will be born, as just as soon as I was born, man the husband, lover, friend, will leave as my father did.

"Man is a child, afraid of fatherhood; man is a child, and not a father. Man is an artist, who needs all the care, all the warmth for himself, as my father did. There is no end to his needs. He needs faith, indulgence, humor; he needs worship, good cooking, mended socks, errands, a hostess, a mistress, a mother, a sister, a secretary, a friend. He needs to be the only one in the world.

"He will hate your wailing and your slobbering, and your sickness, and my feeding you rather than his work, his creation. He might cast you aside for this love of his work, which brings him praise and power. He might run away, as my father ran away from his wife and children, and you would be abandoned as I was.

"It would be better to die than to be abandoned, for you would spend your life haunting the world for this lost father, this fragment of your body and soul, this lost fragment of your very self.

"There is no father on earth. We were deluded by this shadow of God the Father cast on the world, a shadow larger than man. This shadow you would worship and seek to touch, dreaming day and night of its warmth, and of its greatness, dreaming of it covering you and lulling you, larger than a hammock, as large as the sky, big enough to hold your soul and all your fears, larger than man or woman, than church or house, the shadow of a magic father who is nowhere to be found. It is the shadow of God the Father. It would be better if you died inside of me, quietly, in the warmth and in the darkness."

The doctor does not hear the breathing of the child. He rushes me to the clinic. I feel resigned, and yet, deep down, terrified of the anaesthetic. Feeling of oppression. Remembrance of other anaesthetics. Anxiety. Like a birth trauma. The child is six months old. They might save it. Anxiety. Fear of death. Fear of yielding to eternal sleep. But I lay smiling and joking. I was wheeled to the operating room. Legs tied and raised, the pose of love in a cold white operating room, with the clatter of instruments and the smell of antiseptics, and the voice of the doctor, and I trembling with cold, blue with cold and anxiety.

The smell of ether. The cold numbness trickling through the veins. The heaviness, the paralysis, but the mind still clear and struggling with the concept of death, against death, against sleep. The voices grow dimmer. I have no longer the capacity to answer. The desire to sigh, sob, to murmur. "*Ça va madame, ça va madame? Ç a v a m a d a m e, çavamadame çavamadame çavamadameeeeeee..................*"

The heart beats desperately, loudly, as if about to burst. Then you sleep, you fall, you roll, you dream, dream, dream, you are anxious. Dream of a drilling machine drilling between your legs but into numbness. Drilling. You awaken to voices. The voices grow louder. "*Ca va, madame? Faut-il lui en donner encore? Non, c'est fini.*" I weep. The heart, the heart is oppressed and weary. Breathing so difficult. My first thought is to reassure the doctor, so I say: "*C'est très bien, très bien, très bien.*"

I lie in my bed. I came back from death, from darkness, an absence from life. I ask for cologne. The doctor had expected to provoke a natural birth. But nothing happens. No natural cramps, spasms. At ten o'clock he examines me. Exhausts me. During the night, all night, I heard the groaning of a woman dying of cancer. Long, plaintive groaning, desperate howls of pain . . . silence . . . and groaning again.

The next morning the doctor had to operate again. The carriage was brought in again. I joked about my need of a commuter's ticket. I tried not to fight the anaesthetic, to surrender to it, to think of it as forgetting, not dying. Had I not always wanted a drug for forgetting? I yielded to sleep. I resigned myself to die. And the anxiety was lessened. I let myself go.

At one moment I was anxious. When they began to operate, I could feel it, and I didn't know if I were awake enough to say, "I am not asleep yet . . ." But the doctor heard me, reassured me. He waited. I slept. I had comical dreams. It was shorter this time.

Towards eight o'clock I had several spasms of pain. The doctor thought it would happen. He sent for a nurse. I combed my hair, I powdered and perfumed myself, painted my eyelashes. At eight o'clock I was taken to the operating room.

I lay stretched on a table. I had no place on which to rest my legs. I had to keep them raised. Two nurses leaned over me. In front of me stood the German doctor, with the face of a woman and eyes protruding like those of Peter Lorre in *M*. For two hours I made violent efforts. The child inside of me was six months old and yet it was too big for me. I was exhausted, the veins were swelling with strain. I had pushed with my whole being, I had pushed as if I wanted this child out of my body and hurled into another world. "Push, push, with all your strength." Was I pushing with all my strength? All my strength? No, a part of me did not want to push out the child. The doctor knew it. That was why he was angry, mysteriously angry. He knew.

A part of me lay passive, did not want to push out anyone, not even this dead fragment of myself, out in the cold, outside of me. All of me which chose to keep, to lull, to embrace, to love; all of me which carried, preserved, protected; all of me which wanted to imprison the whole world in its passionate tenderness; this part of me would not thrust out the child, nor this past which had died in me. Even though it threatened my life, I could not break, tear out, separate, surrender, open and dilate and yield up this fragment of life, like a fragment of the past, this part of me rebelled against pushing the child, or anyone, out in the cold, to be picked up by strange hands, to be buried in strange places, to be lost, lost, lost.

The doctor knew. A few hours before, he adored me, was devoted and worshipful, and now he was angry. And I was angry, with a black anger, at this part of me which refused to push, to kill, to separate, to lose. "Push! Push! Push with all your strength!" I pushed with anger, with despair, with frenzy, with the feeling that I would die pushing, as one exhales a last breath, that I would push out everything inside of me, and my soul with all the blood around it, and the sinews with my heart inside of them, choked, and that my body itself would open, and smoke would rise, and I would feel the ultimate incision of death.

The nurses leaned over me and they talked to each other while I rested. Then I pushed until I heard the bones cracking, until my veins swelled. I closed my eyes so hard I saw lightning and waves of red and purple.

There was a stir in my ear, a beating as if my eardrum had burst. I closed my lips so tightly the blood was trickling. I must have bitten my tongue. My legs felt enormously heavy, like marble columns, like immense marble columns crushing my body. I was pleading for someone to hold them. The nurse laid her knee on my stomach and shouted: "Push! Push! Push! Push!" Her perspiration fell on me. The doctor paced up and down, angrily and impatiently. "We will be here all night. Three hours now." The head was showing, but I had fainted. Everything was blue, then black. The instruments seemed to be gleaming before my closed eyes. Knives were sharpened in my ears. Ice and silence.

Then I heard voices, first talking too fast for me to understand. A curtain was parted, the voices still tripped over each other, falling fast like a waterfall, with sparks, and they hurt my ears. The table was rolling gently, rolling. The women were lying in the air. Heads. Heads hung where the enormous white bulbs of the lamps were hung. The doctor was still walking, the lamps moved, the heads came near, very near, and the words came more slowly.

They were laughing. One nurse was saying, "When I had my first child I was all ripped to pieces. I had to be sewed up again, and then I had another, and had to be sewn up, and then I had another." The other nurse said, "Mine passed like an envelope through a letter box. Then afterwards the bag would not come out. The bag would not come out. Out. Out. Out." Why did they keep repeating themselves? And why did the lamps turn? And why were the steps of the doctor so very fast, fast, fast?

"She can't labor any more; at six months nature does not help. She should have another injection." I felt the needle thrust. The lamps were still. The ice and the blue which was around the lamps came into my veins. My heart was beating wildly.

The nurses talked: "Now that baby of Mrs. L's last week, who would have thought she was too small, a big woman like that." The words kept turning as on a phonograph record. They kept saying, over and over again, that the bag would not come out, that the child slipped out like a letter in a letter box, that they were so tired with so many hours of work. They laughed at what the doctor said. They said that there was no more of that bandage; it was too late to get any. They washed instruments, and they talked, talked, talked.

Please hold my legs! Please hold my legs! PLEASE HOLD MY LEGS! I am ready again. By throwing my head back I can see the clock. I have been struggling four hours. It would be better to die. Why am I alive and struggling so desperately? I could not remember why I should want to live. Why *live?* I could not remember anything. I saw eyes bulging out, and I heard women talk, and blood. Everything was blood and pain. What was it to *live?* How could one feel to *live?*

I have to push. I have to push. That is a black point, a fixed point in eternity. At the end of a dark tunnel. I have to push. Am I pushing or dying? A voice saying: "Push! Push! Push!" A knee on my stomach, and the marble of the legs, and the head too large and I have to push. The light up there, the immense, round, blazing white light is drinking me. It drinks me. It drinks me slowly, sucks me into space. If I do not close my eyes, it will drink all of me. I seep upward, in a long icy thread, too light; and yet inside of me there is a fire too, the nerves are twisted, there is no repose from this long tunnel dragging me; or am I pushing myself out of the tunnel; or is the child being pushed out of me while the light is drinking me? If I do not close my eyes the light will drink my whole being and I will no longer be able to push myself out of the tunnel.

Am I dying? The ice in the veins, the cracking of the bones, this pushing in blackness, with a small shaft of light in the eyes like the edge of a knife, the feeling of a knife cutting the flesh, the flesh somewhere tearing as if it were burned through by a flame: somewhere my flesh is tearing and the blood is spilling out. I am pushing in the darkness, in utter darkness, I am pushing, pushing, until I open my eyes and I see the doctor who is holding a-long instrument which he swiftly thrusts into me and the pain makes me howl. A long animal howl.

"That will make her push," he says to the nurse. But it does not. It paralyzes me with pain. He wants to do it again. I sit up with fury and shout at him, "Don't you dare do that again, don't you dare!" The heat of my anger warms me, all the ice and pain are melted in fury. I have an instinct that what he has done is unnecessary, that he has done it because he is in a rage, because the needles on the clock keep turning. The dawn is coming and the child does not come out and I am losing strength and the injections do not produce the spasm. The body—neither the nerves nor the muscles do anything to eject the child. Only my will and strength. My fury frightened him and he stands away and waits.

These legs I opened to joy, this honey that flowed out in the joy —now these legs are twisted in pain and the honey flows with the blood. The same pose and the same wetness of passion but this is dying and not loving.

I look at the doctor pacing up and down, or bending to look at the head of the child, which is barely showing. The legs like scissors, and the head barely showing. He looks baffled, as before a savage mystery, baffled by this struggle. He wants to interfere with his instruments, while I struggle with nature, with myself, with my child, and with the meaning I put into all, with my desire to give and to hold, to keep and to lose, to live and to die. No instruments can help me. His eyes are furious. He would like to take a knife. He has to watch and wait.

I want to remember all the time why I should want to live. I am all pain and no memory. The lamp has ceased drinking me. I am too weary to move, even towards the light, or to turn my head and look at the clock. Inside of my body there are fires, there are bruises, the flesh is in pain. The child is not a child, it is a demon lying half-choked between my legs, keeping me from living, strangling me, showing only its head, until I die in its grasp. The demon lies inert at the door of the womb, blocking life, and I cannot rid myself of it.

The nurses begin to talk again. I say, "Let me alone." I place my two hands on my stomach and very slowly, very softly, with the tips of my fingers I drum, drum, drum on my stomach, in circles. Round and round, softly, with eyes open in great serenity. The doctor comes near and looks with amazement. The nurses are silent. Drum drum drum drum drum in soft circles, in soft quiet circles. "Like a savage," they whisper. The mystery.

Eyes open, nerves quiet, I drum gently on my stomach for a long while. The nerves begin to quiver. A mysterious agitation runs through them. I hear the ticking of the clock. It ticks inexorably, separately. The little nerves awaken, stir. I say, "I can push now!" and I push violently. They are shouting, "A little more! Just a little more!"

Will the ice come, and the darkness, before I am through? At the end of the dark tunnel, a knife gleams. I hear the clock and my heart. I say, "Stop!" The doctor holds the instrument, and he is leaning over. I sit up and shout at him. He is afraid again. "Let me alone, all of you!"

I lie back so quietly. I hear the ticking. Softly I drum, drum, drum. I feel my womb stirring, dilating. My hands are so weary, they will fall off. They will fall off, and I will lie there in darkness. The womb is stirring and dilating. Drum drum drum drum drum. "I am ready!" The nurse puts her knee on my stomach. There is blood in my eyes. A tunnel. I push into this tunnel. I bite my lips and push. There is fire, flesh ripping and no air. Out of the tunnel! All my blood is spilling out. "Push! Push! It is coming! It is coming!" I feel the slipperiness, the sudden deliverance, the weight is gone. Darkness.

I hear voices. I open my eyes. I hear them saying, "It was a little girl. Better not show it to her." All my strength is coming back. I sit up. The doctor shouts, "For God's sake, don't sit up, don't move!"

"Show me the child," I say.

"Don't show it," says the nurse, "it will be bad for her."

The nurses try to make me lie down. My heart is beating so loudly I can hardly hear myself repeating, "Show it to me!" The doctor holds it up. It looks dark, and small, like a diminutive man. But it is a little girl. It has long eyelashes on its closed eyes, it is perfectly made, and all glistening with the waters of the womb. It was like a doll, or like a miniature Indian, about one foot long, skin on bones, no flesh. But completely formed. The doctor told me afterwards that it had hands and feet exactly like mine. The head was bigger than average. As I looked at the dead child, for a moment I hated it for all the pain it had caused me, and it was only later that this flare of anger turned into great sadness.

Regrets, long dreams of what this little girl might have been. A dead creation, my first dead creation. The deep pain caused by any death, and any destruction. The failure of my motherhood, or at least the embodiment of it, all my hopes of real, human, simple, direct motherhood lying dead, and the only one left to me, Lawrence's symbolic motherhood, bringing more hope into the world. But the simple human flowering denied to me.

Perhaps I was designed for other forms of creation. Nature connived to keep me a man's woman, and not a mother; not a mother to children but to men. Nature shaping my body for the love of man, not of child. This child which was a primitive connection to the earth, a prolongation of myself, now denied me as if to point up my destiny in other realms.

I love man as creator, lover, husband, friend, but man the father I do not trust. I do not believe in man as father. I do not trust man as father. When I wished this child to die, it was because I felt it would experience the same lack.

The doctor and the nurses were amazed by my aliveness and curiosity. They expected tears. I still had my eyelash make-up on. But afterwards, I lay back and fainted. And alone in my bed, I wept. In the mirror I saw the veins on my face cracked. I fell asleep. Sleep.

Morning toilette. Perfume and powder. The face all well. Visitors. Marguerite, Otto Rank, Henry. Immense weakness. Another day of rest. But on the third day a new anxiety appeared. The breasts began to hurt.

The little nurse from the south of France left all her other patients to comb my hair lovingly. All the nurses kissed me and fondled me. I was bathing in love, feeling languid and calm and light. And then my breasts got hard with milk, too much milk. An amazing amount of milk for such a small person. So hard and painful. That night the nightmare began again.

All the nurses were against the German doctor: because he was German, because he treated them harshly, because they thought he had made all kinds of errors. A French doctor in the hospital had threatened to intervene by force to save me from him. All the nurses began to whisper, to revolt against his orders. They did the opposite of what he asked. He tied my breasts one way and they tied them another. They said he was all wrong about everything, that what he was doing would give me ulcers of the breast. This idea terrified me. All my joy vanished. I felt again in the grip of some dark menace. I imagined my breasts spoiled forever. Ulcers. The nurses, leaning over my bed, seemed malevolent to me; they seemed to be wishing I would have ulcers to prove the German doctor in the wrong. The way they leaned over, examined me, predicted the worst, affected me, frightened me.

The woman who was dying of cancer was still moaning. I could not sleep. I began to think about religion, about pain. I had not yet come to the end of pain. I thought of the God I received with such fervor at Communion and whom I confused with my father. I thought of Catholicism. Wondering. I remembered that Saint Teresa had saved my life when I was nine years old. I thought of God, of a man with a beard from my child's picture books. No, not Catholicism, not Mass, not confession, not priests. But God, where was God? Where was the fervor I had as a child?

I tired of thinking. I fell asleep with my hands folded on my breasts as for death. And I died again, as I had died other times. My breathing was another breathing, an inner breathing. I died and was reborn again in the morning, when the sun came on the wall in front of my window.

A blue sky and the sun on the wall. The nurse had raised me to see the new day. I lay there, feeling the sky, and myself one with the sky, feeling the sun and myself one with the sun, and abandoning myself to the immensity and to God. God penetrated my whole body. I trembled and shivered with an immense joy. Cold, and fever and light, an illumination, a visitation, through the whole body, the shiver of a presence. The light and the sky in the body, God in the body and I melting into God. I melted into God. No image, I felt space, gold, purity, ecstasy, immensity, a profound ineluctable communion. I wept with joy. I knew everything I had done was right. I knew that I needed no dogmas to communicate with Him, but to live, to love, and to suffer. I needed no man, no priest to communicate with Him. By living my life, my passions, my creations to the limit I communed with the sky, the light, and with God. I believed in the transfusion of blood and flesh. I had come upon the infinite, through the flesh and through the blood. Through flesh and blood and love, I was made whole. I cannot say more. There is nothing more to say. The greatest communions come so simply.

But from that moment on, I felt my connection with God, an isolated, wordless, individual, full connection which gives me an immense joy and a sense of the greatness of life, eternity. I was born. I was born woman. To love God and to love man, supremely and separately. Not to confuse them. I was born to great quietude, a super-human joy, above and beyond all human sorrows, transcending pain and tragedy. This joy which I found in the love of man, in creation, was completed by communion with God.

The doctor came, examined me, could not believe his eyes. I was intact, as if nothing had ever happened to me. I could leave the clinic. I was so well, I walked out of it, with everybody looking on. It was a soft summer day. I walked with joy at having escaped the great mouth of death. I wept with joy and gratitude.

Fruit. Flowers. Visitors. I went to sleep that night thinking of God, feeling that I was falling asleep in the bower of heaven. Feeling taken up in huge arms, yielding to a mysterious protection. The moonlight shone in the room. Heaven was a bower, a hammock. I swung in infinite spaces, beyond the world. Slept inside of God.

At five o'clock I left for Louveciennes. The day was soft and lulling. I sat on a deck chair in the garden. Marguerite took care of me. I dreamed and rested. We had dinner out in the garden.

My rhythm is slow. I am resisting entering life again, pain, activity, conflicts. Everything is beginning anew; the day is soft but perishable, like a sigh, the last sigh of summer, heat and foliage. Soft and sad, the end of summer, and leaves falling.

Henry and I are walking down the Rue de la Tombe Issoire, on the way to see the plumber and the pillow-cleaner. Henry is moving into the studio of the Villa Seurat. We are all helping to paint, to hammer, to hang up pictures, to clean. The studio room is large, with its skylight window giving it space and height. A small closet kitchen is built in under the balcony, where some people like to store away paintings, etc. A ladder leads up to it. The window opens on a roof terrace, which connects with the terrace of the studio next door. The bedroom is on the right-hand side of the entrance, with a bathroom. It has a balcony which gives on the Villa Seurat. One can see trees, and the small façades of the pink, green, yellow, ochre villas across the way.

While cleaning the closet, I found a photograph of Antonin Artaud who had once stayed there! It was a beautiful photograph of him as the monk in Dreyer's "Joan of Arc." His cheeks looked hollow, his eyes visionary and fanatical. Antonin Artaud had always refused to give photographs of himself because he feared voodoo curses (*envoûtements,* as he said) and believed that harm could come to him if some demonic person stuck pins into the portrait. And here was the beautiful monk at my mercy. I would not even put a thumbtack through it. I stored it away.

Henry was sad because he had insulted Jack Kahane. "I destroy all your work," he said to me. The sun poured into the studio. Several friends were helping to move Henry into it.

Tropic of Cancer is at the printer's. Henry feels this is a new cycle. Fred is hurt not to be invited to live at the Villa Seurat. Henry wants to be alone.

We are hanging up water colors, and the charts of characters he will write about.

I wonder, who are the other artists living in the Villa Seurat?

Having lunch with Bone and listening to his talk about Dr. Rank's ideas made me realize I knew Rank more as a human being now than as a man of ideas.

Talking with Rank unloosed a flood of curious facts. He had been thinking that, in Paris, it was the Doctor Rank who had taken control, and that he had not lived his life as a man. He began to think of New York as a liberation from the past, the hope of a new life. "I don't want to come back here, to my past ever again." For the first time, he saw New York as a liberating factor. But I was necessary to this liberation. He wanted to begin anew but was not sure he could do it without my help. I was the only one who had taken an interest in the man behind Dr. Rank. He had many plans. He told me about a humorous book he wanted to write on Mark Twain. The suicide of the Twin.

Henry's *Tropic of Cancer* appeared the same day he took possession of his first real home, the book which had been begun in that same house four years ago in Fraenkel's studio. A complete circle.

We all sat down and wrapped and addressed copies of his book to be mailed.

Went with Rank to see a first edition of Mark Twain he wanted at the Nixons. Met Rank's daughter. Later we went to his apartment and met Mrs. Rank, and had drinks with Chana Orloff, Dr. Endler, and other people.

So now I am divided into three selves. One self lives at Louveciennes, has a Spanish maid, eats breakfast in bed, eats pheasants killed by Lani and Louis Andard, listens to the radio, gives orders to the gardener, pays her bills with checks, sits by an open fire, copies the diaries, and translates the second diary volumes from French into English, dreams by the window, gets restless for heightened living.

In Villa Seurat with Henry and Fred and a constant stream of people walking in and out. I peel potatoes, grind coffee French style, wrap books, drink out of chipped cups and glasses discarded in Louveciennes, wipe my hands with old towels left over from Louveciennes, walk down the cobblestone streets to market, repair the phonograph (because Henry is absolutely helpless in practical matters), take the bus, sit at cafés, talk a great deal about books and films, writing and writers, smoke a great deal and watch the invasion of people walking in and out of the place. Henry has made friends with the neighbors: De Maigret, who can come in by walking out of his bedroom, onto his terrace, and into Henry's balcony; and down the ladder, with a woman on the floor below who has lived in Greece; and with a photographer who lives on the ground floor.

The third self wants to learn a profession so that she may always write as she believes, wants to help Rank make a new life because he helped her make a new life, and wants the unknown, the unfamiliar. I finally promised to go to New York for two months. I feel two months are short in the span of eternity.

All the flowers I received during my illness are withering. I often look at them and secretly desire to be back in the days of my convalescence, the moment of quietude, beatitude, before the stronger, more vivid life presented its conflicts and dramas again. I resisted entering real life again, then drove myself into it. Now I feel the exhilaration of perpetual struggles. But for days I enjoyed the indifference, the detachment, and I wondered if this detachment and non-caring was what Henry felt all the time. I watched everything from afar: my father's moralistic letters; Henry's joys over the publication of *Tropic of Cancer*, Rank saying that Henry had learned stability from me, and I mobility from him, that friends often exchanged values. It is Henry who talks about a life of dignity, responsibility, etc.

Rank telephones me that he has good news for me. He is exultant because the sculptured head of me by Chana Orloff will be exhibited. He has purchased it for his library.

She wants me to go on posing for her. She wants to make many drawings.

Telephoned the plumber to fix a leak in the furnace, ordered coal, wrote in the diary, talked with Marguerite. Moved to small salon with the Persian fireplace because I gave Henry the big studio rug and curtains.

The *voyante* lived in a dark and shabby apartment in a workman's quarter, near Clichy. Poor people waiting in the brown living room with the artificial palm trees, the aquariums, and astrological charts on the walls. *Femme de ménage*, doormen, workmen, pregnant women, storekeepers. How they needed hope, needed to know. I felt ashamed to be there, questioning anyone about my destiny. I thought of Freud's explanation of seers. They are able to read what is in your mind.

Perhaps I did not know what the loss of Rank meant to me, whether it would be as serious a loss as the loss of my father. Perhaps I was just as fearful of the future as the poor, the working people waiting there.

The *voyante* asked me to come into the dining room. She was a tired-looking woman, rather thin, with her hair uncombed and her nails dirty. There was a bowl of artificial flowers on the table. On the sideboard, very neatly arranged, a carefully polished glass ball. This she picked up and placed in the center of the dining table on a piece of red cloth. Then she told me, with a slight lisp which came from a missing tooth, that she saw a man on the sea, on his way to America, who is thinking of me (Rank?). She sees my trip to America and success in a new occupation, sees others close to me, indistinct but in distress, sees a man who devours himself and a man who wishes to help me, sees my father returning, a man of about fifty who does me harm, with whom I am not compatible, on whom I have wasted emotion and strength. She sees me signing a paper.

Is that all, is that all, is that all she can tell to the patient, resigned, tired people sitting in her waiting room?

I ran away, to forget her, and went to visit Manuela Del Rio to arrange for a rehearsal of my old dances. Rank had insisted I take up my dancing again. I loved the gaudy colors, the smell of the stage again. I loved her soiled shoes, her worn castanets, her bright red and purple costumes, and even her one-eyed mother who looked like a procuress, and the poodle, and the trunk being packed for a dance number in London.

Then much work to leave all those I love in comfort, to protect them from Teresa's nebulous housekeeping, to foresee their needs.

I stick a fork in my hair in lieu of a Spanish comb and talk about the smell of the stage when I haven't really smelled it yet. But just to hear Manuela say, "Monday at eleven at the Place Pigalle, studio Pigalle," is enough. I sew black lace on my *maja* dress. I give Henry all my typing paper because I do not intend to write books for the present. I start slowly to pack my trunk for New York, taking my photographs out of their frames.

The little details which make joy. They are not important in the world of ideas, they only count in life, for pleasure. The beauty and the ugliness of life's details, the homely and the warm cabbage smells of the world! After the vertigoes of dreams and ideas, the palpable, the warm, and even the homely.

At first, as a girl, I loved blue, and now orange; but I find orange is the complement of blue. I only completed blue then, I made blue more forcible.

I packed the manuscript of *House of Incest*, the diary, the manuscript of *Winter of Artifice*.

I went to Rank to solve my conflict with my father, and only added another father to my life, and another loss.

My real father returned from Cannes, sick, very sweet, and we had quiet mellow talks. He showed me his hands covered with eczema, and I felt the depth of my illusionless love for him. He laments my trip to New York.

It hurt me to rent Louveciennes to strangers. I had to empty it and put everything in storage. And the last night we spent there the windows were without curtains. The moon blazed at the windows like snow-light, impossible, dramatic, behind the bare black branches. And we saw the dawn too, a Pelléas and Mélisande moon and dawn. And I knew I was ejecting myself from my fairy-tale world, surrendering my shell, my nest, my hammock, my refuge. Lying in the Persian bed, watching the garden, feverish with memories. And having to watch the orange pillows and the Chinese red coffer and the Persian cabinet carried out. And the furniture on the street, the wide green gate open, the house emptied, opened, like a skeleton. And the moving men covering the lovely pieces with old tattered blankets.

How to live in the present when no one else is there at the same time, nobody catches up with you, is there to answer? The present is made by the pleasure of collisions of two uncelestial bodies in uncelestial fusions.

I am distributing Sloan's Liniment, radios, free analysis, and the assurance that I will return in two months, a full-fledged analyst, Doctor Nin, thinking I might as well make a profession of a hobby.

No, I have not started a hospital in collaboration with Dr. Endler, but everyone's reaction to my leaving is to get sick.

When I told Joaquin of my experience in the hospital, he thought it was a return to religion, and he took me to Mass on Sunday; but it all seemed drab and literal and did not seem like a continuation of my mystical trance. I thought perhaps that experience meant that, by reverting to dogma and ritual, I could rediscover religious ecstasy, and I tried, but it did not return. To please Joaquin I went to visit the Abbé Alterman.

He is a very famous personage, a friend of Debussy and a converted Jew who, by his brilliance, converted Max Jacob and many other artists. So I donned my new black wool costume with enormous sleeves and a slit in the front which runs from throat to breast, and the bracelet set with stars, and went to visit him in his monastically bare room. He was sitting in front of a very large desk covered with very large books. He was lean, dark-eyed, and intense. All in black, I felt like a voluptuous widow. He looked at me and studied me. I am sure he knew I had come as Thaïs, to tempt him into error. We talked at length.

He started by saying, "*Vous êtes une âme très disputé.*"

I told him about my experience in the hospital, and how I had never been able to find that marvelous state again.

"A visit from God," said l'Abbé Alterman.

We were talking very interestingly until I told him I was studying psychoanalysis with Dr. Otto Rank, that I felt it helped people, had helped me. Then this man, who had fascinated so many artists with his scholarly learning and his wit and his talent for debate, uttered these unbelievable words:

"You know, of course, that psychoanalysts and psychoanalysis are the work of the devil, that if you have any connection with them you are doomed, that God will never visit you again if you do not surrender that evil science immediately. You will be practicing black magic instead of white magic if you do not collaborate with religion. If you insist on standing alone."

When I left him I had no more doubts about the new path I should take.

Before I go up too far, I must go down deep into the earth, to find the earth, and stay on it. I am in life. I am alive.

I said to Henry: "In the books, you are really creating yourself. In *Tropic of Cancer* you were only a sex and a stomach. In the second book, *Black Spring*, you begin to have eyes, a heart, ears, hands. By and by, with each book, you will create a complete man, and then you will be able to write about woman, but not until then. But why do you give the EYES in the book to Brassai, the photographer? They are your eyes, you are describing what you saw, not Brassai. Why do you make Lowenfels the poet? It is your own poetry you are glorifying."

Visit to Marcel Duchamp and his American mistress. A studio full of portfolios, paintings, and her collection of earrings hanging on the white walls, earrings from all over the world, so lovely, every beauty of design duplicated by a twin, and some of them twinkling, some cascades of delicate filigree, some heavy and carved. She was tall and with a beautiful calm face, almost a madonna face with grey hair. She gave me a pair of earrings spontaneously, took them off the hooks and gave them to me.

Marcel Duchamp stood quietly, smoking his pipe, talking little. His eyes shining, very bright, although the rest of him seems carved of wood, much like the chess pieces he loves so much to play with. He had a collection of pipes, and he stood, and sat, and smoked, and welcomed us, and parted from us with a great stylized detachment, as if we were pawns too, and he were reflecting on how to move us. It is said he spends all night on a game, thinking of a move, and then will telephone a friend in another country with whom he is playing a game by long distance. His passion is in chess. About his painting he is detached. He showed me a portfolio, a box, really, which he said should now take the place of completed books. "This is not a time in which to complete anything," he said. "It is a time for fragments." This box contained an unfinished book. Scraps of drawings on any old paper, notes torn from a notebook, odds and ends, half-finished comments, a word all by itself, in large handwriting, the elements with which to compose a book which he would never write. A symbol of the times.

He gave me a portfolio of reproduced copies to take to New York and to show to artists.

The walls were white and high. There was a garden outside, which seemed to extend into the vast studio because of the answering plants. I see their figures against this white background. Although there must have been color, I see them in black and white, people stripped of ornamentation and unessentials, engravings, he of wood, and she of compassionate but serene flesh. And it is difficult to believe that Marcel Duchamp is the one who sent a urinal bowl to an exhibition, as I was told, or played so many surrealist pranks.

Henry was enthusiastic over the idea of the casual, unfinished book. There is no doubt that this was not a surrender to an easy way of creating, accepting the chaos, the fragmentary quality of life, but had much more to do with D. H. Lawrence's quest for a way to capture a description of life and character without killing it, a way to capture the living moments. For this, it was important to follow the waywardness of life itself, its oscillations and whims and mobility. Henry was good at reproducing the chaos of nature and life. Now he wanted to publish his letters, in the same way as Duchamp had published his notes and sketches for an incomplete book.

This great passivity in action which makes Henry take all the blows, never fight for what he loves, write despairingly but act in no way to change his surroundings; which makes him write violently, curse, and take whatever woman comes his way: this great passivity seems to be necessary to the flowering of life, because it means enjoyment, effortlessness. His yieldingness to life. He expresses nonchalance, relaxation, looseness, easygoingness. The will only expresses itself in a negative way, by contradicting others, attacking others, opposing what others have done. His physical relaxation is the expression of a defect, a defect in action. Perhaps the world needed that loosening, that untying, unknotting, unleashing of controls, oiling, de-mentalization. In any case, that is Henry's gift.

Certain qualities were lost by organization, by the forms of the old novel, the old way to tell things.

[November, 1934]

Rank's desperate letters from New York, needing me, reminding me that he canceled all his important official engagements in London to rush to my bedside when I was in the hospital. "Well," he writes, "I am dying now. Come to my rescue." I have to leave Henry struggling to launch his book in spite of the timorousness of Kahane; my father suffering from eczema and wearing white cotton gloves on his hands, his pianist hands; Joaquin's struggles to bring me back into the comforts of Catholicism. The feelings of others affect me, and even the one I appear to send away empty-handed takes away with him a piece of my strength and a piece of my compassion.

I listen to the "Psalms" of Florent Schmitt over the radio in the dark, sitting next to my father, and I weep. This struggle to live by my own truth is so difficult, so wearing. A terrible algebra, always. I am like the adventurer who leaves all those he loves, and returns with his arms full of gold; and then they are happy and they forget how they tried to keep this adventurer from exploring, from his voyage and his search.

Dorothy Dudley wrote a book on Theodore Dreiser. She wrote me a letter full of admiration for my book on D. H. Lawrence. "I feel we have a similar way of writing." We sat in her kitchen and had dinner on a rose paper tablecloth. She gave me a letter of introduction to Theodore Dreiser and Waldo Frank.

I touch the Egyptian earrings given to me by the mistress of Marcel Duchamp and think of their room papered with maps, and all the places yet to see. Blaise Cendrars wrote: "I won't rest until I have lived in every hotel in Paris so I may know every inch of it," and for me, not only of Paris, but of the world. I remember the cat sleeping peacefully and Marcel Duchamp smoking over his chess game: I write about little things because the big ones are like abysses.

I make my father promise to go to Zurich to see Jung if all other medicines fail.

Psychoanalysis did save me because it allowed the birth of the real me, a most dangerous and painful one for a woman, filled with dangers; for no one has ever loved an adventurous woman as they have loved adventurous men. The birth of the real me might have ended like that of my unborn child. I may not become a saint, but I am very full and very rich. I cannot install myself anywhere yet; I must climb dizzier heights. But I still love the relative, not the absolute: the cabbage and the warmth of a fire, Bach on the phonograph, and laughter, and talk in the cafés, and a trunk packed for departure, with copies of *Tropic of Cancer*, and Rank's last SOS and the telephone ringing all day, good-bye, good-bye, good-bye . . .

Index

Huxley, Aldous, 175

Idées et Commentaires, 88
Incest, 273, 274, 275, 296

Jacob, Max, 355
Jaloux, Edmond, 185
James, Henry, quoted, 122
Jardin des Supplices, 265, 311
Jean (sculptress and poetess), 24, 25, 27, 30, 37, 41, 44, 45, 54, 70, 138
Jeanne, 167, 168, 169, 170, 171, 172, 177, 185, 186, 287
Jeunes Filles en Uniformes, 135
Jolas, Eugene, 69
Joyce, James, 139, 140, 143, 151, 190
Jung, C. G., 132, 156, 329, 359; quoted, 156

Kafka, Franz, 256
Kahane, Jack, 135 and *n.*, 141, 319, 321, 350, 359
Keyserling, Hermann, 143
Knopf, Alfred, 205, 328

Lady Chatterley's Lover, 7
L'Age d'Or (film), 7, 159
Lalou, René, 144
L'Art et le Mort, 188
Laughton, Charles, 321
Lawrence, D. H., xiii, 7, 12, 66, 78, 91, 113 122, 124, 140, 143, 144, 151, 158, 165, 175, 177, 189, 190, 194, 213, 240, 267, 314, 331, 357; quoted, 71, 238, 338; on woman as "man's invention," 276; on world disintegration, 331
Leblanc, Georgette, 289
Leonardo da Vinci, 211, 236, 309
Lesbianism, 41, 43, 271, 281

Letters to Anaïs Nin, Miller's, xii
Letters to Rivière, Artaud's, 177
Literature: as exaggeration and dramatization, 109; French, 267; influence on writer, Bradley's view of, 223
London, 157, 321
Lorenzo in Taos, 66
Lorrain, Jean, 255
Louveciennes, France, 3, 5, 20, 41, 62, 79, 92, 93, 94, 105, 125, 167, 188, 241, 252, 304, 314, 348, 354
Lowenfels, Walter, 103, 108, 109, 188, 189, 247, 315, 356
Lucie, Countess, 171, 174, 185, 186
Luhan, Mabel Dodge, 66
Lunt, Alfred, 321

Machen, Arthur, 80
Mädchen in Uniform (film), 135 *n.*
Mahreb, Prince, 171, 172
Marguerite S., 74, 75, 89-90, 100, 126, 127, 177, 246, 305, 319, 329, 333, 349; and Allendy, 194-96
Maruca (Nin), 181, 182, 183, 208, 242, 248, 249, 255, 261, 286, 290, 304, 308, 311, 317, 318, 319
Masochism, 164-65, 257, 271
Maupassant, Guy de, 3, 122
Miller, Henry, viii, xii, 7, 11-16 *passim,* 41, 69, 77, 79, 80, 92, 93, 94, 99, 100, 101, 108, 113, 124, 155, 158, 165, 242, 246, 258, 267; and Allendy, 126, 127, 131, 138-39, 162, 176; anger of, 14, 55, 66, 122, 240, 267; appearance of, 8, 68; on compassion, 52, 53; cruelty of, 69, 70, 71, 72, 73, 83; and dreams, discussion of, 224, 225, 266, 306, 311, 312; energy of, 72, 73, 125-26; Ger-

man background of, 48; letters
from Anaïs Nin, 48-49, 54-55, 204-
05, 240; letters to Anaïs Nin, 47,
48, 49, 55, 100, 135, 156, 157, 173;
in London, 157; and Lowenfels,
188; and Miller, June, 9-25 *passim*, 28, 29, 33, 34, 35, 36, 39-58
passim, 63, 64, 65, 66, 70, 77, 84,
85, 92, 94, 123, 128, 129, 132-53
passim, 157; mother of, 53; obscenities by, 55, 124; and organization, lack of, 257; passion of,
80, 125; and Perlès, 64, 67, 68, 69,
70, 71, 72, 73, 78, 80, 143, 155;
personality of, 11, 14, 15, 16, 48,
68, 357-58; philosophic phase of,
189, 190; quoted, vii, 7, 8, 9-10,
19, 51, 52, 63, 64, 65, 67, 69, 70,
77, 78, 79, 80, 88-89, 92, 94, 95,
117, 126-27, 129, 139, 198, 201;
and Rank, 185, 271, 291, 323, 333;
on saintliness, 57; and whores at
Rue Blondel, 58-60; on world disintegration, 331; writing by,
power of, 10-11, 55, 166, 230, 314;
see also Miller, June

Miller, June, 9-17 *passim*, 22, 25, 37,
38, 39, 40, 73, 74, 130, 145, 148,
149; beauty of, 20, 21, 22, 30, 37,
38, 54; drugs taken by, 44, 123;
elusiveness of, 10, 14, 15, 16, 17,
18, 24, 27, 29, 43; false side of,
20, 21; and Miller, Henry, 9-25
passim, 28, 29, 33, 34, 35, 36, 39-
58 *passim*, 63, 64, 65, 66, 70, 77,
84, 85, 92, 94, 123, 128, 129, 132-
53 *passim*, 157; personality of, 20,
23, 25-26, 27, 28, 29, 30, 45, 49;
purity of, 32, 42; quoted, 22, 23,
24, 25, 30, 31, 36, 44, 51, 133, 134,

136-37, 152; relationship to Anaïs
Nin, 21, 25-26, 28, 29, 31, 32, 33,
36, 40, 41, 45-46, 152, 281
Miralles, Antonio Francisco, 262,
263, 264
Mirbeau, Octave, 265, 311
*Modern Education, a Critique of
Its Fundamental Ideas*, 280
Montparnasse, 6, 25, 118
Mysteries, Hamsun's, 301

Narcissism, 271
*Naturalisme et Mysticisme chez
D. H. Lawrence*, 165
Neuilly, vii, 6, 115, 154
New York, 219, 243, 252, 359
Nietzsche, Friedrich, 150, 164, 177
Nin, Anaïs: Catholicism rejected
by, 71, 239; deserted by father,
182; diary abandoned by, 285,
301, 302, 308; and dreams, discussion of, 224, 225, 266, 306 *n.*,
311, 312; and fear of cruelty, 72;
letters from Antonin Artaud, 188-
89, 197-98, 221-22, 232-33, 240;
letters to Antonin Artaud, 188,
222; letters from father, 201, 213-
14, 217, 223-24, 239, 260; letters
to father, 241, 260; letters from
Henry Miller, 47, 48, 49, 55, 100,
135, 156, 157, 173; letters to
Henry Miller, 48-49, 54-55, 204-05,
240; and Miralles, 262-64; and
Perlès, 62, 65, 66, 71, 72, 73, 78,
79; pregnancy of, and operation,
337-48; psychoanalysis studied by,
325, 328, 352, 355; psychoanalyzed
by Allendy, 75-77, 81-92 *passim*,
97-98, 108-15 *passim*, 118-22, 281,
282, 283, 288; and Rank, 269-78,

364